MUSASHI #9

volume 4

by Takahashi Miyuki

The history of mankind has
been one of wars. Race.
Religion. Philosophy.
The causes are untold.

The combatants have their own
justifications, but on occasion,
some create a volatile
situation that threatens to
destroy the world.

Ultimate Blue.
An organization shrouded in
complete secrecy. Also known
as "the other United Nations."
Nobody knows when it was
created. Nobody knows
where it is based.

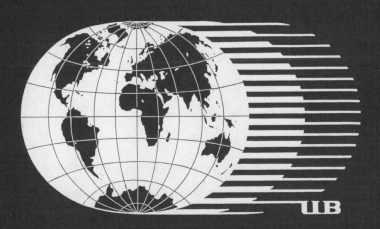

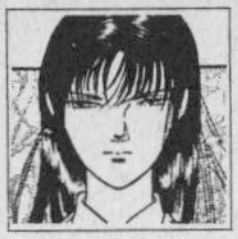

Musashi (Shinozuka Kou, Shinozaki Kei)

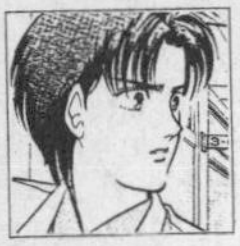

Tachibana Shingo

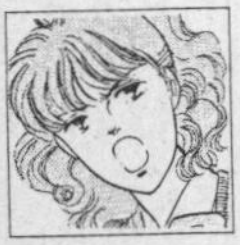

Shirakawa Ahiko

The story so far...

The history of mankind has been one of wars. Relentless warring would have doomed the planet to annihilation were it not for Ultimate Blue, a secret organization also known as "the other United Nations," and its team of super agents. ***Musashi Nine***, or ***Shinozuka Kou*** as she is known, is one of them.

A Hong Kong triad by the name of White Dragon is smuggling guns into Japan. An incriminating photo gets a young photographer killed, but not before it passes into the hands of his best friend, ***Shingo Tachibana***. The smugglers then turn their attention to Shingo, who with Musashi finds the evidence. The smugglers are arrested. Two of the three assassins sent to neutralize Shingo are silenced—but not the third.

Musashi Nine is protecting Shingo from the assassin on the loose when the U.S. armed forces ask her to also protect ***Akiho Shirakawa***.

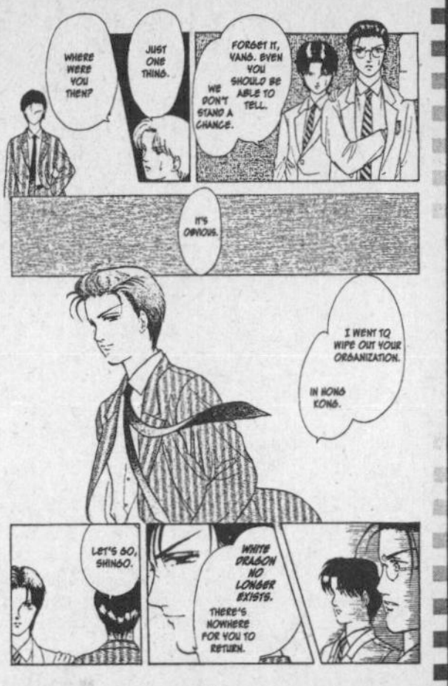
FORGET IT, YANG. EVEN YOU SHOULD BE ABLE TO TELL.
WE DON'T STAND A CHANCE.
JUST ONE THING.
WHERE WERE YOU THEN?
IT'S OBVIOUS.
I WENT TO WIPE OUT YOUR ORGANIZATION.
IN HONG KONG.
WHITE DRAGON NO LONGER EXISTS.
THERE'S NOWHERE FOR YOU TO RETURN.
LET'S GO, SHINGO.

American Naval Chain of Command and Ranks

President

Secretary of Defense

Chief of Naval Operations

Vice Admiral   Rear Admiral

Captain   Commander   Lieutenant Commander

Lieutenant   Lieutenant (Junior Grade)   Ensign

Chief Warrant Officer   Warrant Officer

Master Chief Petty Officer   Senior Chief Petty Officer   Chief Petty Officer

Petty Officer 1st Class   Petty Officer 2nd Class   Petty Officer 3rd Class

Seaman   Seaman Apprentice   Seaman Recruit

contents

MUSASHI #9

4

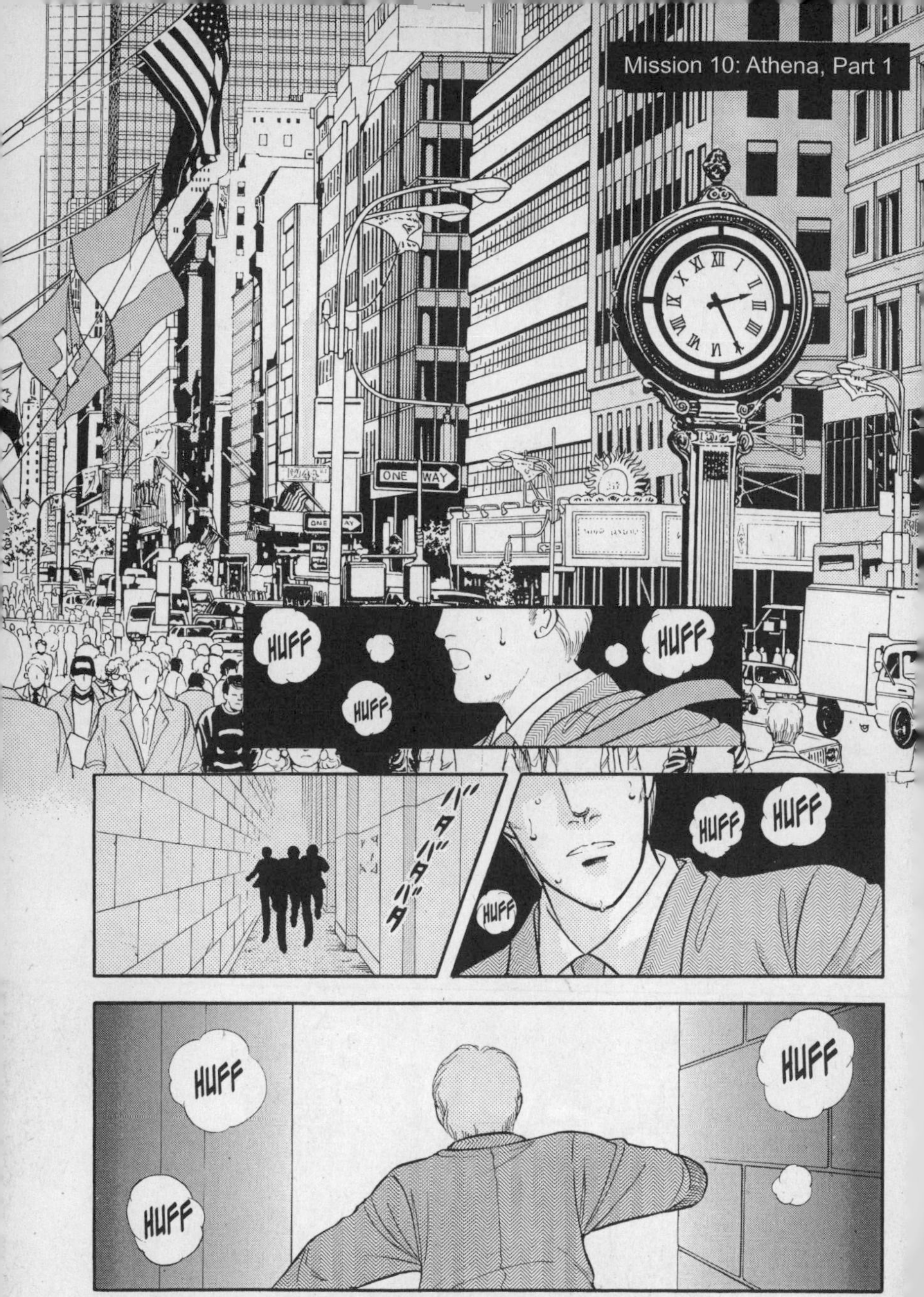
Mission 10: Athena, Part 1
ONE WAY
ONE WAY
HUFF
HUFF
HUFF
HUFF
HUFF
HUFF
バタバタバタ
HUFF
HUFF

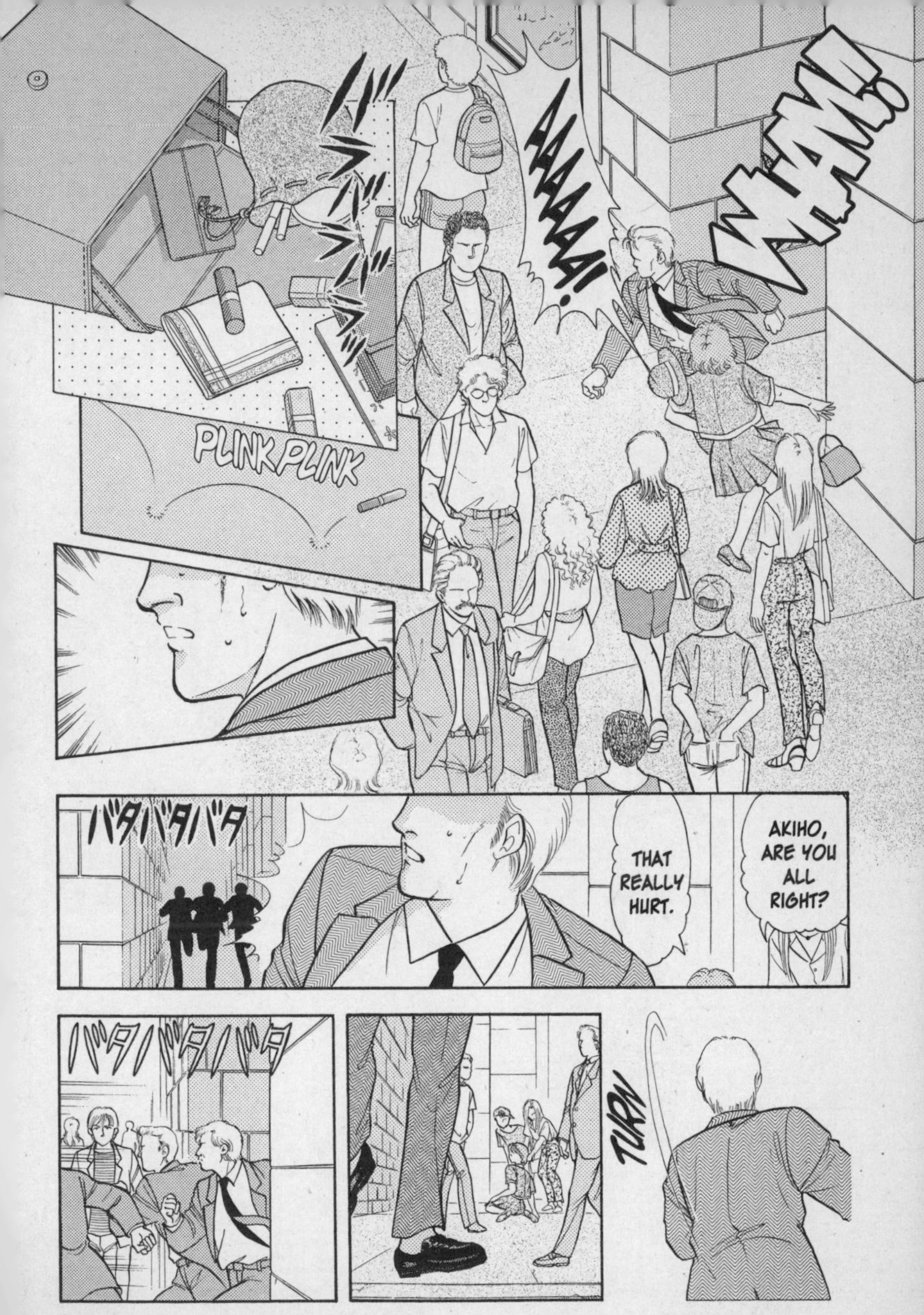
WHAM!!
AAAAAA!
PLINK PLINK
AKIHO, ARE YOU ALL RIGHT?
THAT REALLY HURT.
バタバタバタ
TURN
バタバタバタ

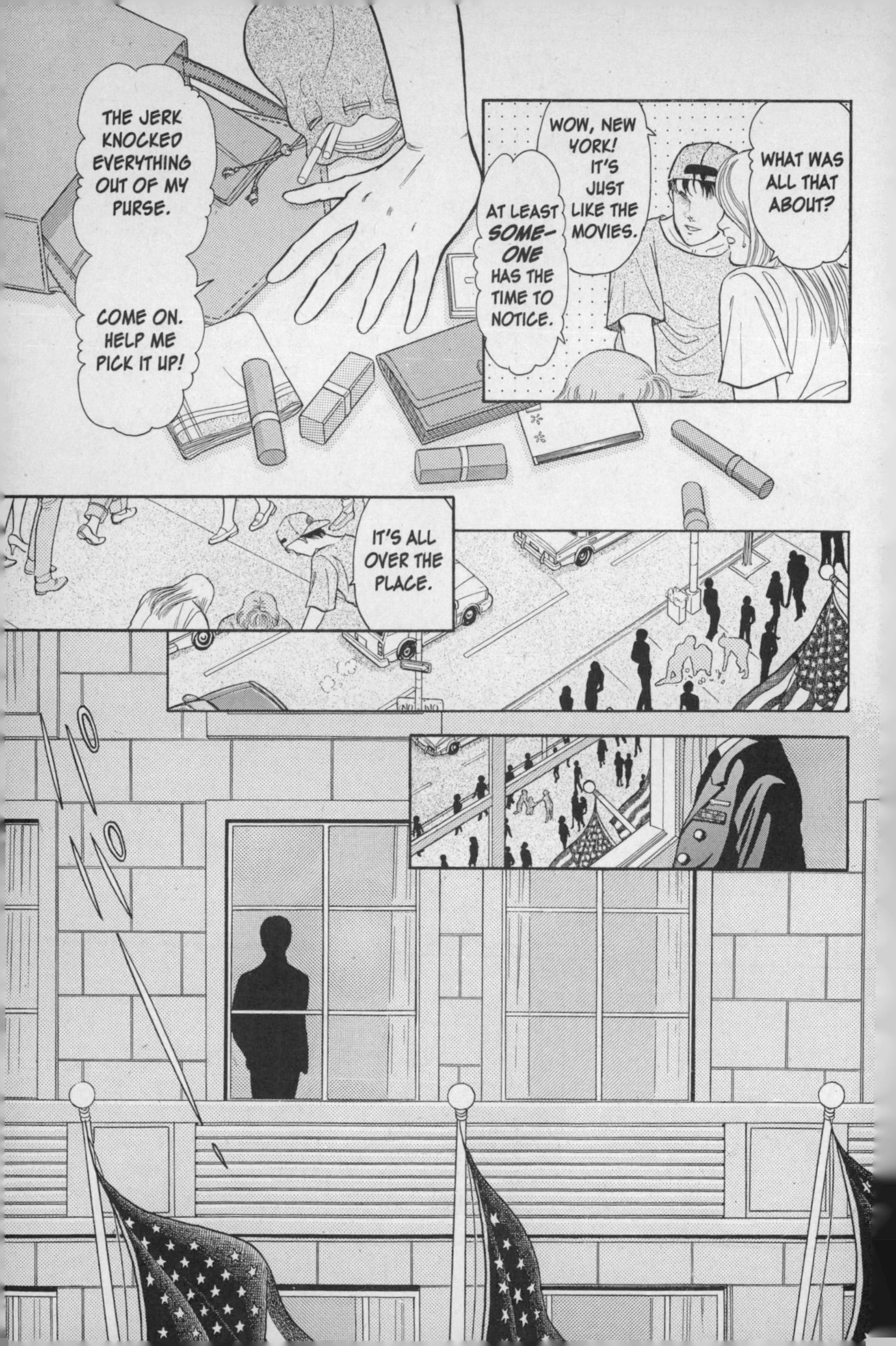
WHAT WAS ALL THAT ABOUT?
WOW, NEW YORK! IT'S JUST LIKE THE MOVIES.
AT LEAST SOME-ONE HAS THE TIME TO NOTICE.
THE JERK KNOCKED EVERYTHING OUT OF MY PURSE.
COME ON. HELP ME PICK IT UP!
IT'S ALL OVER THE PLACE.

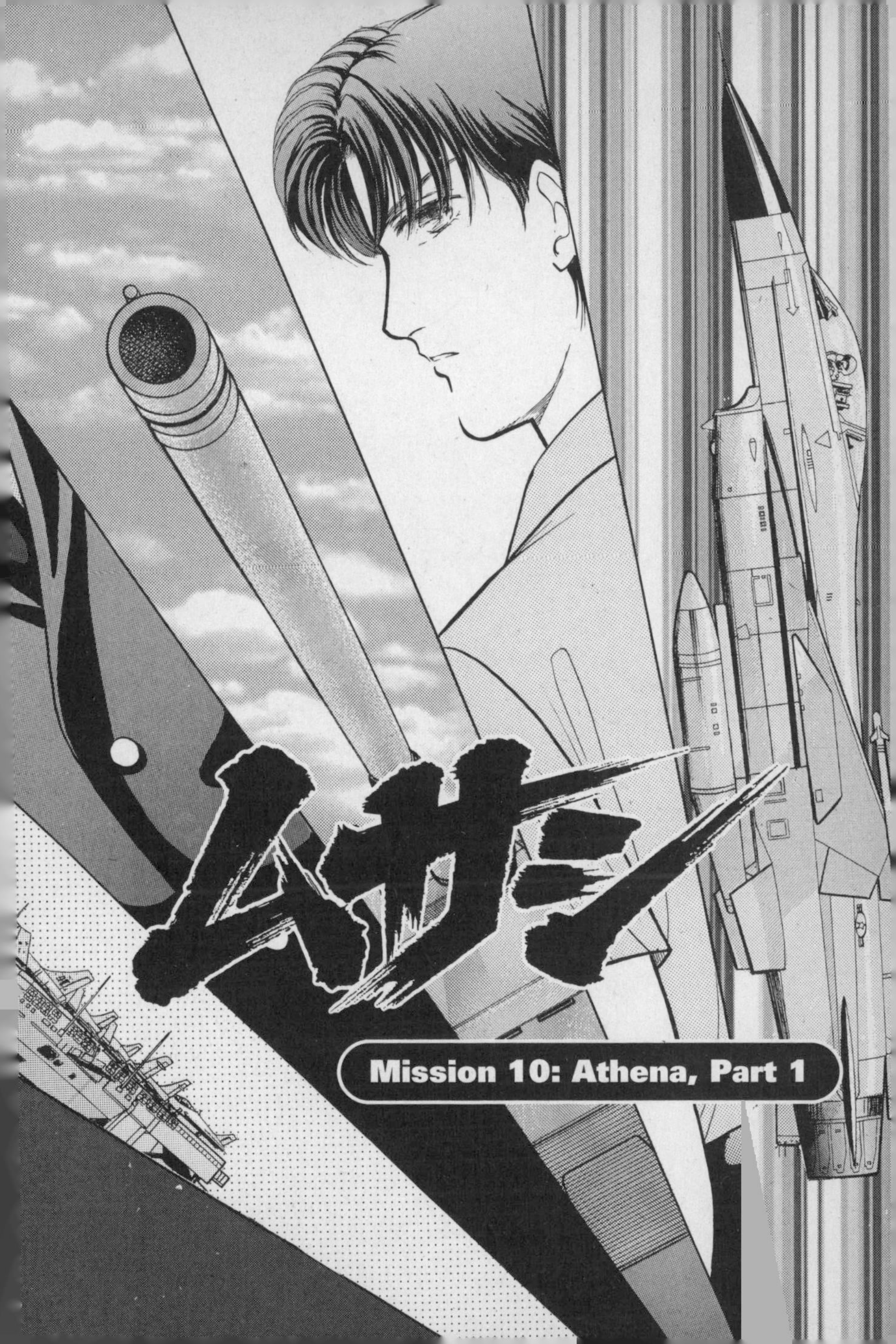
ムサシ
Mission 10: Athena, Part 1

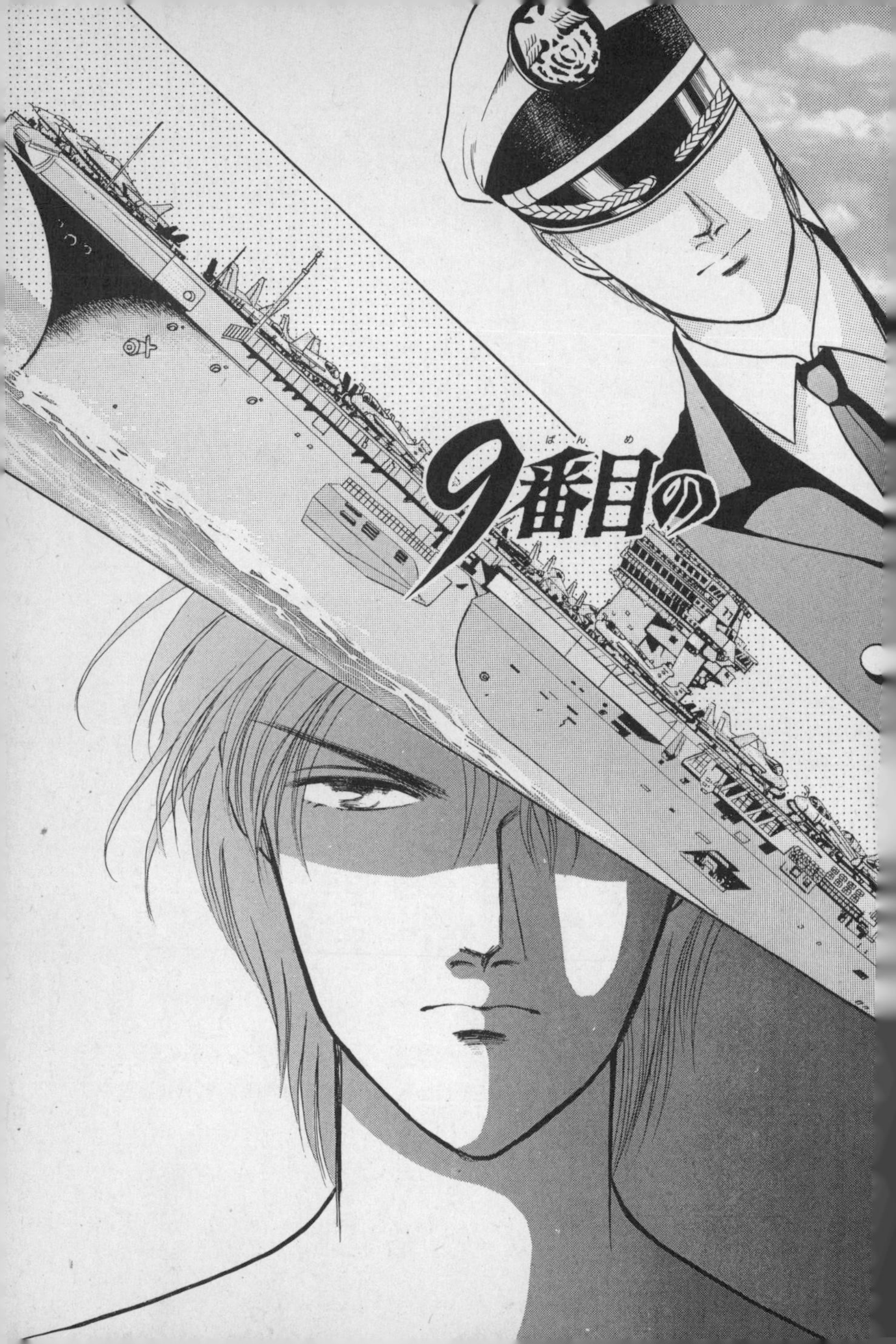
9番目の

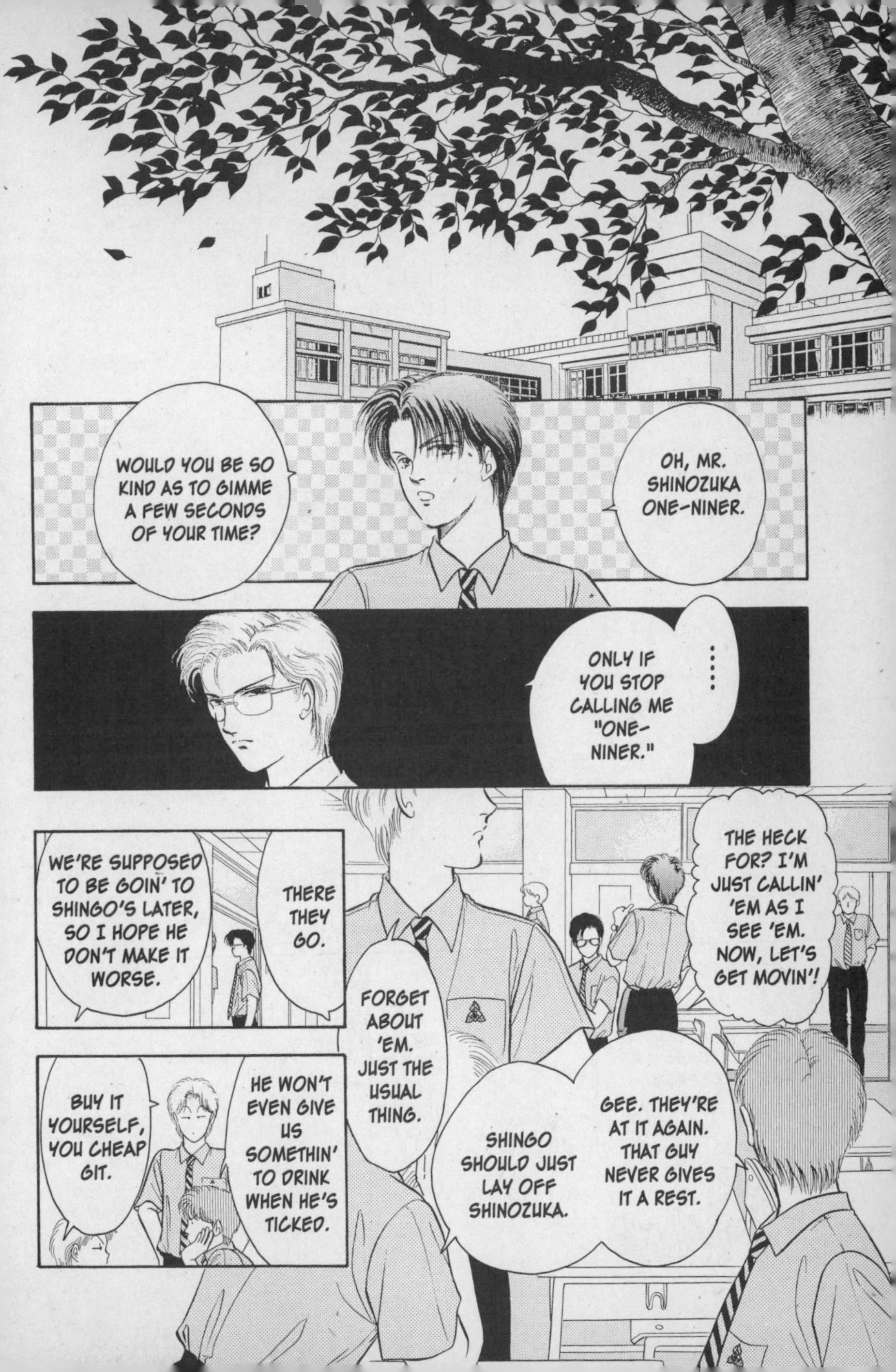
OH, MR. SHINOZUKA ONE-NINER.
WOULD YOU BE SO KIND AS TO GIMME A FEW SECONDS OF YOUR TIME?
.....
ONLY IF YOU STOP CALLING ME "ONE-NINER."
THE HECK FOR? I'M JUST CALLIN' 'EM AS I SEE 'EM. NOW, LET'S GET MOVIN'!
GEE. THEY'RE AT IT AGAIN. THAT GUY NEVER GIVES IT A REST.
SHINGO SHOULD JUST LAY OFF SHINOZUKA.
FORGET ABOUT 'EM. JUST THE USUAL THING.
THERE THEY GO.
WE'RE SUPPOSED TO BE GOIN' TO SHINGO'S LATER, SO I HOPE HE DON'T MAKE IT WORSE.
HE WON'T EVEN GIVE US SOMETHIN' TO DRINK WHEN HE'S TICKED.
BUY IT YOURSELF, YOU CHEAP GIT.

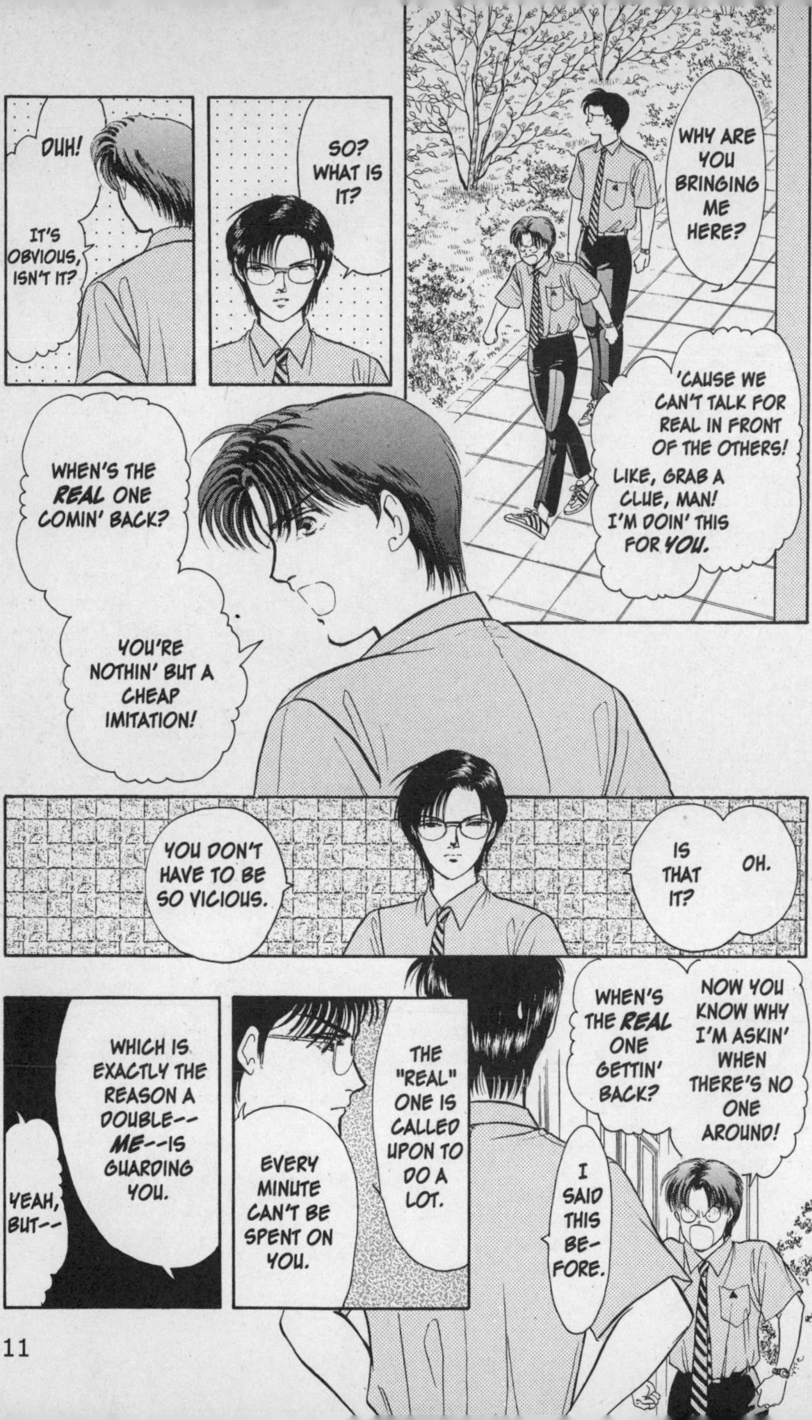
WHY ARE YOU BRINGING ME HERE?
'CAUSE WE CAN'T TALK FOR REAL IN FRONT OF THE OTHERS!
LIKE, GRAB A CLUE, MAN! I'M DOIN' THIS FOR YOU.
SO? WHAT IS IT?
DUH!
IT'S OBVIOUS, ISN'T IT?
WHEN'S THE REAL ONE COMIN' BACK?
YOU'RE NOTHIN' BUT A CHEAP IMITATION!
OH.
IS THAT IT?
YOU DON'T HAVE TO BE SO VICIOUS.
NOW YOU KNOW WHY I'M ASKIN' WHEN THERE'S NO ONE AROUND!
WHEN'S THE REAL ONE GETTIN' BACK?
I SAID THIS BE-FORE.
THE "REAL" ONE IS CALLED UPON TO DO A LOT.
EVERY MINUTE CAN'T BE SPENT ON YOU.
WHICH IS EXACTLY THE REASON A DOUBLE--ME--IS GUARDING YOU.
YEAH, BUT--

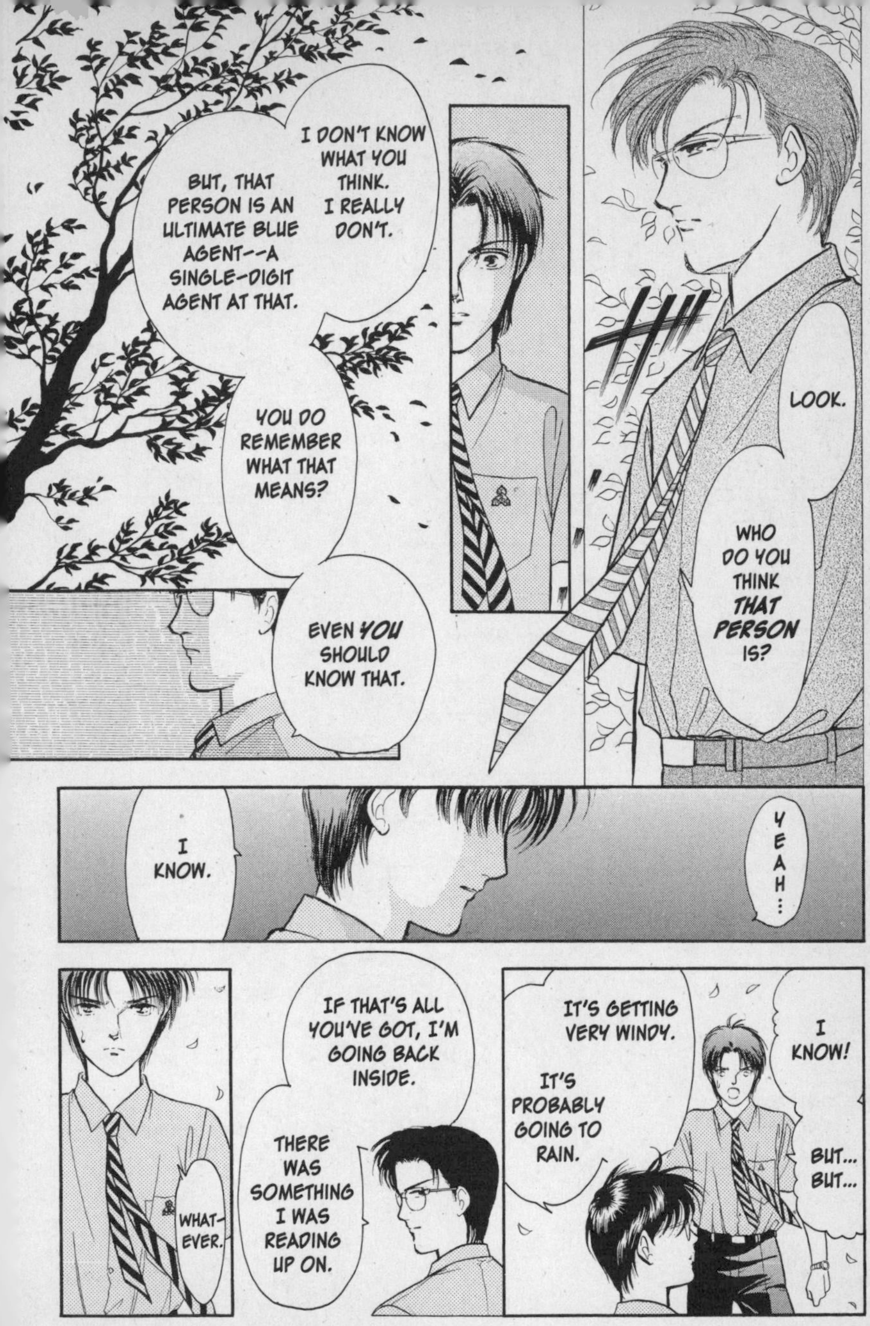
LOOK.
WHO DO YOU THINK *THAT PERSON* IS?
I DON'T KNOW WHAT YOU THINK. I REALLY DON'T.
BUT, THAT PERSON IS AN ULTIMATE BLUE AGENT--A SINGLE-DIGIT AGENT AT THAT.
YOU DO REMEMBER WHAT THAT MEANS?
EVEN *YOU* SHOULD KNOW THAT.
YEAH...
I KNOW.
I KNOW!
BUT... BUT...
IT'S GETTING VERY WINDY.
IT'S PROBABLY GOING TO RAIN.
IF THAT'S ALL YOU'VE GOT, I'M GOING BACK INSIDE.
THERE WAS SOMETHING I WAS READING UP ON.
WHATEVER.

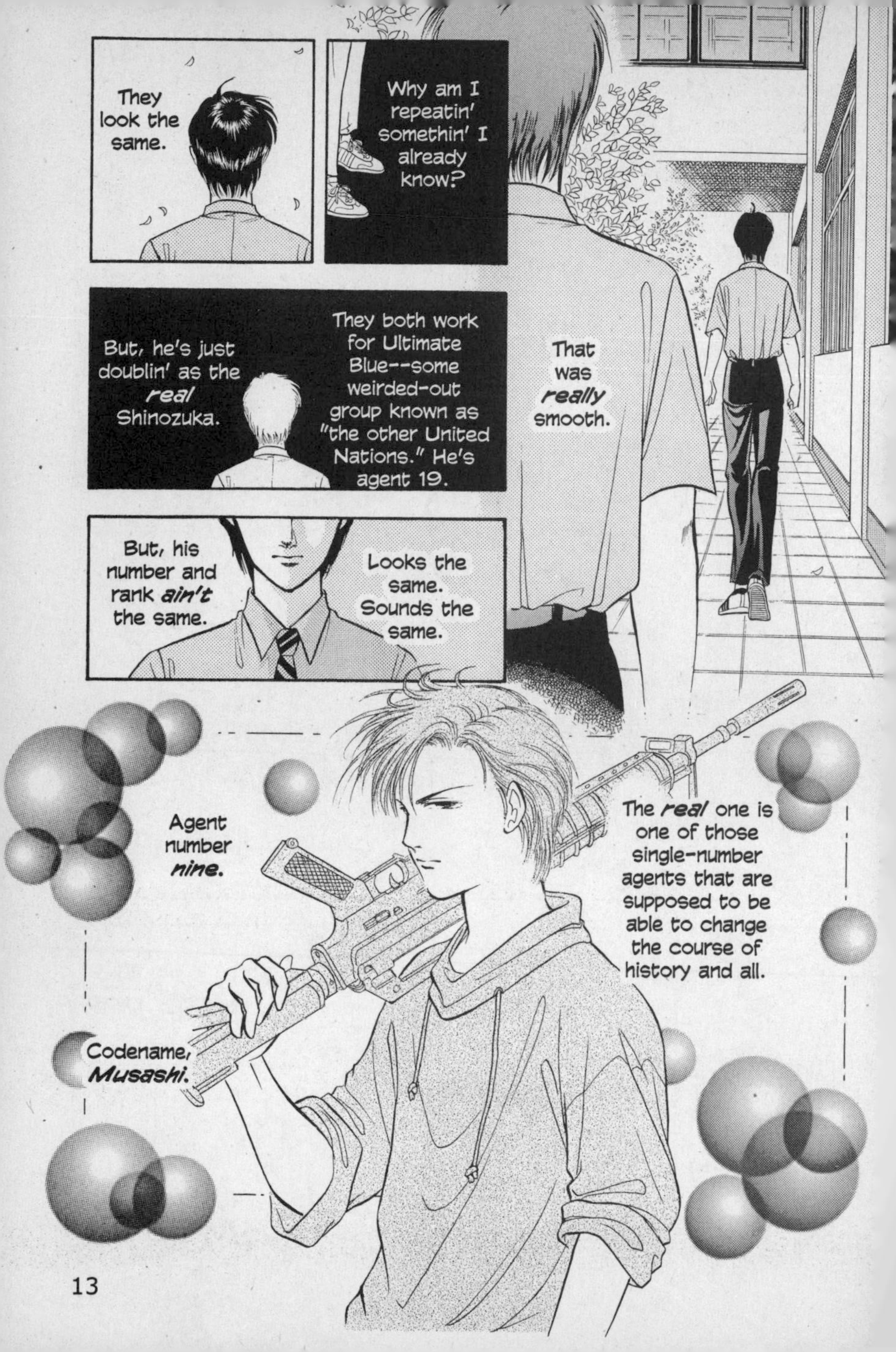

That was *really* smooth.
Why am I repeatin' somethin' I already know?
They look the same.
They both work for Ultimate Blue--some weirded-out group known as "the other United Nations." He's agent 19.
But, he's just doublin' as the *real* Shinozuka.
Looks the same. Sounds the same.
But, his number and rank *ain't* the same.
The *real* one is one of those single-number agents that are supposed to be able to change the course of history and all.
Agent number *nine*.
Codename, *Musashi*.

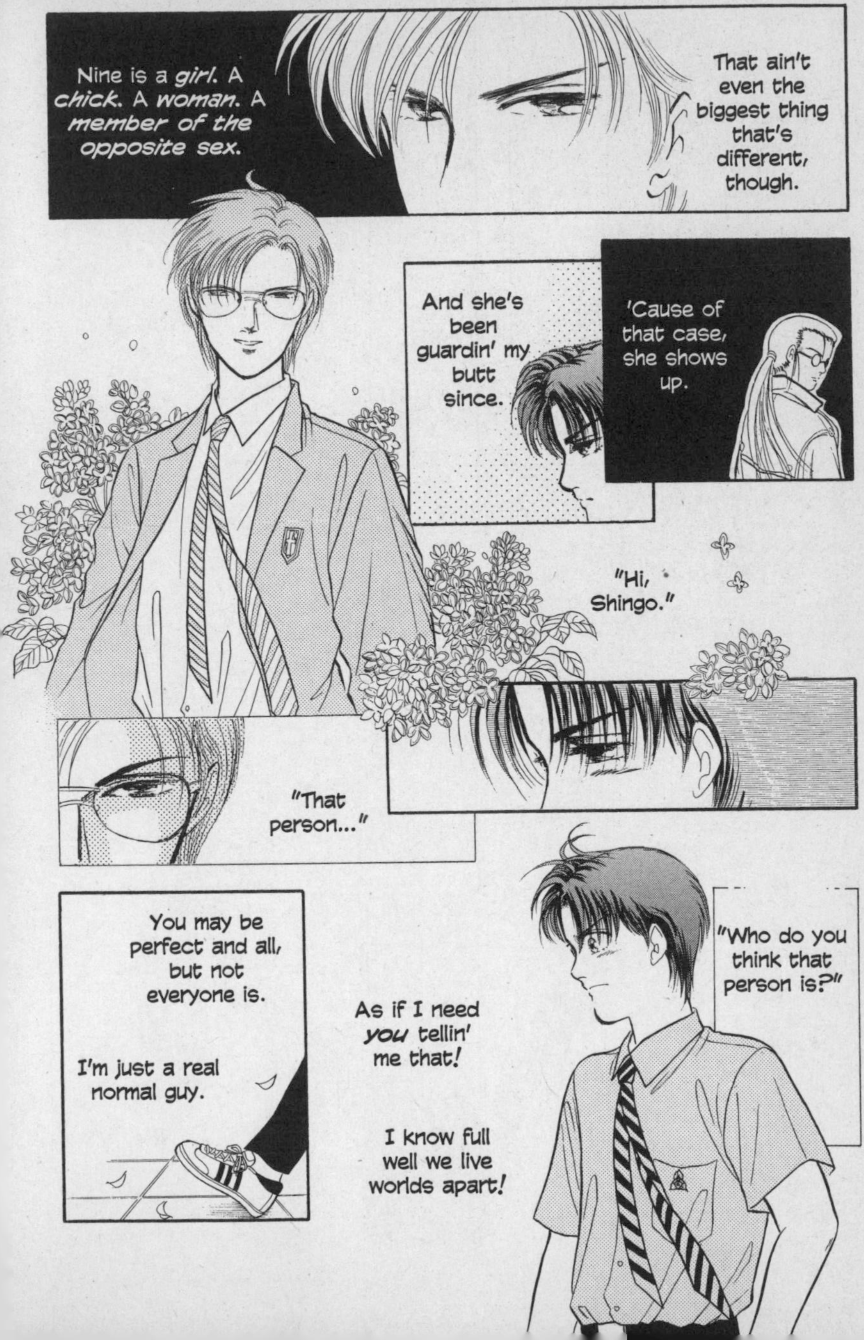
That ain't even the biggest thing that's different, though.
Nine is a *girl*. A *chick*. A *woman*. A *member of the opposite sex*.
'Cause of that case, she shows up.
And she's been guardin' my butt since.
"Hi, Shingo."
"That person..."
"Who do you think that person is?"
As if I need *you* tellin' me that!
I know full well we live worlds apart!
You may be perfect and all, but not everyone is.
I'm just a real normal guy.

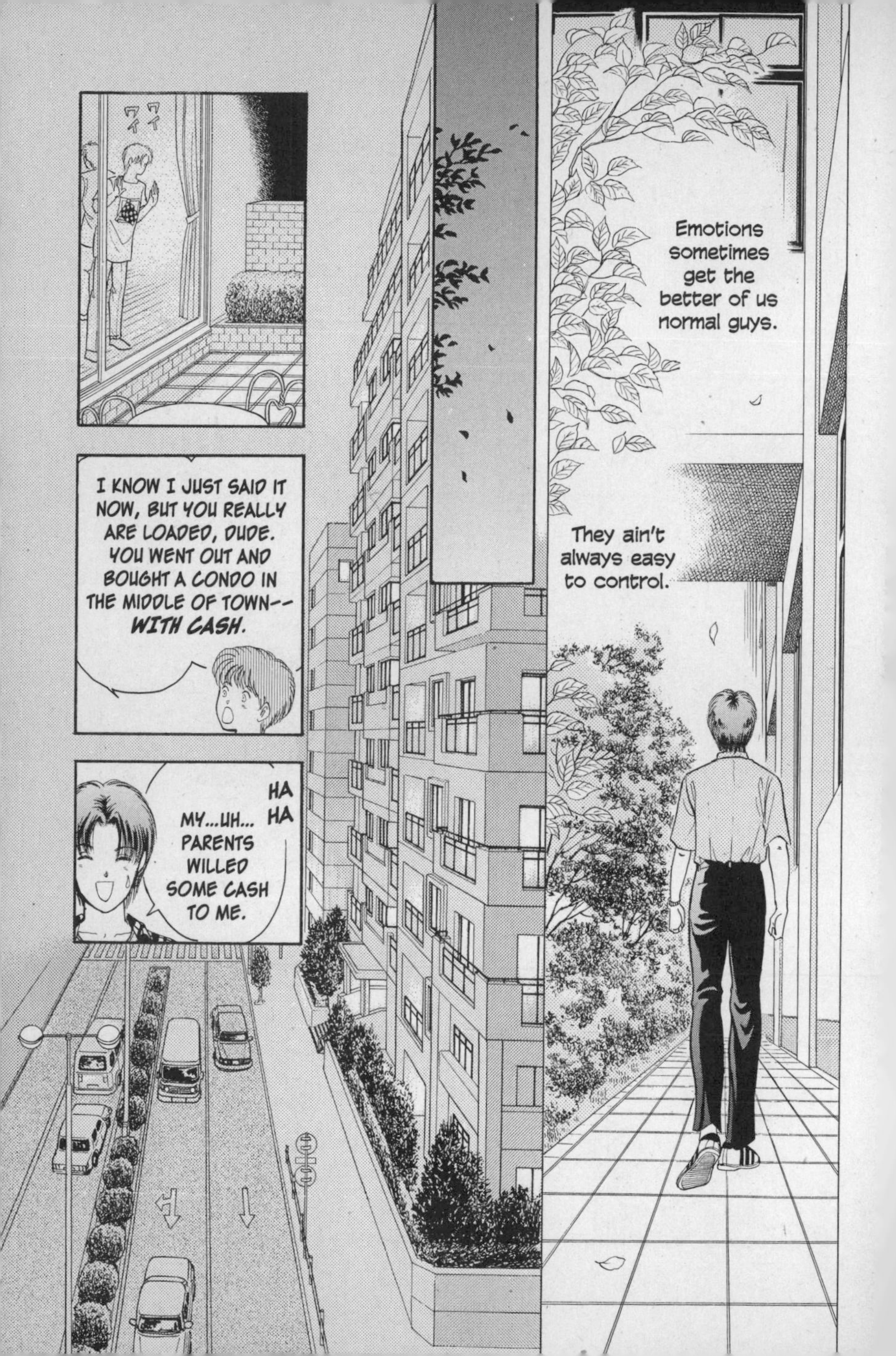
Emotions sometimes get the better of us normal guys.
They ain't always easy to control.
I KNOW I JUST SAID IT NOW, BUT YOU REALLY ARE LOADED, DUDE. YOU WENT OUT AND BOUGHT A CONDO IN THE MIDDLE OF TOWN-- WITH CASH.
HA HA
MY...UH... PARENTS WILLED SOME CASH TO ME.

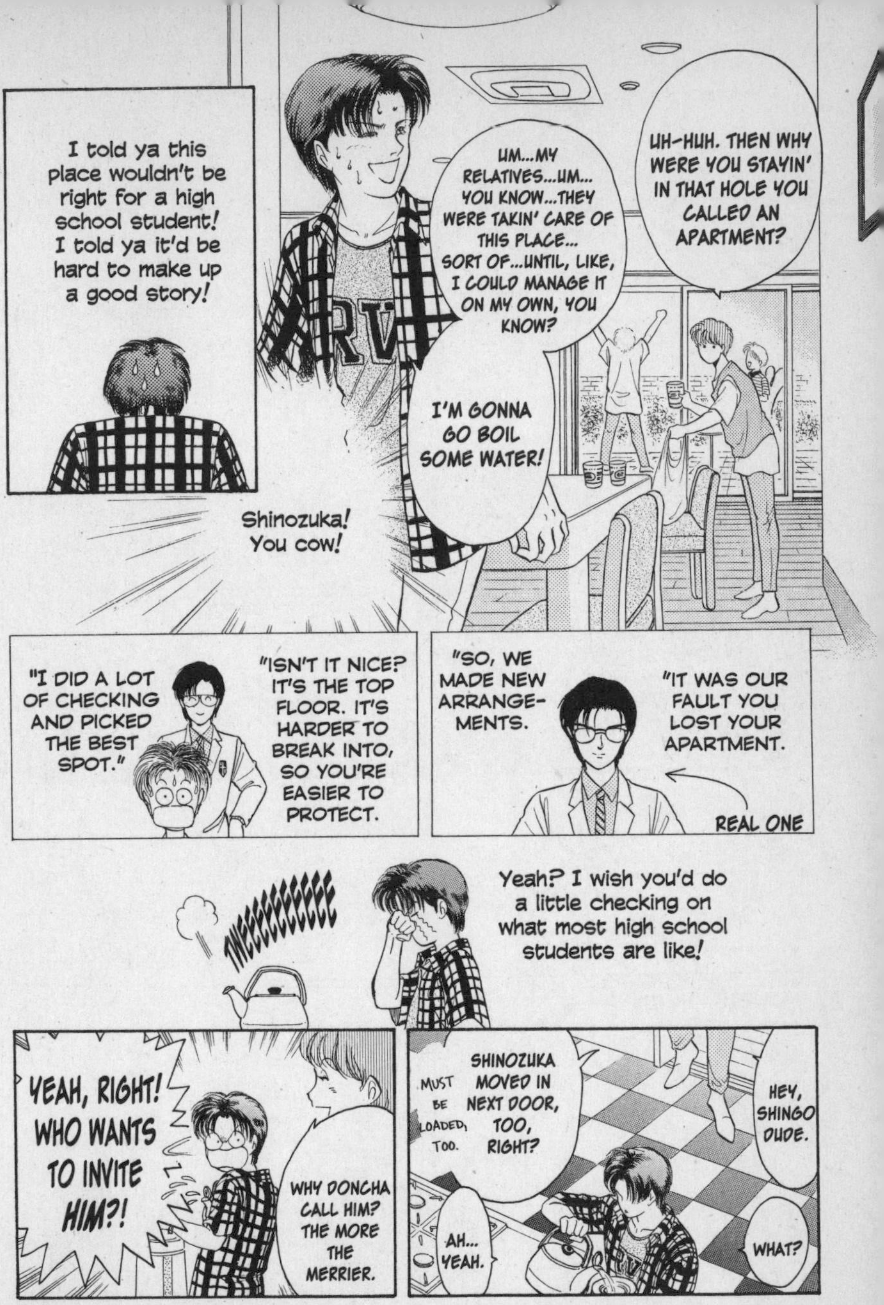
UH-HUH. THEN WHY WERE YOU STAYIN' IN THAT HOLE YOU CALLED AN APARTMENT?
UM...MY RELATIVES...UM... YOU KNOW...THEY WERE TAKIN' CARE OF THIS PLACE... SORT OF...UNTIL, LIKE, I COULD MANAGE IT ON MY OWN, YOU KNOW?
I'M GONNA GO BOIL SOME WATER!
I told ya this place wouldn't be right for a high school student! I told ya it'd be hard to make up a good story!
Shinozuka! You cow!
"IT WAS OUR FAULT YOU LOST YOUR APARTMENT.
"SO, WE MADE NEW ARRANGE-MENTS.
REAL ONE
"ISN'T IT NICE? IT'S THE TOP FLOOR. IT'S HARDER TO BREAK INTO, SO YOU'RE EASIER TO PROTECT.
"I DID A LOT OF CHECKING AND PICKED THE BEST SPOT."
Yeah? I wish you'd do a little checking on what most high school students are like!
TWEEEEEEEEEE
HEY, SHINGO DUDE.
SHINOZUKA MOVED IN NEXT DOOR, TOO, RIGHT?
MUST BE LOADED, TOO.
WHAT?
AH... YEAH.
WHY DONCHA CALL HIM? THE MORE THE MERRIER.
YEAH, RIGHT! WHO WANTS TO INVITE HIM?!

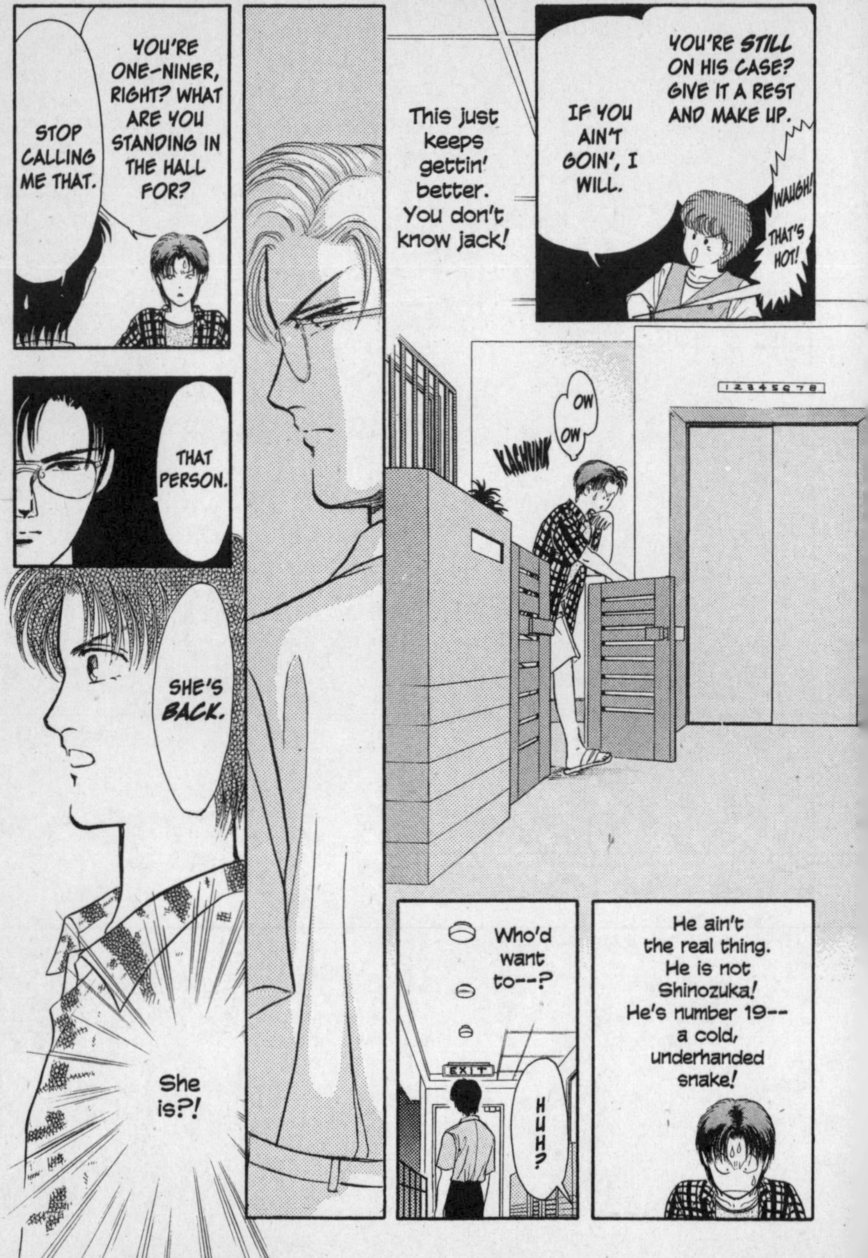
YOU'RE STILL ON HIS CASE? GIVE IT A REST AND MAKE UP.
IF YOU AIN'T GOIN', I WILL.
WAUGH! THAT'S HOT!
This just keeps gettin' better. You don't know jack!
KACHUNK
OW OW
He ain't the real thing. He is not Shinozuka! He's number 19-- a cold, underhanded snake!
Who'd want to--?
HUH?
EXIT
YOU'RE ONE-NINER, RIGHT? WHAT ARE YOU STANDING IN THE HALL FOR?
STOP CALLING ME THAT.
THAT PERSON.
SHE'S BACK.
She is?!

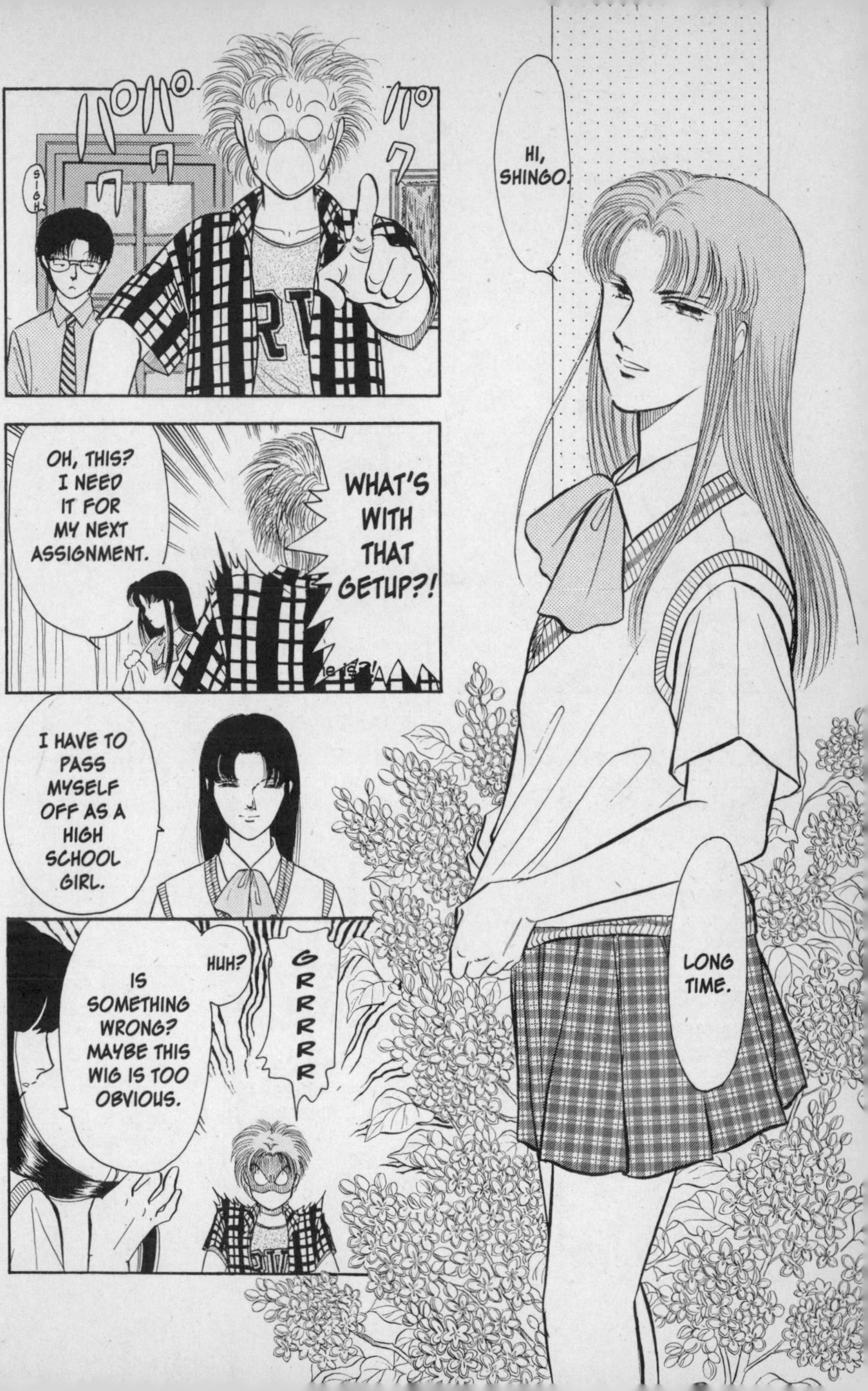
HI, SHINGO.
LONG TIME.
SIGH
WHAT'S WITH THAT GETUP?!
OH, THIS? I NEED IT FOR MY NEXT ASSIGNMENT.
I HAVE TO PASS MYSELF OFF AS A HIGH SCHOOL GIRL.
GRRRRR
HUH?
IS SOMETHING WRONG? MAYBE THIS WIG IS TOO OBVIOUS.

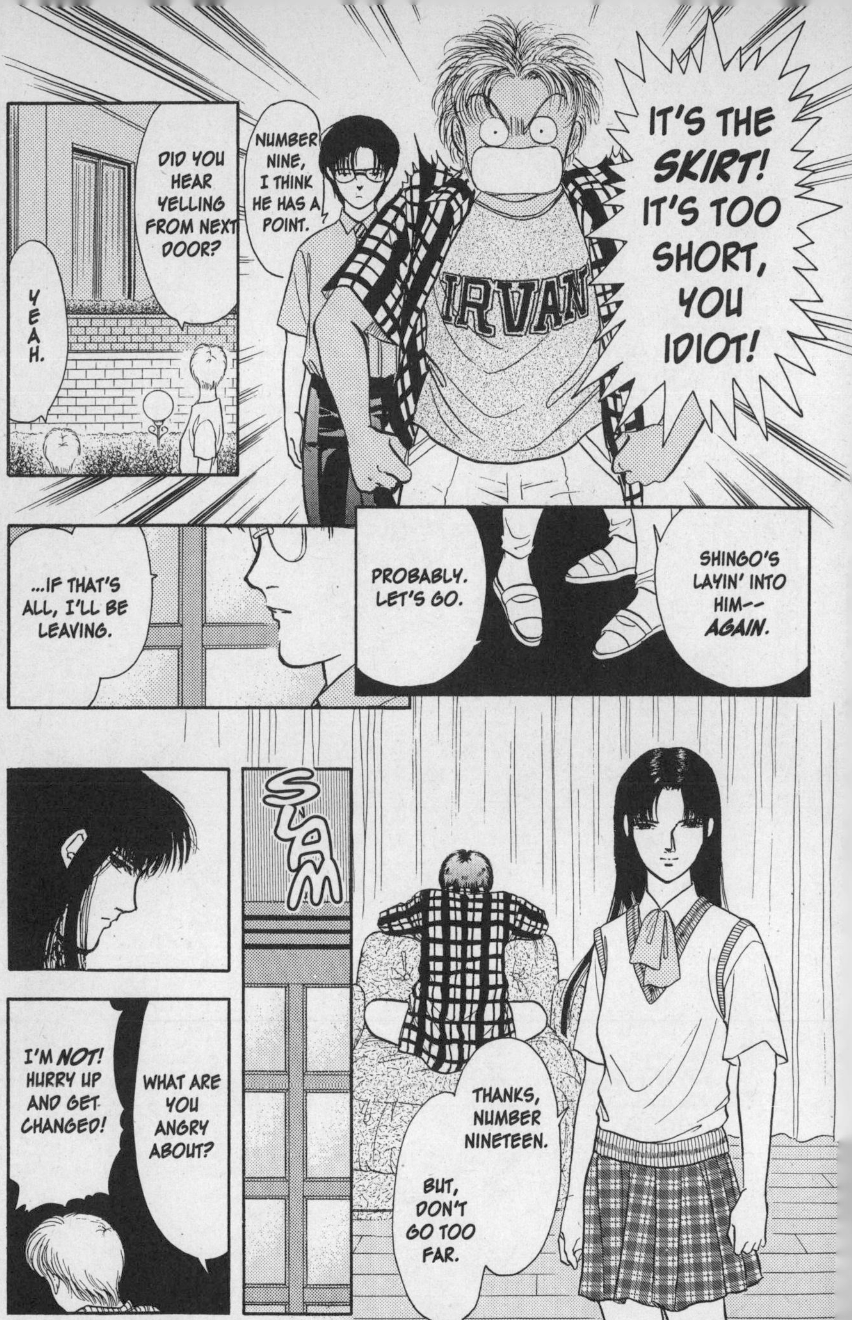
IT'S THE SKIRT! IT'S TOO SHORT, YOU IDIOT!
NUMBER NINE, I THINK HE HAS A POINT.
DID YOU HEAR YELLING FROM NEXT DOOR?
YEAH.
SHINGO'S LAYIN' INTO HIM-- AGAIN.
PROBABLY. LET'S GO.
...IF THAT'S ALL, I'LL BE LEAVING.
THANKS, NUMBER NINETEEN.
BUT, DON'T GO TOO FAR.
SLAM
WHAT ARE YOU ANGRY ABOUT?
I'M NOT! HURRY UP AND GET CHANGED!

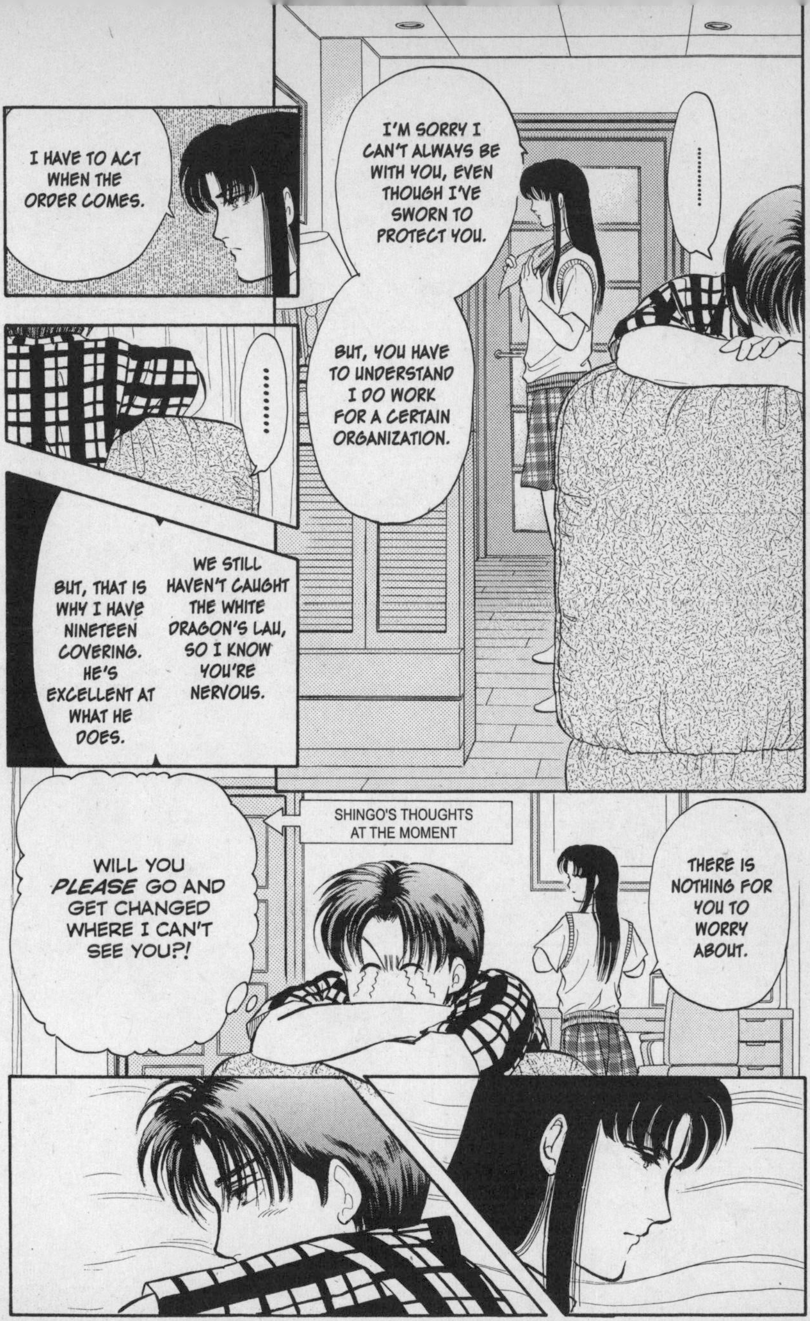
......
I'M SORRY I CAN'T ALWAYS BE WITH YOU, EVEN THOUGH I'VE SWORN TO PROTECT YOU.
BUT, YOU HAVE TO UNDERSTAND I DO WORK FOR A CERTAIN ORGANIZATION.
I HAVE TO ACT WHEN THE ORDER COMES.
......
WE STILL HAVEN'T CAUGHT THE WHITE DRAGON'S LAU, SO I KNOW YOU'RE NERVOUS.
BUT, THAT IS WHY I HAVE NINETEEN COVERING. HE'S EXCELLENT AT WHAT HE DOES.
THERE IS NOTHING FOR YOU TO WORRY ABOUT.
SHINGO'S THOUGHTS AT THE MOMENT
WILL YOU *PLEASE* GO AND GET CHANGED WHERE I CAN'T SEE YOU?!

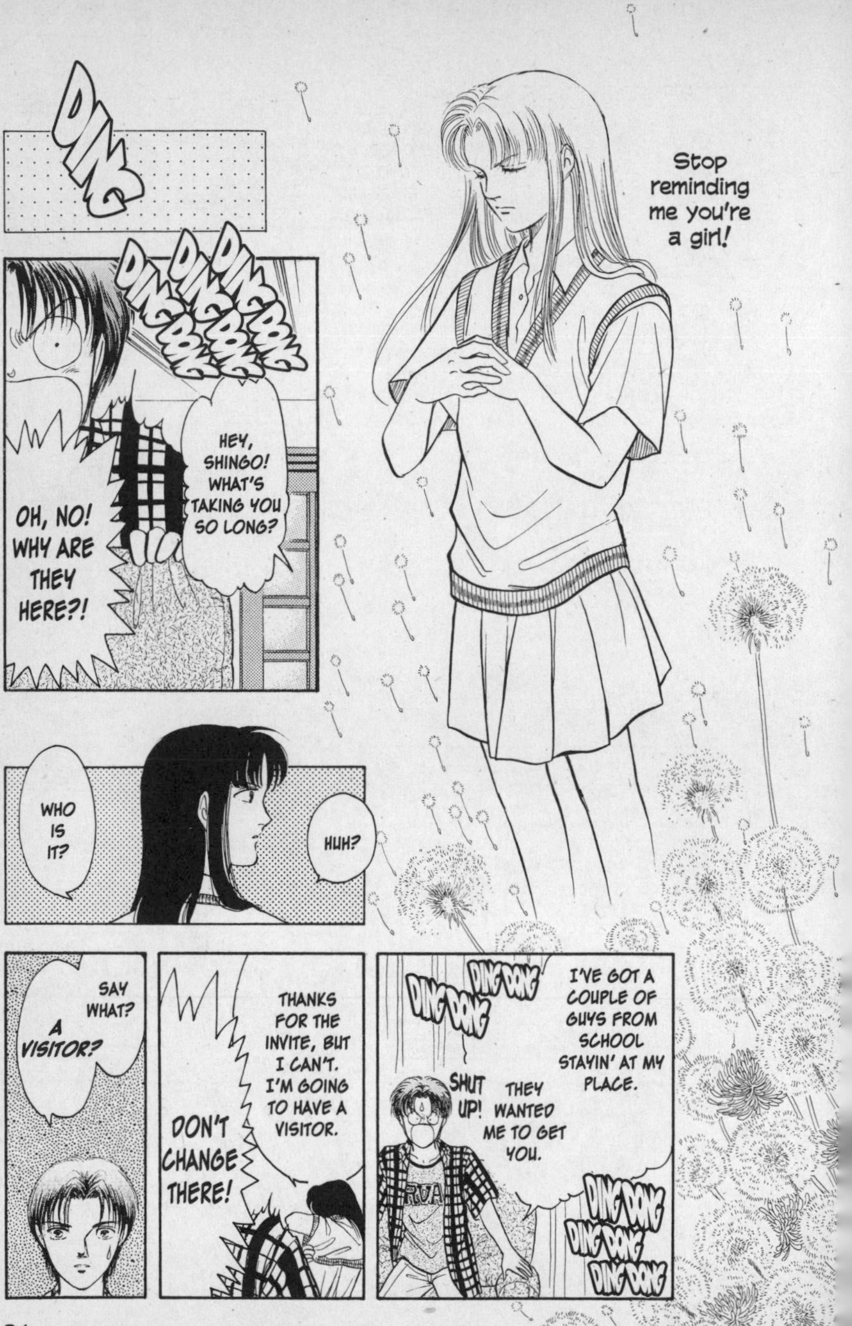

Stop reminding me you're a girl!
DING
DING DONG DING DONG DING DONG
HEY, SHINGO! WHAT'S TAKING YOU SO LONG?
OH, NO! WHY ARE THEY HERE?!
HUH?
WHO IS IT?
DING DONG DING DONG
I'VE GOT A COUPLE OF GUYS FROM SCHOOL STAYIN' AT MY PLACE.
THEY WANTED ME TO GET YOU.
SHUT UP!
DING DONG DING DONG DING DONG
THANKS FOR THE INVITE, BUT I CAN'T. I'M GOING TO HAVE A VISITOR.
DON'T CHANGE THERE!
SAY WHAT? A VISITOR?

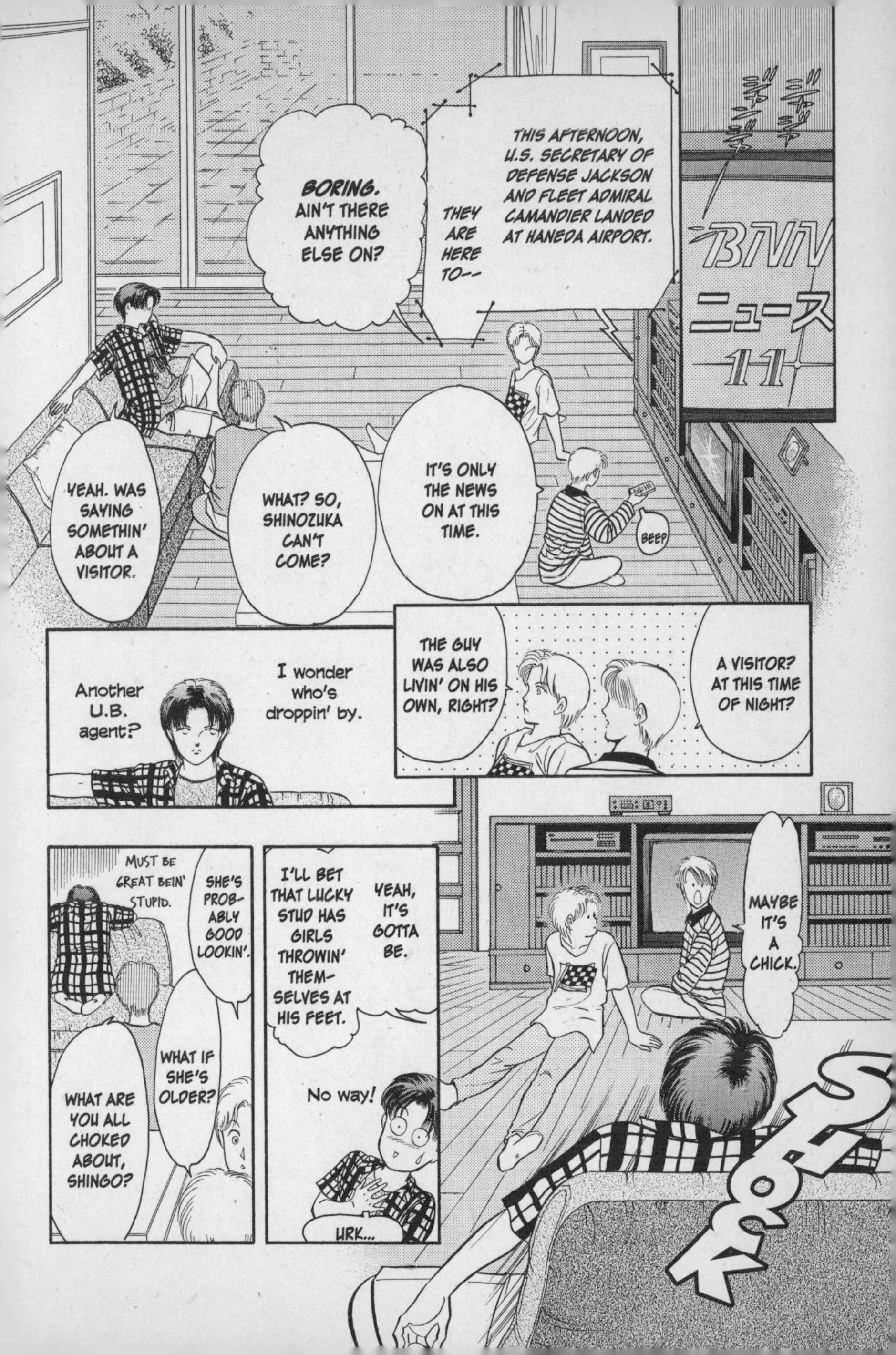
BNN ニュース 11
THIS AFTERNOON, U.S. SECRETARY OF DEFENSE JACKSON AND FLEET ADMIRAL CAMANDIER LANDED AT HANEDA AIRPORT.
THEY ARE HERE TO--
BORING. AIN'T THERE ANYTHING ELSE ON?
IT'S ONLY THE NEWS ON AT THIS TIME.
BEEP
WHAT? SO, SHINOZUKA CAN'T COME?
YEAH. WAS SAYING SOMETHIN' ABOUT A VISITOR.
A VISITOR? AT THIS TIME OF NIGHT?
THE GUY WAS ALSO LIVIN' ON HIS OWN, RIGHT?
I wonder who's droppin' by.
Another U.B. agent?
MAYBE IT'S A CHICK.
SHOCK
YEAH, IT'S GOTTA BE.
I'LL BET THAT LUCKY STUD HAS GIRLS THROWIN' THEM-SELVES AT HIS FEET.
No way!
URK...
SHE'S PROB-ABLY GOOD LOOKIN'.
MUST BE GREAT BEIN' STUPID.
WHAT IF SHE'S OLDER?
WHAT ARE YOU ALL CHOKED ABOUT, SHINGO?

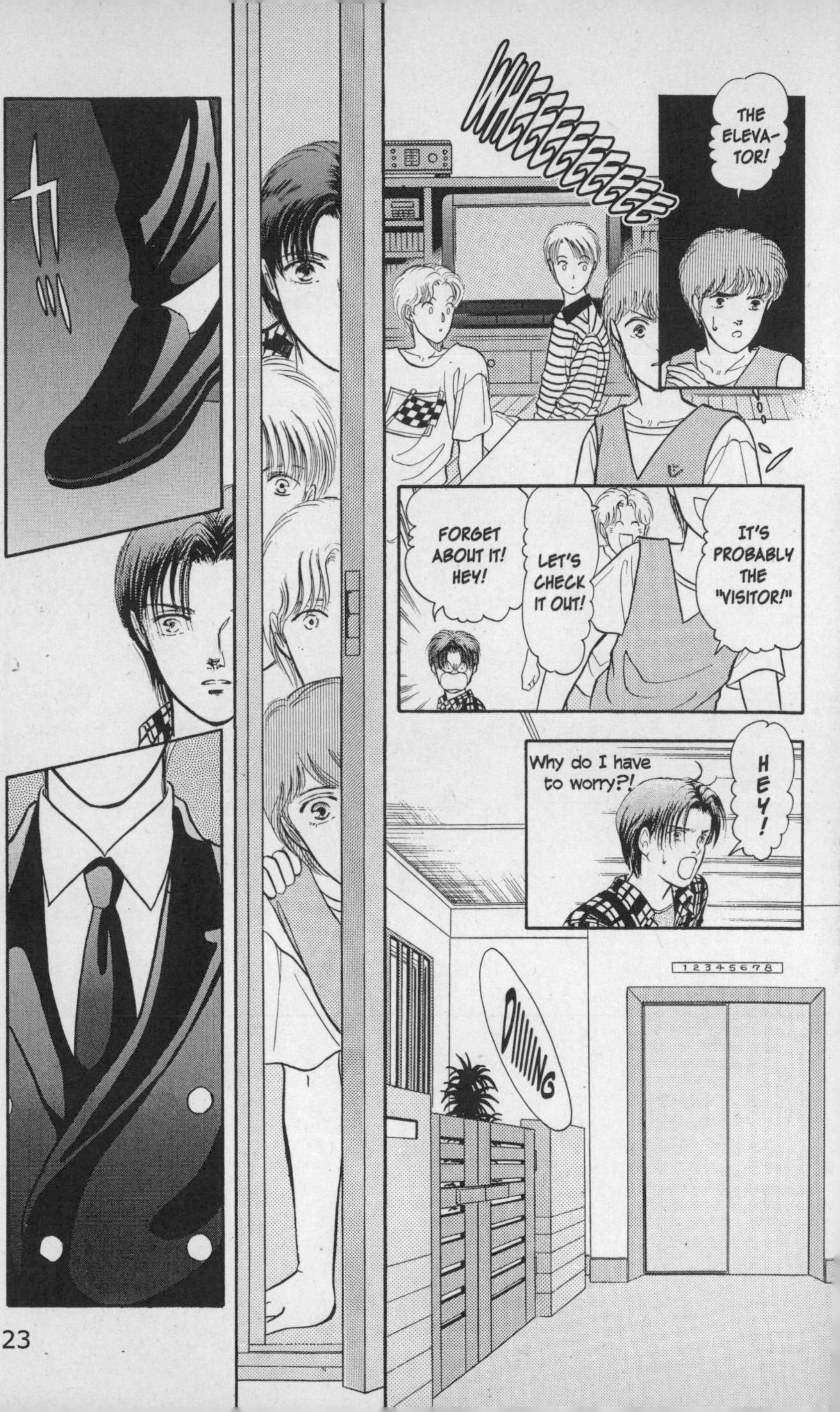
WHEEEEEEEEE
THE ELEVA-TOR!
IT'S PROBABLY THE "VISITOR!"
LET'S CHECK IT OUT!
FORGET ABOUT IT! HEY!
HEY!
Why do I have to worry?!
DIIIING
カッ

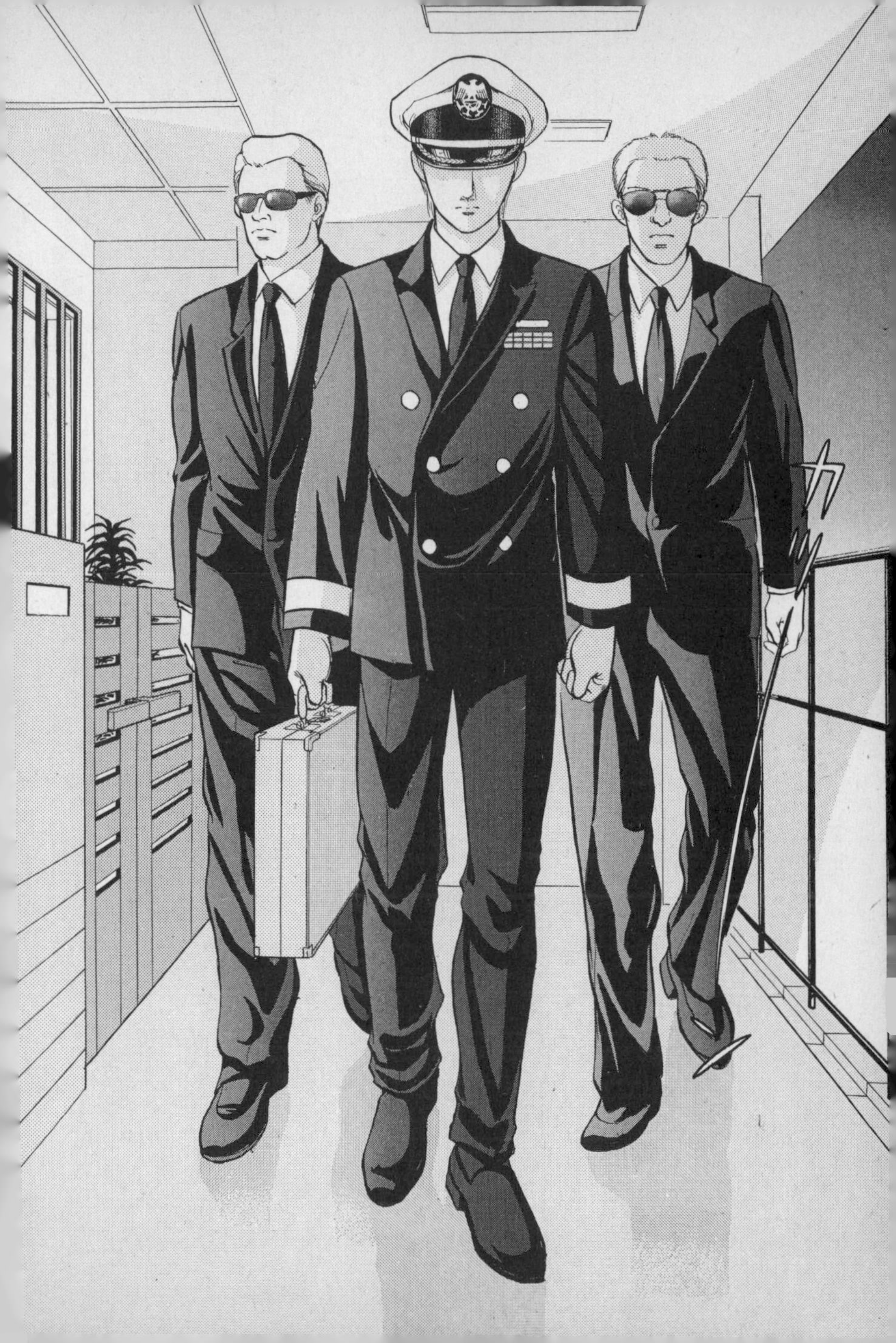

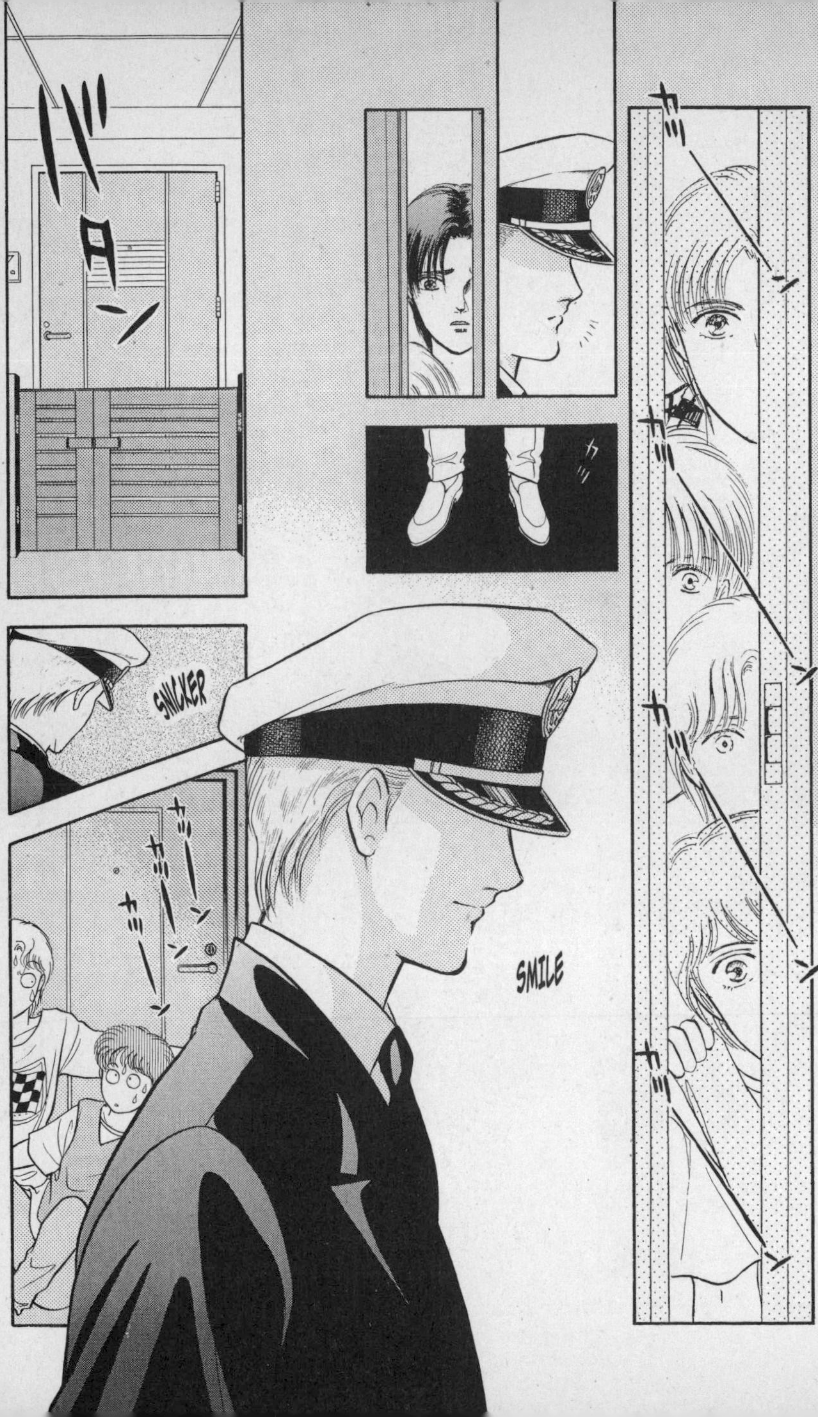
SMILE
SNICKER

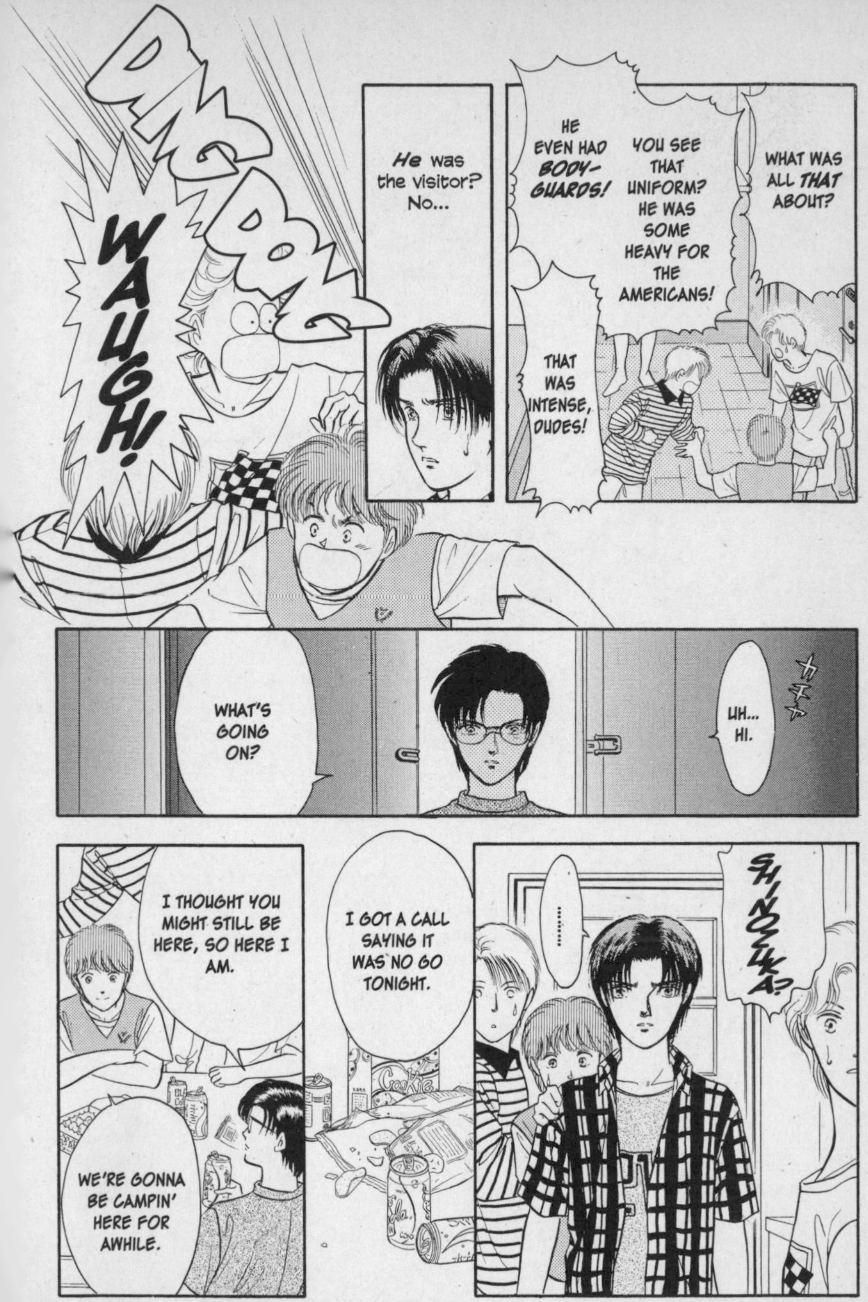
WHAT WAS ALL THAT ABOUT?
YOU SEE THAT UNIFORM? HE WAS SOME HEAVY FOR THE AMERICANS!
HE EVEN HAD BODY-GUARDS!
THAT WAS INTENSE, DUDES!
He was the visitor? No...
DING DONG
WAUGH!
UH... HI.
WHAT'S GOING ON?
SHINOZUKA?
......
I GOT A CALL SAYING IT WAS NO GO TONIGHT.
I THOUGHT YOU MIGHT STILL BE HERE, SO HERE I AM.
WE'RE GONNA BE CAMPIN' HERE FOR AWHILE.

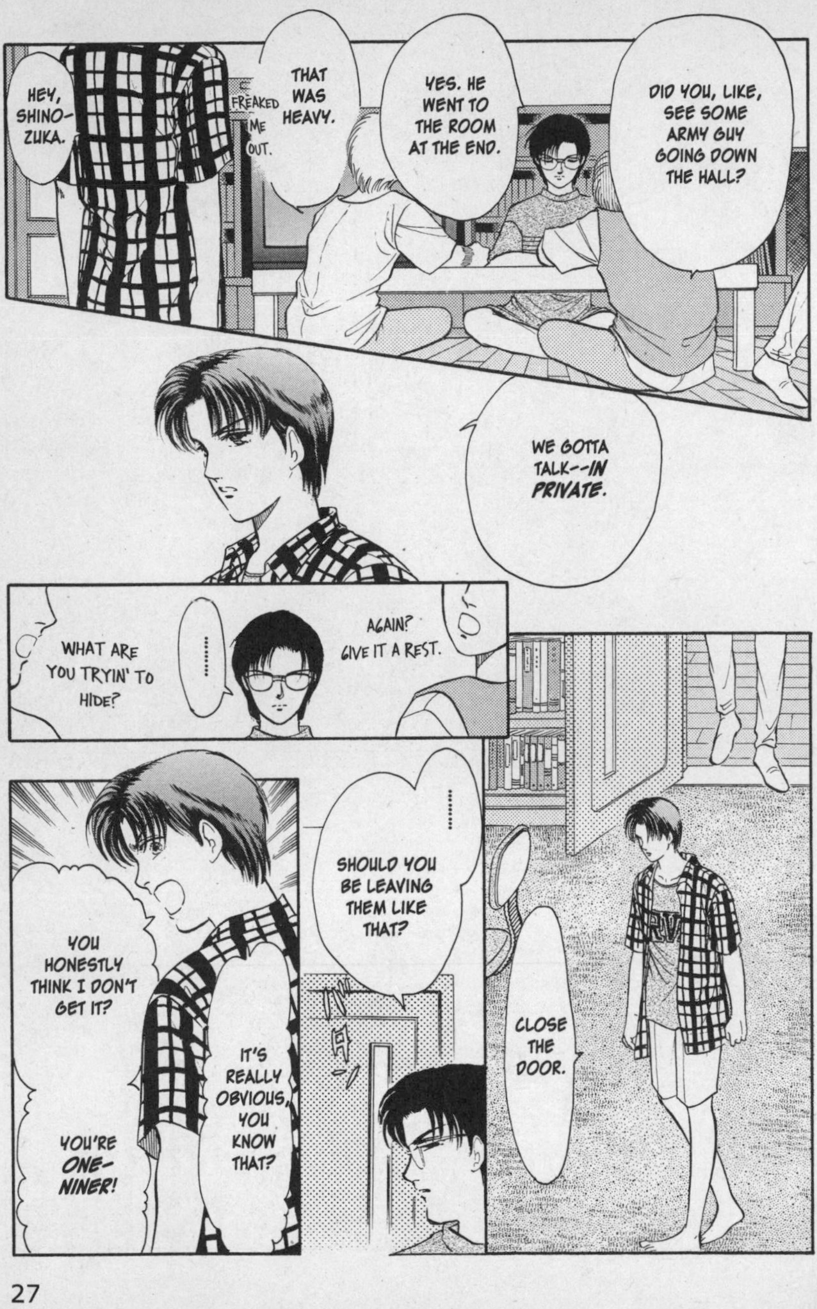
DID YOU, LIKE, SEE SOME ARMY GUY GOING DOWN THE HALL?
YES. HE WENT TO THE ROOM AT THE END.
THAT WAS HEAVY.
FREAKED ME OUT.
HEY, SHINOZUKA.
WE GOTTA TALK--*IN PRIVATE*.
AGAIN? GIVE IT A REST.
......
WHAT ARE YOU TRYIN' TO HIDE?
CLOSE THE DOOR.
......
SHOULD YOU BE LEAVING THEM LIKE THAT?
YOU HONESTLY THINK I DON'T GET IT?
IT'S REALLY OBVIOUS, YOU KNOW THAT?
YOU'RE *ONE-NINER!*

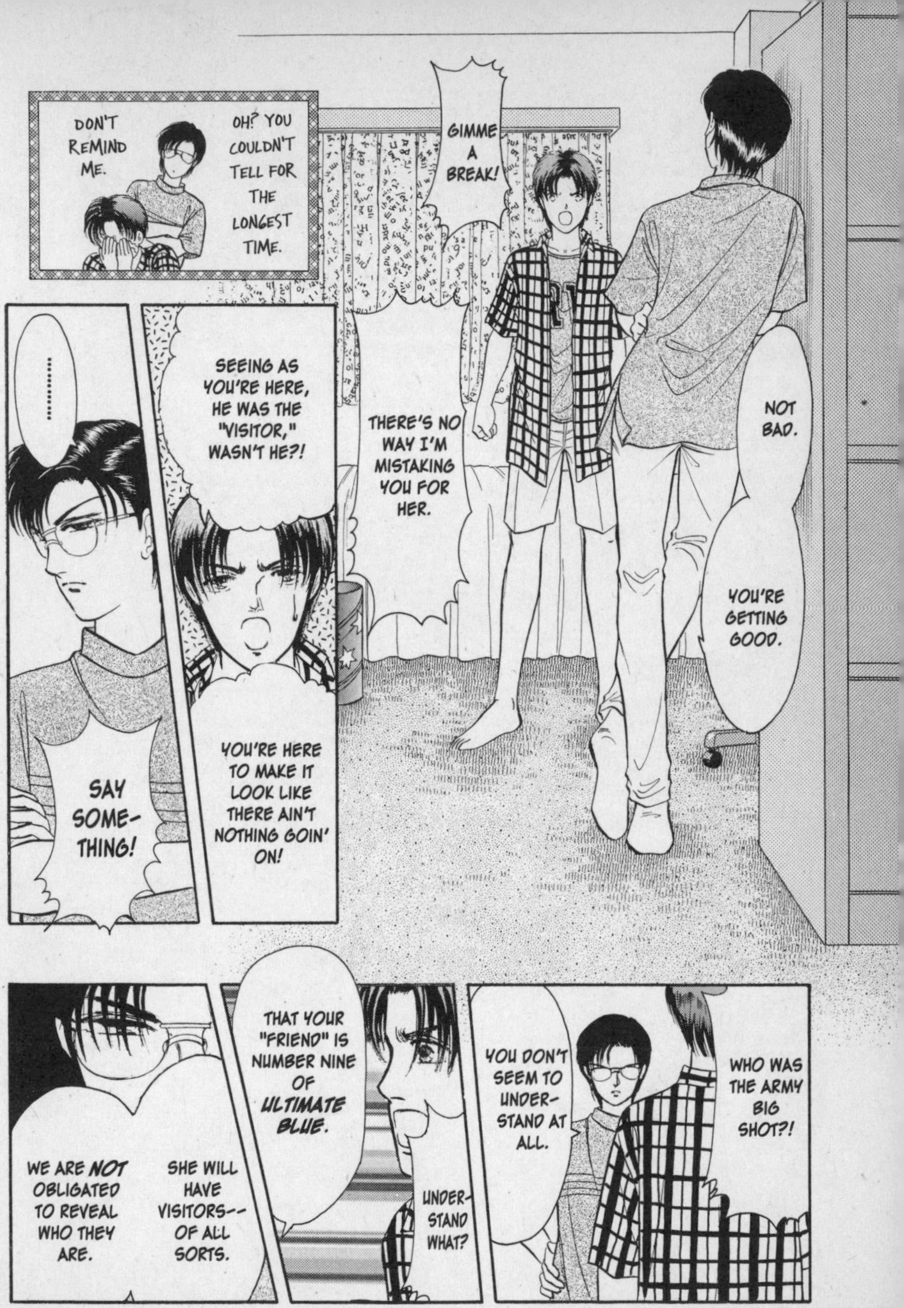
NOT BAD.
YOU'RE GETTING GOOD.
GIMME A BREAK!
THERE'S NO WAY I'M MISTAKING YOU FOR HER.
OH? YOU COULDN'T TELL FOR THE LONGEST TIME.
DON'T REMIND ME.
SEEING AS YOU'RE HERE, HE WAS THE "VISITOR," WASN'T HE?!
YOU'RE HERE TO MAKE IT LOOK LIKE THERE AIN'T NOTHING GOIN' ON!
....
SAY SOME-THING!
WHO WAS THE ARMY BIG SHOT?!
YOU DON'T SEEM TO UNDER-STAND AT ALL.
UNDER-STAND WHAT?
THAT YOUR "FRIEND" IS NUMBER NINE OF ULTIMATE BLUE.
SHE WILL HAVE VISITORS--OF ALL SORTS.
WE ARE NOT OBLIGATED TO REVEAL WHO THEY ARE.

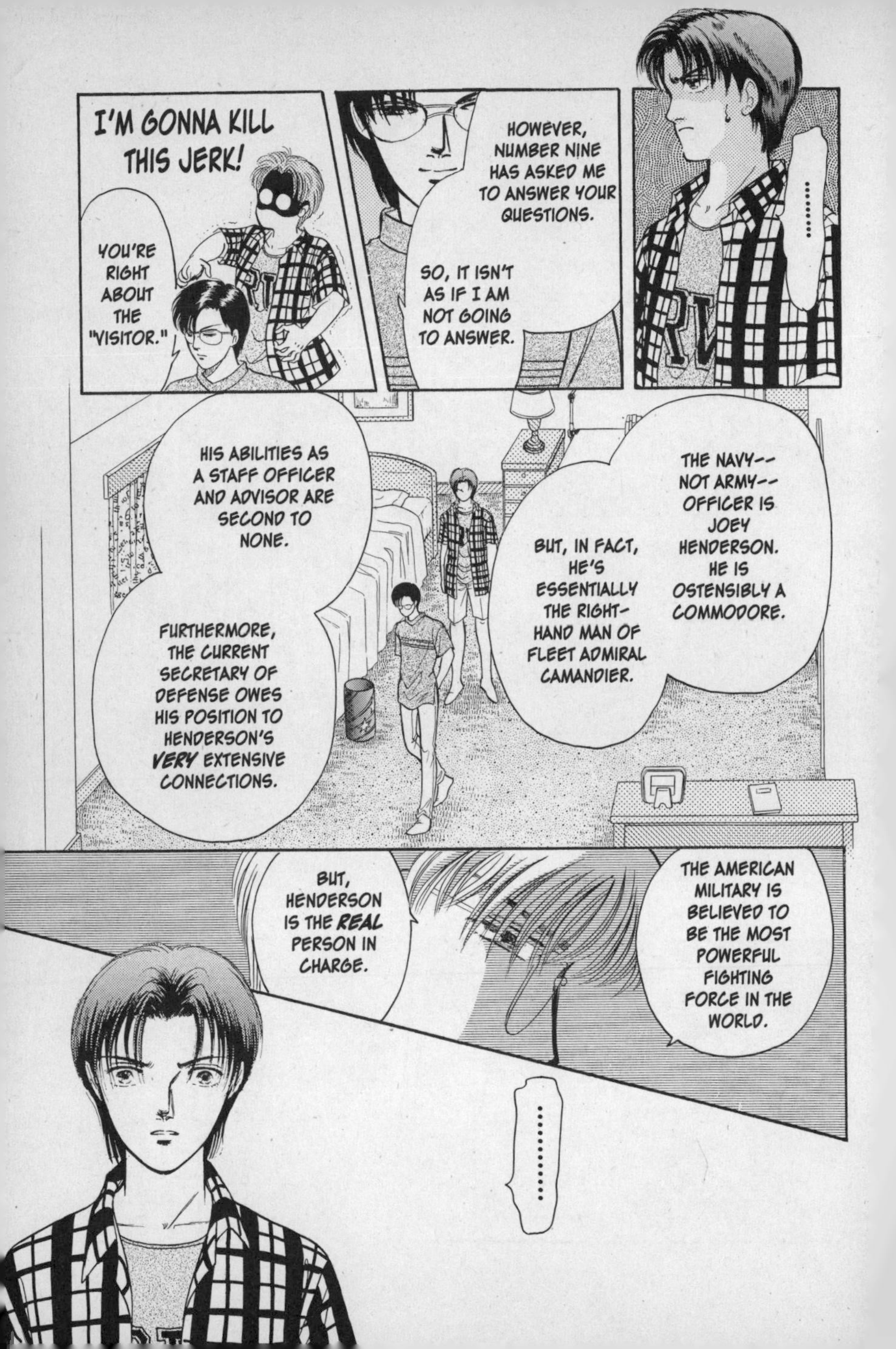
......
HOWEVER, NUMBER NINE HAS ASKED ME TO ANSWER YOUR QUESTIONS.
SO, IT ISN'T AS IF I AM NOT GOING TO ANSWER.
I'M GONNA KILL THIS JERK!
YOU'RE RIGHT ABOUT THE "VISITOR."
THE NAVY--NOT ARMY--OFFICER IS JOEY HENDERSON. HE IS OSTENSIBLY A COMMODORE.
BUT, IN FACT, HE'S ESSENTIALLY THE RIGHT-HAND MAN OF FLEET ADMIRAL CAMANDIER.
HIS ABILITIES AS A STAFF OFFICER AND ADVISOR ARE SECOND TO NONE.
FURTHERMORE, THE CURRENT SECRETARY OF DEFENSE OWES HIS POSITION TO HENDERSON'S *VERY* EXTENSIVE CONNECTIONS.
THE AMERICAN MILITARY IS BELIEVED TO BE THE MOST POWERFUL FIGHTING FORCE IN THE WORLD.
BUT, HENDERSON IS THE *REAL* PERSON IN CHARGE.
......

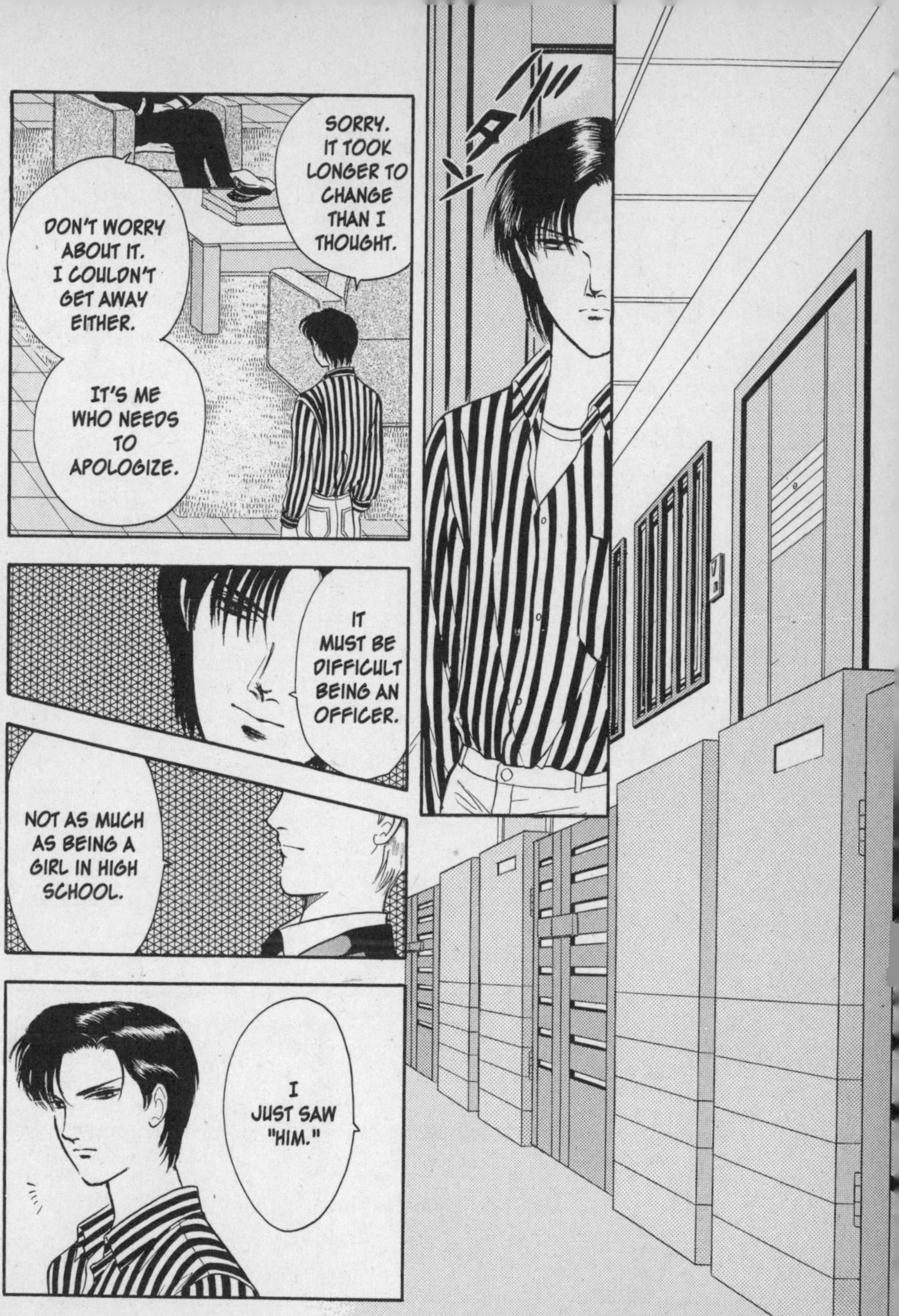
SORRY. IT TOOK LONGER TO CHANGE THAN I THOUGHT.
DON'T WORRY ABOUT IT. I COULDN'T GET AWAY EITHER.
IT'S ME WHO NEEDS TO APOLOGIZE.
IT MUST BE DIFFICULT BEING AN OFFICER.
NOT AS MUCH AS BEING A GIRL IN HIGH SCHOOL.
I JUST SAW "HIM."

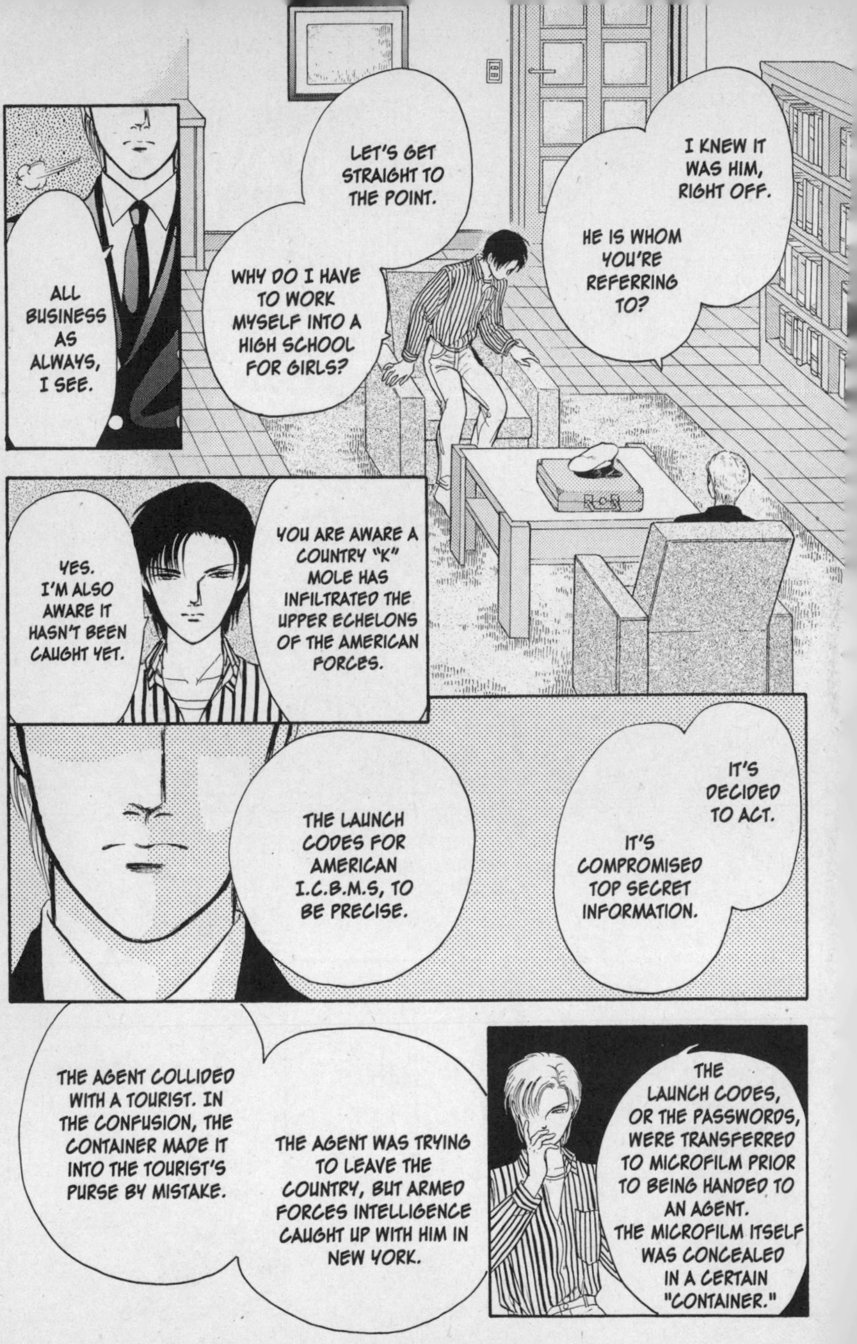
I KNEW IT WAS HIM, RIGHT OFF.
HE IS WHOM YOU'RE REFERRING TO?
LET'S GET STRAIGHT TO THE POINT.
WHY DO I HAVE TO WORK MYSELF INTO A HIGH SCHOOL FOR GIRLS?
ALL BUSINESS AS ALWAYS, I SEE.
YOU ARE AWARE A COUNTRY "K" MOLE HAS INFILTRATED THE UPPER ECHELONS OF THE AMERICAN FORCES.
YES. I'M ALSO AWARE IT HASN'T BEEN CAUGHT YET.
IT'S DECIDED TO ACT.
IT'S COMPROMISED TOP SECRET INFORMATION.
THE LAUNCH CODES FOR AMERICAN I.C.B.M.S, TO BE PRECISE.
THE LAUNCH CODES, OR THE PASSWORDS, WERE TRANSFERRED TO MICROFILM PRIOR TO BEING HANDED TO AN AGENT.
THE MICROFILM ITSELF WAS CONCEALED IN A CERTAIN "CONTAINER."
THE AGENT WAS TRYING TO LEAVE THE COUNTRY, BUT ARMED FORCES INTELLIGENCE CAUGHT UP WITH HIM IN NEW YORK.
THE AGENT COLLIDED WITH A TOURIST. IN THE CONFUSION, THE CONTAINER MADE IT INTO THE TOURIST'S PURSE BY MISTAKE.

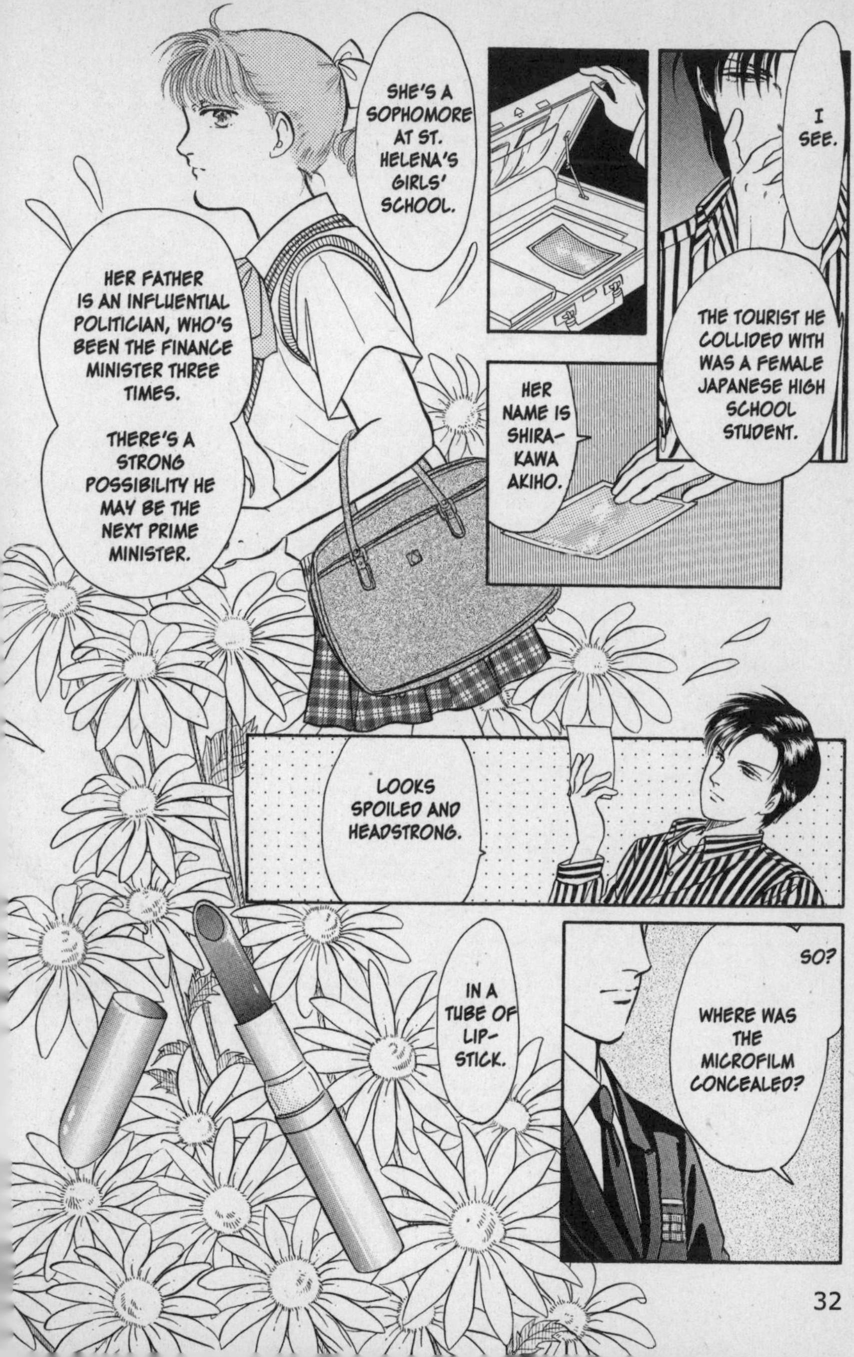
I SEE.
THE TOURIST HE COLLIDED WITH WAS A FEMALE JAPANESE HIGH SCHOOL STUDENT.
HER NAME IS SHIRA-KAWA AKIHO.
SHE'S A SOPHOMORE AT ST. HELENA'S GIRLS' SCHOOL.
HER FATHER IS AN INFLUENTIAL POLITICIAN, WHO'S BEEN THE FINANCE MINISTER THREE TIMES.
THERE'S A STRONG POSSIBILITY HE MAY BE THE NEXT PRIME MINISTER.
LOOKS SPOILED AND HEADSTRONG.
SO?
WHERE WAS THE MICROFILM CONCEALED?
IN A TUBE OF LIP-STICK.

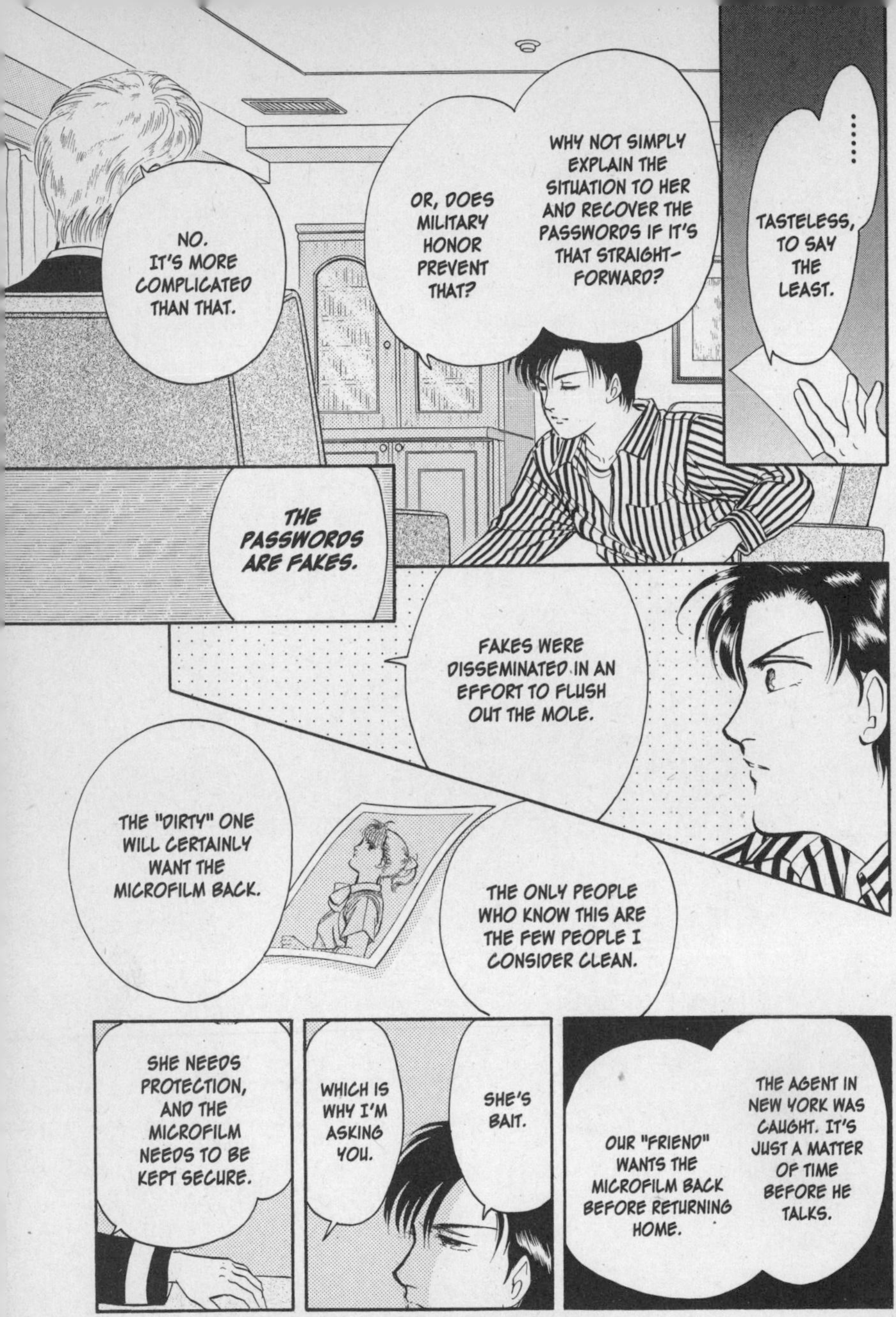
……
TASTELESS, TO SAY THE LEAST.
WHY NOT SIMPLY EXPLAIN THE SITUATION TO HER AND RECOVER THE PASSWORDS IF IT'S THAT STRAIGHT-FORWARD?
OR, DOES MILITARY HONOR PREVENT THAT?
NO. IT'S MORE COMPLICATED THAN THAT.
THE PASSWORDS ARE FAKES.
FAKES WERE DISSEMINATED IN AN EFFORT TO FLUSH OUT THE MOLE.
THE ONLY PEOPLE WHO KNOW THIS ARE THE FEW PEOPLE I CONSIDER CLEAN.
THE "DIRTY" ONE WILL CERTAINLY WANT THE MICROFILM BACK.
THE AGENT IN NEW YORK WAS CAUGHT. IT'S JUST A MATTER OF TIME BEFORE HE TALKS.
OUR "FRIEND" WANTS THE MICROFILM BACK BEFORE RETURNING HOME.
SHE'S BAIT.
WHICH IS WHY I'M ASKING YOU.
SHE NEEDS PROTECTION, AND THE MICROFILM NEEDS TO BE KEPT SECURE.

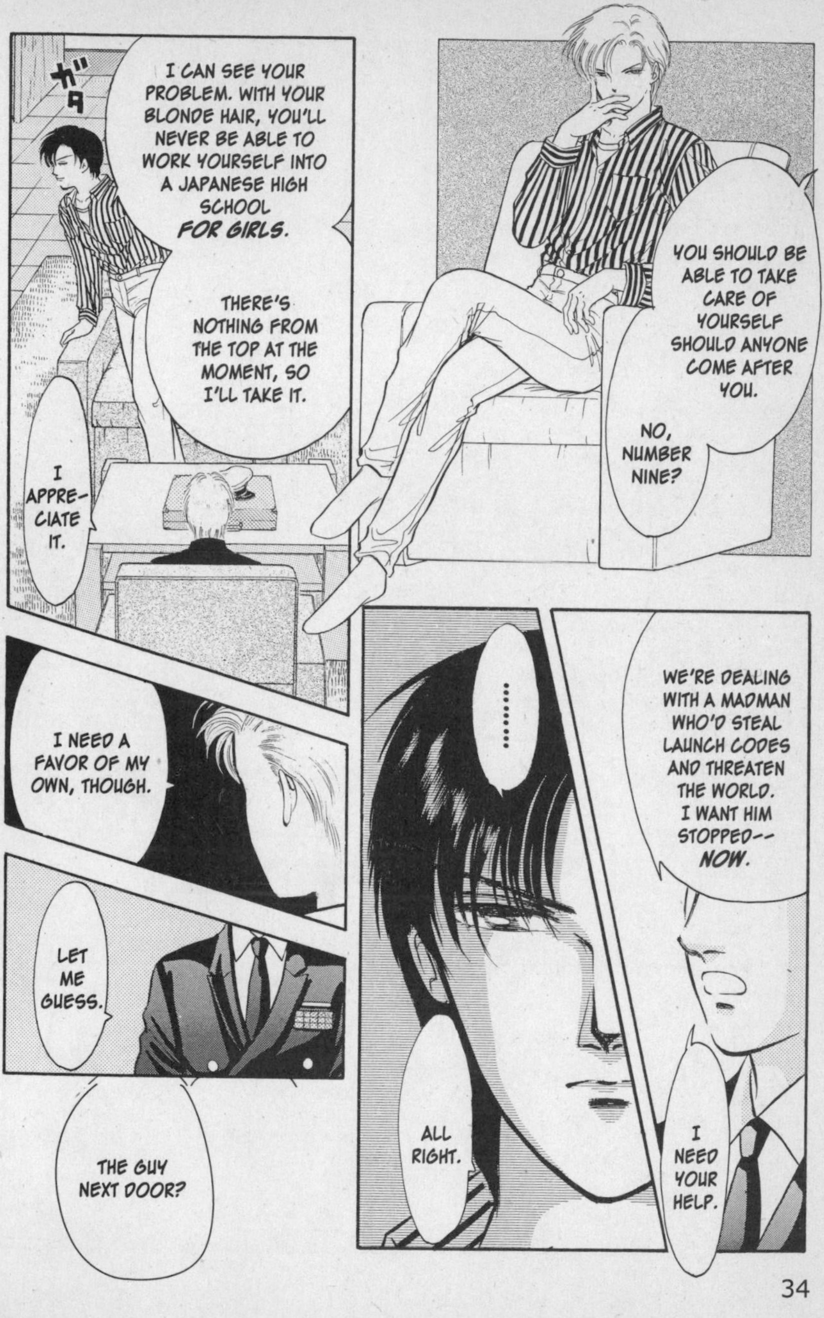
YOU SHOULD BE ABLE TO TAKE CARE OF YOURSELF SHOULD ANYONE COME AFTER YOU.
NO, NUMBER NINE?
I CAN SEE YOUR PROBLEM. WITH YOUR BLONDE HAIR, YOU'LL NEVER BE ABLE TO WORK YOURSELF INTO A JAPANESE HIGH SCHOOL *FOR GIRLS*.
ガタ
THERE'S NOTHING FROM THE TOP AT THE MOMENT, SO I'LL TAKE IT.
I APPRE-CIATE IT.
WE'RE DEALING WITH A MADMAN WHO'D STEAL LAUNCH CODES AND THREATEN THE WORLD. I WANT HIM STOPPED-- *NOW*.
I NEED YOUR HELP.
....
ALL RIGHT.
I NEED A FAVOR OF MY OWN, THOUGH.
LET ME GUESS.
THE GUY NEXT DOOR?

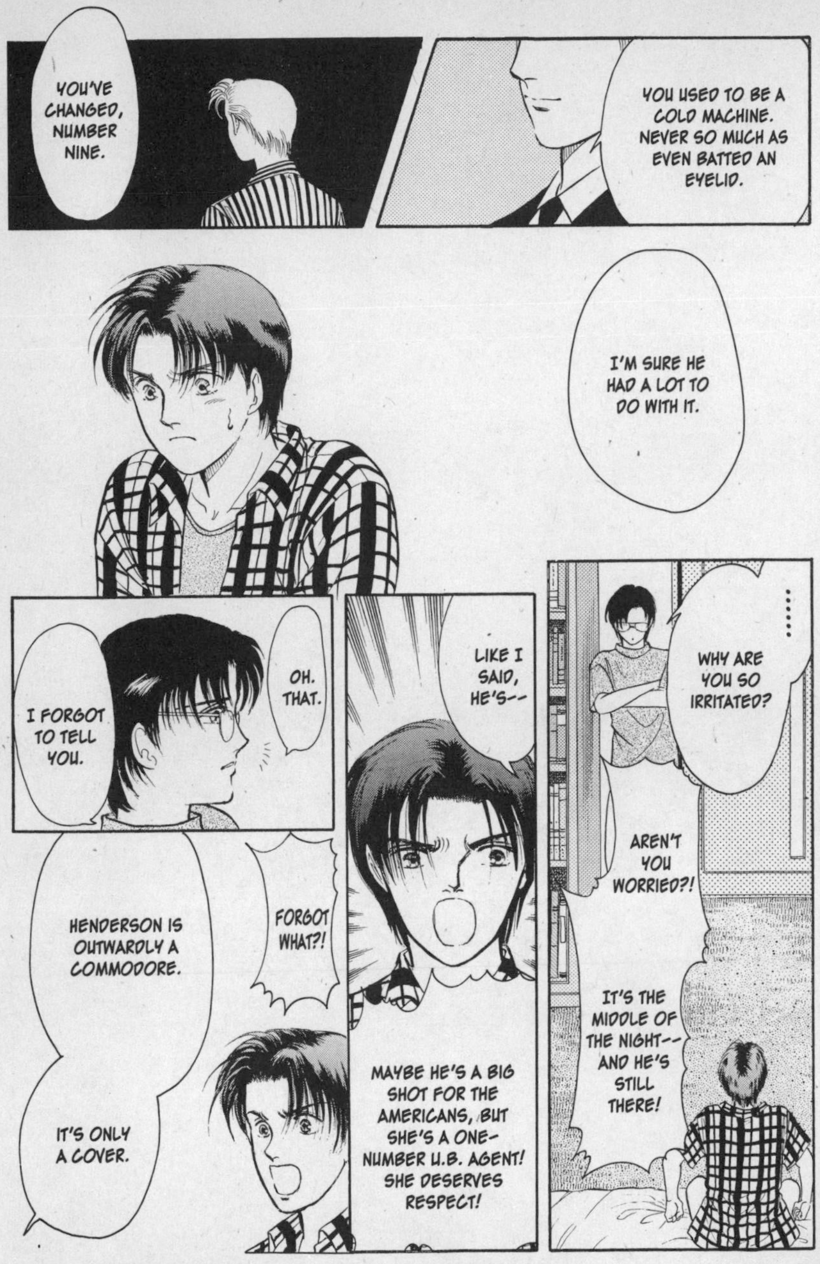
YOU USED TO BE A COLD MACHINE. NEVER SO MUCH AS EVEN BATTED AN EYELID.
YOU'VE CHANGED, NUMBER NINE.
I'M SURE HE HAD A LOT TO DO WITH IT.
......
WHY ARE YOU SO IRRITATED?
AREN'T YOU WORRIED?!
IT'S THE MIDDLE OF THE NIGHT-- AND HE'S STILL THERE!
LIKE I SAID, HE'S--
MAYBE HE'S A BIG SHOT FOR THE AMERICANS, BUT SHE'S A ONE-NUMBER U.B. AGENT! SHE DESERVES RESPECT!
OH. THAT.
I FORGOT TO TELL YOU.
FORGOT WHAT?!
HENDERSON IS OUTWARDLY A COMMODORE.
IT'S ONLY A COVER.

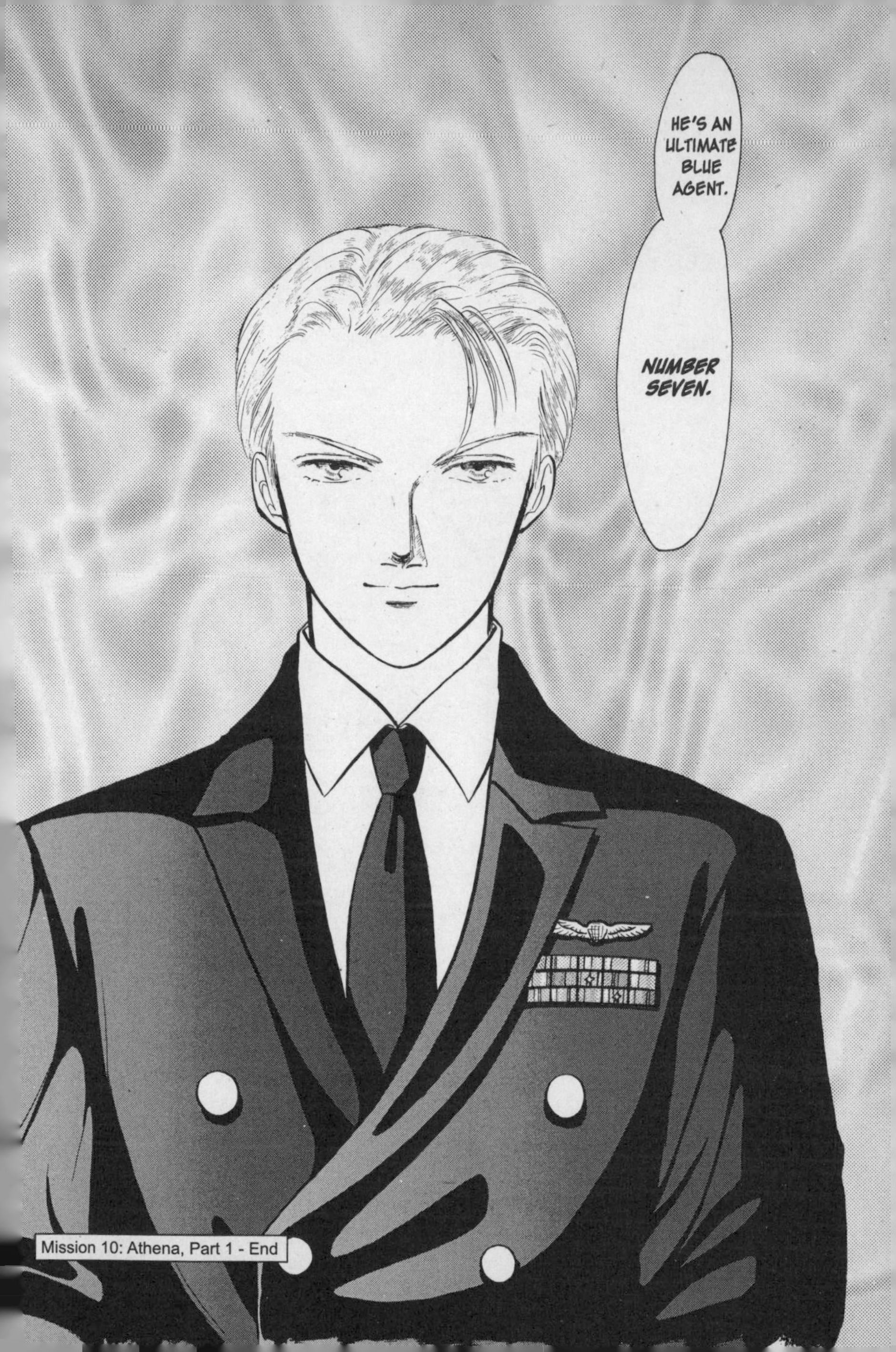
HE'S AN ULTIMATE BLUE AGENT.
NUMBER SEVEN.
Mission 10: Athena, Part 1 - End

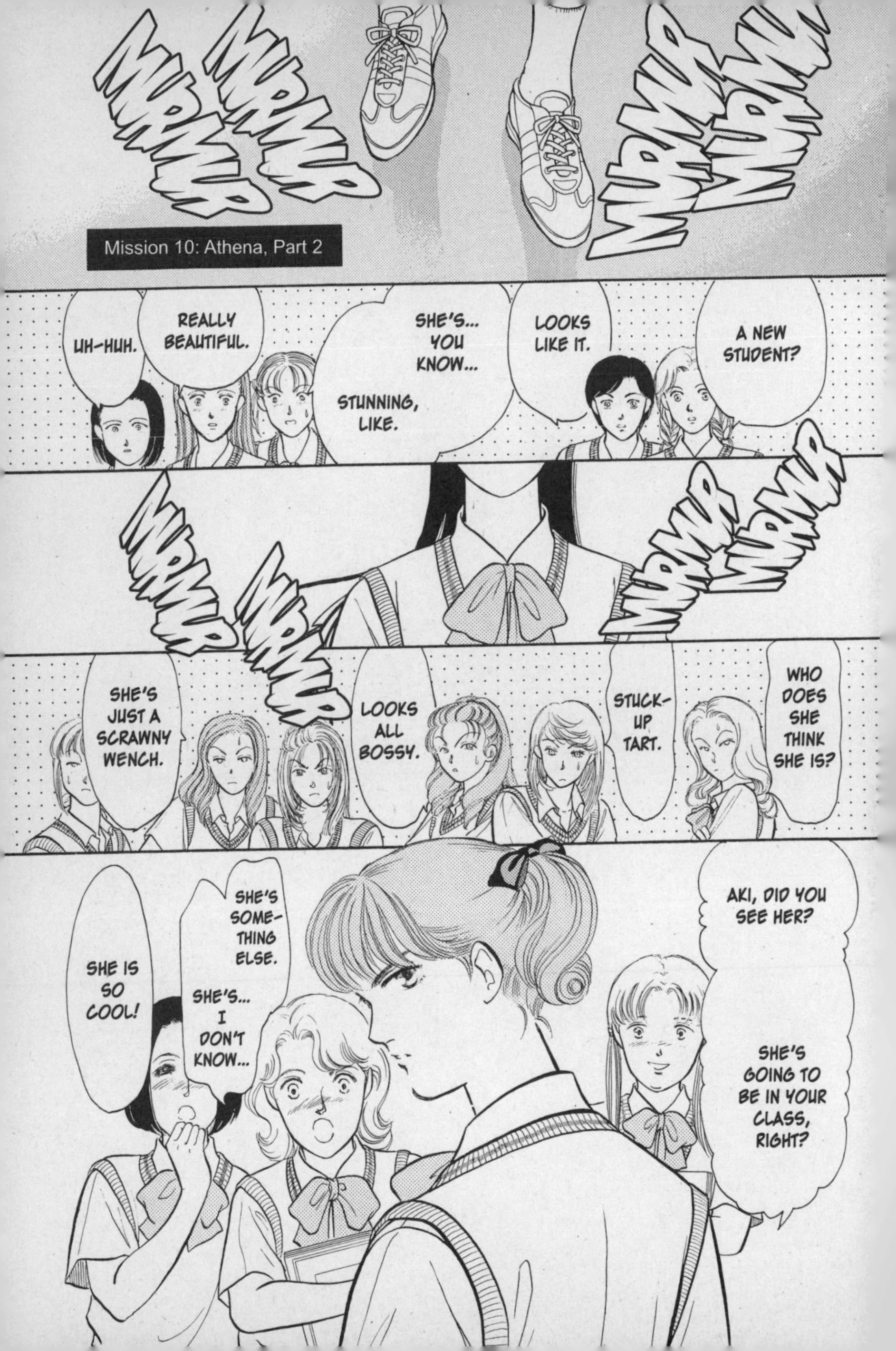
MURMUR
MURMUR
MURMUR
MURMUR
Mission 10: Athena, Part 2
A NEW STUDENT?
LOOKS LIKE IT.
SHE'S... YOU KNOW...
STUNNING, LIKE.
REALLY BEAUTIFUL.
UH-HUH.
MURMUR
MURMUR
MURMUR
MURMUR
WHO DOES SHE THINK SHE IS?
STUCK-UP TART.
LOOKS ALL BOSSY.
SHE'S JUST A SCRAWNY WENCH.
AKI, DID YOU SEE HER?
SHE'S GOING TO BE IN YOUR CLASS, RIGHT?
SHE'S SOME-THING ELSE.
SHE'S... I DON'T KNOW...
SHE IS SO COOL!

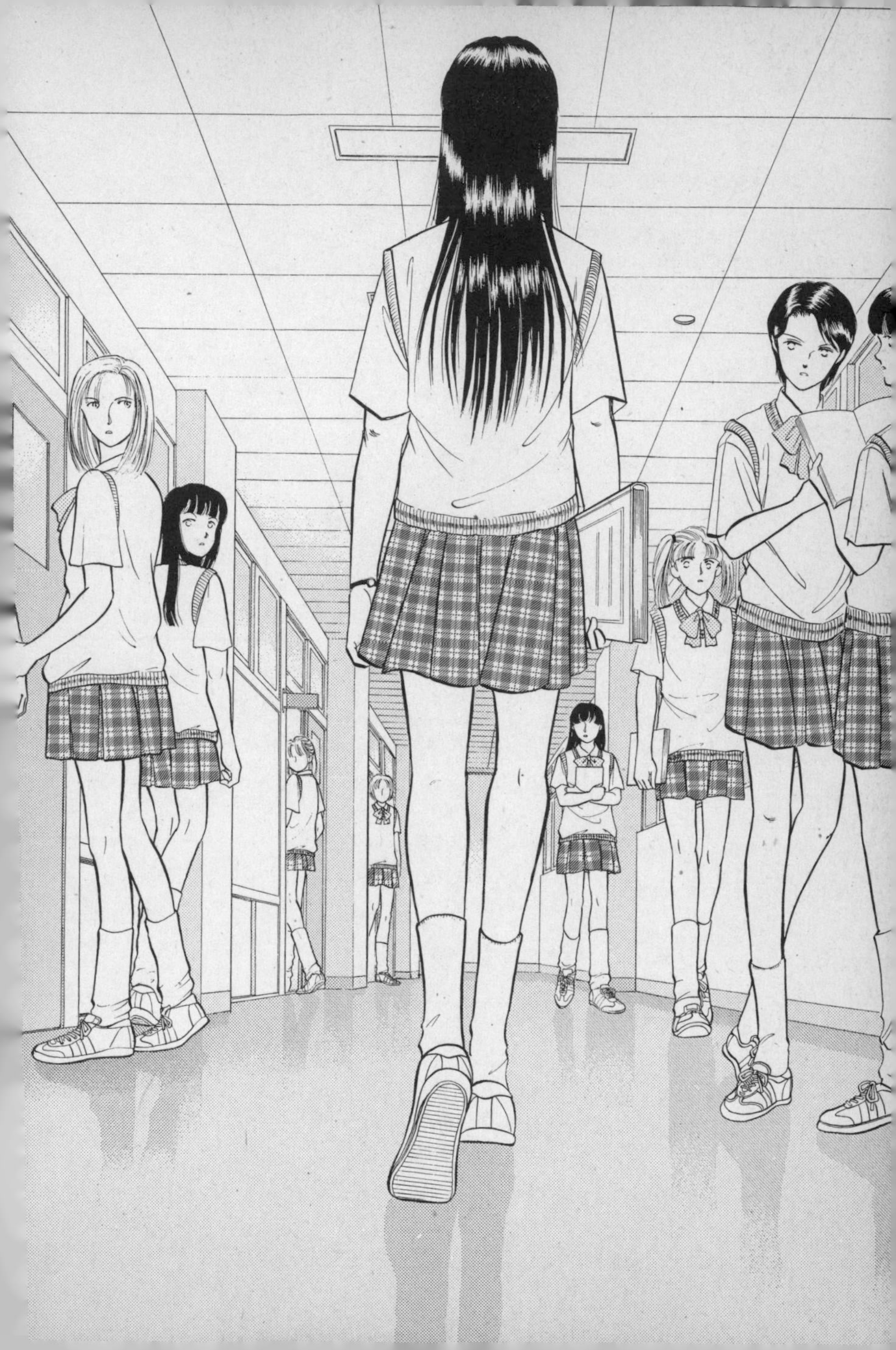

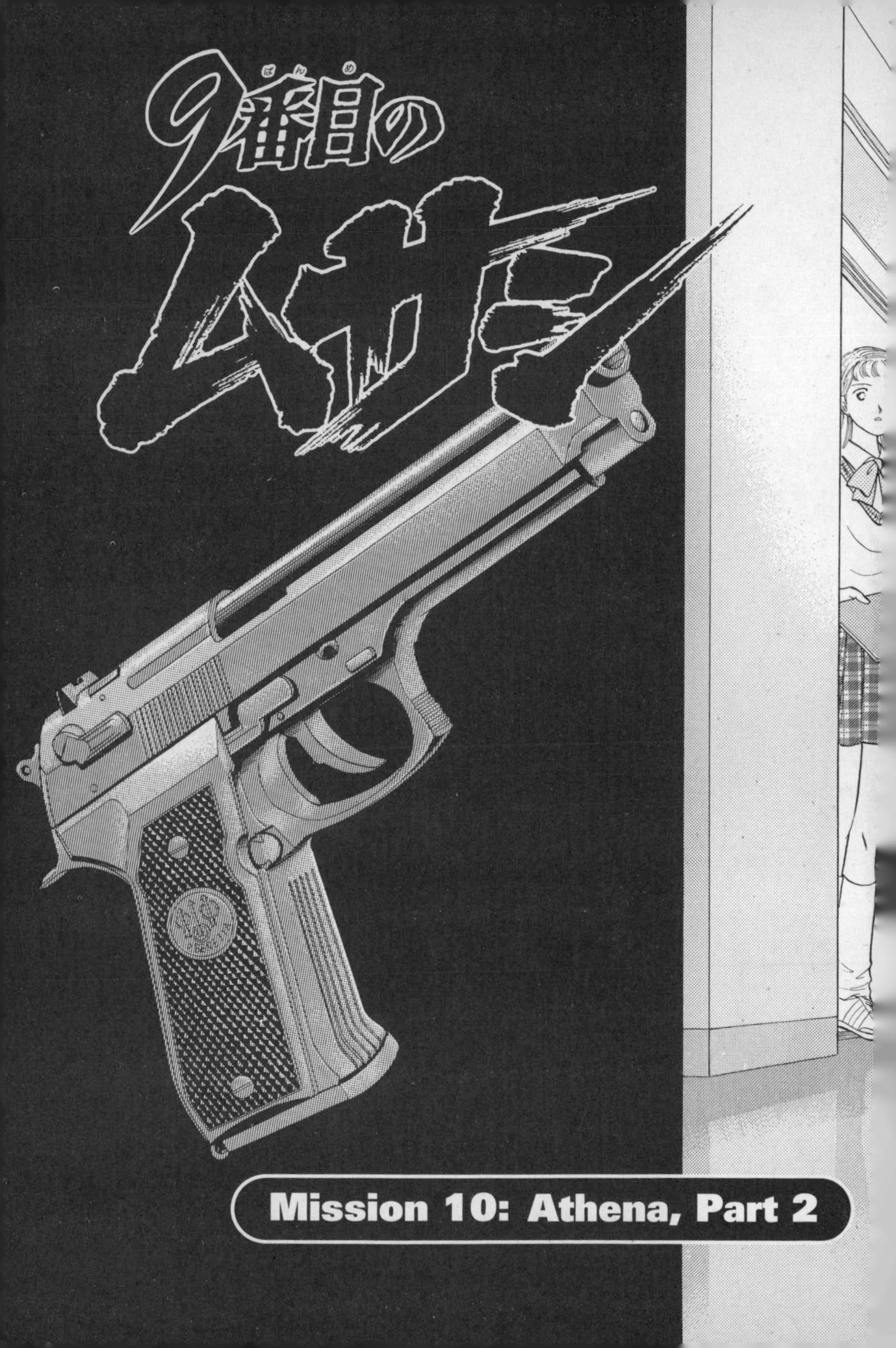
9番目のムサシ
Mission 10: Athena, Part 2

The source of all of my problems is actually a friend of mine, Shinozuka Kou.

Kou looks like a regular sorta high school guy, but is actually a radical super agent for some weirded out organization called Ultimate Blue.

U.B. is supposed to be preservin' world peace, but who knows? How good of an agent is Shinozuka? Who knows? How many of them are there? Again, who knows? But, the top nine are world movers. And, Shinozuka is one of them.

Code number, *nine*. Codename, *Musashi*.

That enough is mind-boggling. But, it gets even...ah, bunk!

Shinozuka may pack around a Colt XM.

Shinozuka may be so important there are agents acting as doubles. But, who...?

Who in the world will ever believe Shinozuka is a girl!?!

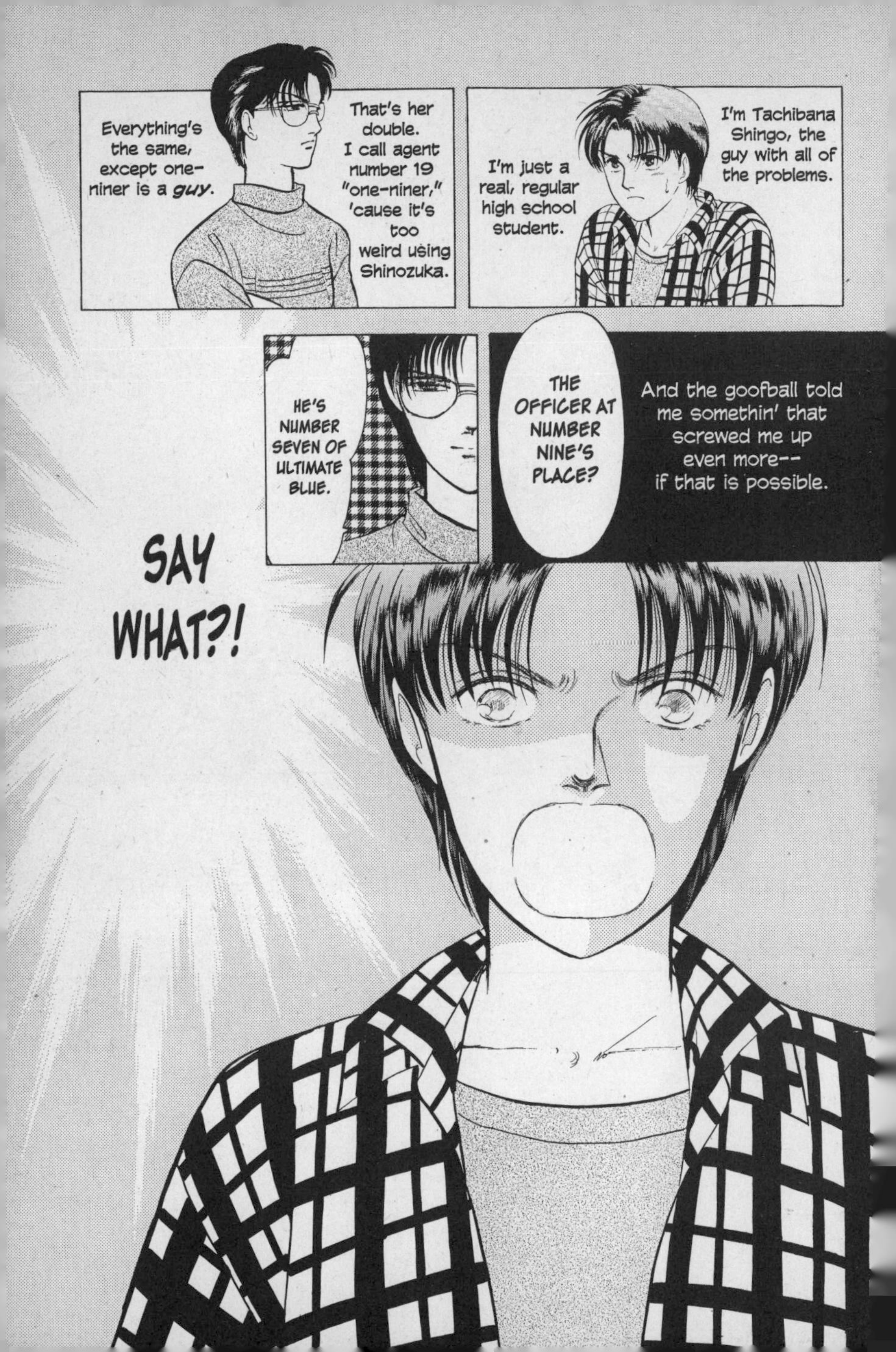
I'm Tachibana Shingo, the guy with all of the problems.
I'm just a real, regular high school student.
That's her double. I call agent number 19 "one-niner," 'cause it's too weird using Shinozuka.
Everything's the same, except one-niner is a *guy*.
And the goofball told me somethin' that screwed me up even more-- if that is possible.
THE OFFICER AT NUMBER NINE'S PLACE?
HE'S NUMBER SEVEN OF ULTIMATE BLUE.
SAY WHAT?!

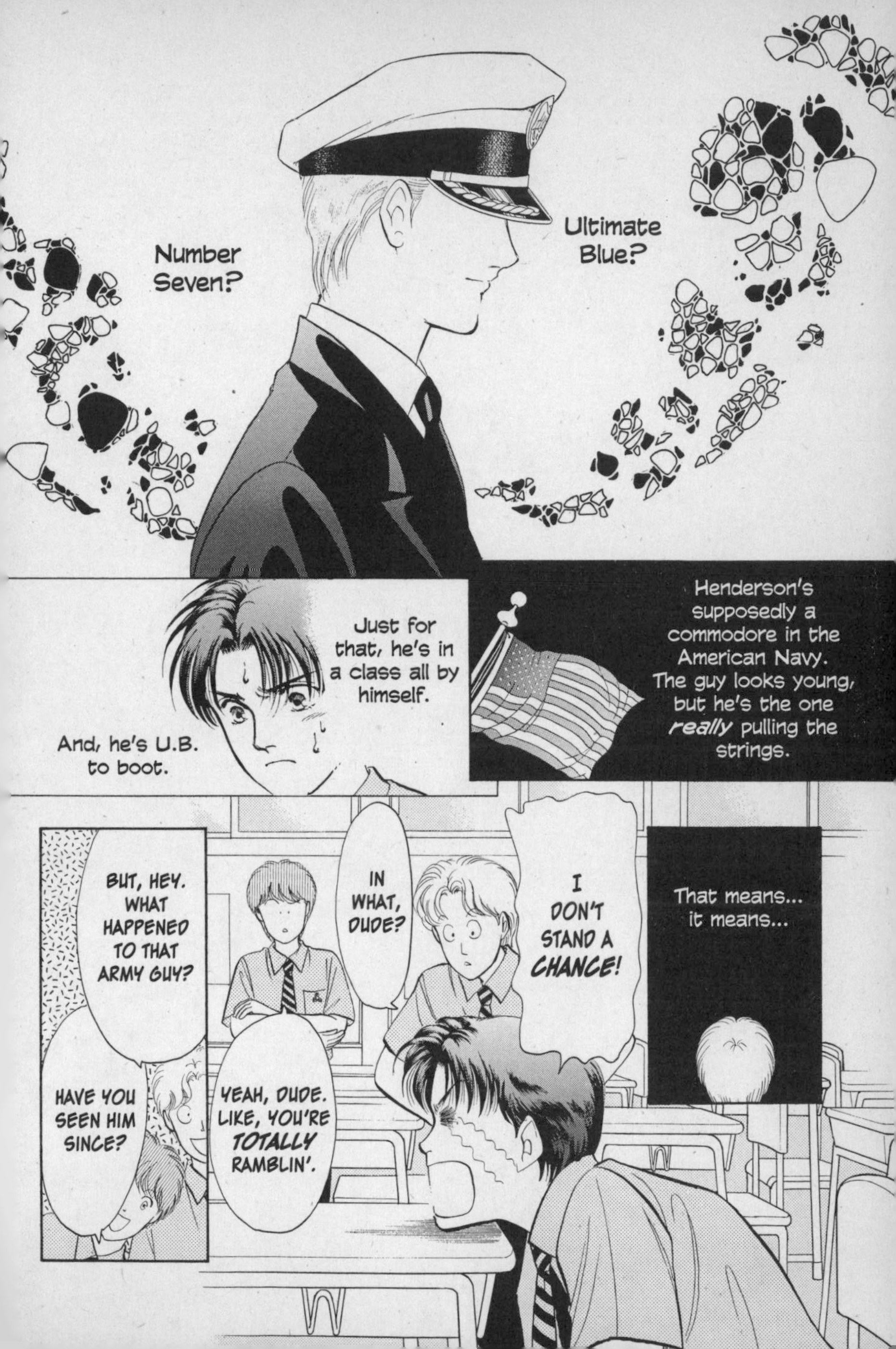
Ultimate Blue?
Number Seven?
Henderson's supposedly a commodore in the American Navy. The guy looks young, but he's the one *really* pulling the strings.
Just for that, he's in a class all by himself.
And, he's U.B. to boot.
That means... it means...
I DON'T STAND A *CHANCE!*
IN WHAT, DUDE?
YEAH, DUDE. LIKE, YOU'RE *TOTALLY* RAMBLIN'.
BUT, HEY. WHAT HAPPENED TO THAT ARMY GUY?
HAVE YOU SEEN HIM SINCE?

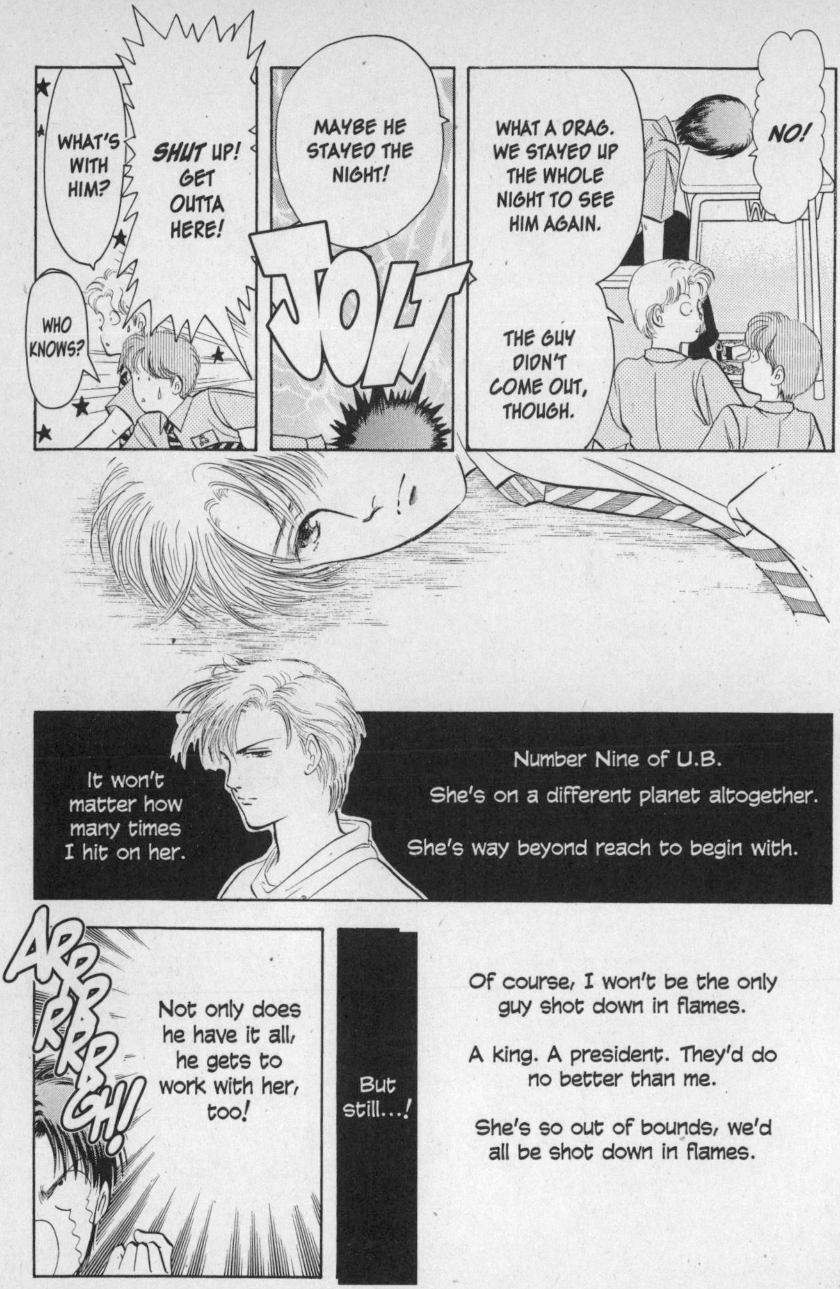
NO!
WHAT A DRAG. WE STAYED UP THE WHOLE NIGHT TO SEE HIM AGAIN.
THE GUY DIDN'T COME OUT, THOUGH.
MAYBE HE STAYED THE NIGHT!
JOLT
SHUT UP! GET OUTTA HERE!
WHAT'S WITH HIM?
WHO KNOWS?
Number Nine of U.B.
She's on a different planet altogether.
She's way beyond reach to begin with.
It won't matter how many times I hit on her.
Of course, I won't be the only guy shot down in flames.
A king. A president. They'd do no better than me.
She's so out of bounds, we'd all be shot down in flames.
But still...!
Not only does he have it all, he gets to work with her, too!
ARRRRRRGH!

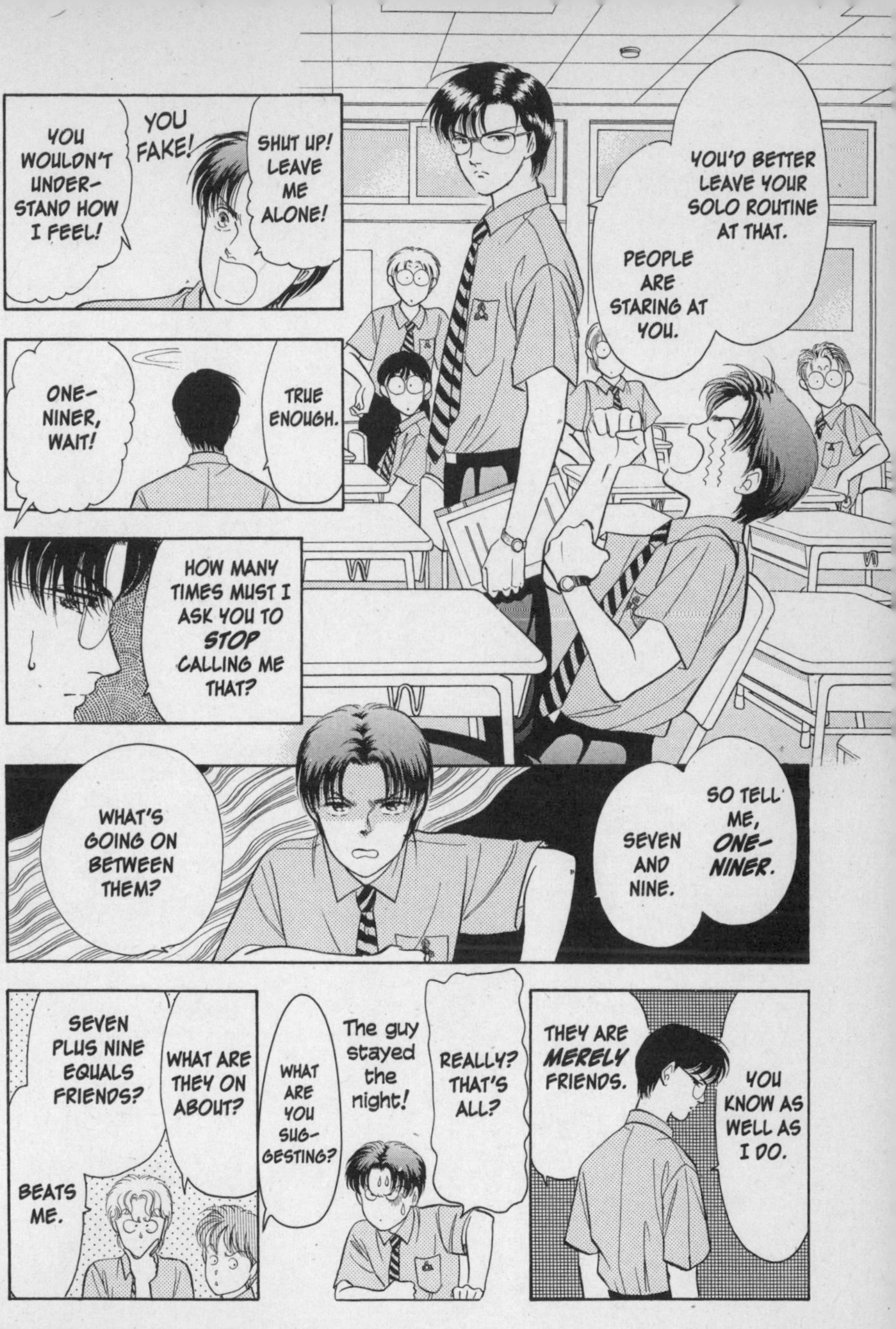
YOU'D BETTER LEAVE YOUR SOLO ROUTINE AT THAT.
PEOPLE ARE STARING AT YOU.
SHUT UP! LEAVE ME ALONE!
YOU FAKE!
YOU WOULDN'T UNDER-STAND HOW I FEEL!
TRUE ENOUGH.
ONE-NINER, WAIT!
HOW MANY TIMES MUST I ASK YOU TO *STOP* CALLING ME THAT?
SO TELL ME, *ONE-NINER.*
SEVEN AND NINE.
WHAT'S GOING ON BETWEEN THEM?
YOU KNOW AS WELL AS I DO.
THEY ARE *MERELY* FRIENDS.
REALLY? THAT'S ALL?
The guy stayed the night!
WHAT ARE YOU SUG-GESTING?
WHAT ARE THEY ON ABOUT?
SEVEN PLUS NINE EQUALS FRIENDS?
BEATS ME.

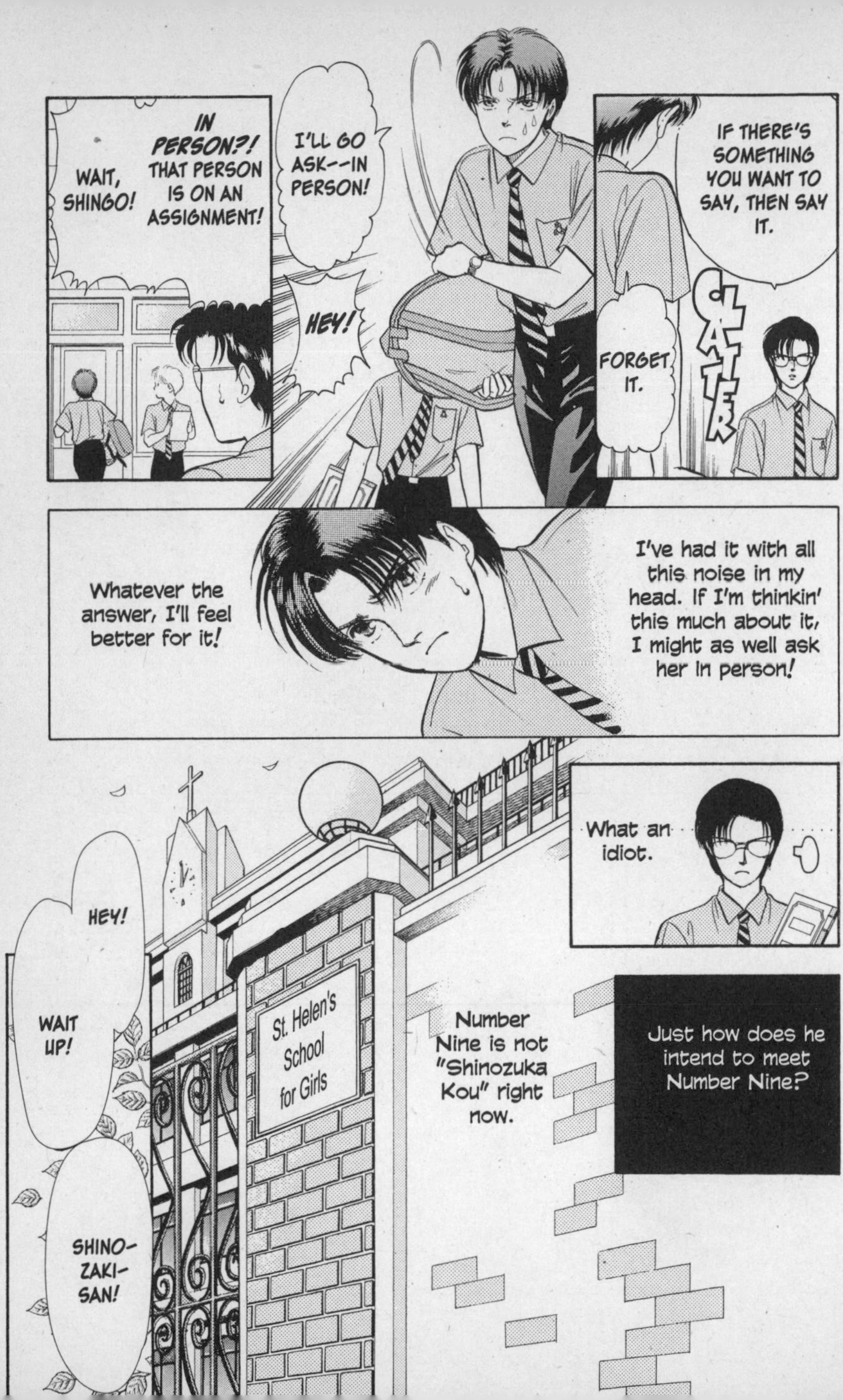
IF THERE'S SOMETHING YOU WANT TO SAY, THEN SAY IT.
CLATTER
FORGET IT.
I'LL GO ASK--IN PERSON!
HEY!
IN PERSON?! THAT PERSON IS ON AN ASSIGNMENT!
WAIT, SHINGO!
I've had it with all this noise in my head. If I'm thinkin' this much about it, I might as well ask her in person!
Whatever the answer, I'll feel better for it!
What an idiot.
Just how does he intend to meet Number Nine?
Number Nine is not "Shinozuka Kou" right now.
St. Helen's School for Girls
HEY!
WAIT UP!
SHINO-ZAKI-SAN!

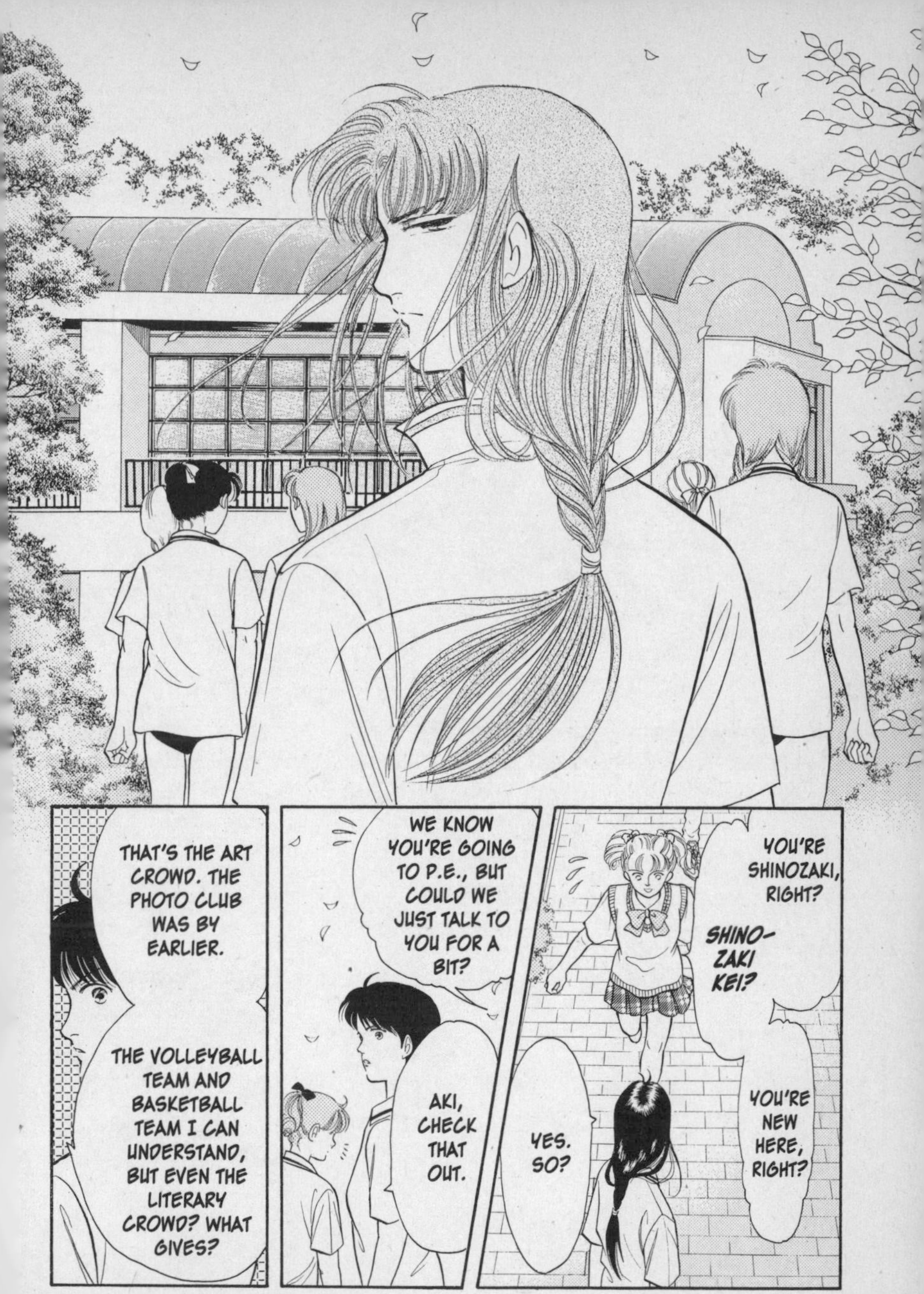
YOU'RE SHINOZAKI, RIGHT?
SHINO-ZAKI KEI?
YOU'RE NEW HERE, RIGHT?
YES. SO?
WE KNOW YOU'RE GOING TO P.E., BUT COULD WE JUST TALK TO YOU FOR A BIT?
AKI, CHECK THAT OUT.
THAT'S THE ART CROWD. THE PHOTO CLUB WAS BY EARLIER.
THE VOLLEYBALL TEAM AND BASKETBALL TEAM I CAN UNDERSTAND, BUT EVEN THE LITERARY CROWD? WHAT GIVES?

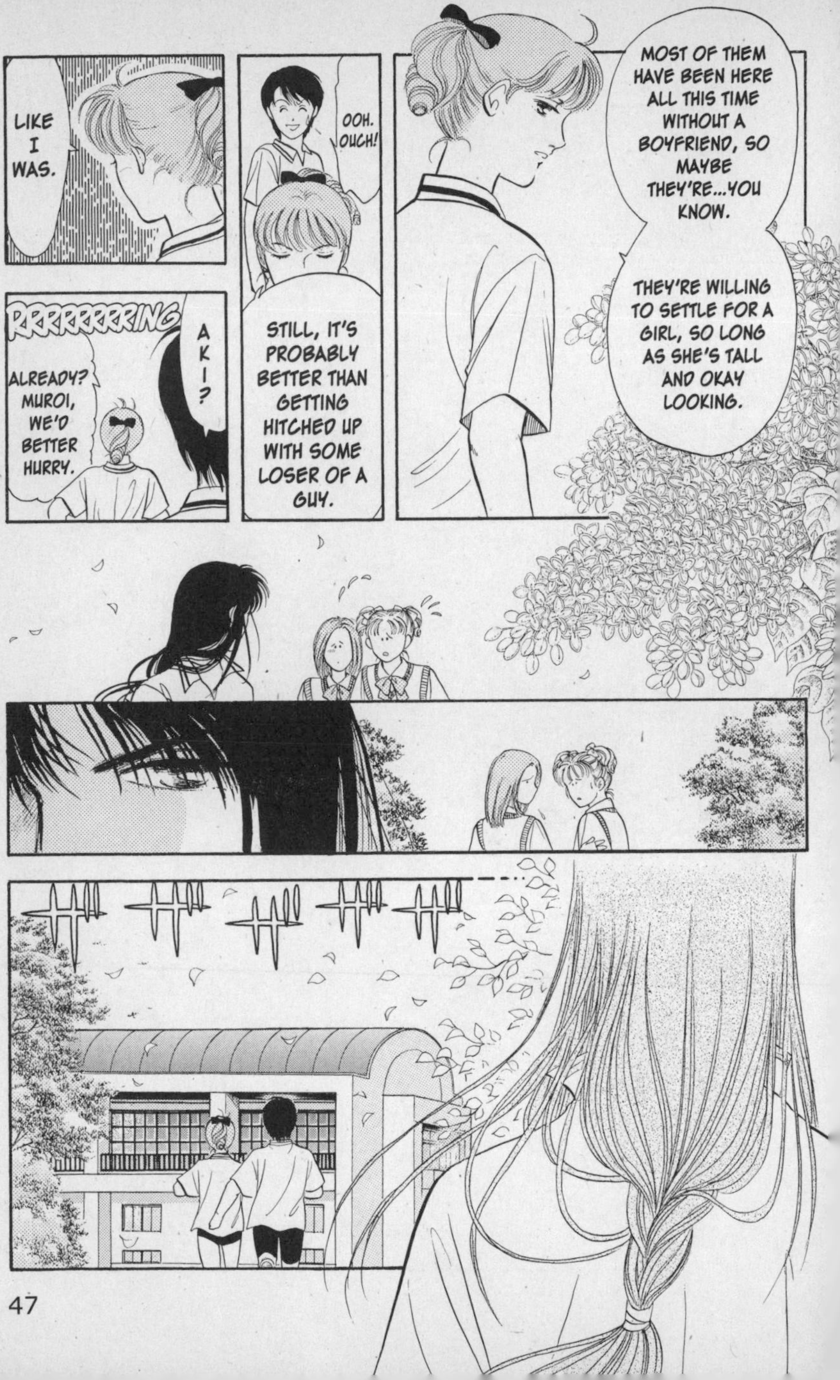
MOST OF THEM HAVE BEEN HERE ALL THIS TIME WITHOUT A BOYFRIEND, SO MAYBE THEY'RE...YOU KNOW.
THEY'RE WILLING TO SETTLE FOR A GIRL, SO LONG AS SHE'S TALL AND OKAY LOOKING.
OOH. OUCH!
STILL, IT'S PROBABLY BETTER THAN GETTING HITCHED UP WITH SOME LOSER OF A GUY.
LIKE I WAS.
RRRRRRRRING
AKI?
ALREADY? MUROI, WE'D BETTER HURRY.

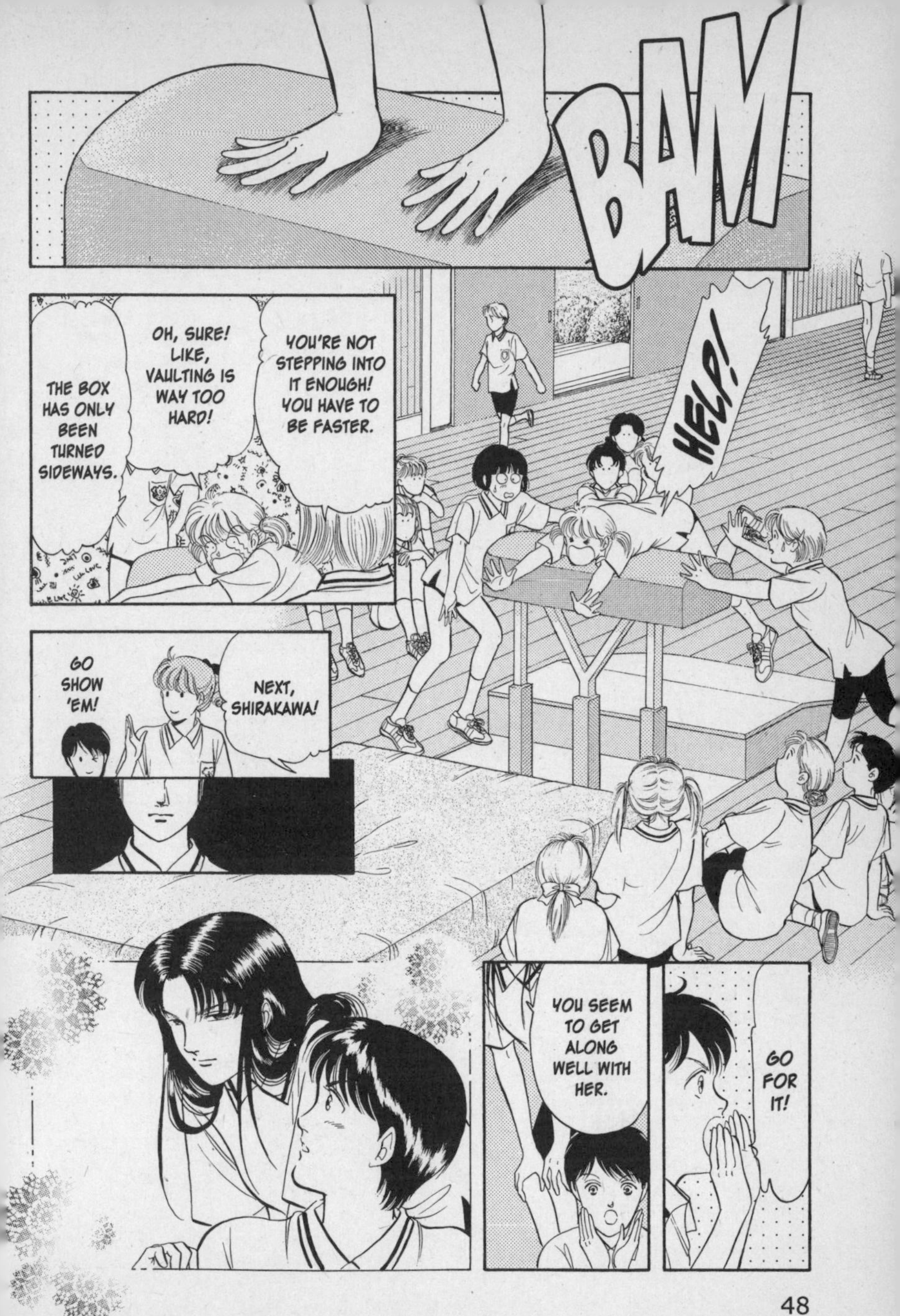
BAM
HELP!
YOU'RE NOT STEPPING INTO IT ENOUGH! YOU HAVE TO BE FASTER.
OH, SURE! LIKE, VAULTING IS WAY TOO HARD!
THE BOX HAS ONLY BEEN TURNED SIDEWAYS.
NEXT, SHIRAKAWA!
GO SHOW 'EM!
GO FOR IT!
YOU SEEM TO GET ALONG WELL WITH HER.

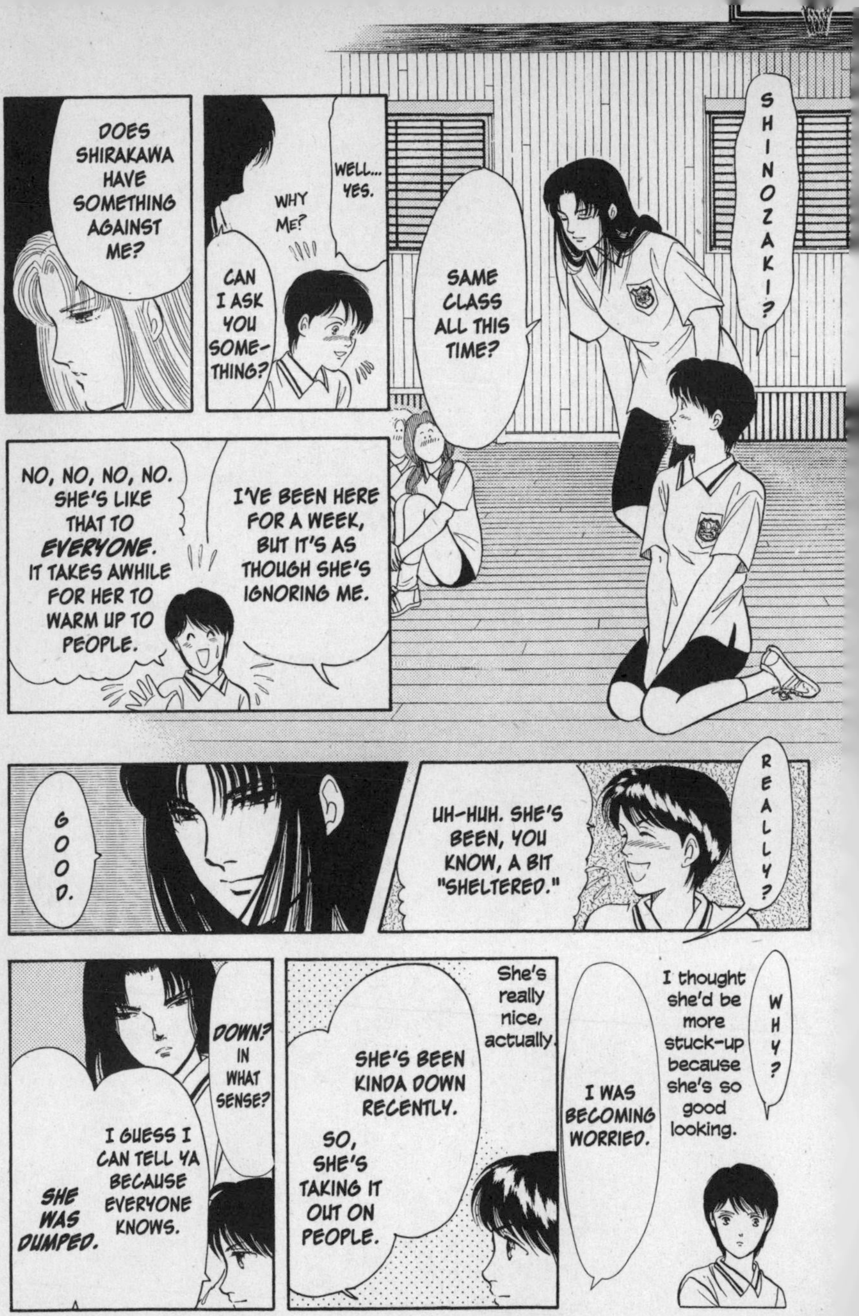
SHINOZAKI?
SAME CLASS ALL THIS TIME?
WELL... YES.
WHY ME?
CAN I ASK YOU SOMETHING?
DOES SHIRAKAWA HAVE SOMETHING AGAINST ME?
I'VE BEEN HERE FOR A WEEK, BUT IT'S AS THOUGH SHE'S IGNORING ME.
NO, NO, NO, NO. SHE'S LIKE THAT TO EVERYONE. IT TAKES AWHILE FOR HER TO WARM UP TO PEOPLE.
REALLY?
UH-HUH. SHE'S BEEN, YOU KNOW, A BIT "SHELTERED."
GOOD.
WHY?
I thought she'd be more stuck-up because she's so good looking.
She's really nice, actually.
I WAS BECOMING WORRIED.
SHE'S BEEN KINDA DOWN RECENTLY.
SO, SHE'S TAKING IT OUT ON PEOPLE.
DOWN? IN WHAT SENSE?
I GUESS I CAN TELL YA BECAUSE EVERYONE KNOWS.
SHE WAS DUMPED.

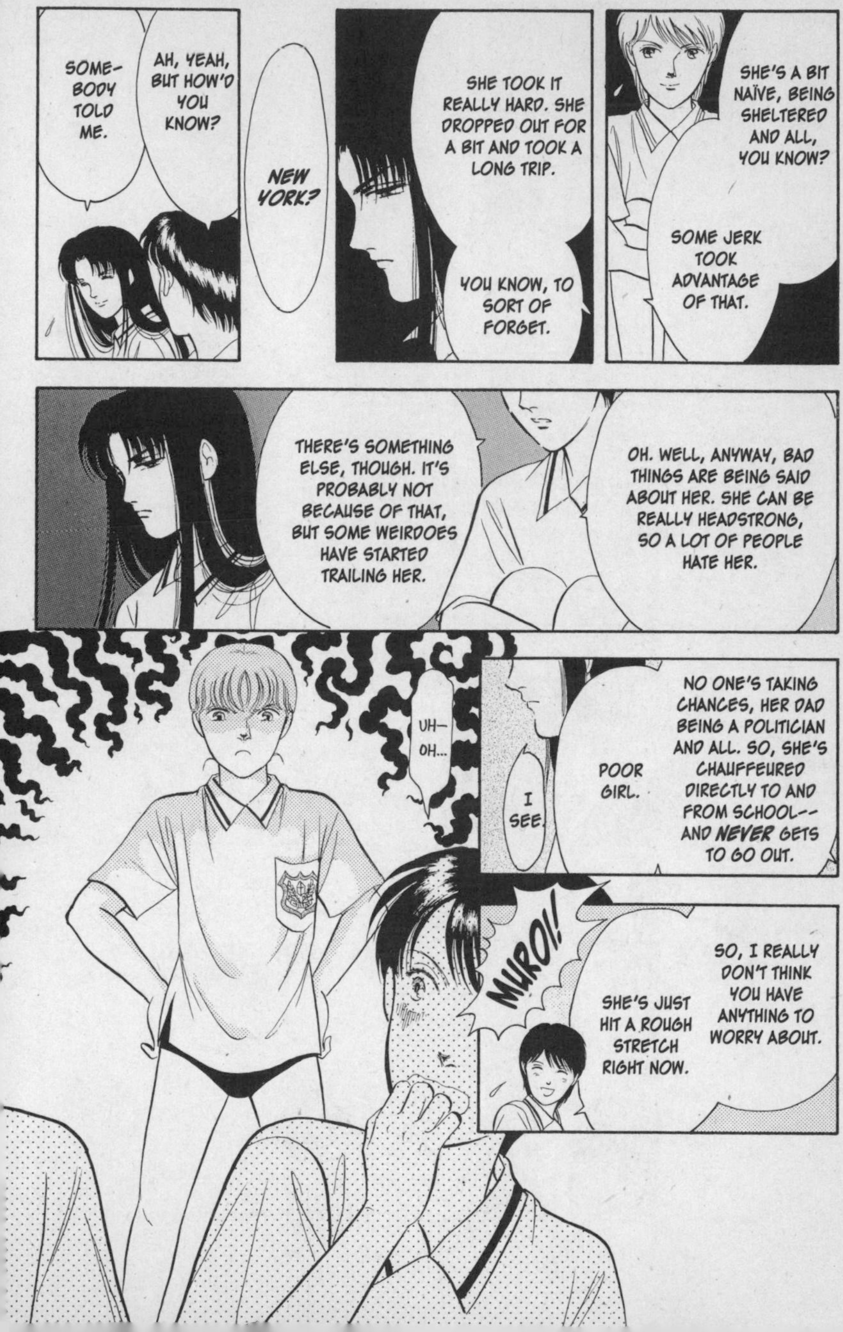
SHE'S A BIT NAÏVE, BEING SHELTERED AND ALL, YOU KNOW?
SOME JERK TOOK ADVANTAGE OF THAT.
SHE TOOK IT REALLY HARD. SHE DROPPED OUT FOR A BIT AND TOOK A LONG TRIP.
YOU KNOW, TO SORT OF FORGET.
NEW YORK?
AH, YEAH, BUT HOW'D YOU KNOW?
SOME-BODY TOLD ME.
OH. WELL, ANYWAY, BAD THINGS ARE BEING SAID ABOUT HER. SHE CAN BE REALLY HEADSTRONG, SO A LOT OF PEOPLE HATE HER.
THERE'S SOMETHING ELSE, THOUGH. IT'S PROBABLY NOT BECAUSE OF THAT, BUT SOME WEIRDOES HAVE STARTED TRAILING HER.
NO ONE'S TAKING CHANCES, HER DAD BEING A POLITICIAN AND ALL. SO, SHE'S CHAUFFEURED DIRECTLY TO AND FROM SCHOOL-- AND *NEVER* GETS TO GO OUT.
POOR GIRL.
I SEE.
SO, I REALLY DON'T THINK YOU HAVE ANYTHING TO WORRY ABOUT.
SHE'S JUST HIT A ROUGH STRETCH RIGHT NOW.
MUROI!
UH-OH...

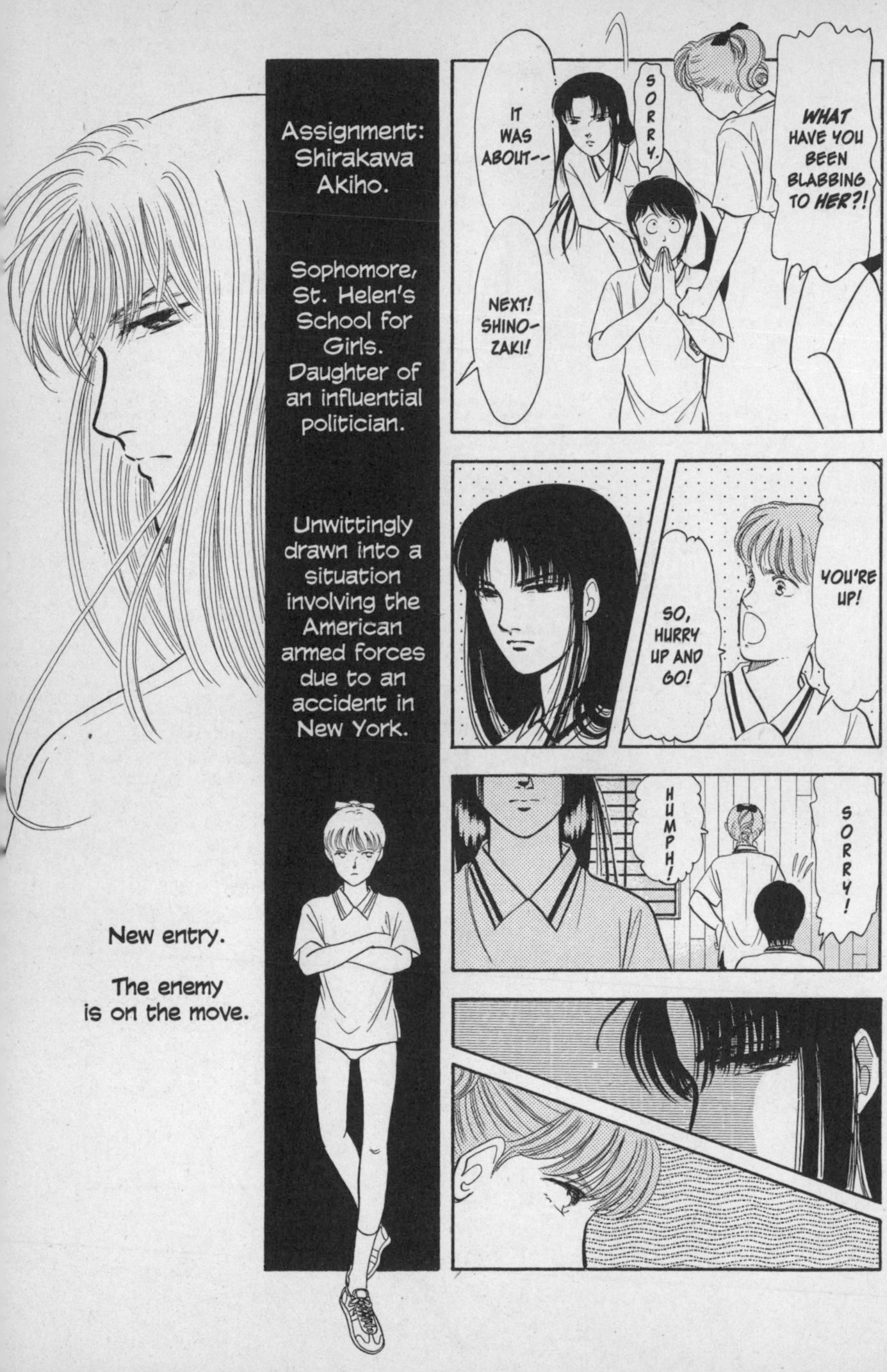
WHAT HAVE YOU BEEN BLABBING TO HER?!
SORRY.
IT WAS ABOUT--
NEXT! SHINOZAKI!
YOU'RE UP!
SO, HURRY UP AND GO!
SORRY!
HUMPH!
Assignment: Shirakawa Akiho.
Sophomore, St. Helen's School for Girls. Daughter of an influential politician.
Unwittingly drawn into a situation involving the American armed forces due to an accident in New York.
New entry.
The enemy is on the move.

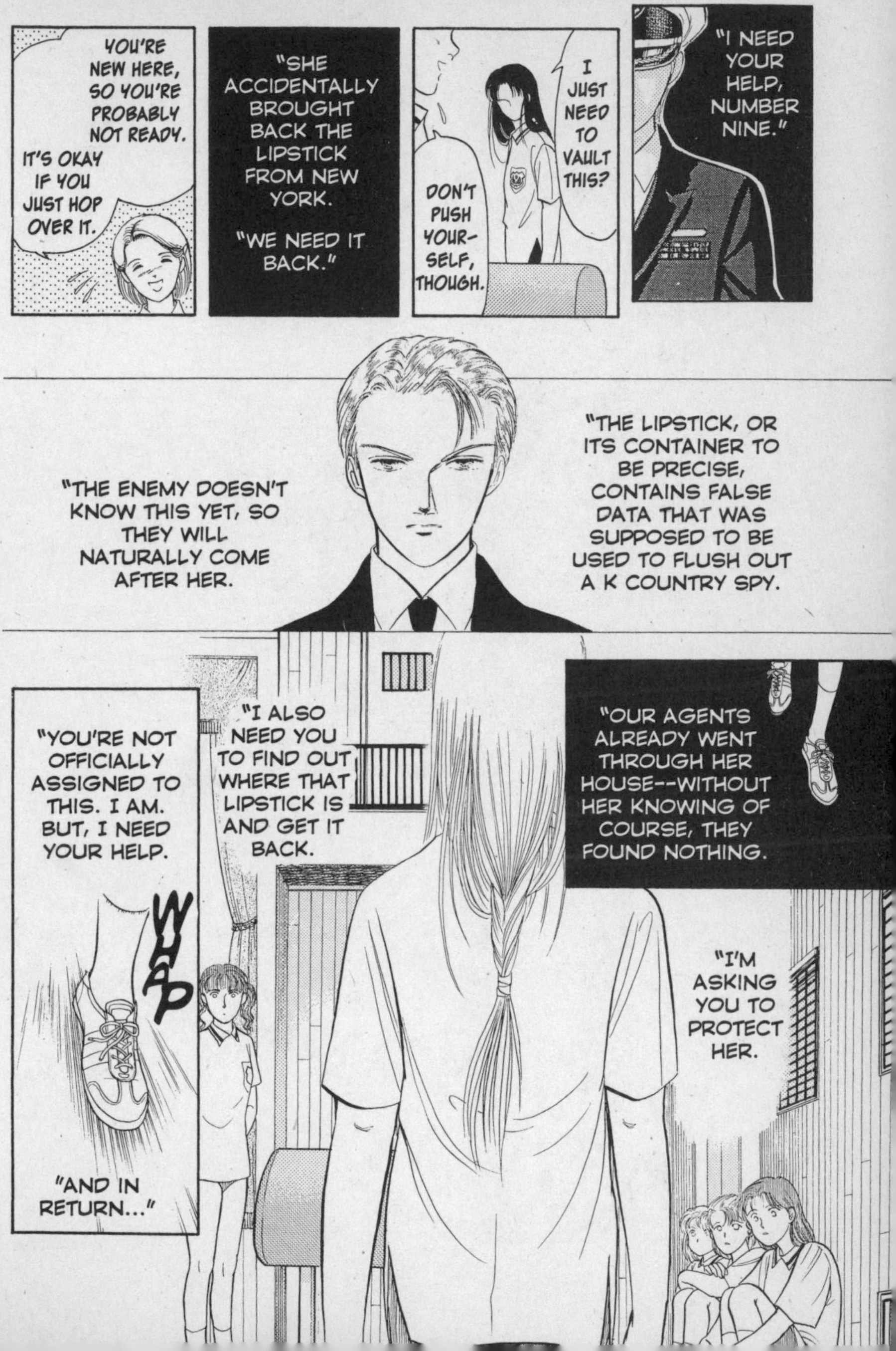
"I NEED YOUR HELP, NUMBER NINE."
I JUST NEED TO VAULT THIS?
DON'T PUSH YOURSELF, THOUGH.
"SHE ACCIDENTALLY BROUGHT BACK THE LIPSTICK FROM NEW YORK.
"WE NEED IT BACK."
YOU'RE NEW HERE, SO YOU'RE PROBABLY NOT READY.
IT'S OKAY IF YOU JUST HOP OVER IT.
"THE LIPSTICK, OR ITS CONTAINER TO BE PRECISE, CONTAINS FALSE DATA THAT WAS SUPPOSED TO BE USED TO FLUSH OUT A K COUNTRY SPY.
"THE ENEMY DOESN'T KNOW THIS YET, SO THEY WILL NATURALLY COME AFTER HER.
"OUR AGENTS ALREADY WENT THROUGH HER HOUSE--WITHOUT HER KNOWING OF COURSE, THEY FOUND NOTHING.
"I'M ASKING YOU TO PROTECT HER.
"I ALSO NEED YOU TO FIND OUT WHERE THAT LIPSTICK IS AND GET IT BACK.
"YOU'RE NOT OFFICIALLY ASSIGNED TO THIS. I AM. BUT, I NEED YOUR HELP.
WHAP
"AND IN RETURN..."

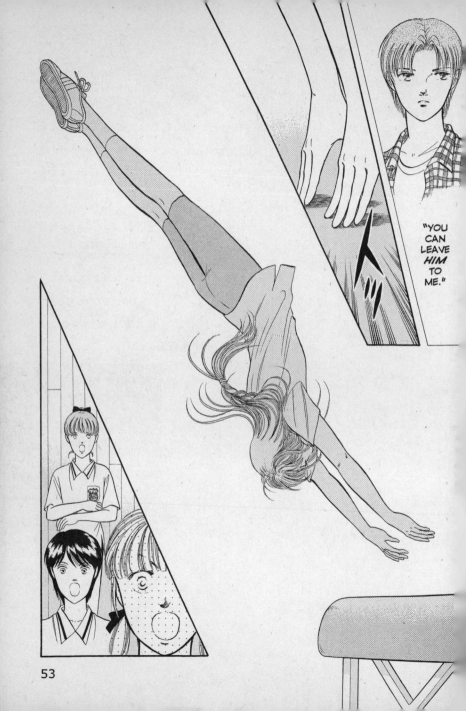

"YOU CAN LEAVE *HIM* TO ME."

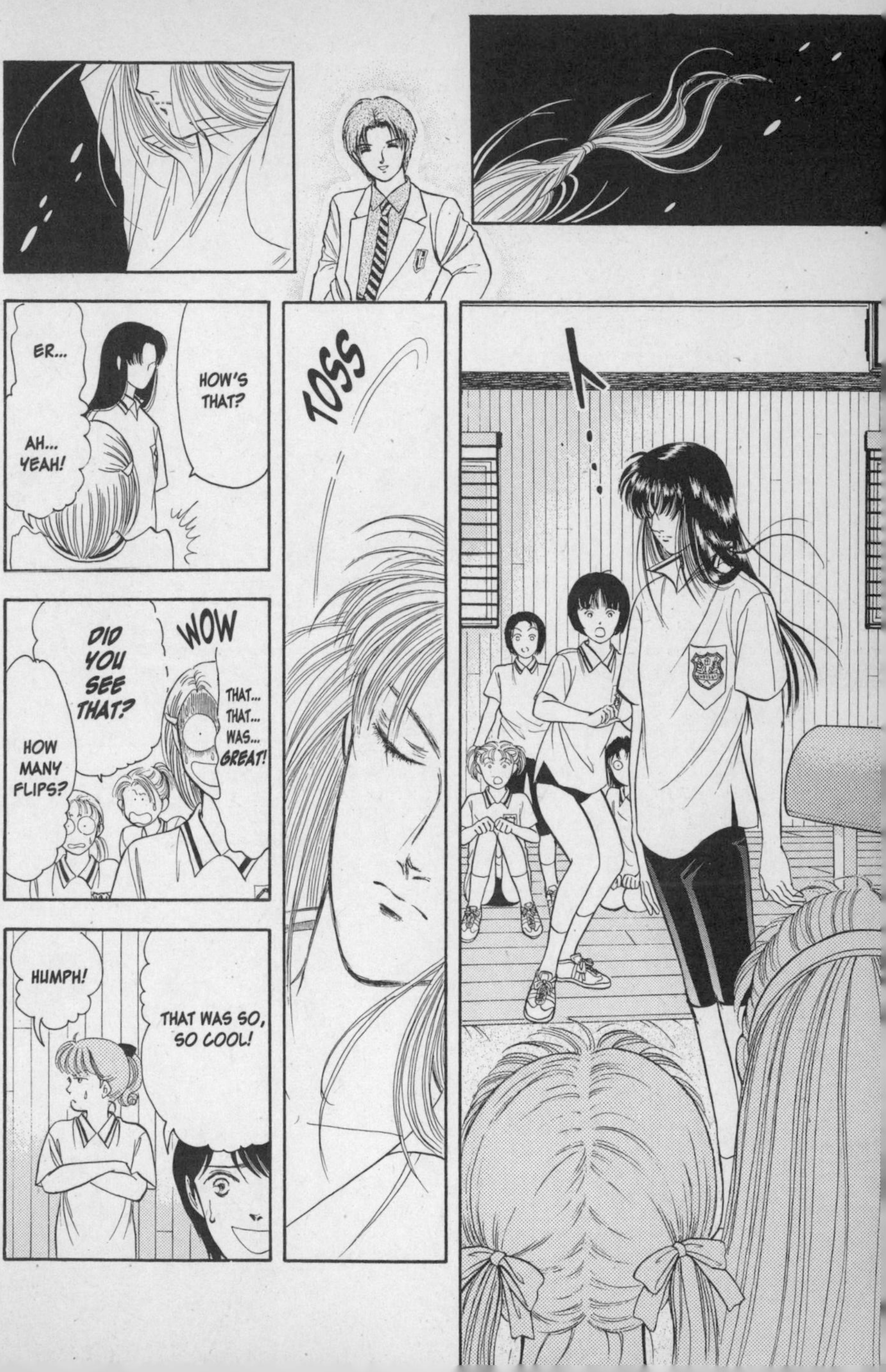
TOSS
HOW'S THAT?
ER...
AH... YEAH!
WOW
THAT... THAT... WAS... GREAT!
DID YOU SEE THAT?
HOW MANY FLIPS?
THAT WAS SO, SO COOL!
HUMPH!

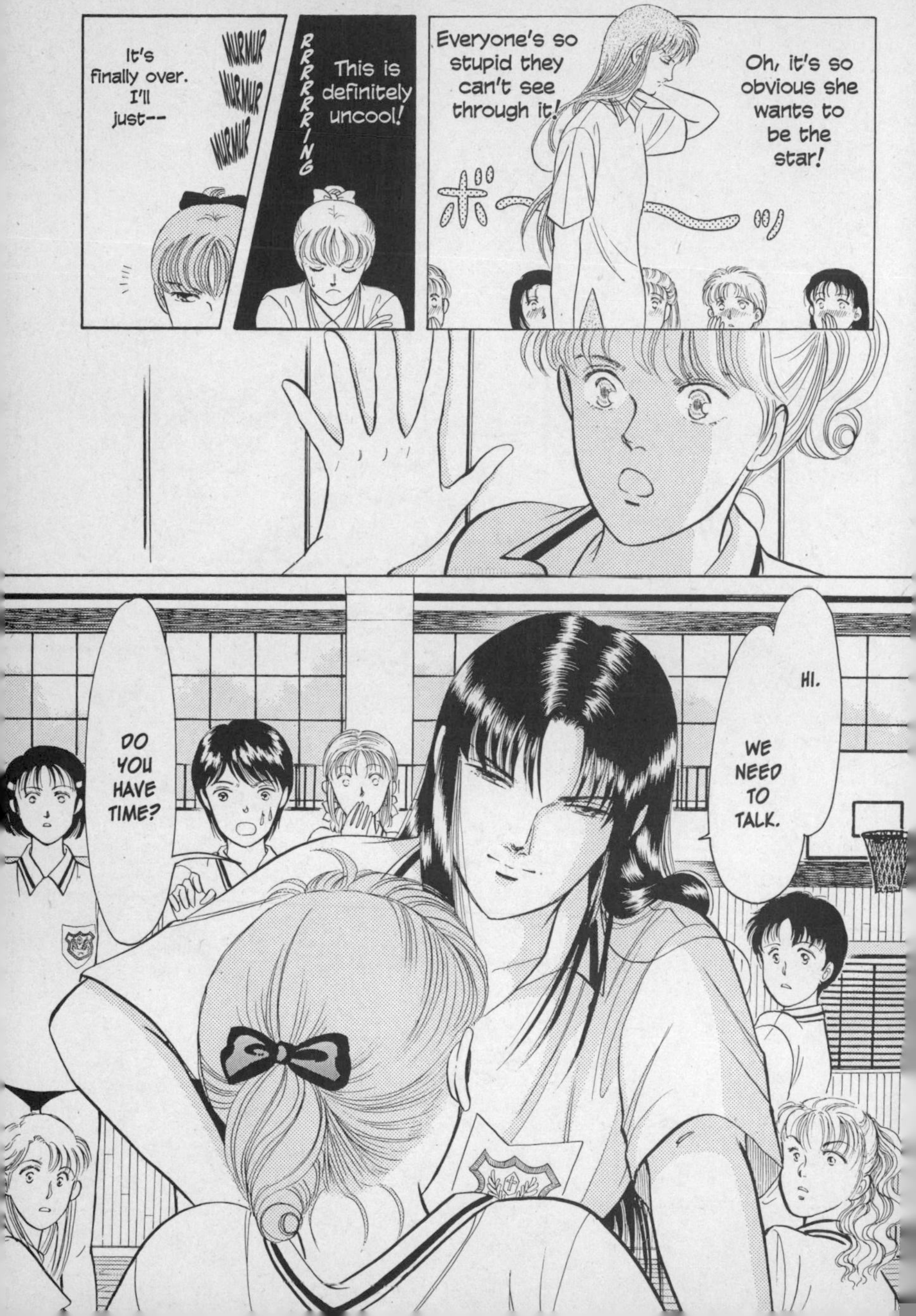

Oh, it's so obvious she wants to be the star!
Everyone's so stupid they can't see through it!
This is definitely uncool!
RRRRRRING
MURMUR
MURMUR
MURMUR
It's finally over. I'll just--
HI.
WE NEED TO TALK.
DO YOU HAVE TIME?

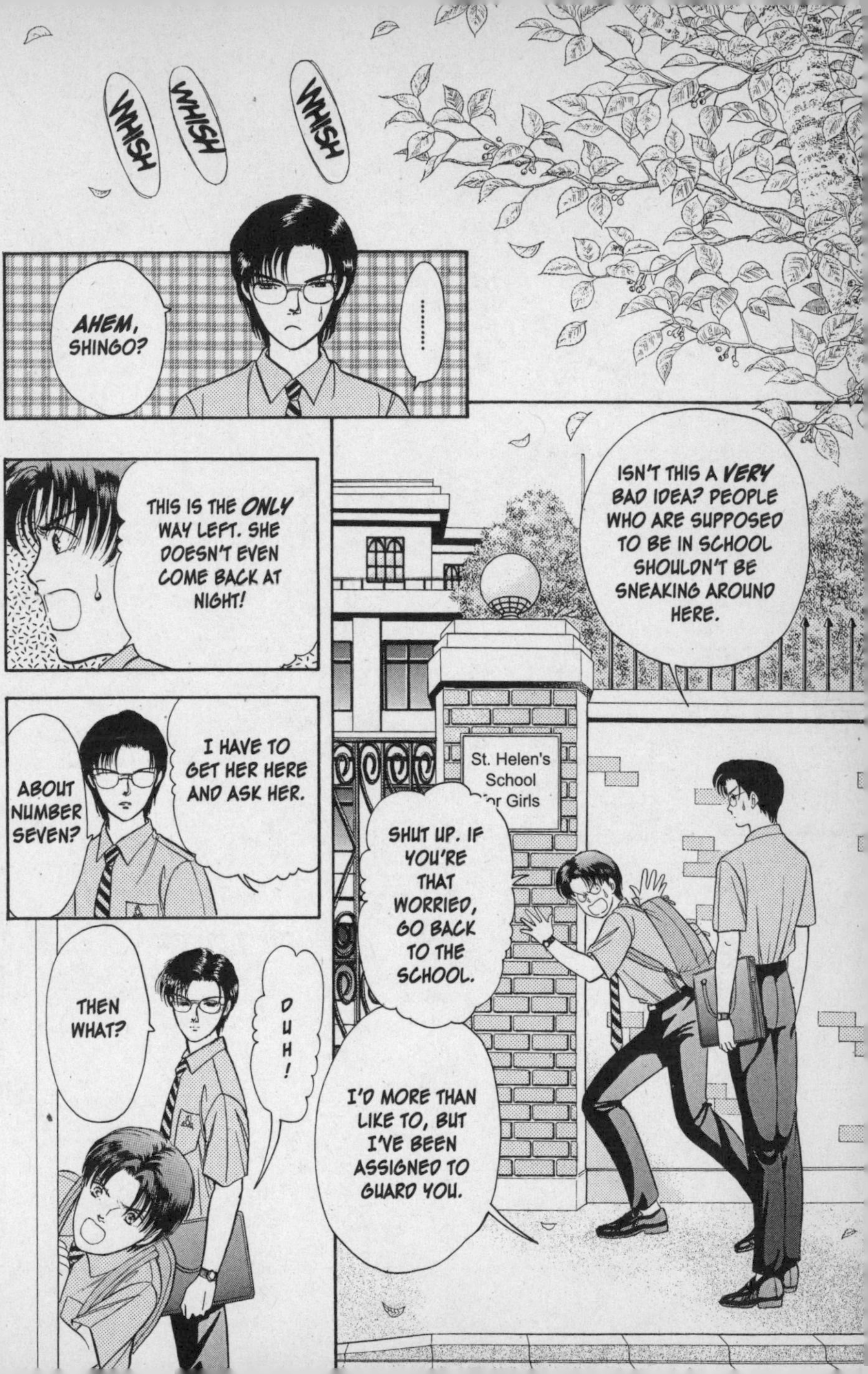
ISN'T THIS A *VERY* BAD IDEA? PEOPLE WHO ARE SUPPOSED TO BE IN SCHOOL SHOULDN'T BE SNEAKING AROUND HERE.
St. Helen's School For Girls
SHUT UP. IF YOU'RE THAT WORRIED, GO BACK TO THE SCHOOL.
I'D MORE THAN LIKE TO, BUT I'VE BEEN ASSIGNED TO GUARD YOU.
WHISH
WHISH
WHISH
......
AHEM, SHINGO?
THIS IS THE *ONLY* WAY LEFT. SHE DOESN'T EVEN COME BACK AT NIGHT!
I HAVE TO GET HER HERE AND ASK HER.
ABOUT NUMBER SEVEN?
DUH!
THEN WHAT?

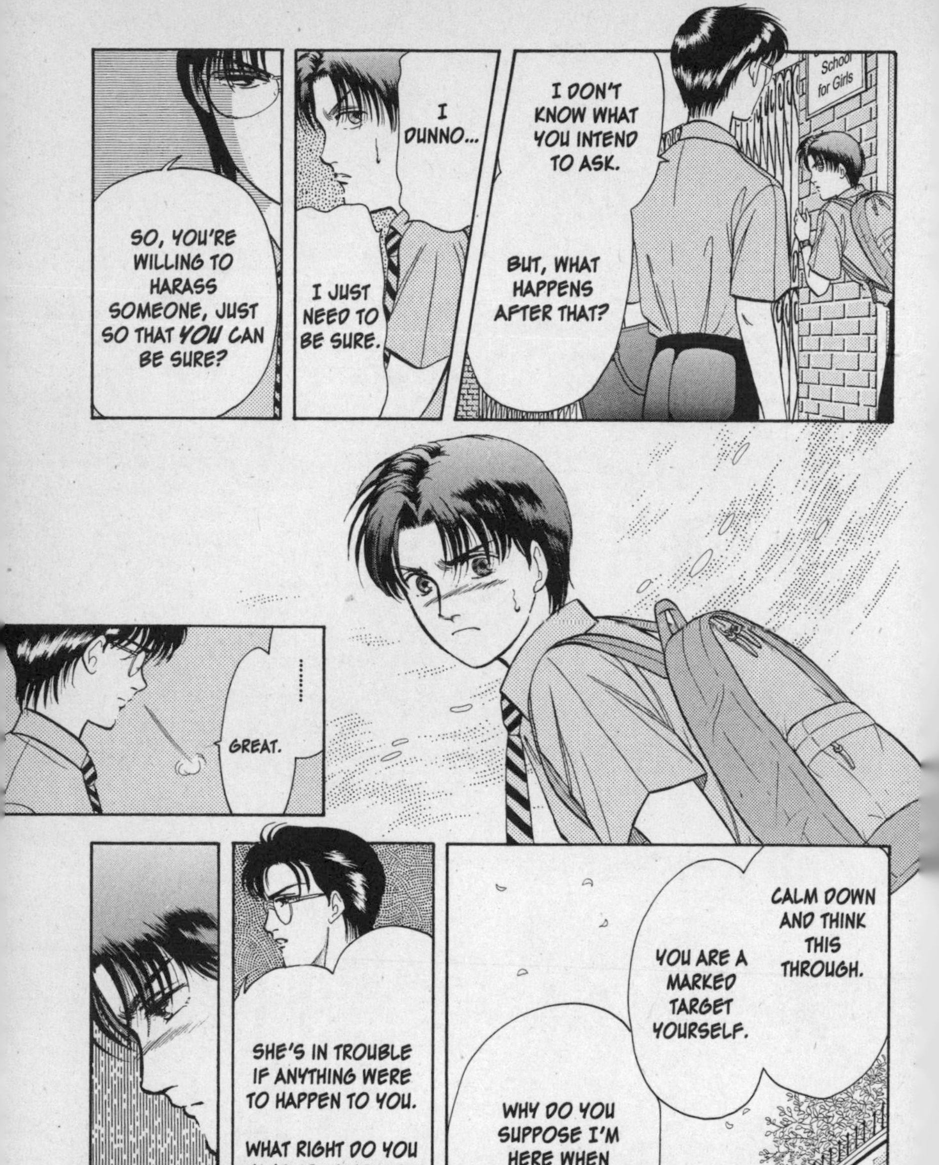
School for Girls
I DON'T KNOW WHAT YOU INTEND TO ASK.
BUT, WHAT HAPPENS AFTER THAT?
I DUNNO...
I JUST NEED TO BE SURE.
SO, YOU'RE WILLING TO HARASS SOMEONE, JUST SO THAT *YOU* CAN BE SURE?
......
GREAT.
CALM DOWN AND THINK THIS THROUGH.
YOU ARE A MARKED TARGET YOURSELF.
WHY DO YOU SUPPOSE I'M HERE WHEN NUMBER NINE IS NOT?
SHE'S IN TROUBLE IF ANYTHING WERE TO HAPPEN TO YOU.
WHAT RIGHT DO YOU HAVE TO INTERFERE WITH HER MISSION?

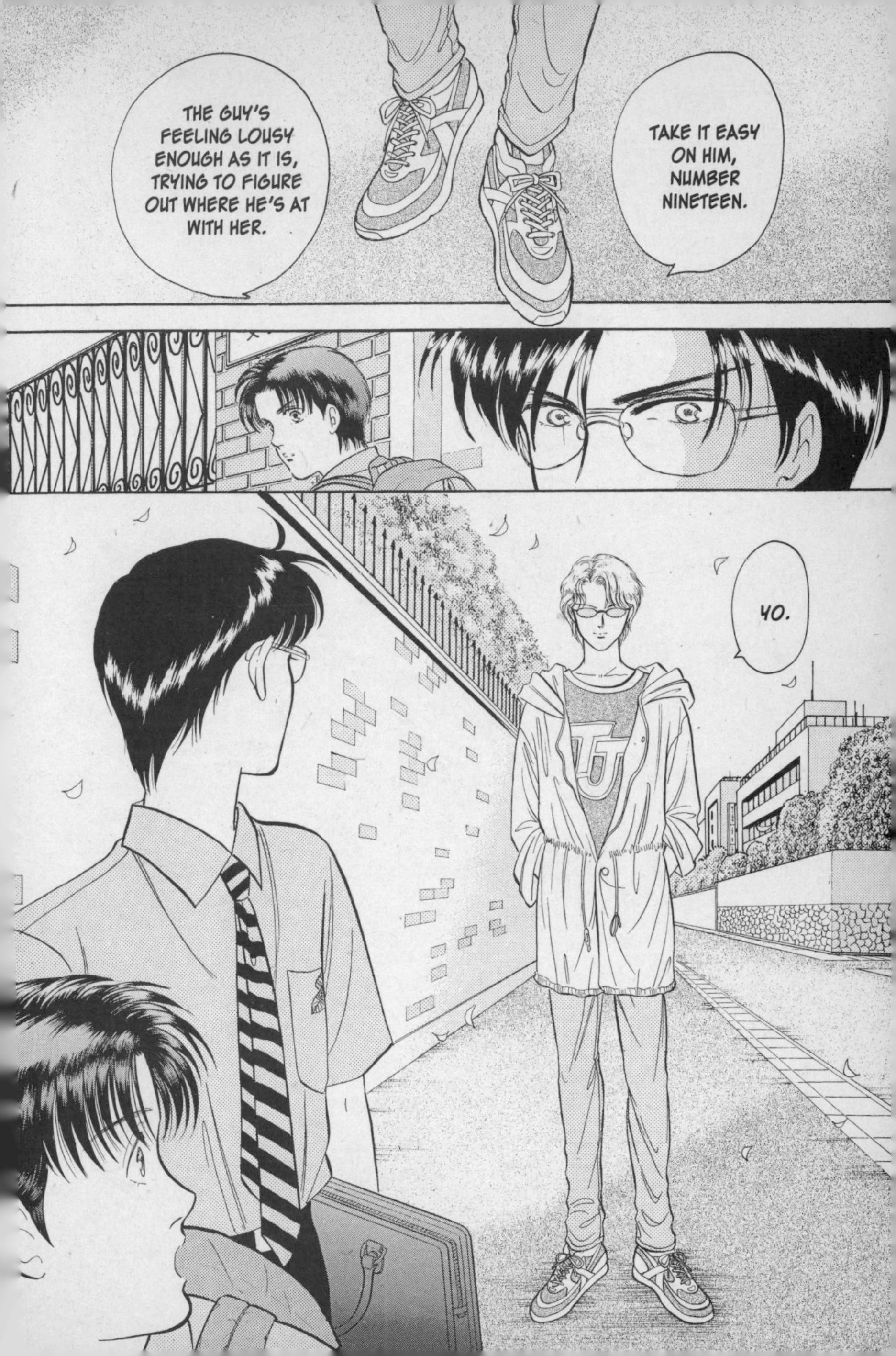
TAKE IT EASY ON HIM, NUMBER NINETEEN.
THE GUY'S FEELING LOUSY ENOUGH AS IT IS, TRYING TO FIGURE OUT WHERE HE'S AT WITH HER.
YO.

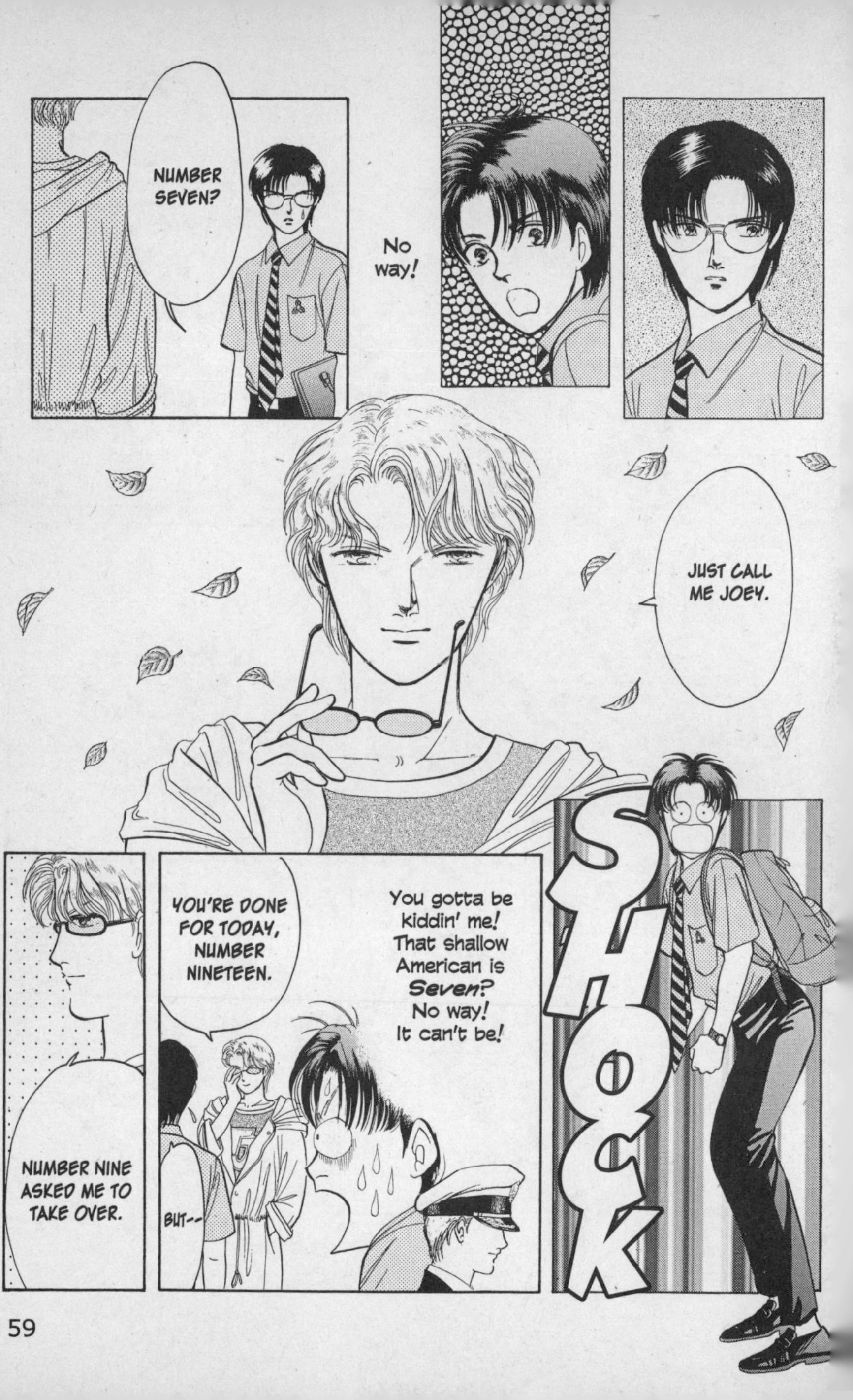
No way!
NUMBER SEVEN?
JUST CALL ME JOEY.
SHOCK
You gotta be kiddin' me! That shallow American is *Seven*? No way! It can't be!
YOU'RE DONE FOR TODAY, NUMBER NINETEEN.
BUT--
NUMBER NINE ASKED ME TO TAKE OVER.

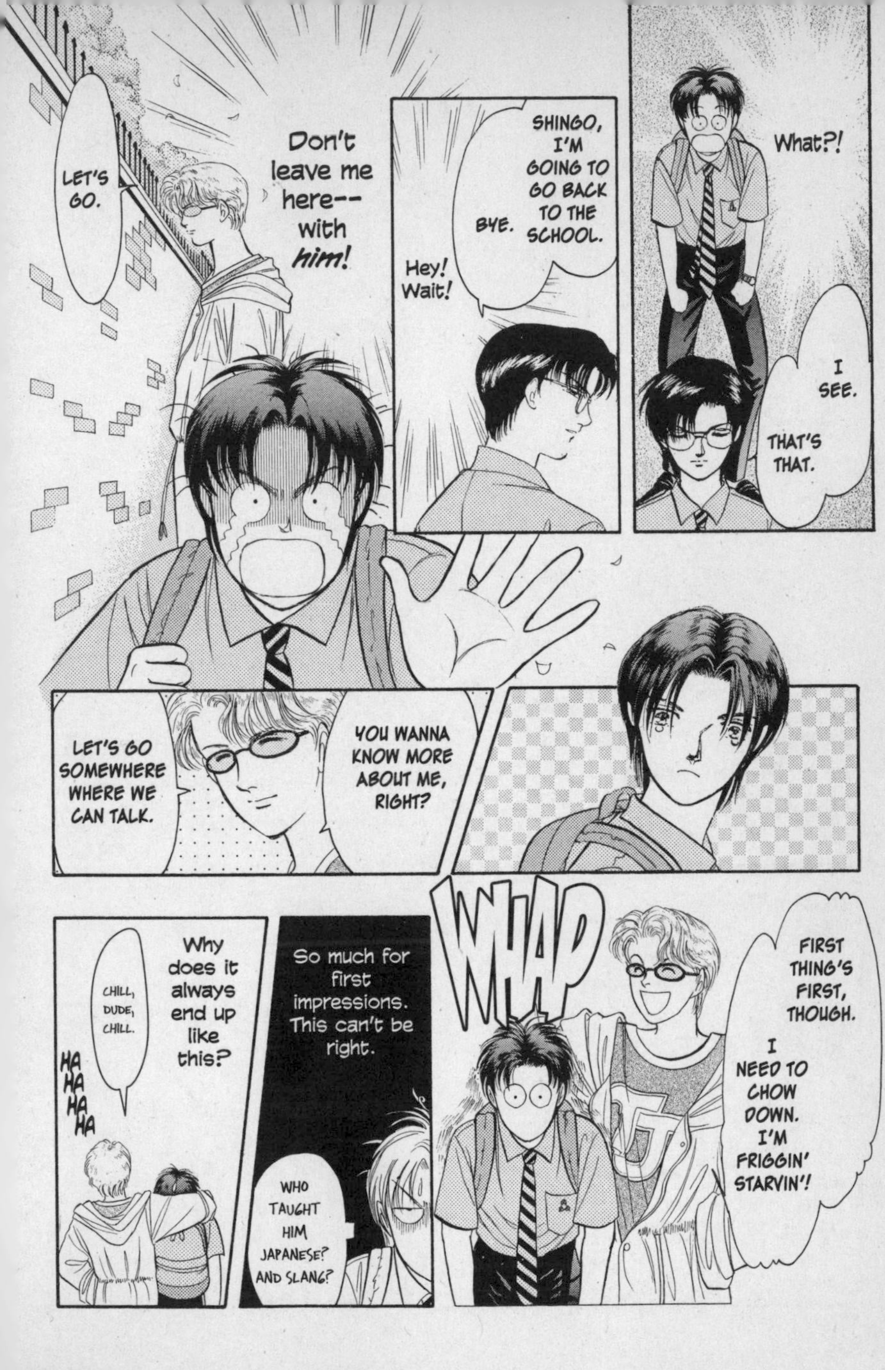
What?!
I SEE.
THAT'S THAT.
SHINGO, I'M GOING TO GO BACK TO THE SCHOOL.
BYE.
Hey! Wait!
LET'S GO.
Don't leave me here--with *him*!
YOU WANNA KNOW MORE ABOUT ME, RIGHT?
LET'S GO SOMEWHERE WHERE WE CAN TALK.
WHAP
FIRST THING'S FIRST, THOUGH.
I NEED TO CHOW DOWN. I'M FRIGGIN' STARVIN'!
So much for first impressions. This can't be right.
WHO TAUGHT HIM JAPANESE? AND SLANG?
Why does it always end up like this?
CHILL, DUDE, CHILL.
HA HA HA HA

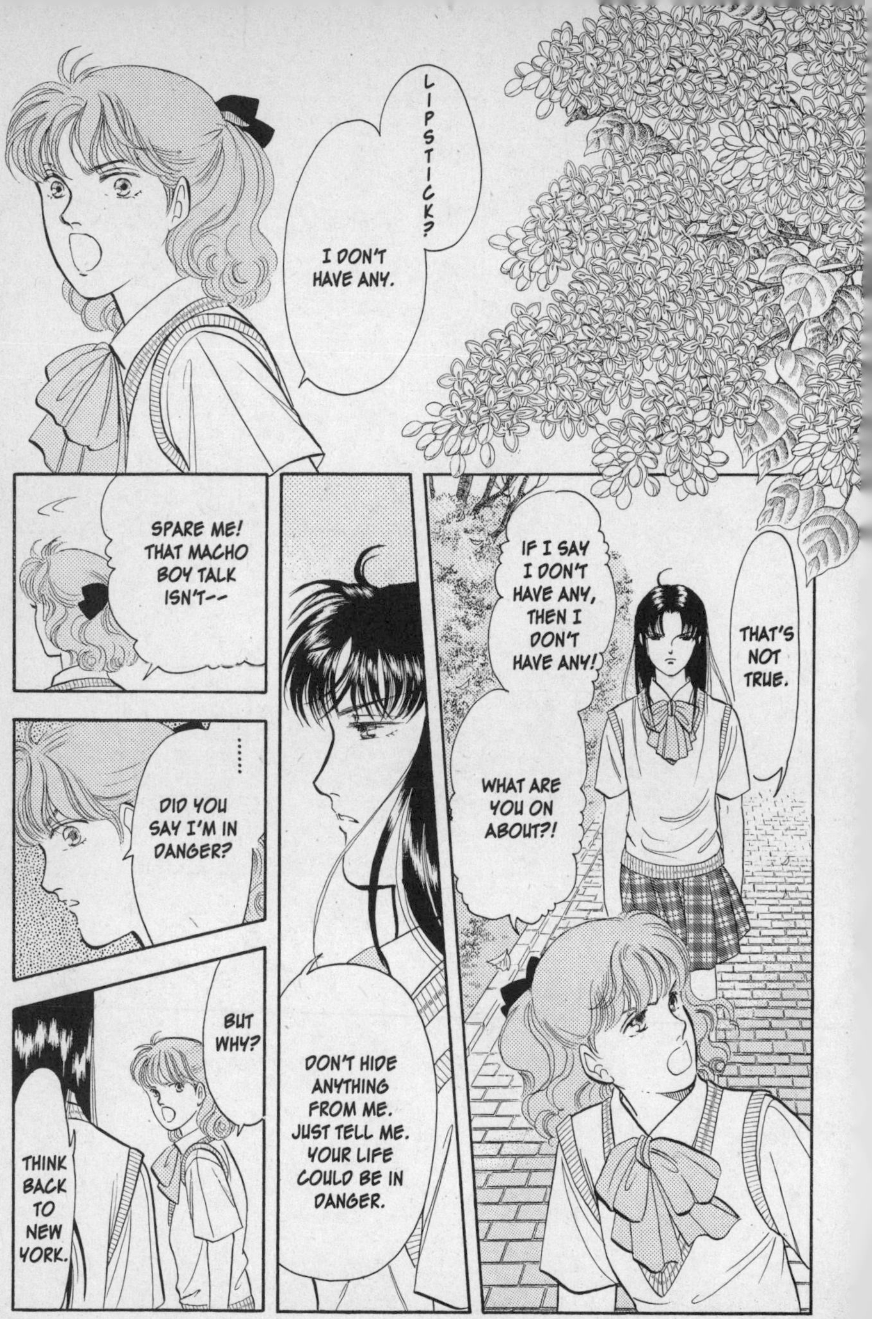
LIPSTICK?
I DON'T HAVE ANY.
THAT'S NOT TRUE.
IF I SAY I DON'T HAVE ANY, THEN I DON'T HAVE ANY!
WHAT ARE YOU ON ABOUT?!
DON'T HIDE ANYTHING FROM ME. JUST TELL ME. YOUR LIFE COULD BE IN DANGER.
SPARE ME! THAT MACHO BOY TALK ISN'T--
......
DID YOU SAY I'M IN DANGER?
BUT WHY?
THINK BACK TO NEW YORK.

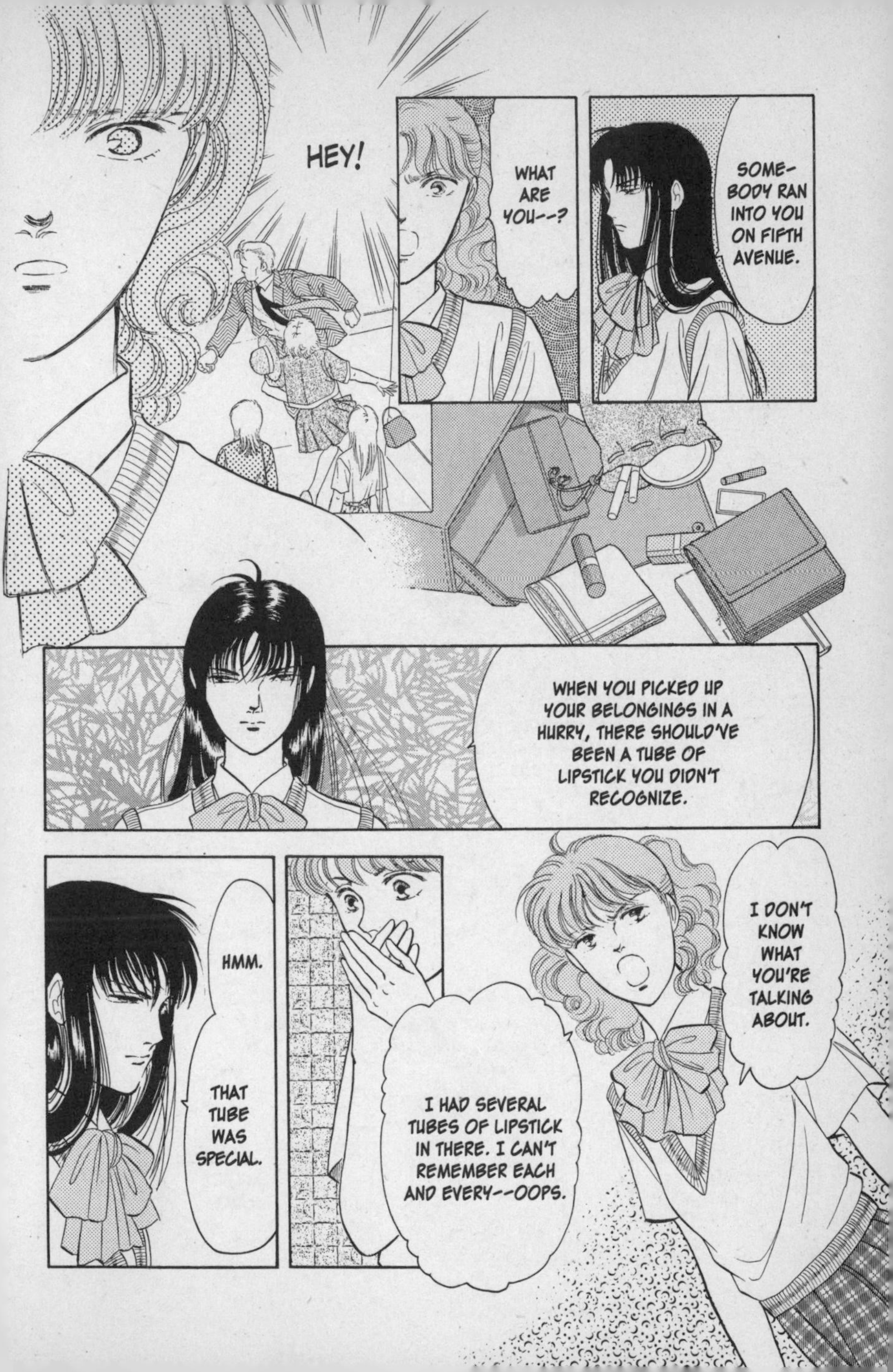
SOME-BODY RAN INTO YOU ON FIFTH AVENUE.
WHAT ARE YOU--?
HEY!
WHEN YOU PICKED UP YOUR BELONGINGS IN A HURRY, THERE SHOULD'VE BEEN A TUBE OF LIPSTICK YOU DIDN'T RECOGNIZE.
I DON'T KNOW WHAT YOU'RE TALKING ABOUT.
I HAD SEVERAL TUBES OF LIPSTICK IN THERE. I CAN'T REMEMBER EACH AND EVERY--OOPS.
HMM.
THAT TUBE WAS SPECIAL.

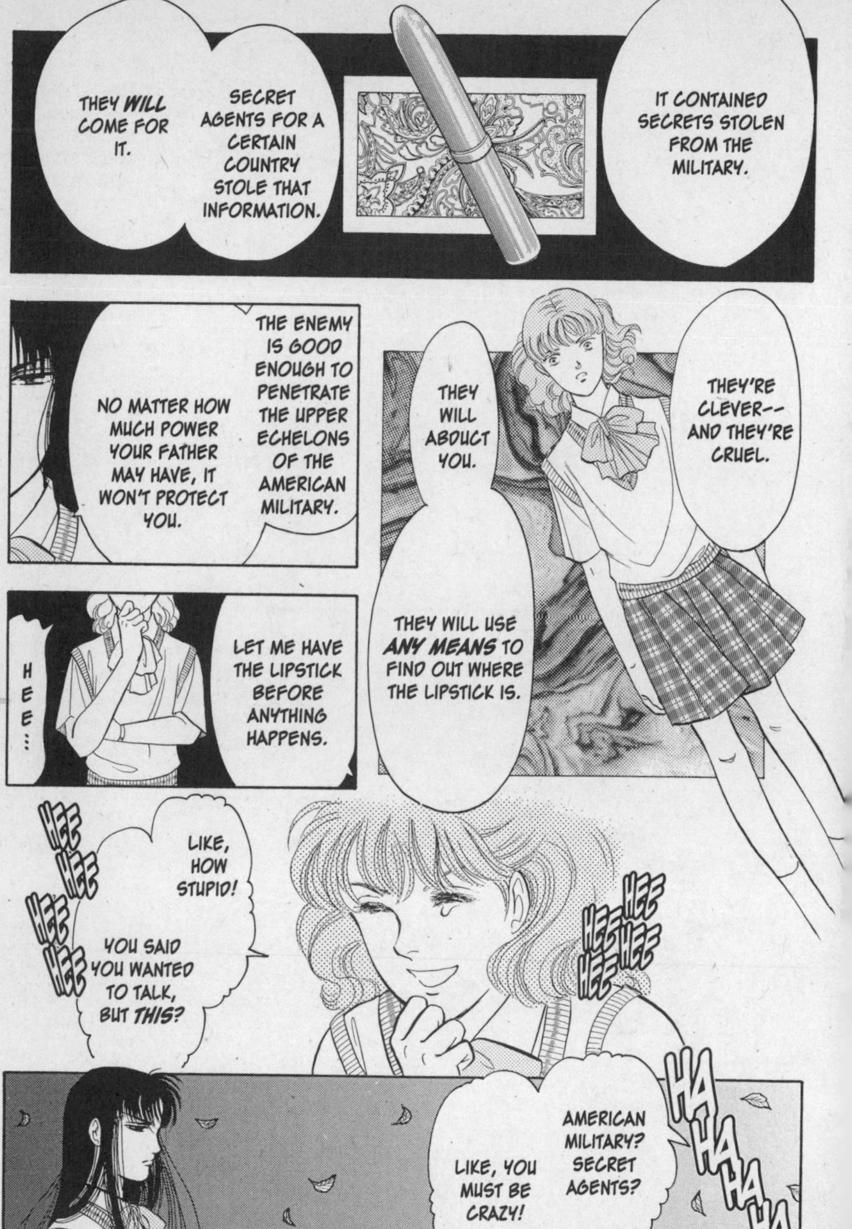
IT CONTAINED SECRETS STOLEN FROM THE MILITARY.
SECRET AGENTS FOR A CERTAIN COUNTRY STOLE THAT INFORMATION.
THEY *WILL* COME FOR IT.
THEY'RE CLEVER--AND THEY'RE CRUEL.
THEY WILL ABDUCT YOU.
THEY WILL USE ***ANY MEANS*** TO FIND OUT WHERE THE LIPSTICK IS.
THE ENEMY IS GOOD ENOUGH TO PENETRATE THE UPPER ECHELONS OF THE AMERICAN MILITARY.
NO MATTER HOW MUCH POWER YOUR FATHER MAY HAVE, IT WON'T PROTECT YOU.
LET ME HAVE THE LIPSTICK BEFORE ANYTHING HAPPENS.
HEE...
HEE HEE HEE HEE
LIKE, HOW STUPID!
YOU SAID YOU WANTED TO TALK, BUT *THIS?*
HEE HEE HEE HEE
HA HA HA HA
AMERICAN MILITARY? SECRET AGENTS?
LIKE, YOU MUST BE CRAZY!

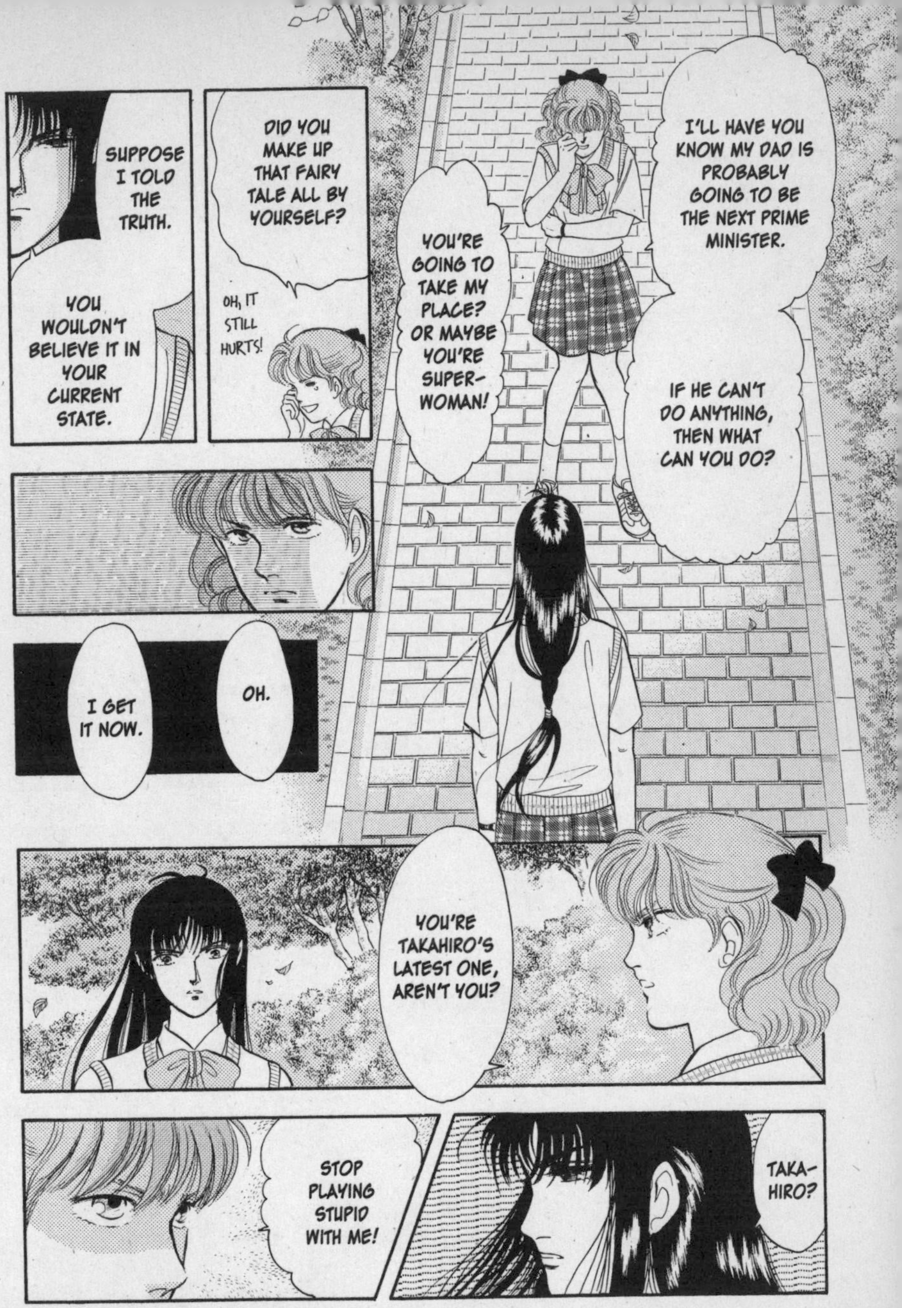
I'LL HAVE YOU KNOW MY DAD IS PROBABLY GOING TO BE THE NEXT PRIME MINISTER.
IF HE CAN'T DO ANYTHING, THEN WHAT CAN YOU DO?
YOU'RE GOING TO TAKE MY PLACE? OR MAYBE YOU'RE SUPER-WOMAN!
DID YOU MAKE UP THAT FAIRY TALE ALL BY YOURSELF?
OH, IT STILL HURTS!
SUPPOSE I TOLD THE TRUTH.
YOU WOULDN'T BELIEVE IT IN YOUR CURRENT STATE.
OH.
I GET IT NOW.
YOU'RE TAKAHIRO'S LATEST ONE, AREN'T YOU?
TAKA-HIRO?
STOP PLAYING STUPID WITH ME!

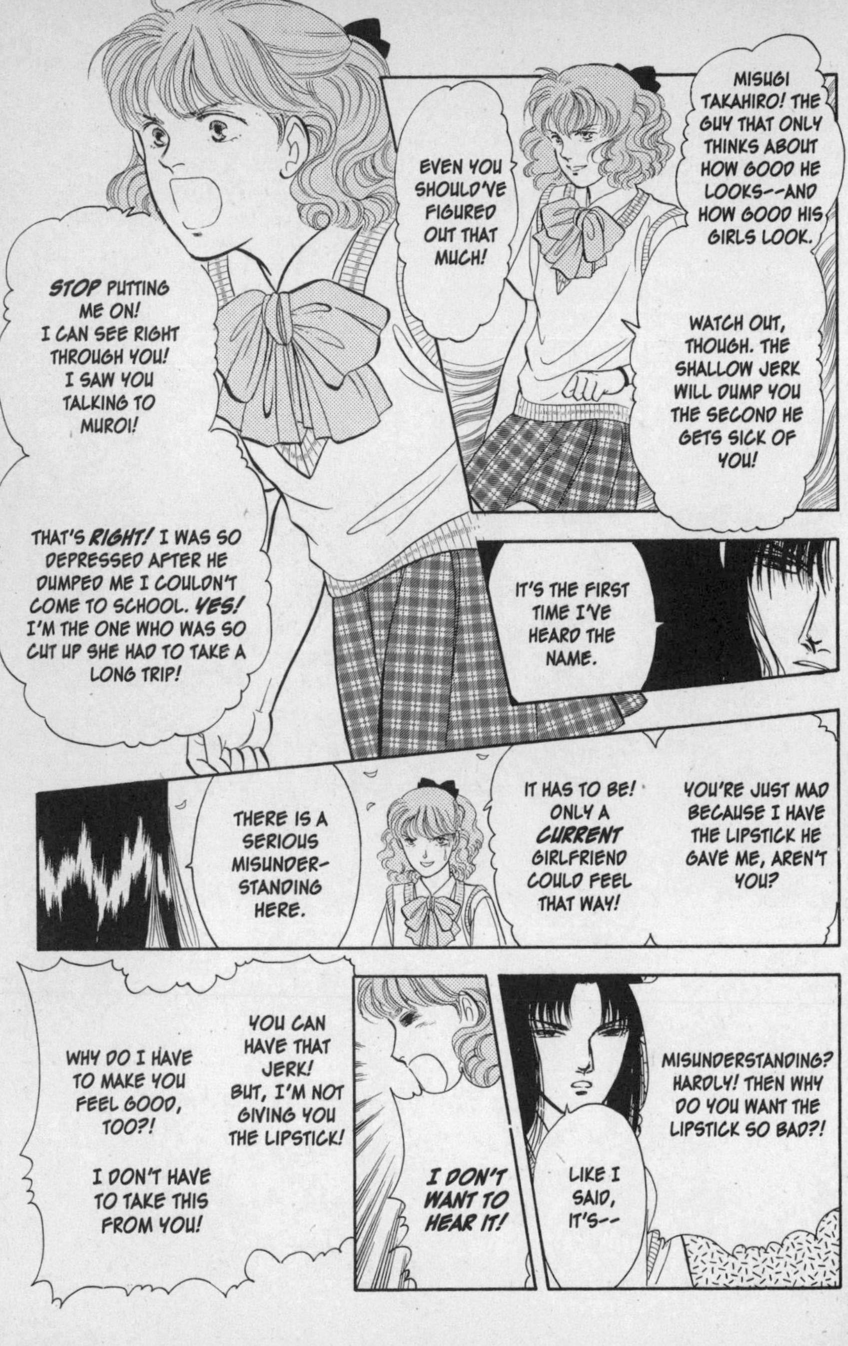
MISUGI TAKAHIRO! THE GUY THAT ONLY THINKS ABOUT HOW GOOD HE LOOKS--AND HOW GOOD HIS GIRLS LOOK.
EVEN YOU SHOULD'VE FIGURED OUT THAT MUCH!
WATCH OUT, THOUGH. THE SHALLOW JERK WILL DUMP YOU THE SECOND HE GETS SICK OF YOU!
IT'S THE FIRST TIME I'VE HEARD THE NAME.
STOP PUTTING ME ON! I CAN SEE RIGHT THROUGH YOU! I SAW YOU TALKING TO MUROI!
THAT'S RIGHT! I WAS SO DEPRESSED AFTER HE DUMPED ME I COULDN'T COME TO SCHOOL. YES! I'M THE ONE WHO WAS SO CUT UP SHE HAD TO TAKE A LONG TRIP!
YOU'RE JUST MAD BECAUSE I HAVE THE LIPSTICK HE GAVE ME, AREN'T YOU?
IT HAS TO BE! ONLY A CURRENT GIRLFRIEND COULD FEEL THAT WAY!
THERE IS A SERIOUS MISUNDER-STANDING HERE.
MISUNDERSTANDING? HARDLY! THEN WHY DO YOU WANT THE LIPSTICK SO BAD?!
LIKE I SAID, IT'S--
YOU CAN HAVE THAT JERK! BUT, I'M NOT GIVING YOU THE LIPSTICK!
I DON'T WANT TO HEAR IT!
WHY DO I HAVE TO MAKE YOU FEEL GOOD, TOO?!
I DON'T HAVE TO TAKE THIS FROM YOU!

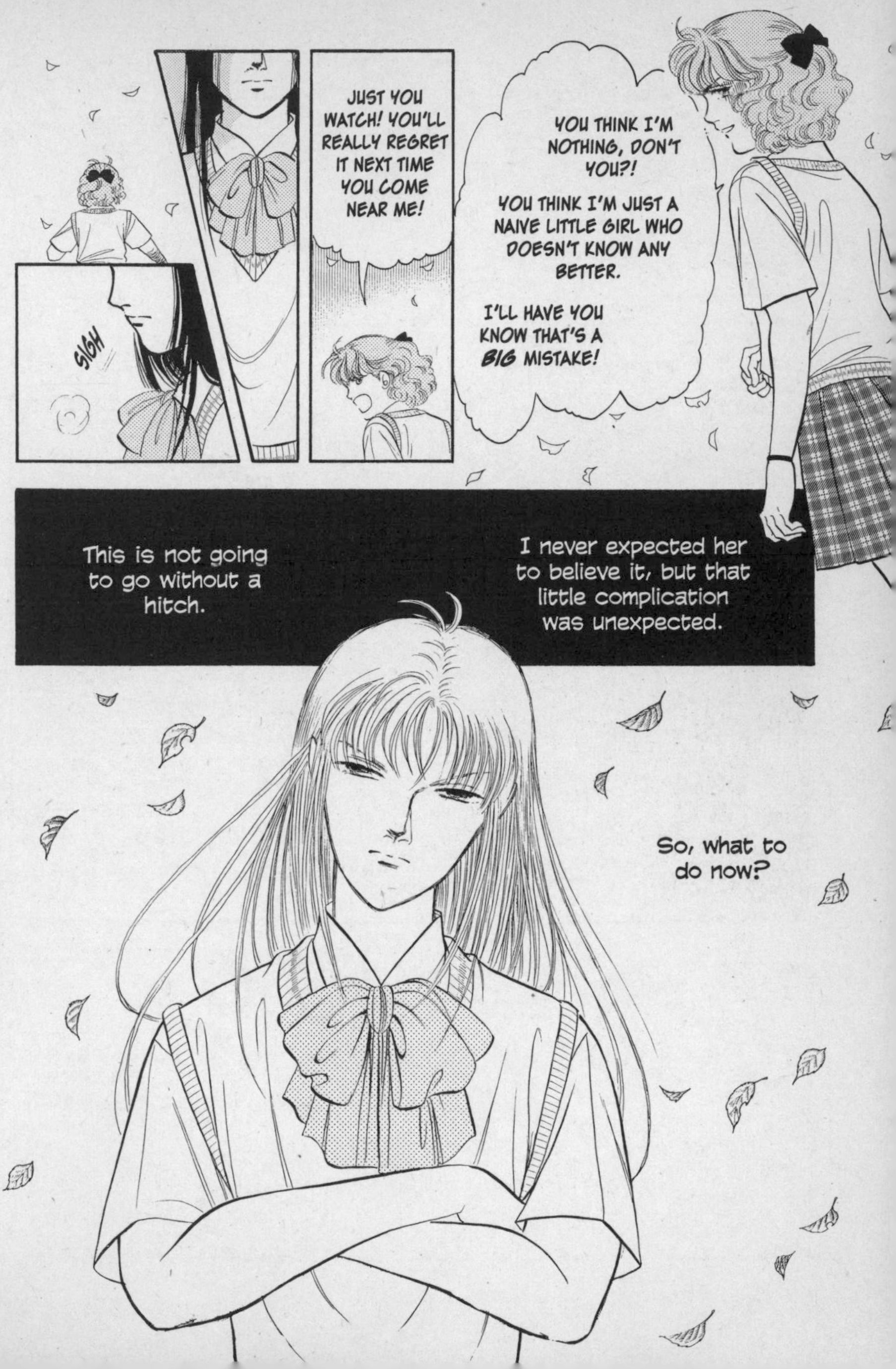
YOU THINK I'M NOTHING, DON'T YOU?!
YOU THINK I'M JUST A NAIVE LITTLE GIRL WHO DOESN'T KNOW ANY BETTER.
I'LL HAVE YOU KNOW THAT'S A BIG MISTAKE!
JUST YOU WATCH! YOU'LL REALLY REGRET IT NEXT TIME YOU COME NEAR ME!
SIGH
I never expected her to believe it, but that little complication was unexpected.
This is not going to go without a hitch.
So, what to do now?

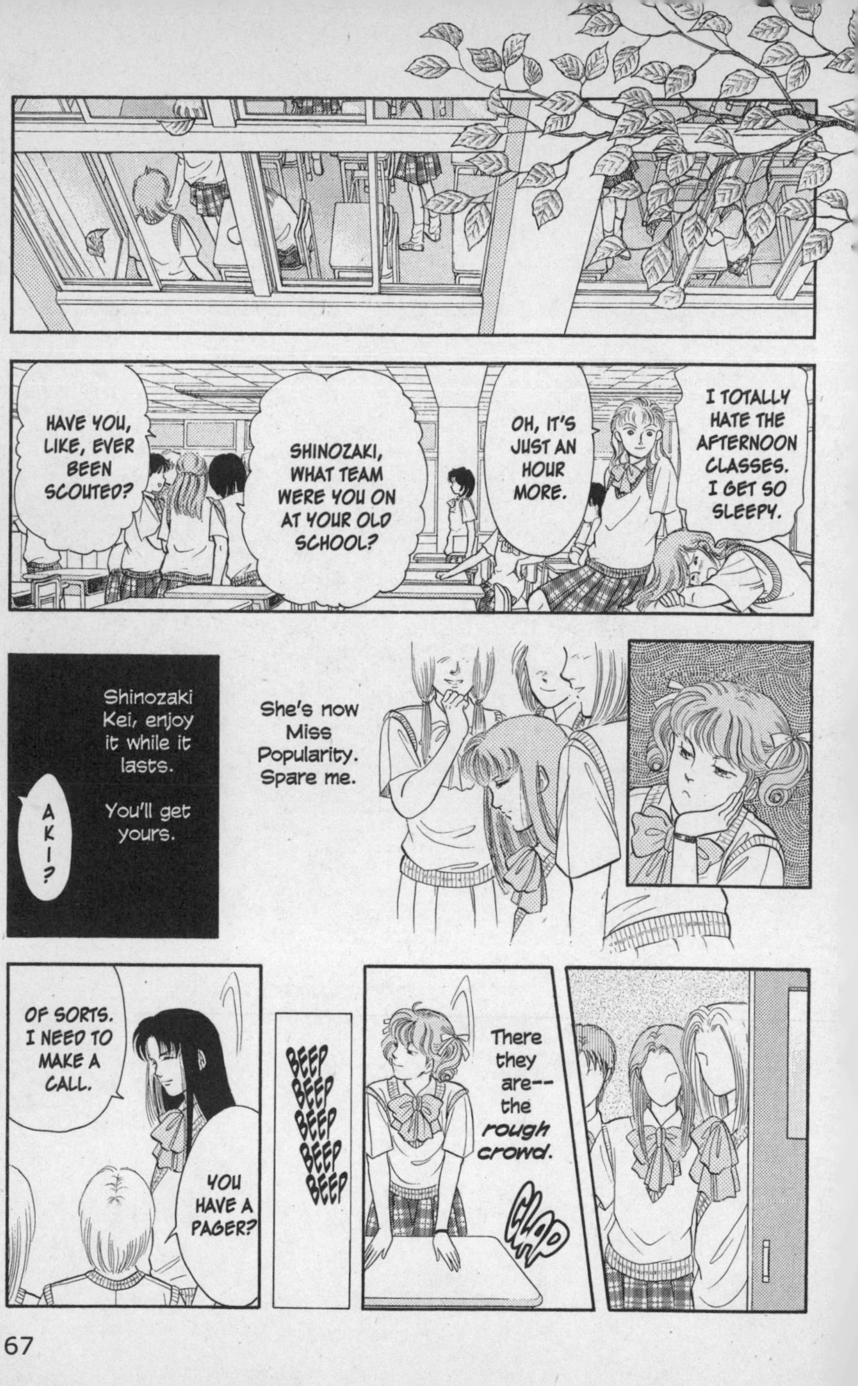

I TOTALLY HATE THE AFTERNOON CLASSES. I GET SO SLEEPY.
OH, IT'S JUST AN HOUR MORE.
SHINOZAKI, WHAT TEAM WERE YOU ON AT YOUR OLD SCHOOL?
HAVE YOU, LIKE, EVER BEEN SCOUTED?
She's now Miss Popularity. Spare me.
Shinozaki Kei, enjoy it while it lasts.
You'll get yours.
AKI?
There they are-- the *rough crowd*.
CLAP
BEEP BEEP BEEP BEEP BEEP
YOU HAVE A PAGER?
OF SORTS. I NEED TO MAKE A CALL.

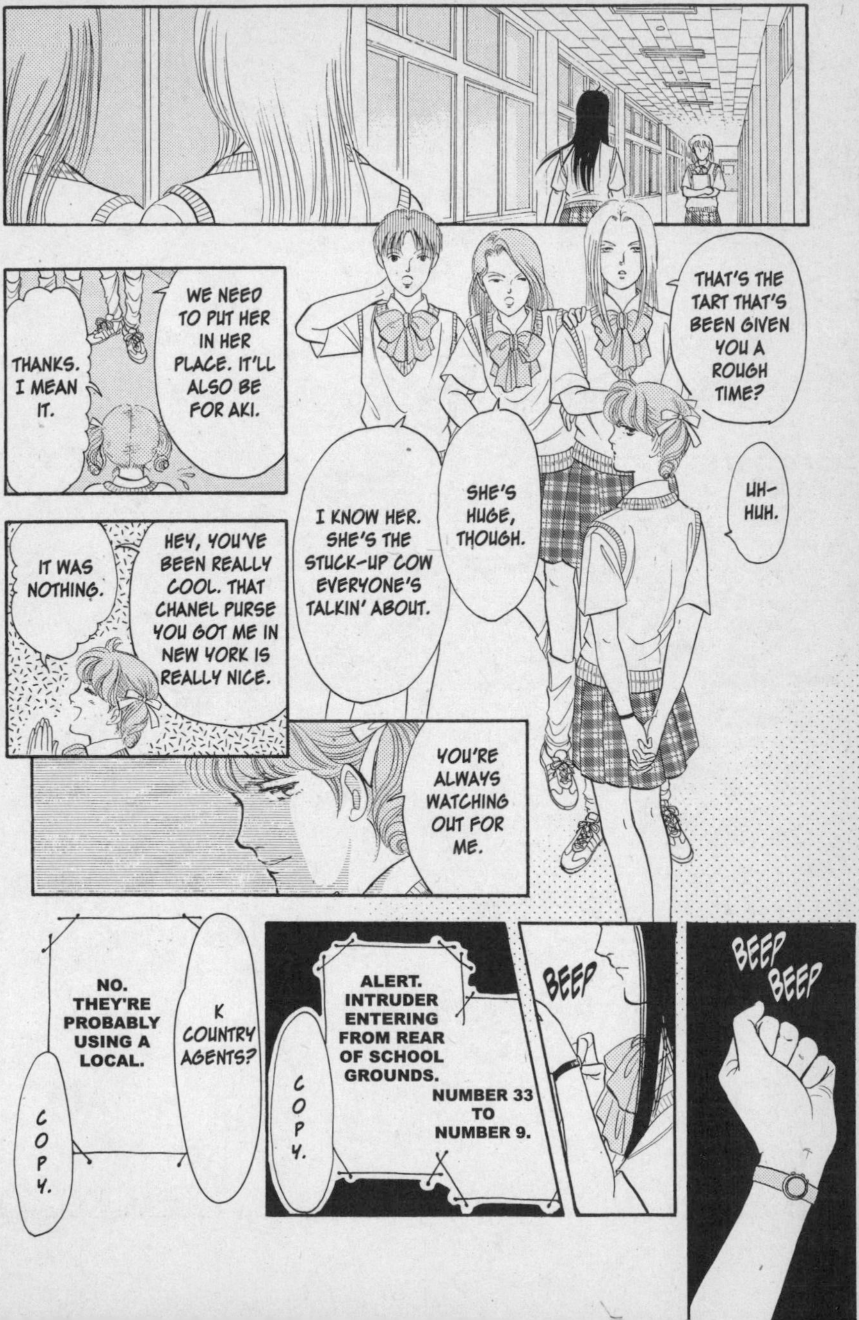
THAT'S THE TART THAT'S BEEN GIVEN YOU A ROUGH TIME?
UH-HUH.
SHE'S HUGE, THOUGH.
I KNOW HER. SHE'S THE STUCK-UP COW EVERYONE'S TALKIN' ABOUT.
WE NEED TO PUT HER IN HER PLACE. IT'LL ALSO BE FOR AKI.
THANKS. I MEAN IT.
HEY, YOU'VE BEEN REALLY COOL. THAT CHANEL PURSE YOU GOT ME IN NEW YORK IS REALLY NICE.
IT WAS NOTHING.
YOU'RE ALWAYS WATCHING OUT FOR ME.
BEEP BEEP
BEEP
ALERT. INTRUDER ENTERING FROM REAR OF SCHOOL GROUNDS.
NUMBER 33 TO NUMBER 9.
COPY.
K COUNTRY AGENTS?
NO. THEY'RE PROBABLY USING A LOCAL.
COPY.

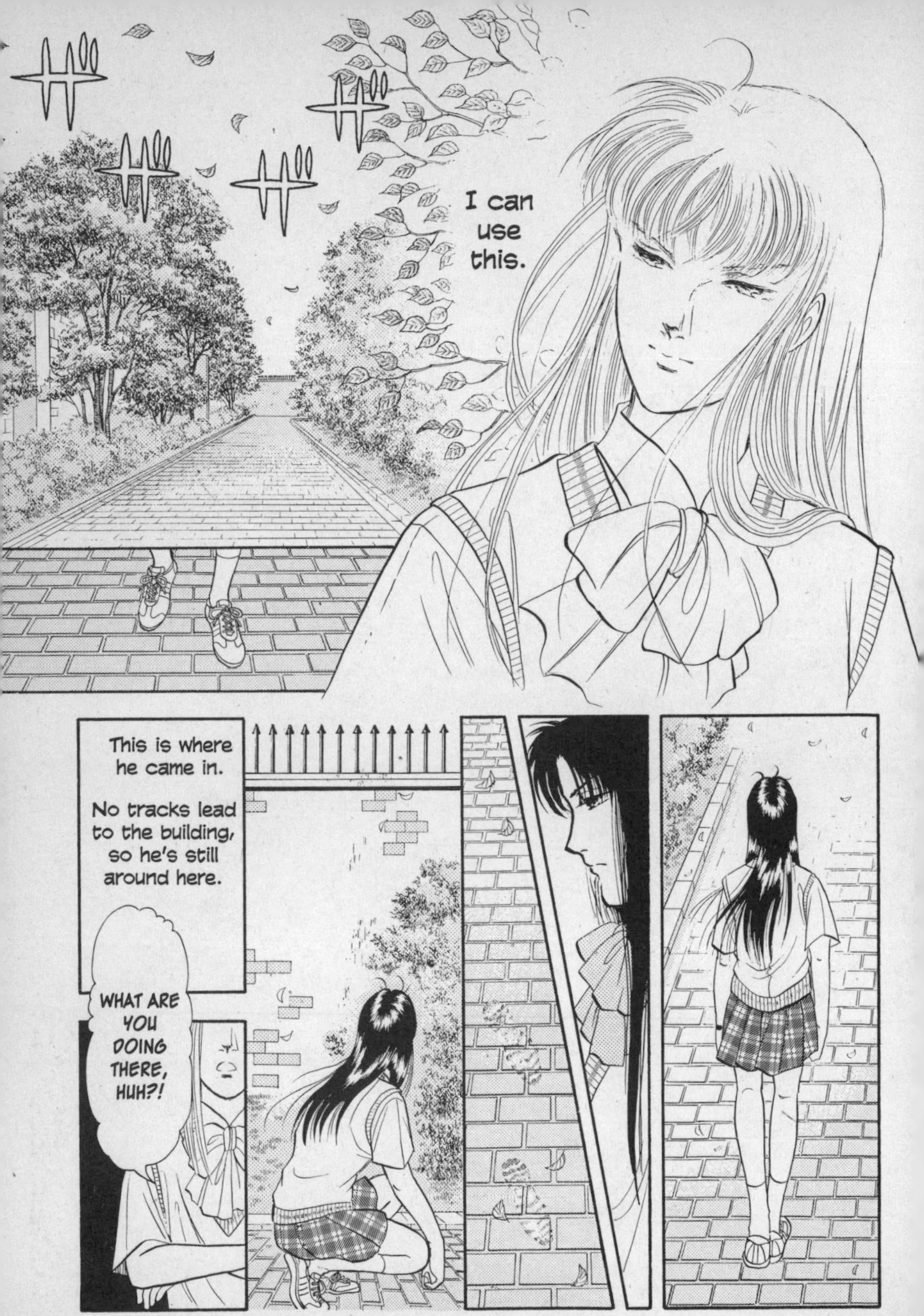
I can use this.
This is where he came in.
No tracks lead to the building, so he's still around here.
WHAT ARE YOU DOING THERE, HUH?!

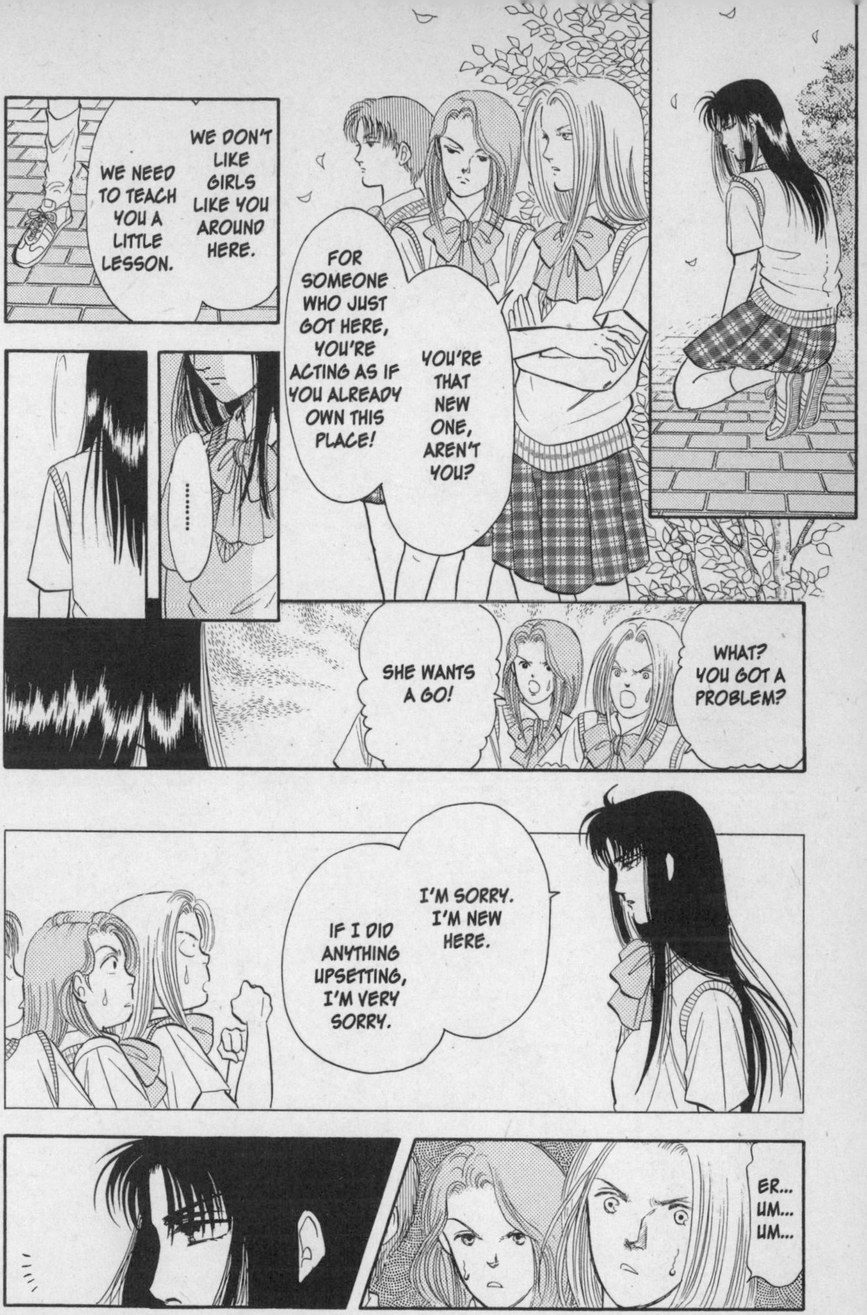
YOU'RE THAT NEW ONE, AREN'T YOU?
FOR SOMEONE WHO JUST GOT HERE, YOU'RE ACTING AS IF YOU ALREADY OWN THIS PLACE!
WE DON'T LIKE GIRLS LIKE YOU AROUND HERE.
WE NEED TO TEACH YOU A LITTLE LESSON.
....
WHAT? YOU GOT A PROBLEM?
SHE WANTS A GO!
I'M SORRY. I'M NEW HERE.
IF I DID ANYTHING UPSETTING, I'M VERY SORRY.
ER... UM... UM...

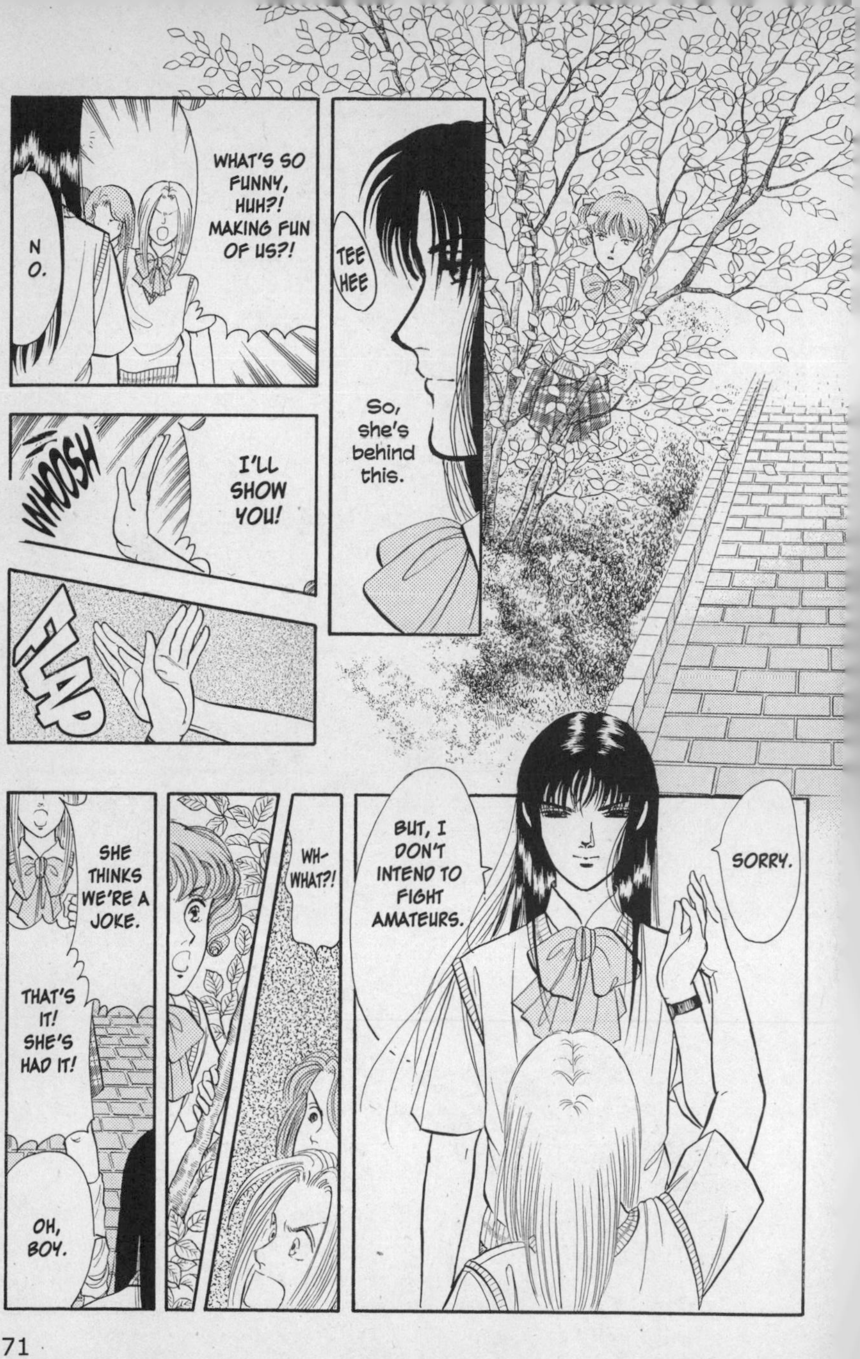
TEE HEE
So, she's behind this.
WHAT'S SO FUNNY, HUH?! MAKING FUN OF US?!
NO.
I'LL SHOW YOU!
WHOOSH
FLAP
SORRY.
BUT, I DON'T INTEND TO FIGHT AMATEURS.
WH-WHAT?!
SHE THINKS WE'RE A JOKE.
THAT'S IT! SHE'S HAD IT!
OH, BOY.

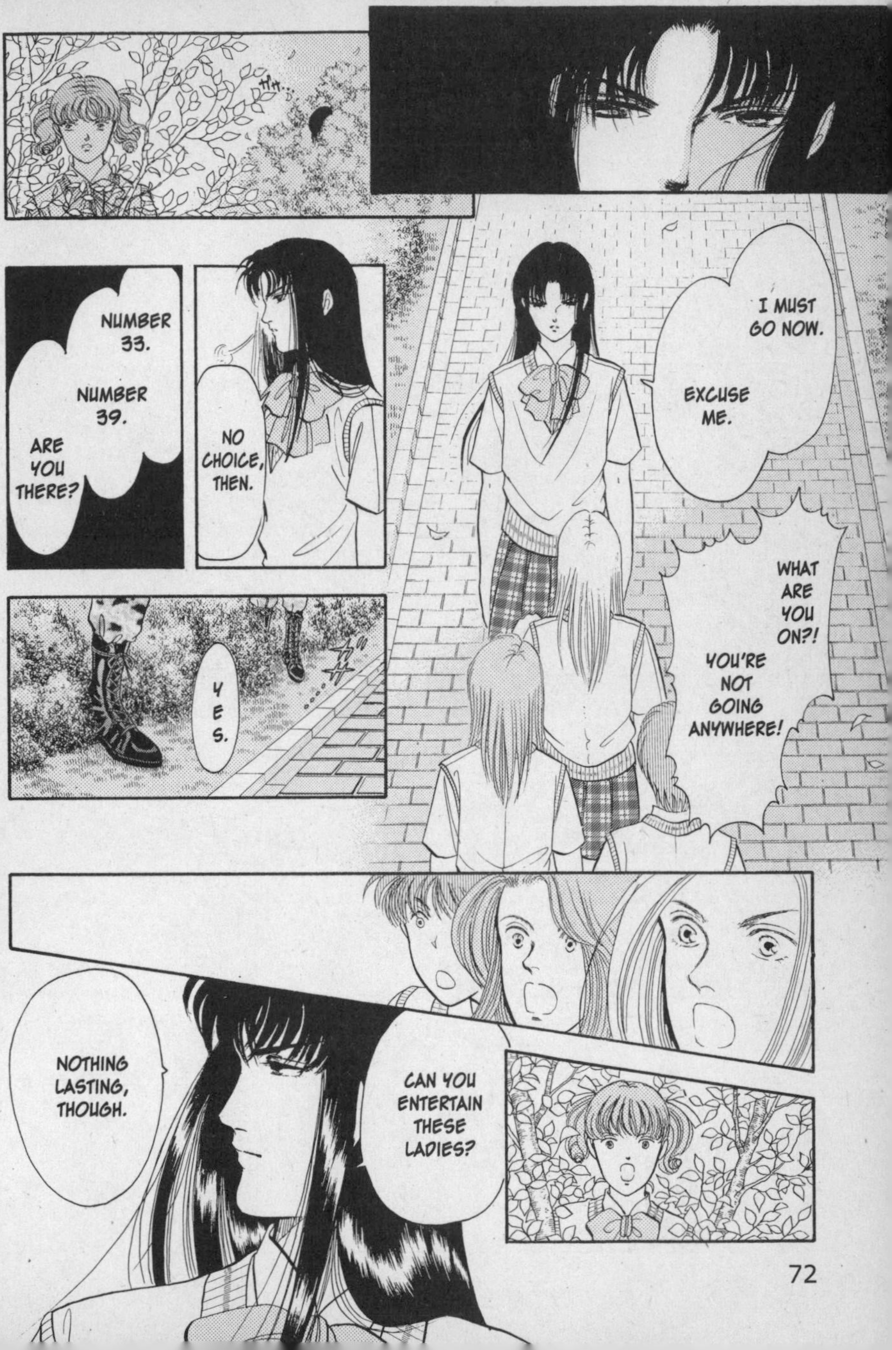
I MUST GO NOW.
EXCUSE ME.
WHAT ARE YOU ON?! YOU'RE NOT GOING ANYWHERE!
NO CHOICE, THEN.
NUMBER 33.
NUMBER 39.
ARE YOU THERE?
YES.
CAN YOU ENTERTAIN THESE LADIES?
NOTHING LASTING, THOUGH.

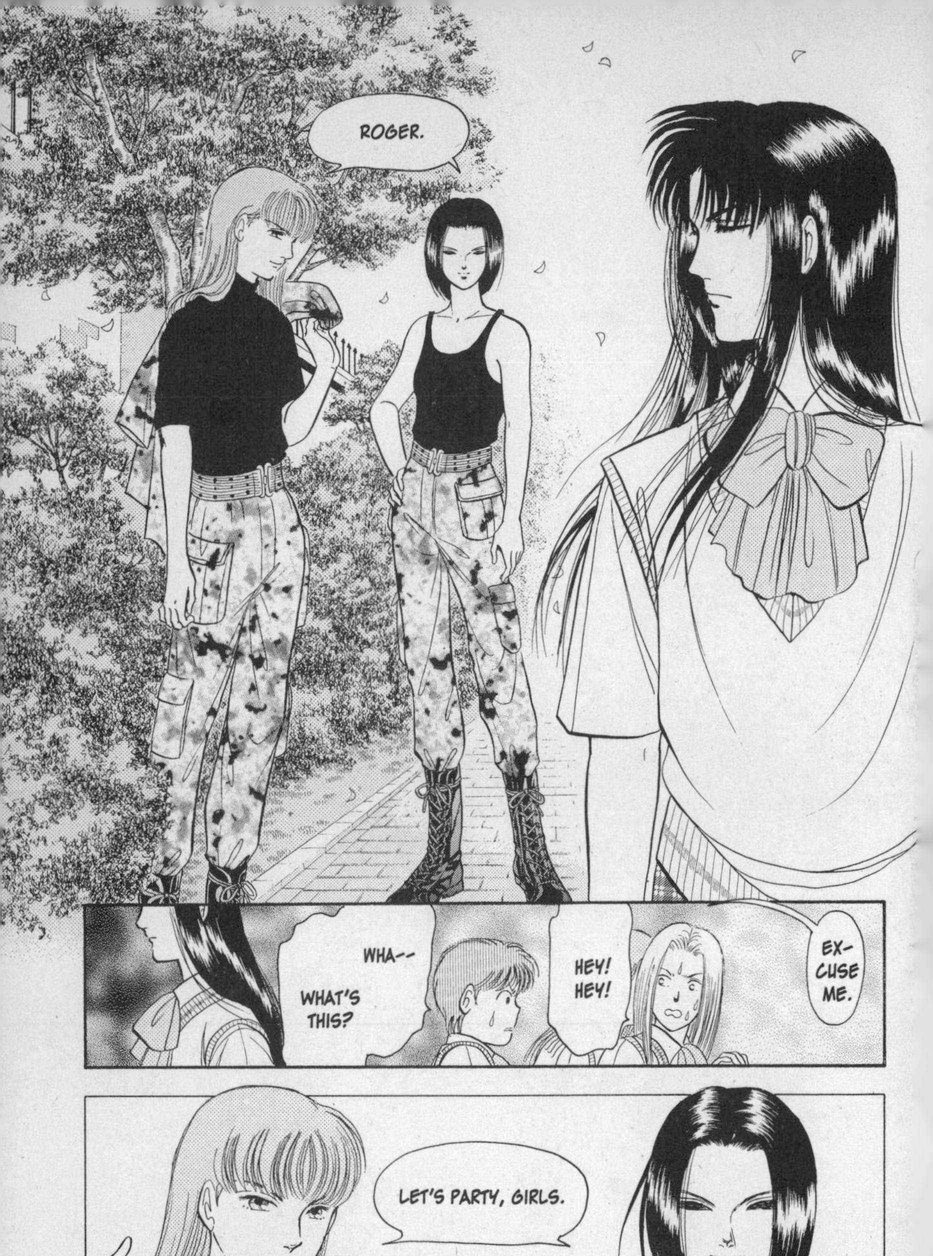
ROGER.
EX-CUSE ME.
HEY! HEY!
WHA-- WHAT'S THIS?
LET'S PARTY, GIRLS.

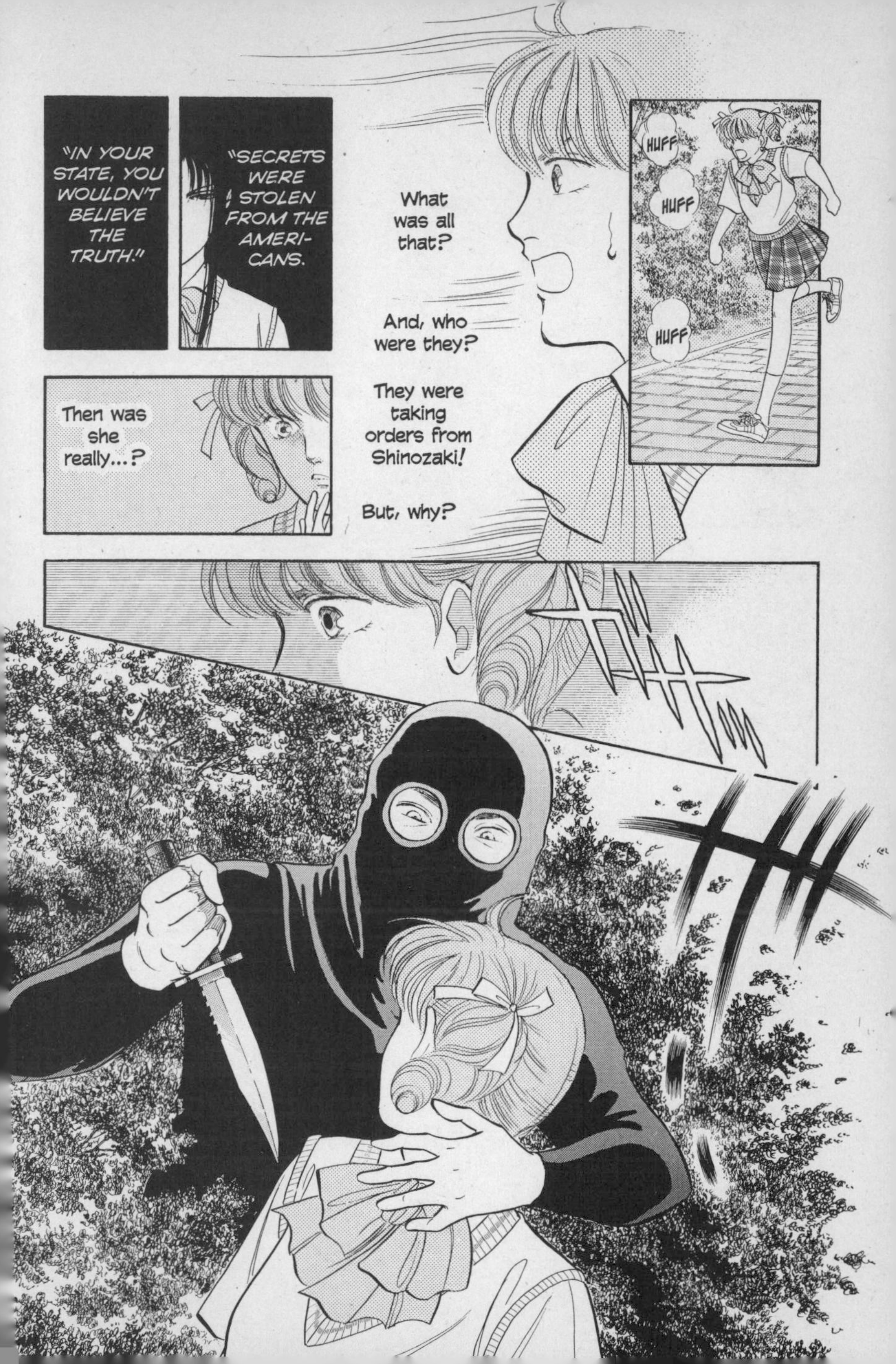
HUFF
HUFF
HUFF
What was all that?
And, who were they?
They were taking orders from Shinozaki!
But, why?
"SECRETS WERE STOLEN FROM THE AMERICANS.
"IN YOUR STATE, YOU WOULDN'T BELIEVE THE TRUTH."
Then was she really...?

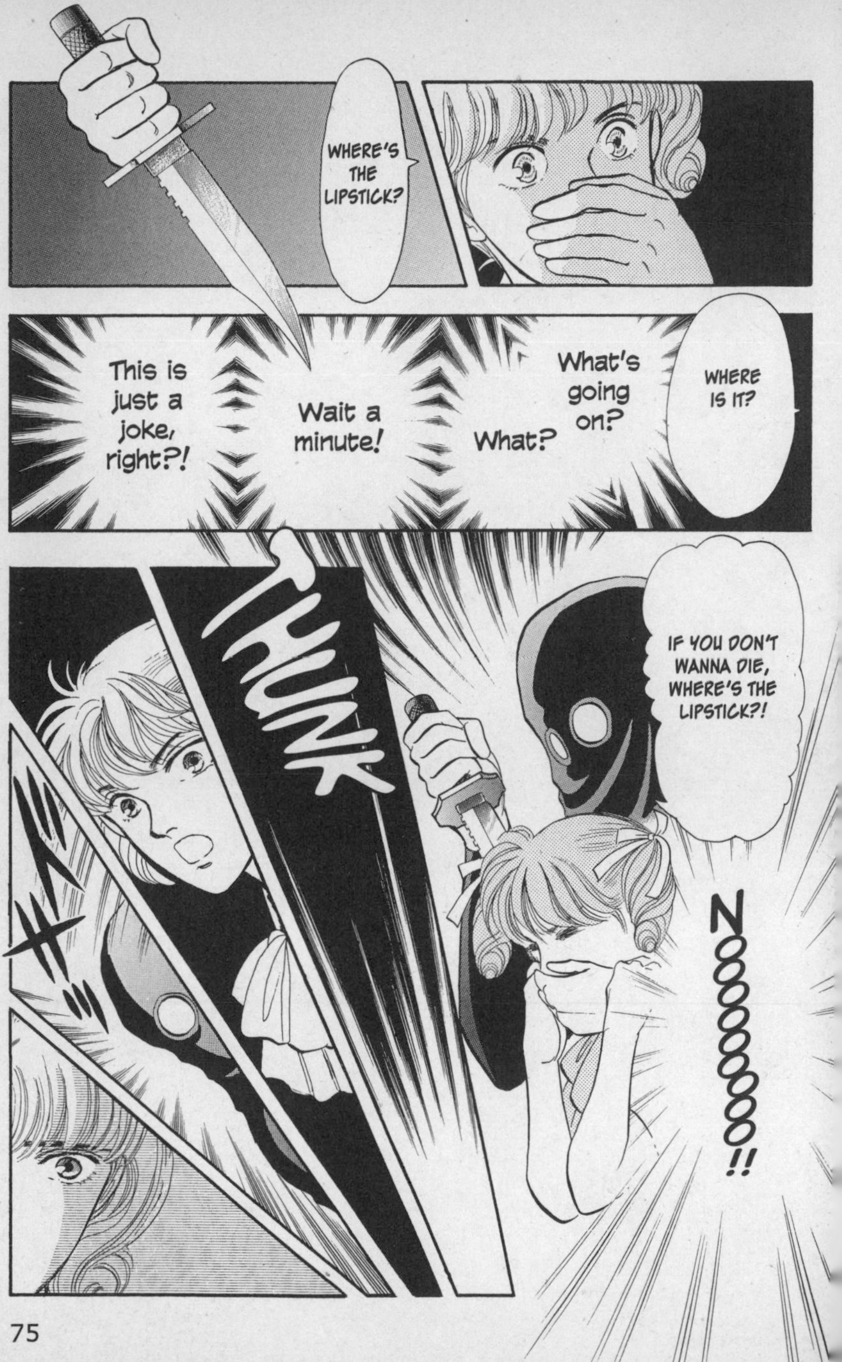
WHERE'S THE LIPSTICK?
WHERE IS IT?
What's going on?
What?
Wait a minute!
This is just a joke, right?!
IF YOU DON'T WANNA DIE, WHERE'S THE LIPSTICK?!
NOOOOOOOOO!!
THUNK

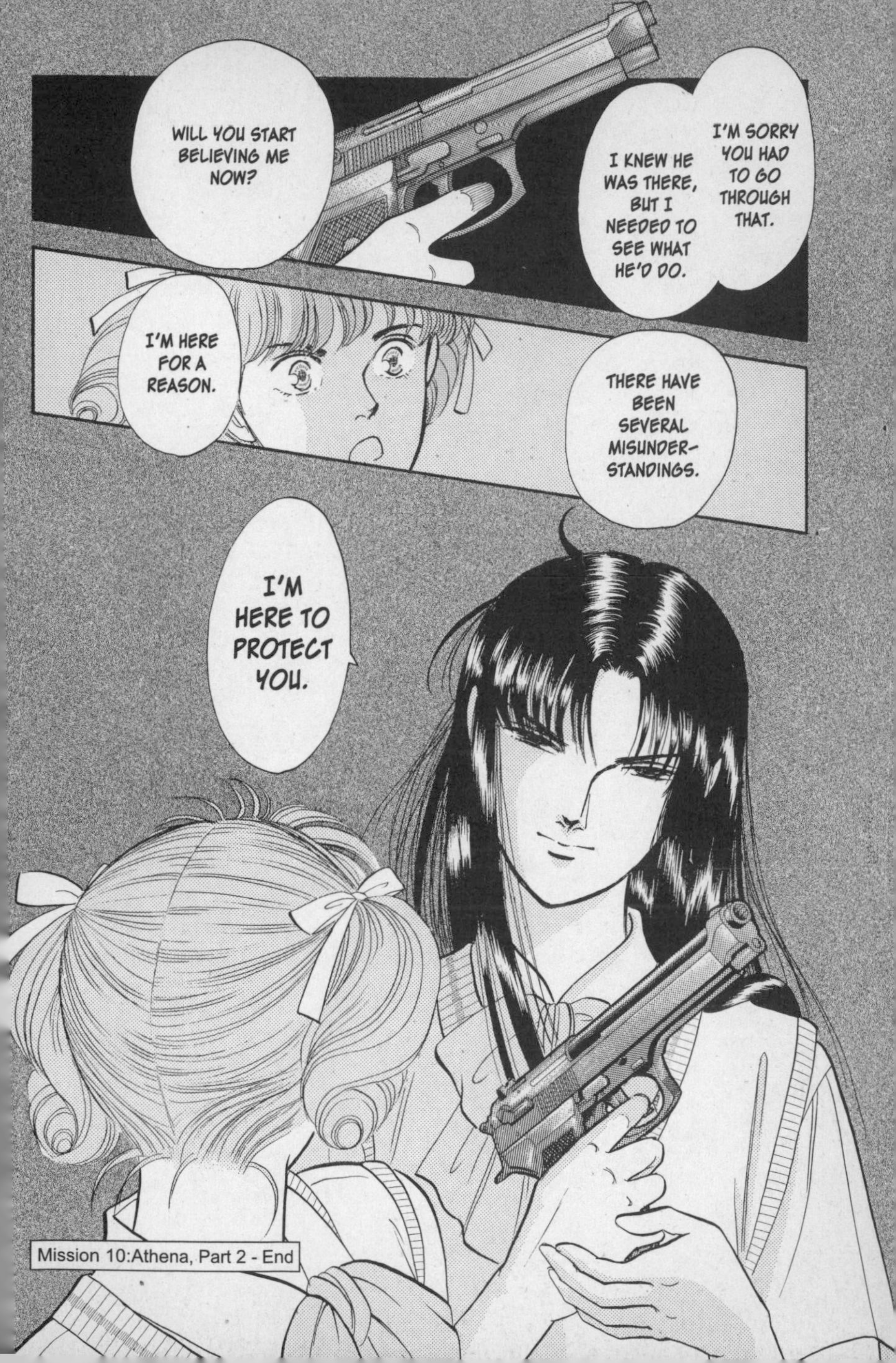
I'M SORRY YOU HAD TO GO THROUGH THAT.
I KNEW HE WAS THERE, BUT I NEEDED TO SEE WHAT HE'D DO.
WILL YOU START BELIEVING ME NOW?
THERE HAVE BEEN SEVERAL MISUNDER-STANDINGS.
I'M HERE FOR A REASON.
I'M HERE TO PROTECT YOU.
Mission 10:Athena, Part 2 - End

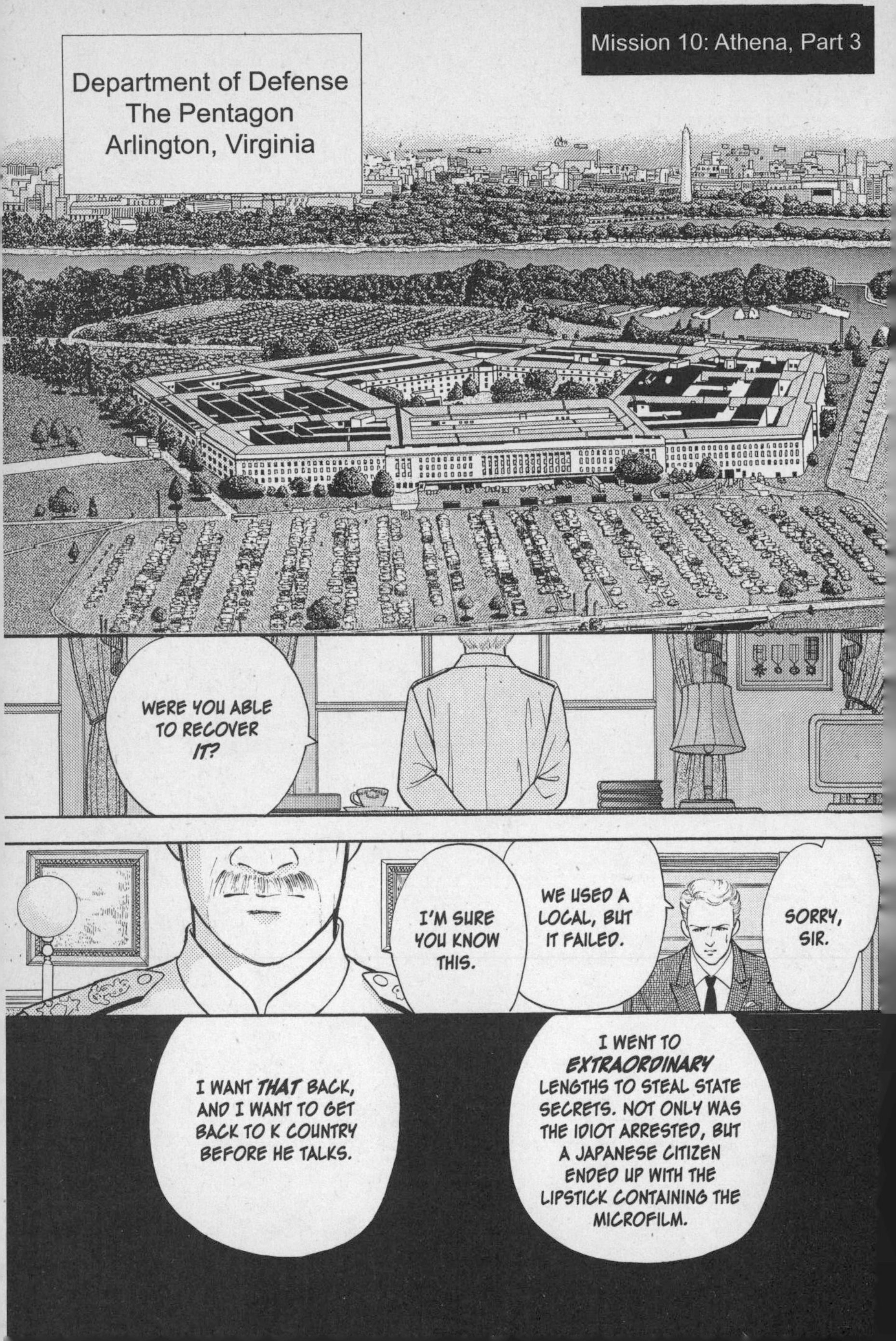
Mission 10: Athena, Part 3
Department of Defense The Pentagon Arlington, Virginia
WERE YOU ABLE TO RECOVER IT?
SORRY, SIR.
WE USED A LOCAL, BUT IT FAILED.
I'M SURE YOU KNOW THIS.
I WENT TO EXTRAORDINARY LENGTHS TO STEAL STATE SECRETS. NOT ONLY WAS THE IDIOT ARRESTED, BUT A JAPANESE CITIZEN ENDED UP WITH THE LIPSTICK CONTAINING THE MICROFILM.
I WANT THAT BACK, AND I WANT TO GET BACK TO K COUNTRY BEFORE HE TALKS.

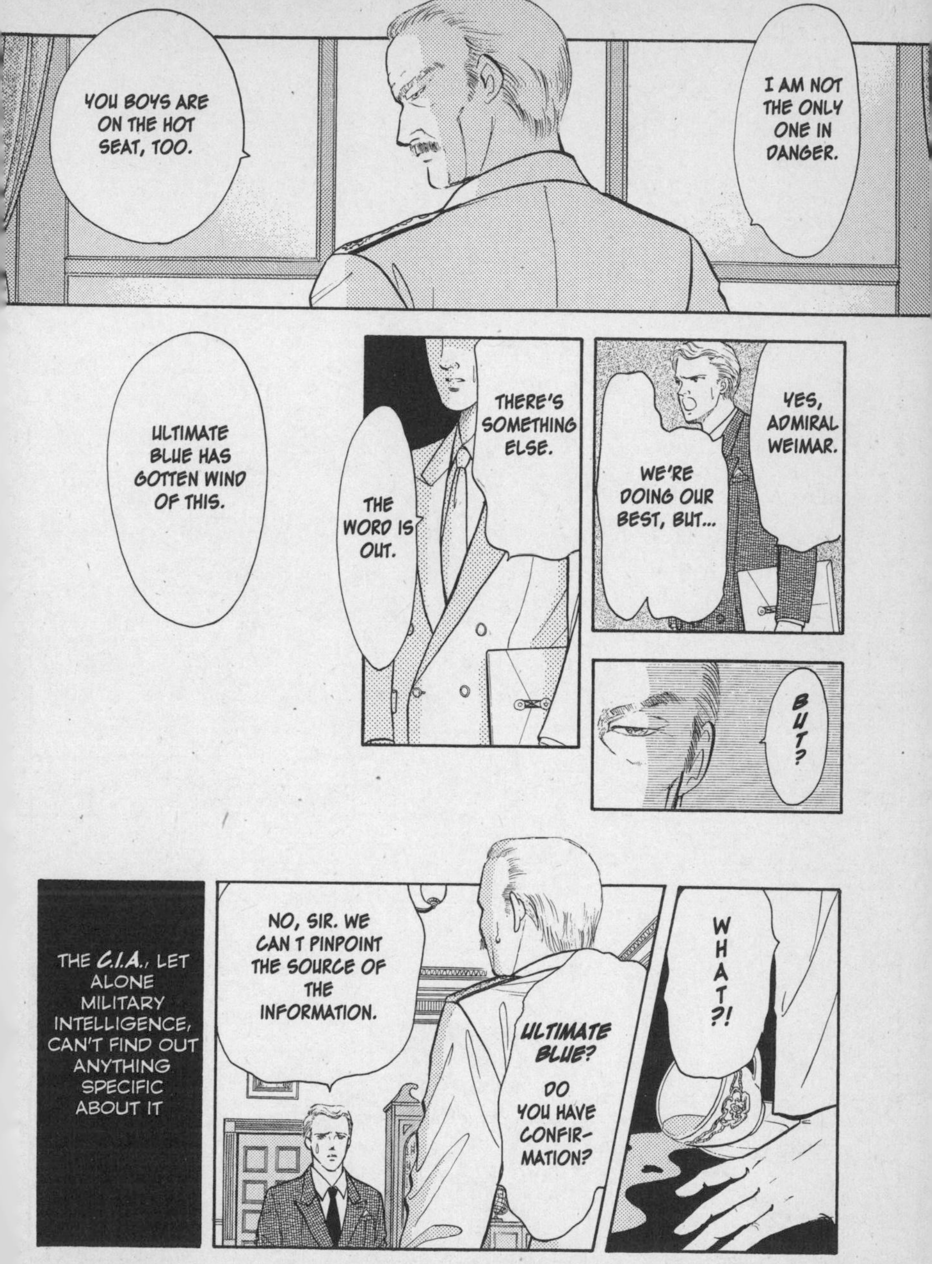
I AM NOT THE ONLY ONE IN DANGER.
YOU BOYS ARE ON THE HOT SEAT, TOO.
YES, ADMIRAL WEIMAR.
WE'RE DOING OUR BEST, BUT...
BUT?
THERE'S SOMETHING ELSE.
THE WORD IS OUT.
ULTIMATE BLUE HAS GOTTEN WIND OF THIS.
WHAT?!
ULTIMATE BLUE?
DO YOU HAVE CONFIRMATION?
NO, SIR. WE CAN T PINPOINT THE SOURCE OF THE INFORMATION.
THE C.I.A., LET ALONE MILITARY INTELLIGENCE, CAN'T FIND OUT ANYTHING SPECIFIC ABOUT IT

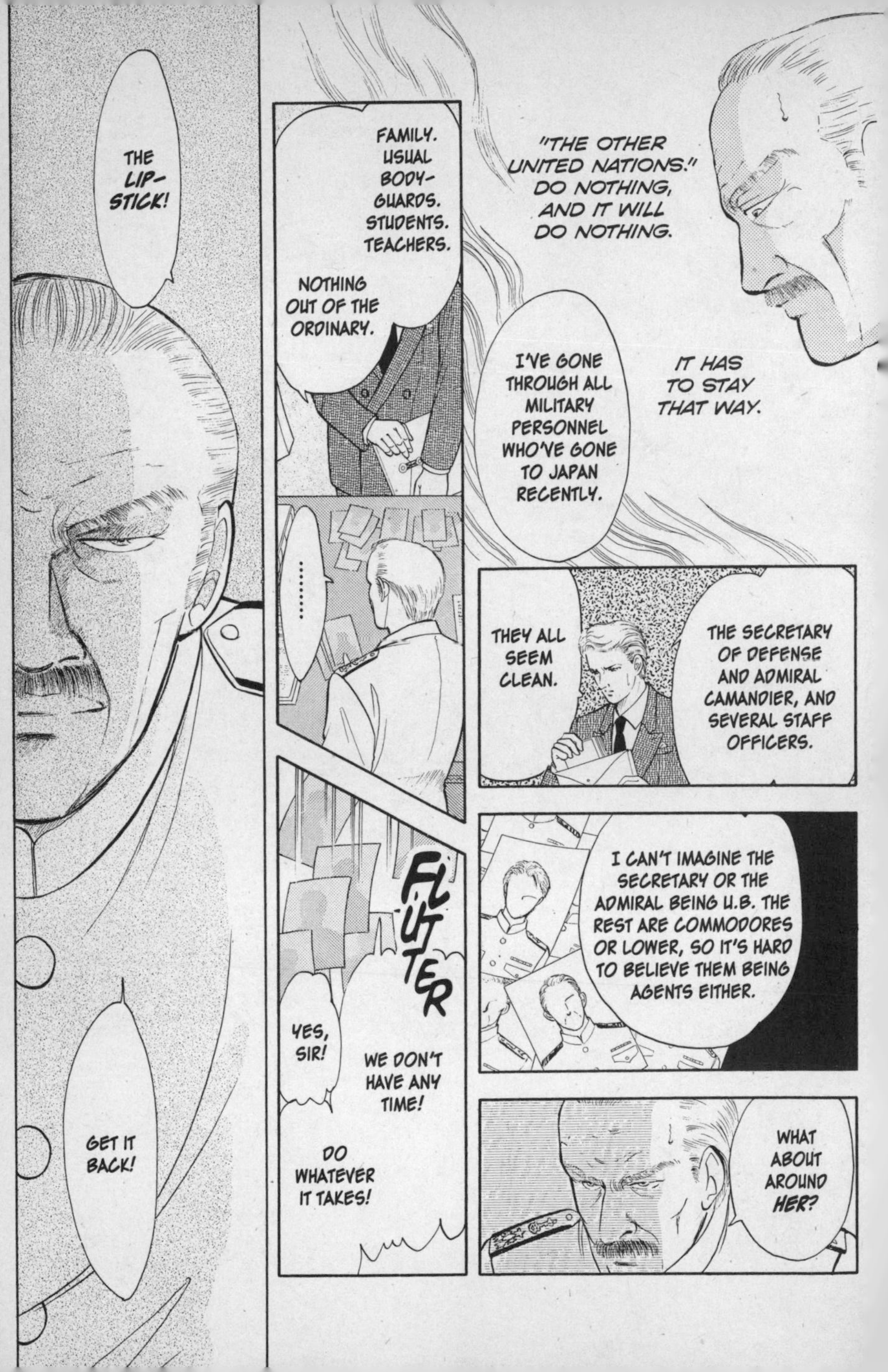
"THE OTHER UNITED NATIONS." DO NOTHING, AND IT WILL DO NOTHING.
IT HAS TO STAY THAT WAY.
I'VE GONE THROUGH ALL MILITARY PERSONNEL WHO'VE GONE TO JAPAN RECENTLY.
THE SECRETARY OF DEFENSE AND ADMIRAL CAMANDIER, AND SEVERAL STAFF OFFICERS.
THEY ALL SEEM CLEAN.
I CAN'T IMAGINE THE SECRETARY OR THE ADMIRAL BEING U.B. THE REST ARE COMMODORES OR LOWER, SO IT'S HARD TO BELIEVE THEM BEING AGENTS EITHER.
WHAT ABOUT AROUND HER?
FAMILY. USUAL BODY-GUARDS. STUDENTS. TEACHERS.
NOTHING OUT OF THE ORDINARY.
......
FLUTTER
YES, SIR!
WE DON'T HAVE ANY TIME!
DO WHATEVER IT TAKES!
THE LIP-STICK!
GET IT BACK!

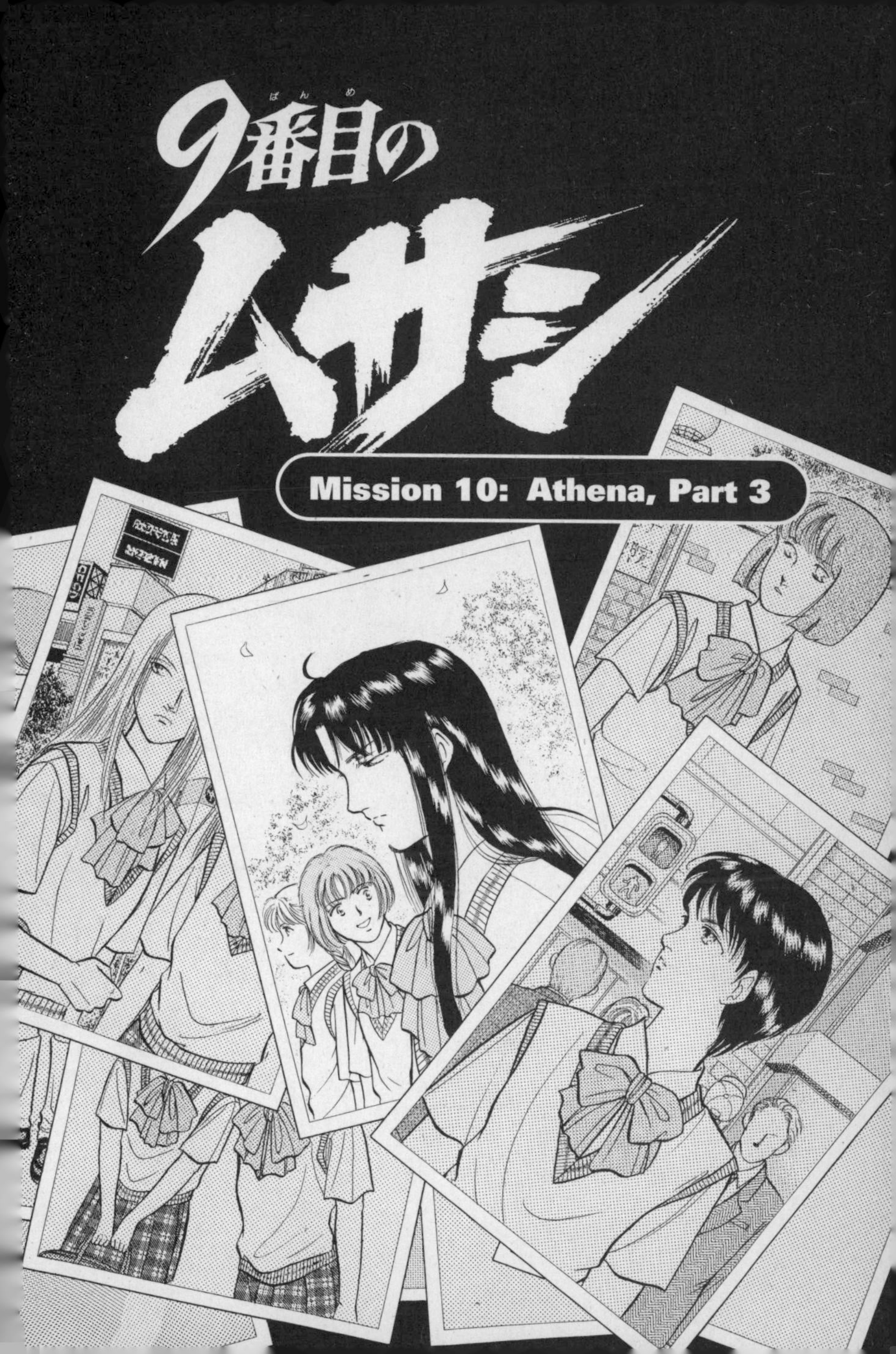
9番目のムサシ
Mission 10: Athena, Part 3

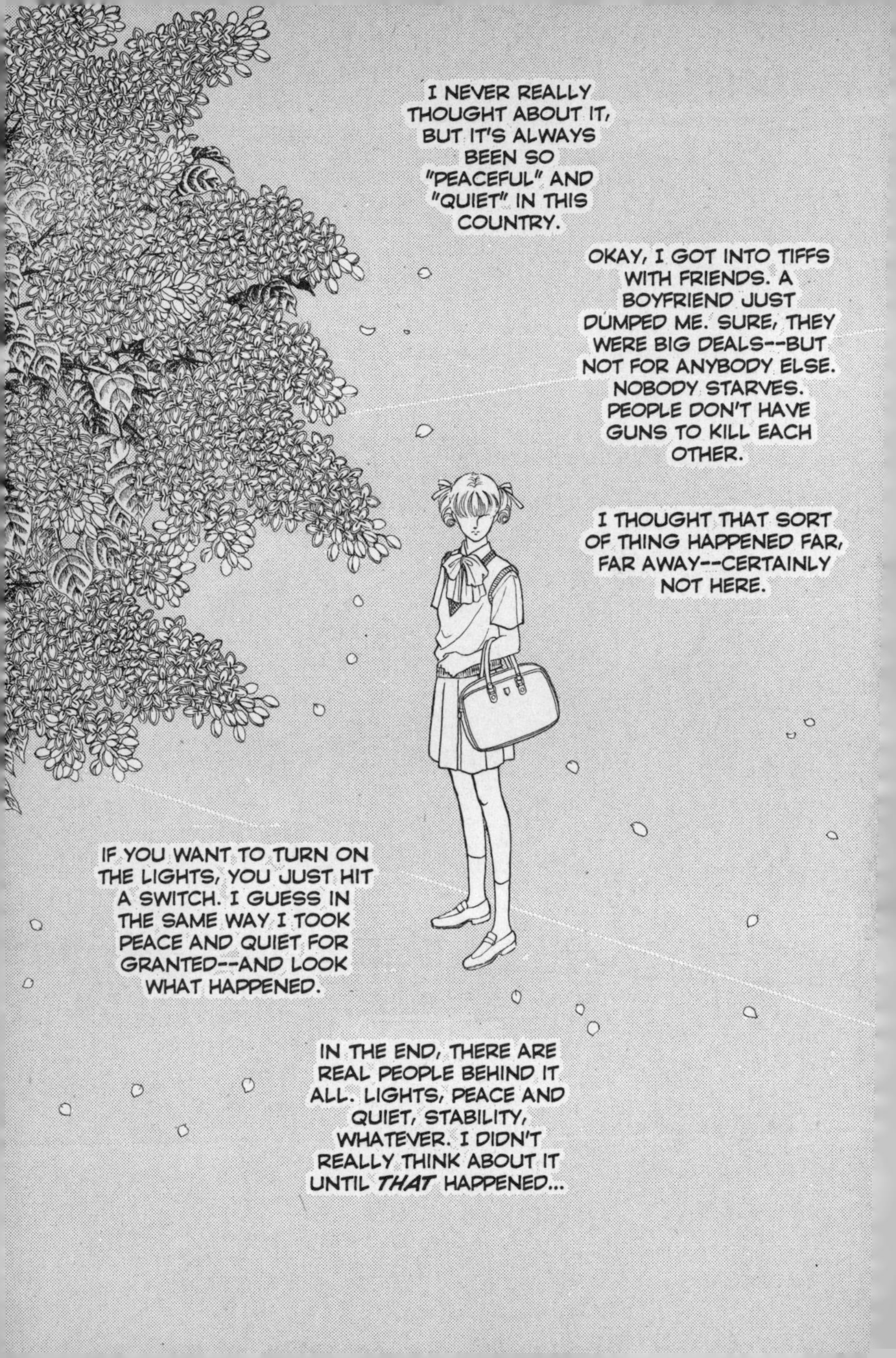
I NEVER REALLY THOUGHT ABOUT IT, BUT IT'S ALWAYS BEEN SO "PEACEFUL" AND "QUIET" IN THIS COUNTRY.
OKAY, I GOT INTO TIFFS WITH FRIENDS. A BOYFRIEND JUST DUMPED ME. SURE, THEY WERE BIG DEALS--BUT NOT FOR ANYBODY ELSE. NOBODY STARVES. PEOPLE DON'T HAVE GUNS TO KILL EACH OTHER.
I THOUGHT THAT SORT OF THING HAPPENED FAR, FAR AWAY--CERTAINLY NOT HERE.
IF YOU WANT TO TURN ON THE LIGHTS, YOU JUST HIT A SWITCH. I GUESS IN THE SAME WAY I TOOK PEACE AND QUIET FOR GRANTED--AND LOOK WHAT HAPPENED.
IN THE END, THERE ARE REAL PEOPLE BEHIND IT ALL. LIGHTS, PEACE AND QUIET, STABILITY, WHATEVER. I DIDN'T REALLY THINK ABOUT IT UNTIL *THAT* HAPPENED...

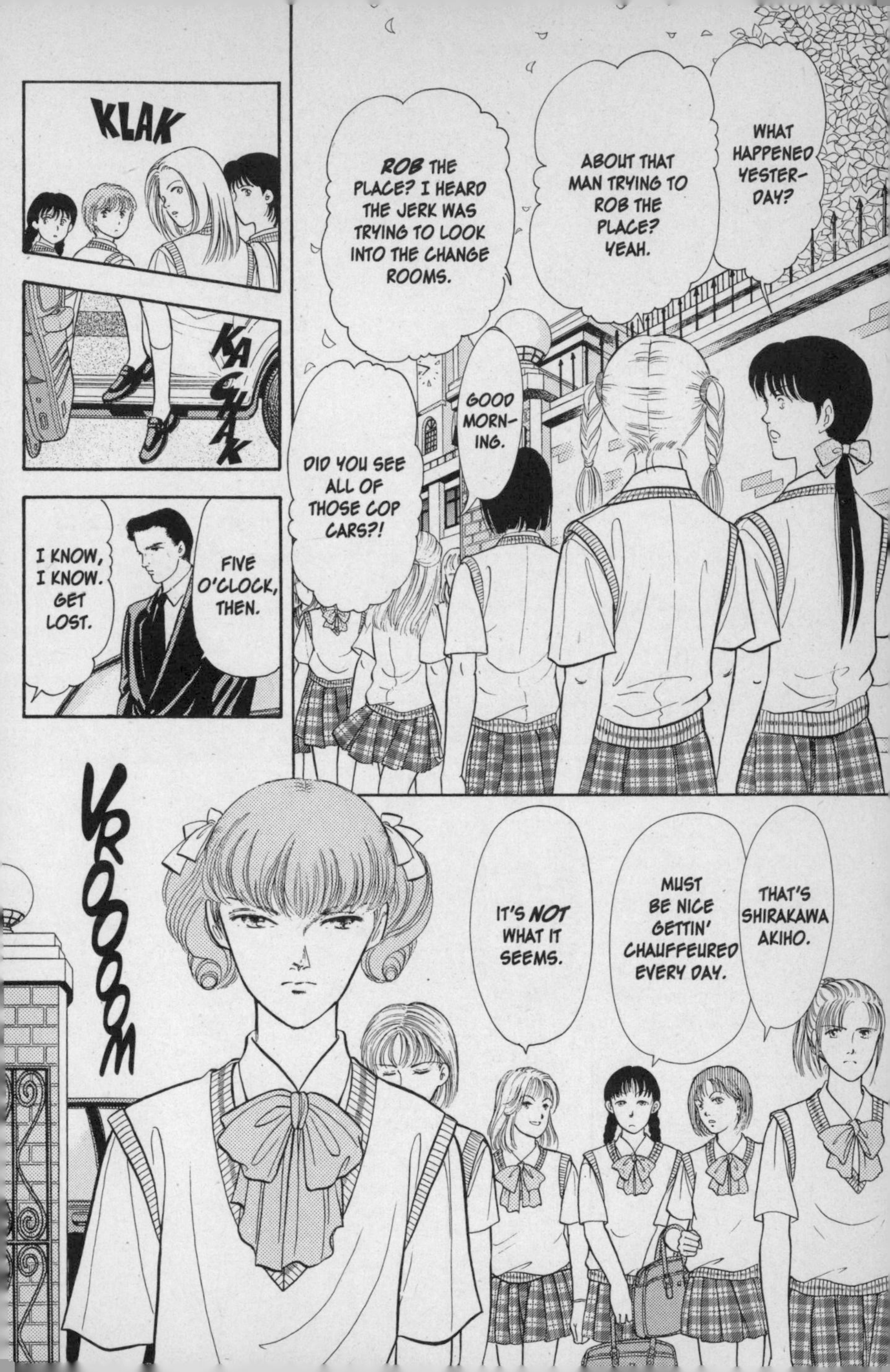
WHAT HAPPENED YESTER-DAY?
ABOUT THAT MAN TRYING TO ROB THE PLACE? YEAH.
ROB THE PLACE? I HEARD THE JERK WAS TRYING TO LOOK INTO THE CHANGE ROOMS.
GOOD MORN-ING.
DID YOU SEE ALL OF THOSE COP CARS?!
KLAK
KACHAK
FIVE O'CLOCK, THEN.
I KNOW, I KNOW. GET LOST.
THAT'S SHIRAKAWA AKIHO.
MUST BE NICE GETTIN' CHAUFFEURED EVERY DAY.
IT'S *NOT* WHAT IT SEEMS.
VROOOOM

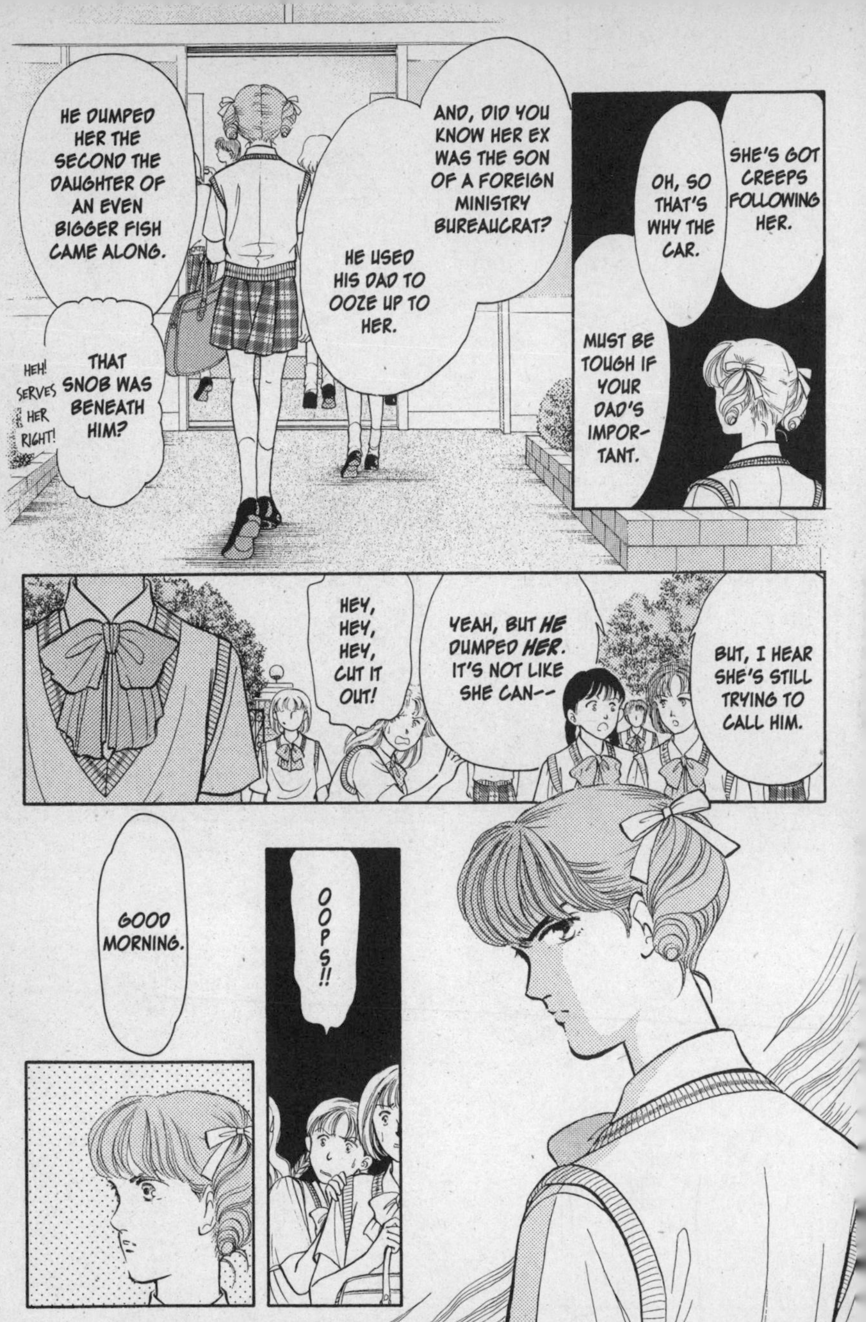
SHE'S GOT CREEPS FOLLOWING HER.
OH, SO THAT'S WHY THE CAR.
MUST BE TOUGH IF YOUR DAD'S IMPORTANT.
AND, DID YOU KNOW HER EX WAS THE SON OF A FOREIGN MINISTRY BUREAUCRAT?
HE USED HIS DAD TO OOZE UP TO HER.
HE DUMPED HER THE SECOND THE DAUGHTER OF AN EVEN BIGGER FISH CAME ALONG.
THAT SNOB WAS BENEATH HIM?
HEH! SERVES HER RIGHT!
BUT, I HEAR SHE'S STILL TRYING TO CALL HIM.
YEAH, BUT HE DUMPED HER. IT'S NOT LIKE SHE CAN--
HEY, HEY, HEY, CUT IT OUT!
GOOD MORNING.
OOPS!!

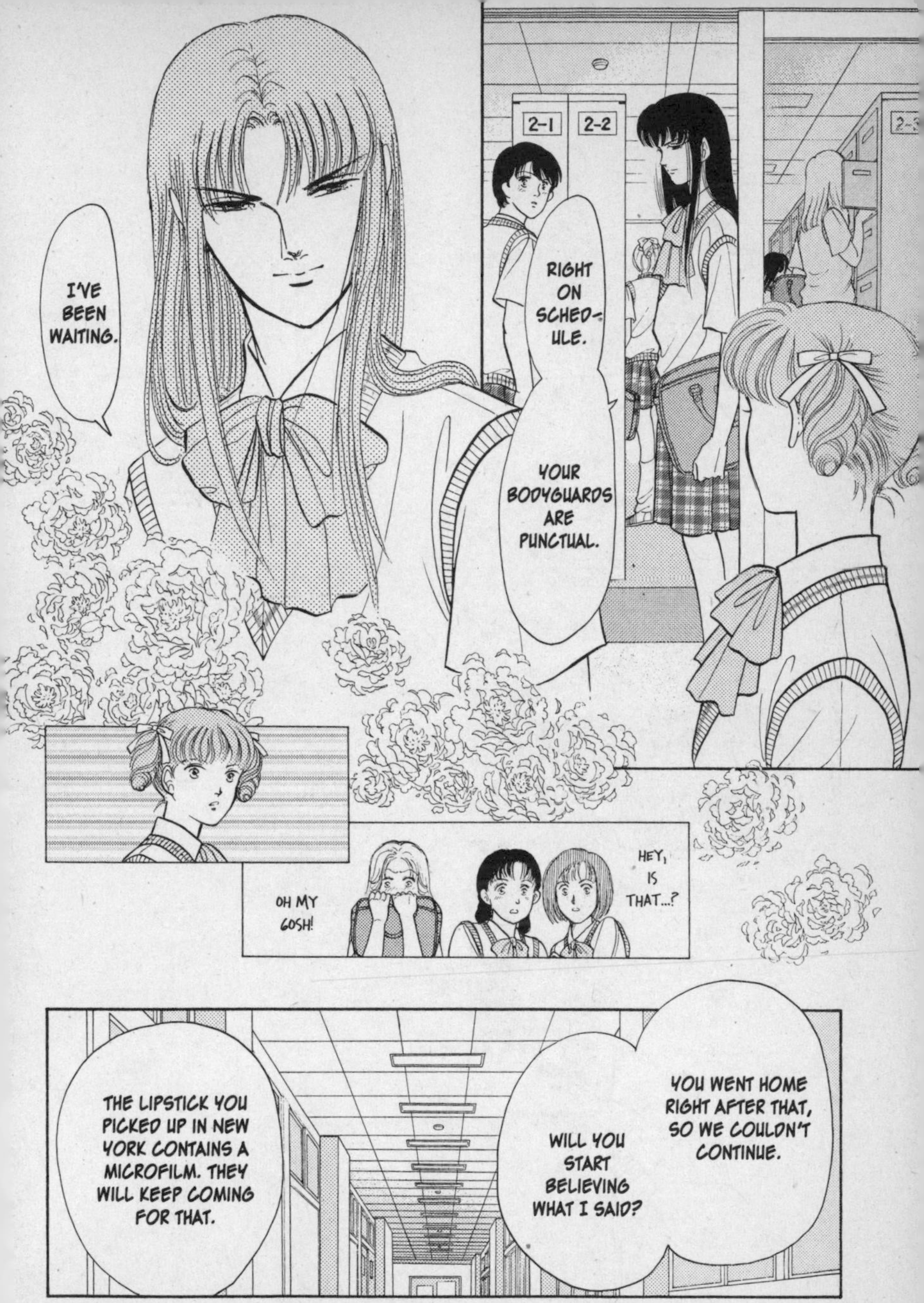
RIGHT ON SCHED-ULE.
YOUR BODYGUARDS ARE PUNCTUAL.
I'VE BEEN WAITING.
HEY, IS THAT...?
OH MY GOSH!
YOU WENT HOME RIGHT AFTER THAT, SO WE COULDN'T CONTINUE.
WILL YOU START BELIEVING WHAT I SAID?
THE LIPSTICK YOU PICKED UP IN NEW YORK CONTAINS A MICROFILM. THEY WILL KEEP COMING FOR THAT.

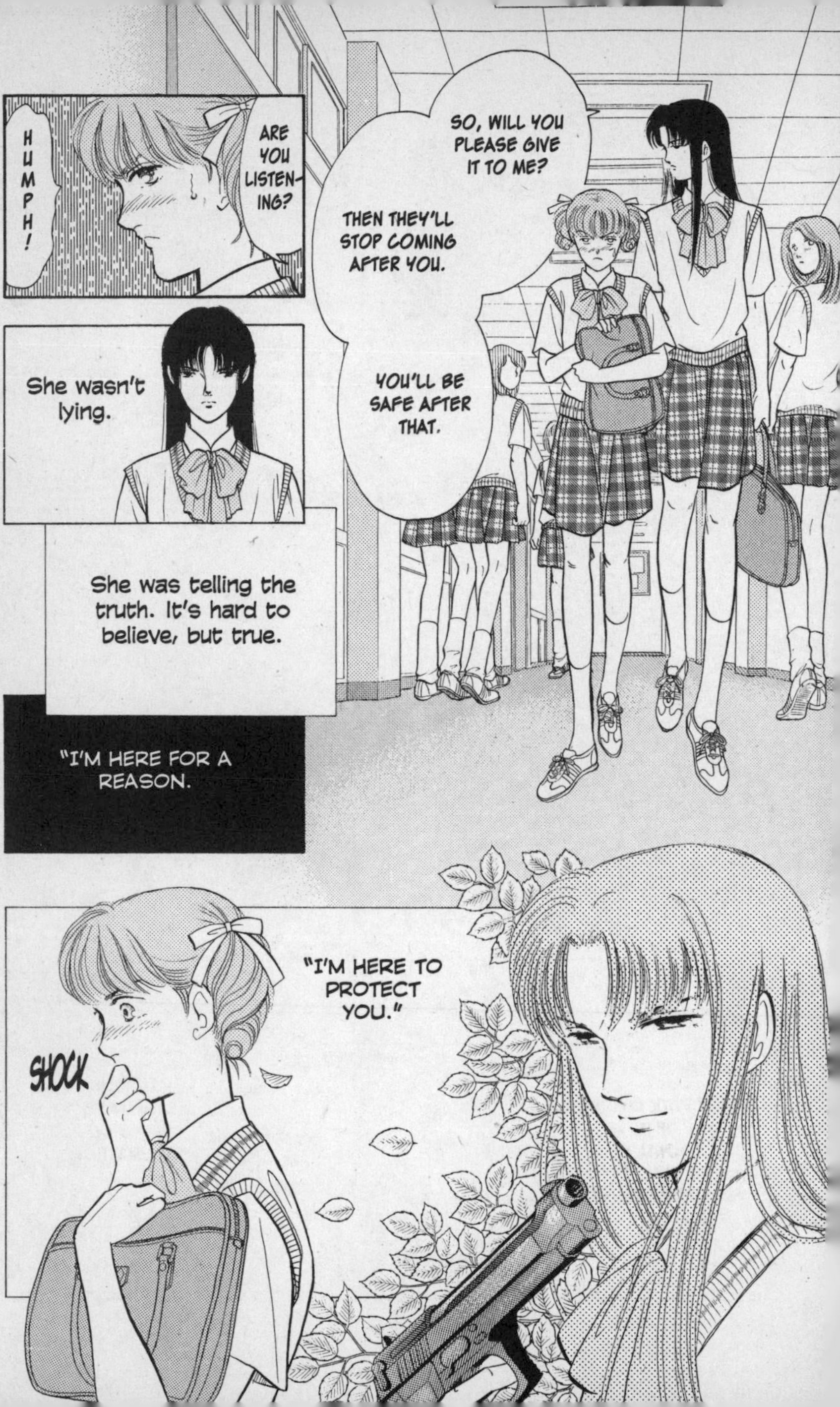
SO, WILL YOU PLEASE GIVE IT TO ME?
THEN THEY'LL STOP COMING AFTER YOU.
YOU'LL BE SAFE AFTER THAT.
ARE YOU LISTENING?
HUMPH!
She wasn't lying.
She was telling the truth. It's hard to believe, but true.
"I'M HERE FOR A REASON.
"I'M HERE TO PROTECT YOU."
SHOCK

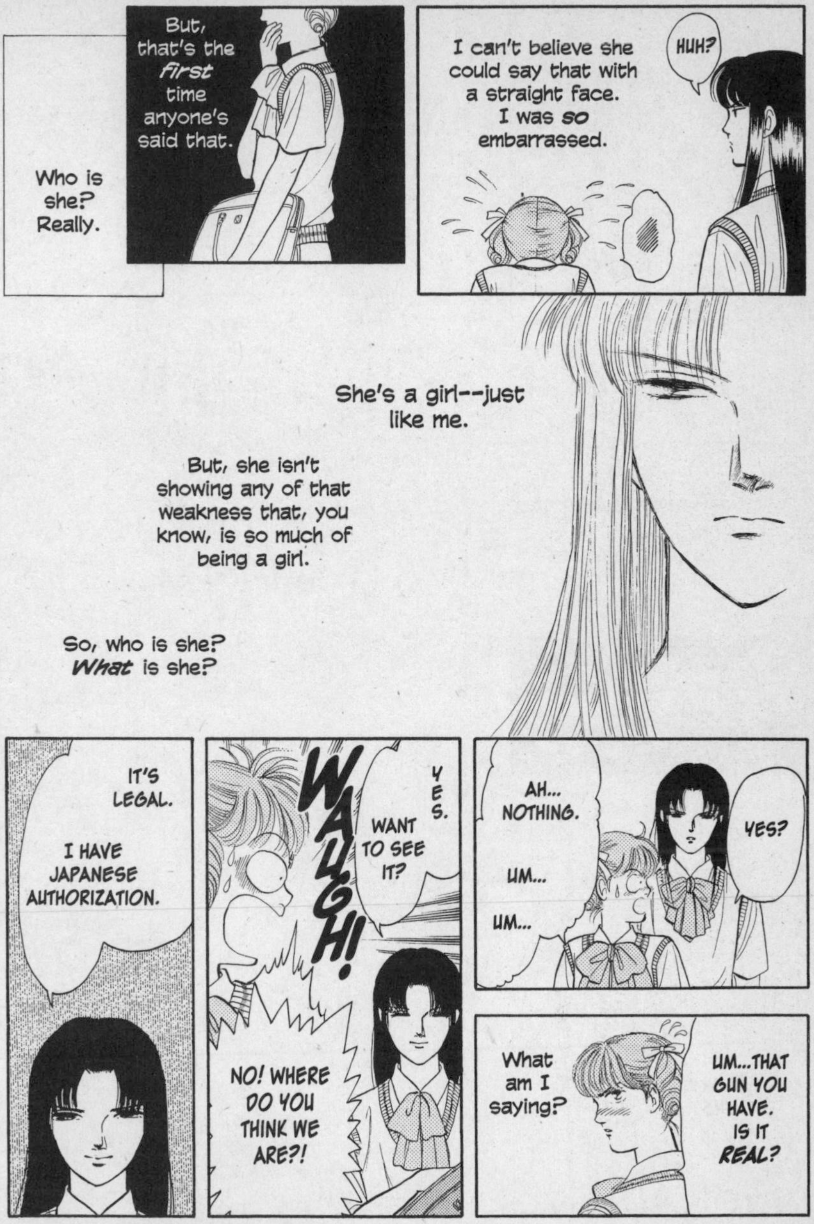
HUH?
I can't believe she could say that with a straight face. I was *so* embarrassed.
But, that's the *first* time anyone's said that.
Who is she? Really.
She's a girl--just like me.
But, she isn't showing any of that weakness that, you know, is so much of being a girl.
So, who is she? *What* is she?
YES?
AH... NOTHING.
UM...
UM...
UM...THAT GUN YOU HAVE. IS IT *REAL?*
What am I saying?
YES.
WANT TO SEE IT?
WAUGH!
NO! WHERE DO YOU THINK WE ARE?!
IT'S LEGAL.
I HAVE JAPANESE AUTHORIZATION.

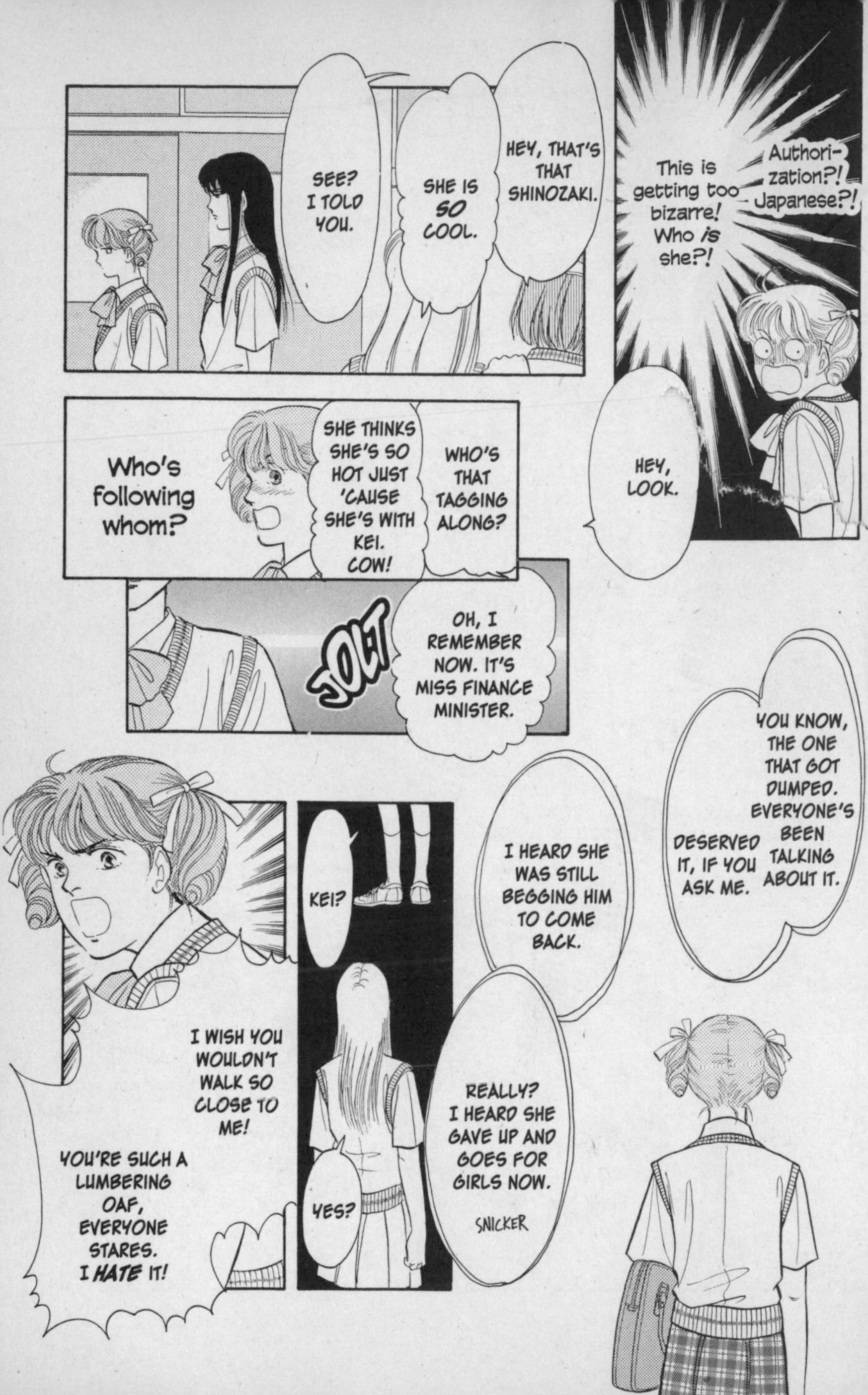

Authori-zation?! Japanese?!
This is getting too bizarre! Who *is* she?!
HEY, LOOK.
HEY, THAT'S THAT SHINOZAKI.
SHE IS *SO* COOL.
SEE? I TOLD YOU.
WHO'S THAT TAGGING ALONG?
SHE THINKS SHE'S SO HOT JUST 'CAUSE SHE'S WITH KEI. COW!
Who's following whom?
OH, I REMEMBER NOW. IT'S MISS FINANCE MINISTER.
JOLT
YOU KNOW, THE ONE THAT GOT DUMPED. EVERYONE'S BEEN TALKING ABOUT IT.
DESERVED IT, IF YOU ASK ME.
I HEARD SHE WAS STILL BEGGING HIM TO COME BACK.
REALLY? I HEARD SHE GAVE UP AND GOES FOR GIRLS NOW.
SNICKER
KEI?
YES?
I WISH YOU WOULDN'T WALK SO CLOSE TO ME!
YOU'RE SUCH A LUMBERING OAF, EVERYONE STARES. I *HATE* IT!

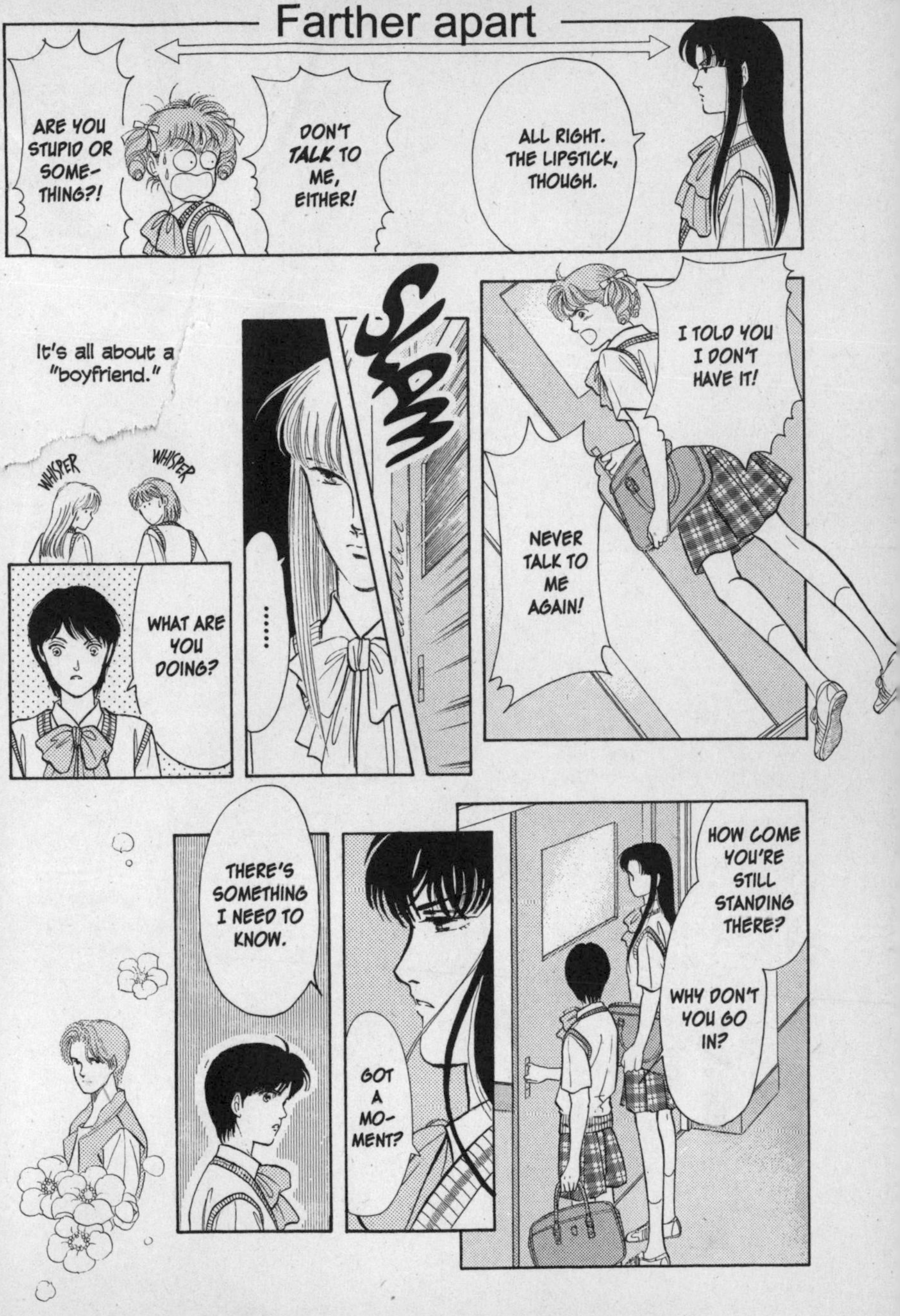
Farther apart
ALL RIGHT. THE LIPSTICK, THOUGH.
DON'T TALK TO ME, EITHER!
ARE YOU STUPID OR SOME-THING?!
I TOLD YOU I DON'T HAVE IT!
NEVER TALK TO ME AGAIN!
SLAM
……
It's all about a "boyfriend."
WHISPER
WHISPER
WHAT ARE YOU DOING?
HOW COME YOU'RE STILL STANDING THERE?
WHY DON'T YOU GO IN?
GOT A MO-MENT?
THERE'S SOMETHING I NEED TO KNOW.

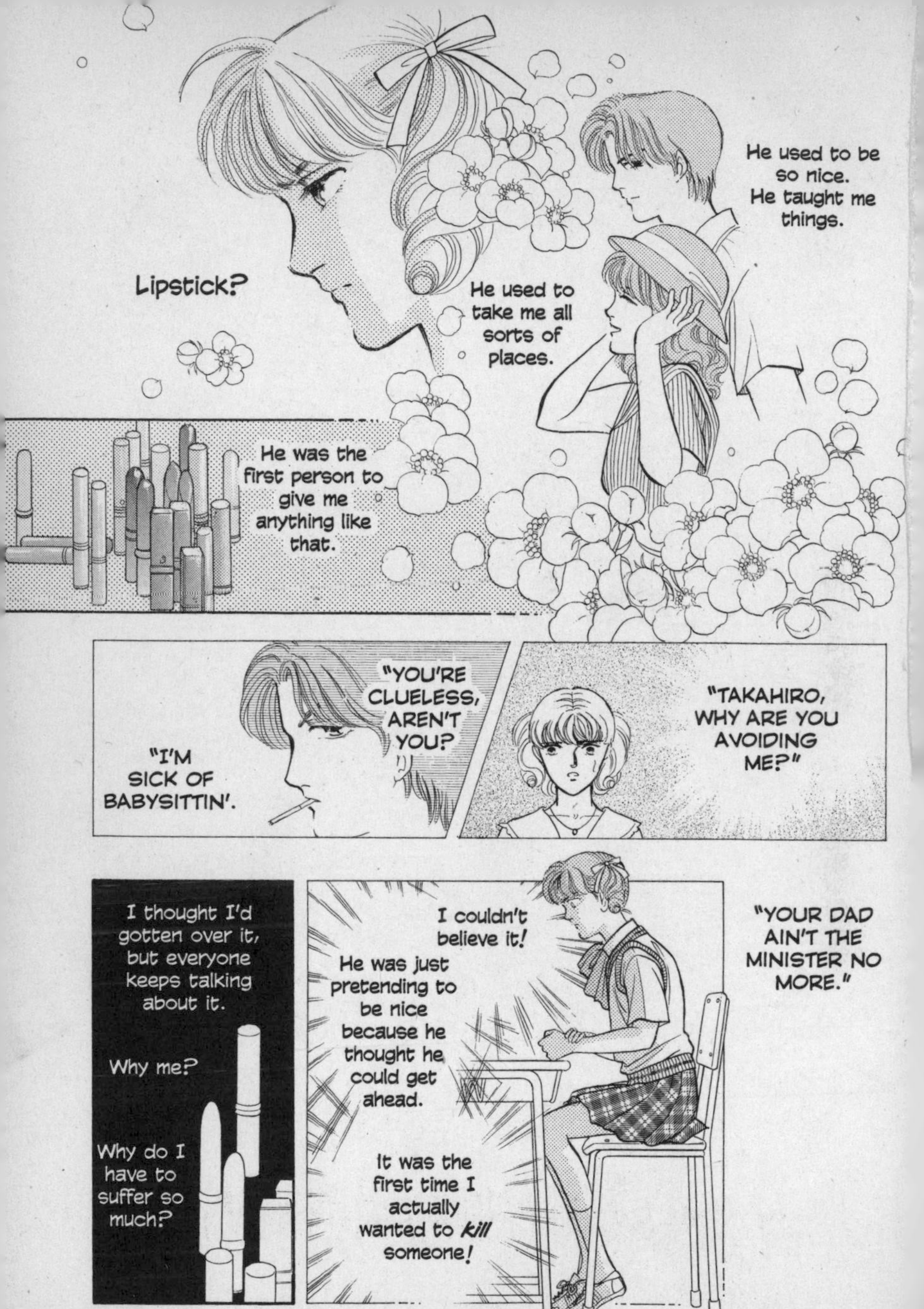
He used to be so nice. He taught me things.
He used to take me all sorts of places.
Lipstick?
He was the first person to give me anything like that.
"TAKAHIRO, WHY ARE YOU AVOIDING ME?"
"YOU'RE CLUELESS, AREN'T YOU?
"I'M SICK OF BABYSITTIN'.
"YOUR DAD AIN'T THE MINISTER NO MORE."
I couldn't believe it!
He was just pretending to be nice because he thought he could get ahead.
It was the first time I actually wanted to *kill* someone!
I thought I'd gotten over it, but everyone keeps talking about it.
Why me?
Why do I have to suffer so much?

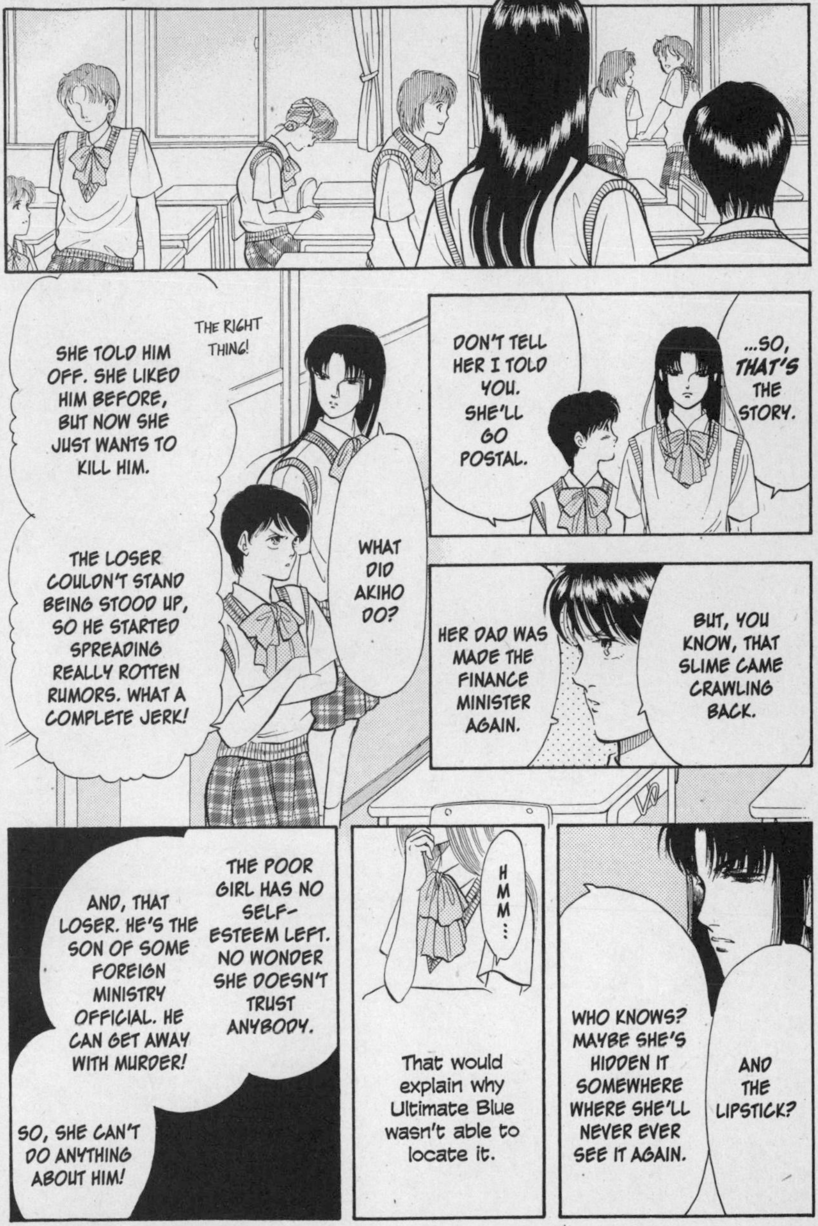
...SO, *THAT'S* THE STORY.
DON'T TELL HER I TOLD YOU. SHE'LL GO POSTAL.
BUT, YOU KNOW, THAT SLIME CAME CRAWLING BACK.
HER DAD WAS MADE THE FINANCE MINISTER AGAIN.
WHAT DID AKIHO DO?
SHE TOLD HIM OFF. SHE LIKED HIM BEFORE, BUT NOW SHE JUST WANTS TO KILL HIM.
THE RIGHT THING!
THE LOSER COULDN'T STAND BEING STOOD UP, SO HE STARTED SPREADING REALLY ROTTEN RUMORS. WHAT A COMPLETE JERK!
AND THE LIPSTICK?
WHO KNOWS? MAYBE SHE'S HIDDEN IT SOMEWHERE WHERE SHE'LL NEVER EVER SEE IT AGAIN.
HMM...
That would explain why Ultimate Blue wasn't able to locate it.
THE POOR GIRL HAS NO SELF-ESTEEM LEFT. NO WONDER SHE DOESN'T TRUST ANYBODY.
AND, THAT LOSER. HE'S THE SON OF SOME FOREIGN MINISTRY OFFICIAL. HE CAN GET AWAY WITH MURDER!
SO, SHE CAN'T DO ANYTHING ABOUT HIM!

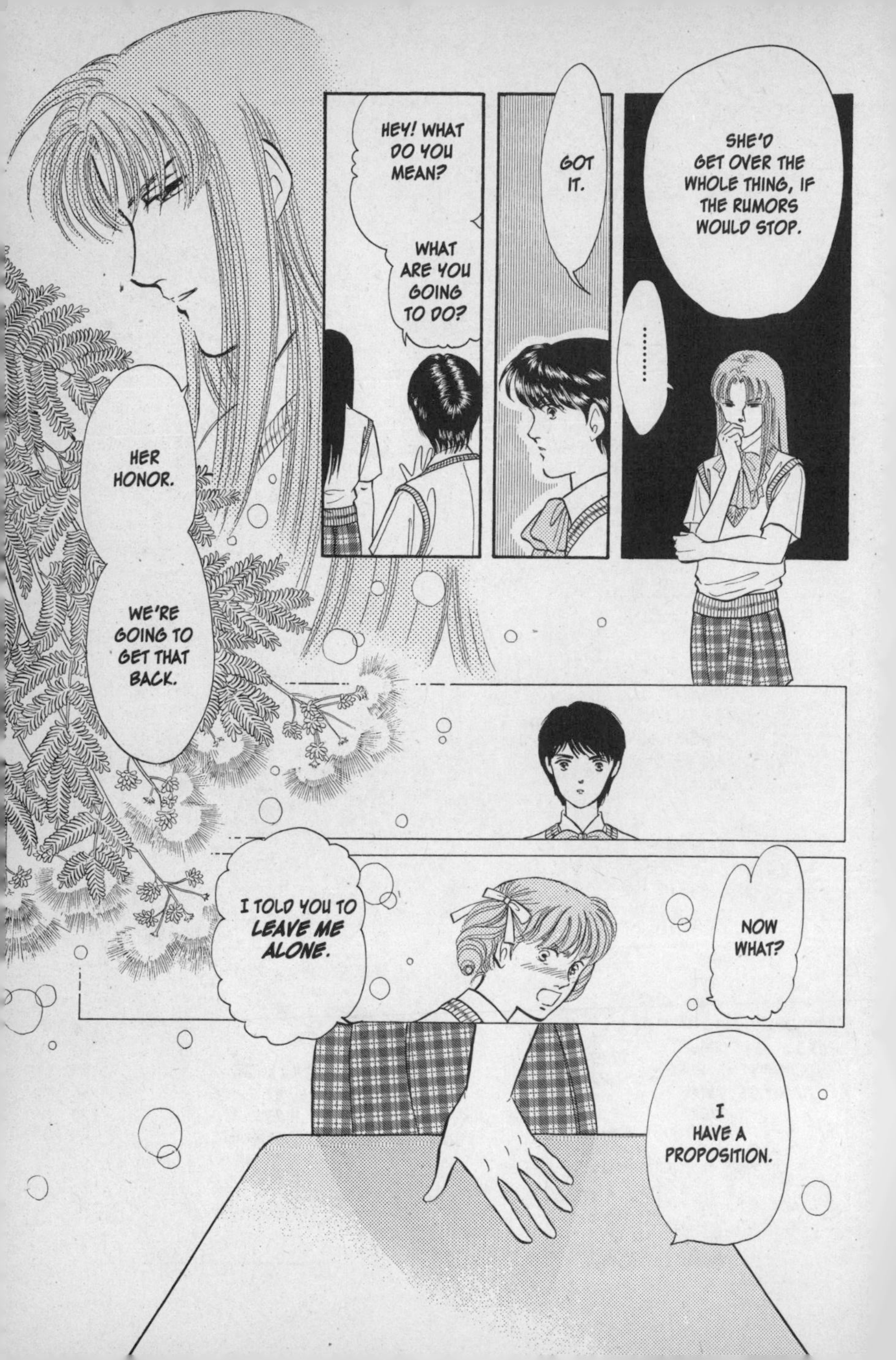
SHE'D GET OVER THE WHOLE THING, IF THE RUMORS WOULD STOP.
......
GOT IT.
HEY! WHAT DO YOU MEAN?
WHAT ARE YOU GOING TO DO?
HER HONOR.
WE'RE GOING TO GET THAT BACK.
NOW WHAT?
I TOLD YOU TO *LEAVE ME ALONE*.
I HAVE A PROPOSITION.

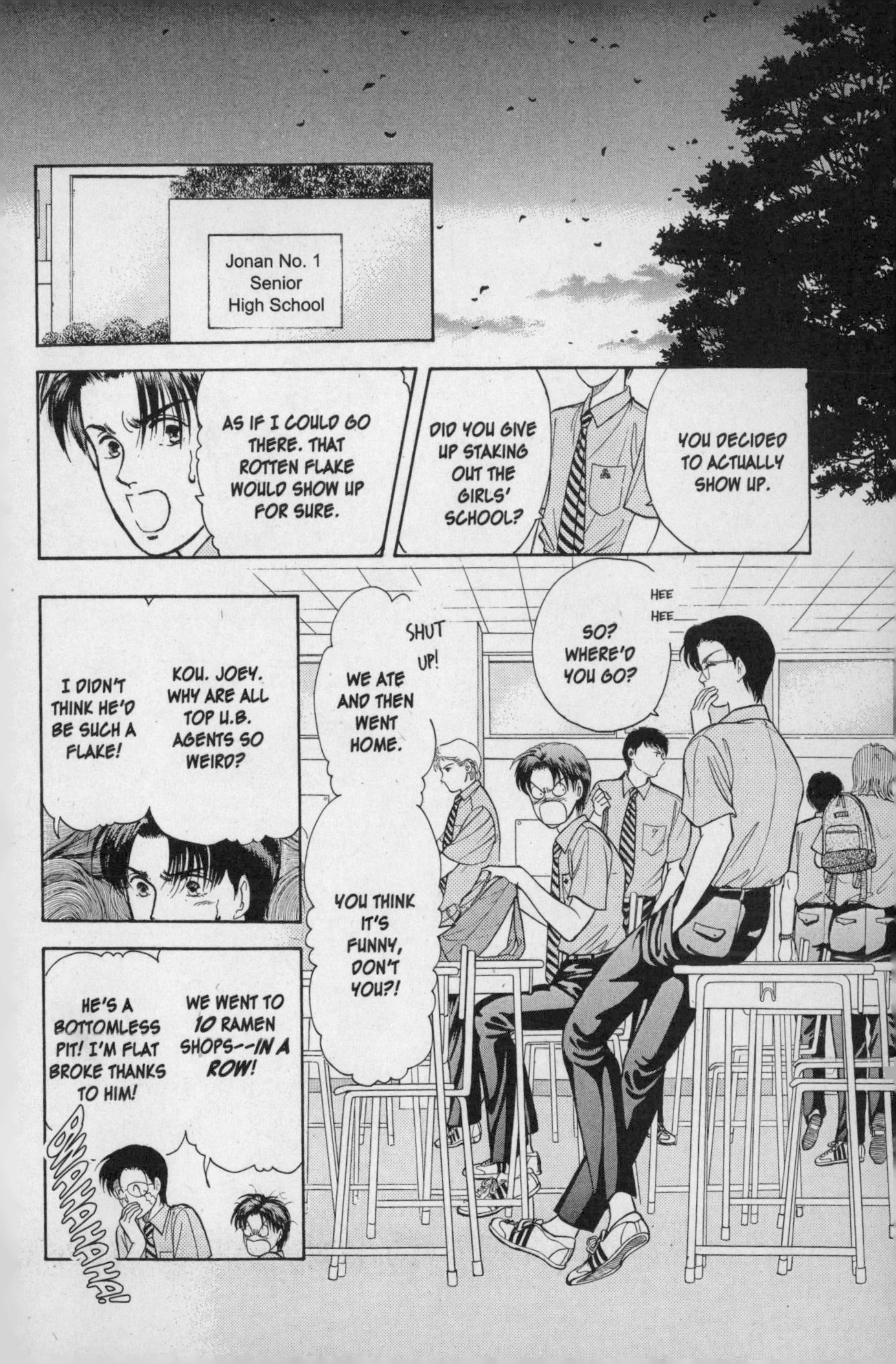
Jonan No. 1
Senior
High School
YOU DECIDED TO ACTUALLY SHOW UP.
DID YOU GIVE UP STAKING OUT THE GIRLS' SCHOOL?
AS IF I COULD GO THERE. THAT ROTTEN FLAKE WOULD SHOW UP FOR SURE.
HEE HEE
SO? WHERE'D YOU GO?
SHUT UP!
WE ATE AND THEN WENT HOME.
YOU THINK IT'S FUNNY, DON'T YOU?!
KOU. JOEY. WHY ARE ALL TOP U.B. AGENTS SO WEIRD?
I DIDN'T THINK HE'D BE SUCH A FLAKE!
WE WENT TO 10 RAMEN SHOPS--IN A ROW!
HE'S A BOTTOMLESS PIT! I'M FLAT BROKE THANKS TO HIM!
BWAHAHAHAHA!

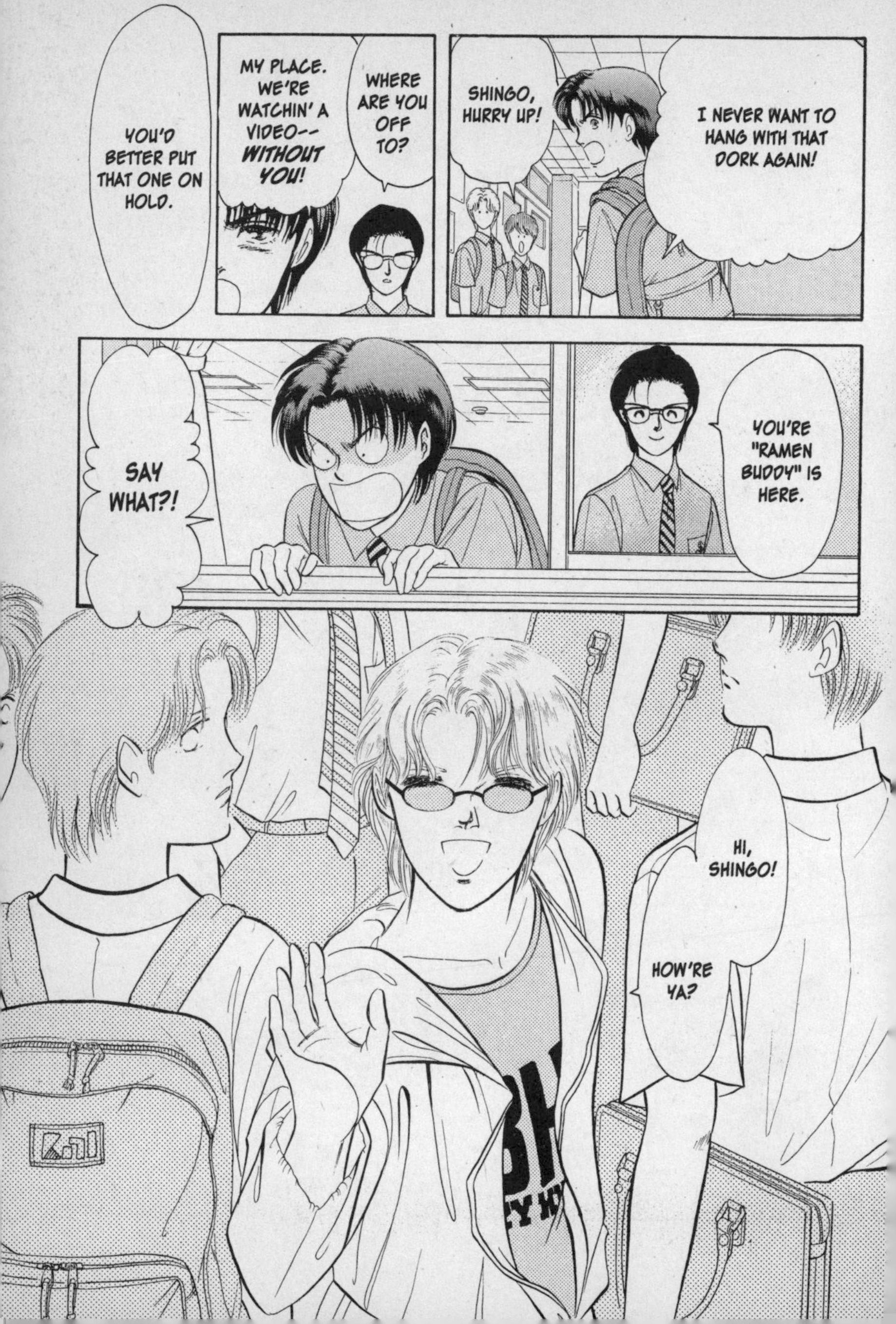
I NEVER WANT TO HANG WITH THAT DORK AGAIN!
SHINGO, HURRY UP!
WHERE ARE YOU OFF TO?
MY PLACE. WE'RE WATCHIN' A VIDEO-- *WITHOUT YOU!*
YOU'D BETTER PUT THAT ONE ON HOLD.
YOU'RE "RAMEN BUDDY" IS HERE.
SAY WHAT?!
HI, SHINGO!
HOW'RE YA?

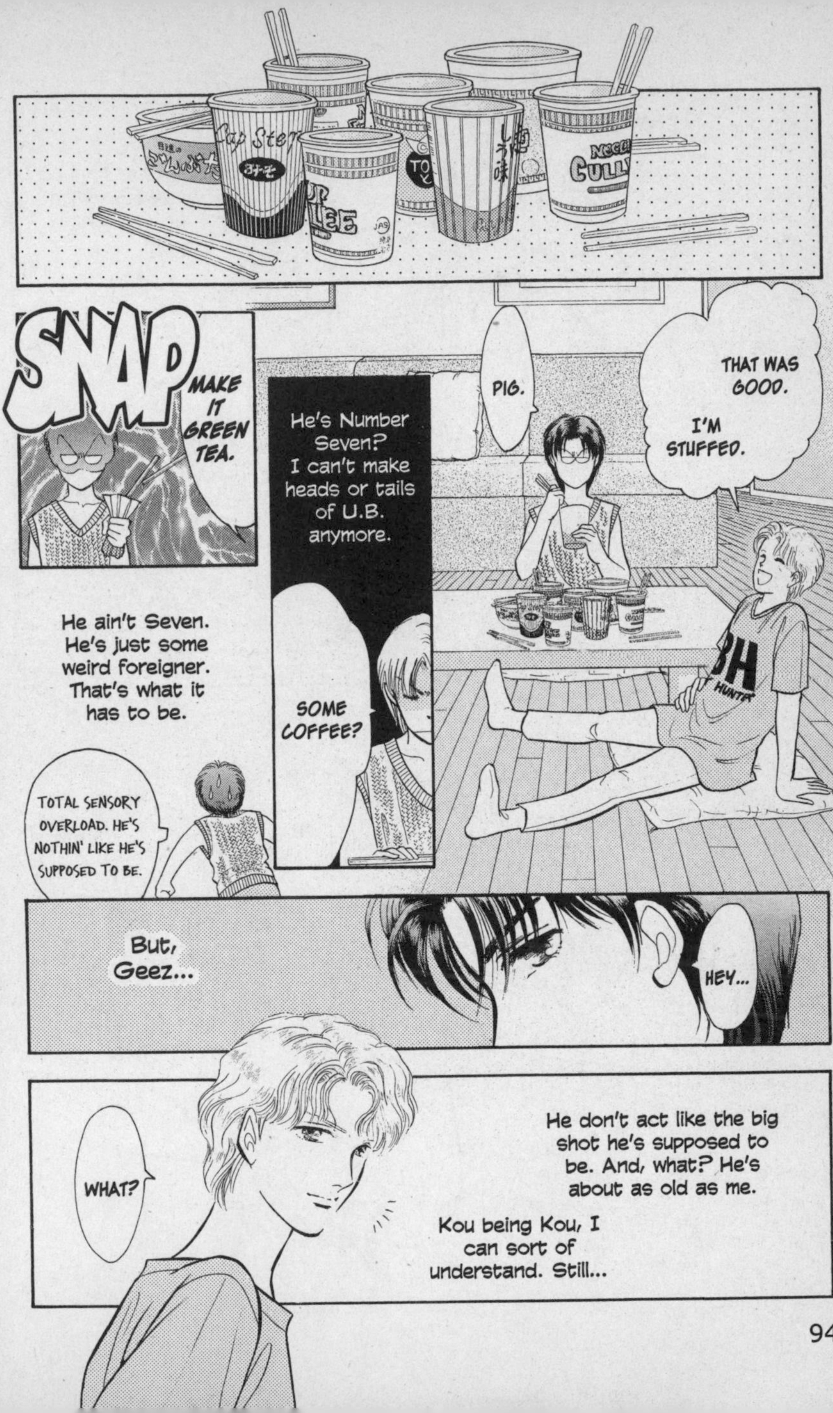
THAT WAS GOOD.
I'M STUFFED.
PIG.
He's Number Seven? I can't make heads or tails of U.B. anymore.
SOME COFFEE?
SNAP
MAKE IT GREEN TEA.
He ain't Seven. He's just some weird foreigner. That's what it has to be.
TOTAL SENSORY OVERLOAD. HE'S NOTHIN' LIKE HE'S SUPPOSED TO BE.
HEY...
But, Geez...
He don't act like the big shot he's supposed to be. And, what? He's about as old as me.
Kou being Kou, I can sort of understand. Still...
WHAT?

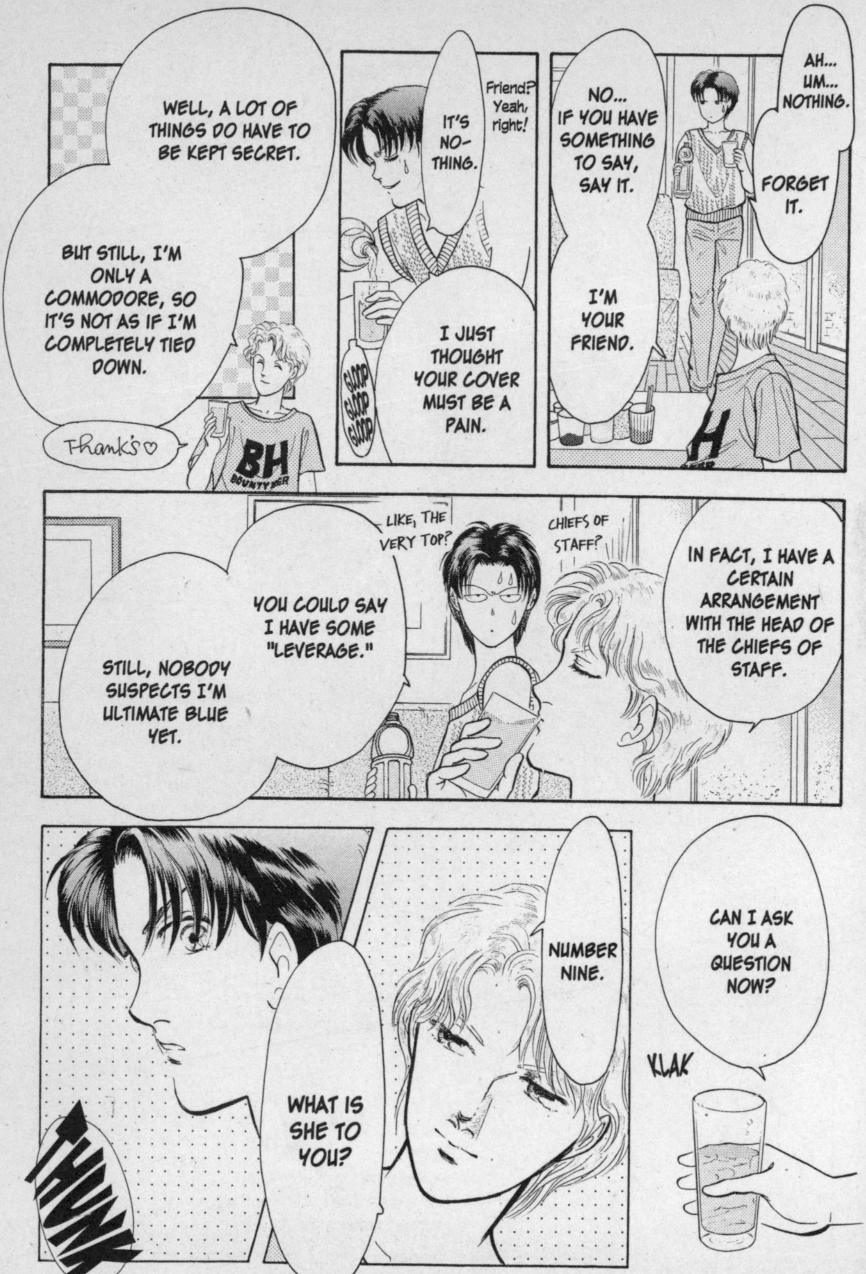
AH... UM... NOTHING.
FORGET IT.
NO... IF YOU HAVE SOMETHING TO SAY, SAY IT.
I'M YOUR FRIEND.
Friend? Yeah, right!
IT'S NO-THING.
I JUST THOUGHT YOUR COVER MUST BE A PAIN.
GLOOP GLOOP GLOOP
WELL, A LOT OF THINGS DO HAVE TO BE KEPT SECRET.
BUT STILL, I'M ONLY A COMMODORE, SO IT'S NOT AS IF I'M COMPLETELY TIED DOWN.
Thank's♡
IN FACT, I HAVE A CERTAIN ARRANGEMENT WITH THE HEAD OF THE CHIEFS OF STAFF.
CHIEFS OF STAFF?
LIKE, THE VERY TOP?
YOU COULD SAY I HAVE SOME "LEVERAGE."
STILL, NOBODY SUSPECTS I'M ULTIMATE BLUE YET.
CAN I ASK YOU A QUESTION NOW?
KLAK
NUMBER NINE.
WHAT IS SHE TO YOU?
THUNK

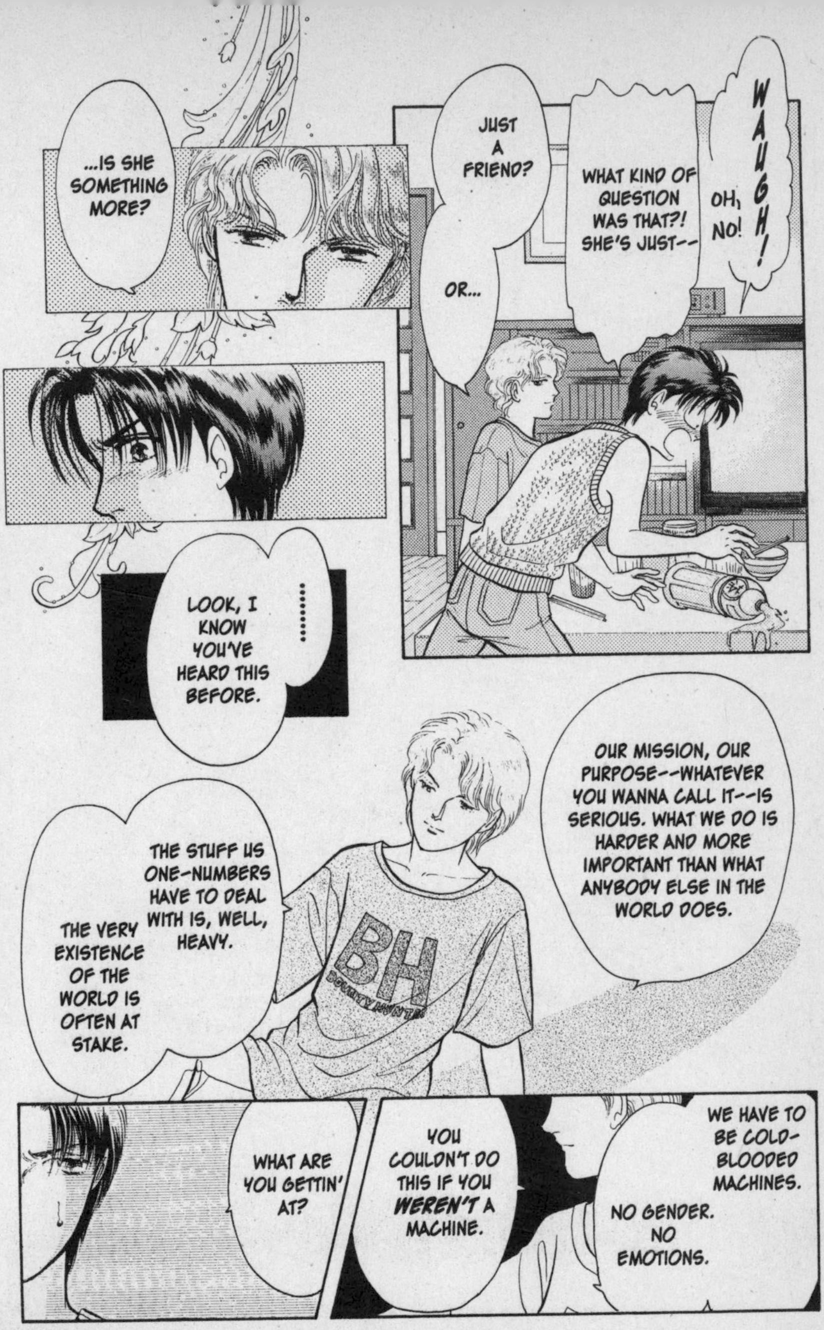
WAUGH!
OH, NO!
WHAT KIND OF QUESTION WAS THAT?! SHE'S JUST--
JUST A FRIEND?
OR...
...IS SHE SOMETHING MORE?
....
LOOK, I KNOW YOU'VE HEARD THIS BEFORE.
OUR MISSION, OUR PURPOSE--WHATEVER YOU WANNA CALL IT--IS SERIOUS. WHAT WE DO IS HARDER AND MORE IMPORTANT THAN WHAT ANYBODY ELSE IN THE WORLD DOES.
THE STUFF US ONE-NUMBERS HAVE TO DEAL WITH IS, WELL, HEAVY.
THE VERY EXISTENCE OF THE WORLD IS OFTEN AT STAKE.
WE HAVE TO BE COLD-BLOODED MACHINES.
NO GENDER. NO EMOTIONS.
YOU COULDN'T DO THIS IF YOU *WEREN'T* A MACHINE.
WHAT ARE YOU GETTIN' AT?

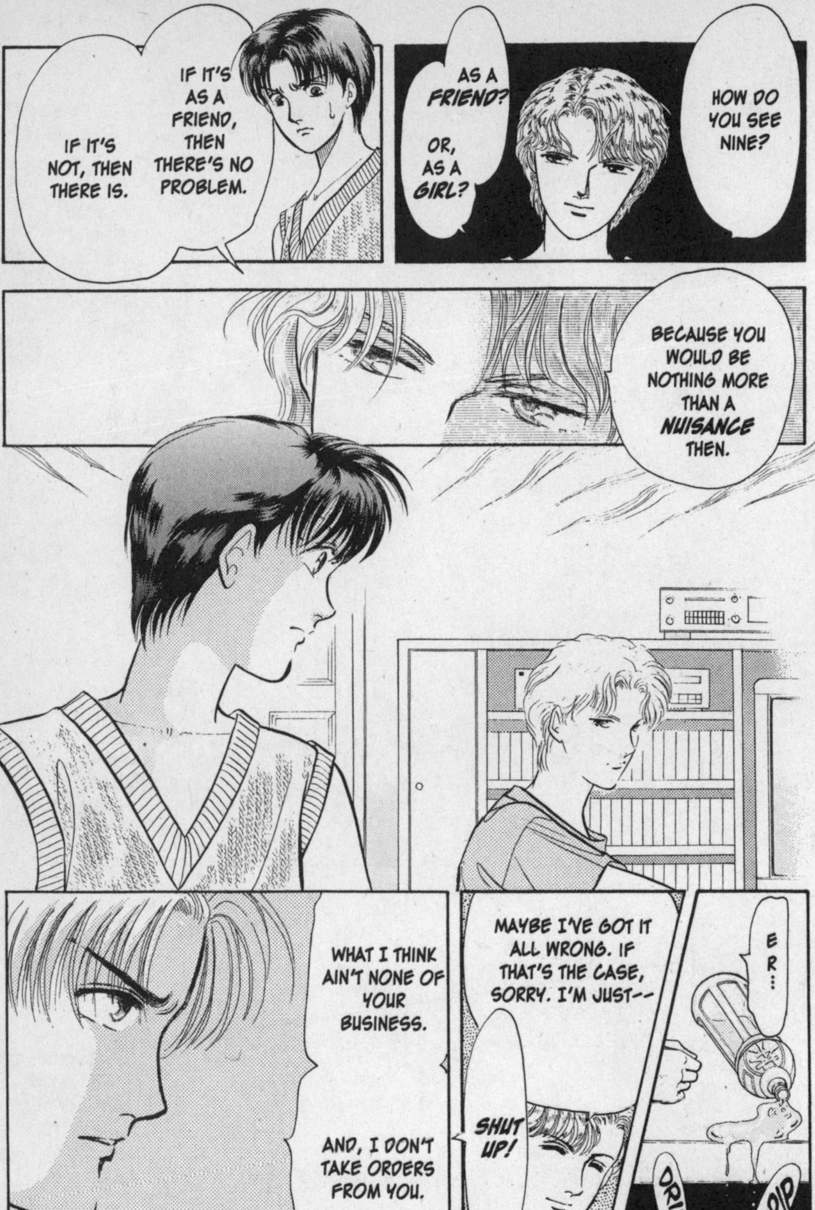
HOW DO YOU SEE NINE?
AS A FRIEND?
OR, AS A GIRL?
IF IT'S AS A FRIEND, THEN THERE'S NO PROBLEM.
IF IT'S NOT, THEN THERE IS.
BECAUSE YOU WOULD BE NOTHING MORE THAN A NUISANCE THEN.
ER...
DRIP
DRIP
MAYBE I'VE GOT IT ALL WRONG. IF THAT'S THE CASE, SORRY. I'M JUST--
SHUT UP!
WHAT I THINK AIN'T NONE OF YOUR BUSINESS.
AND, I DON'T TAKE ORDERS FROM YOU.

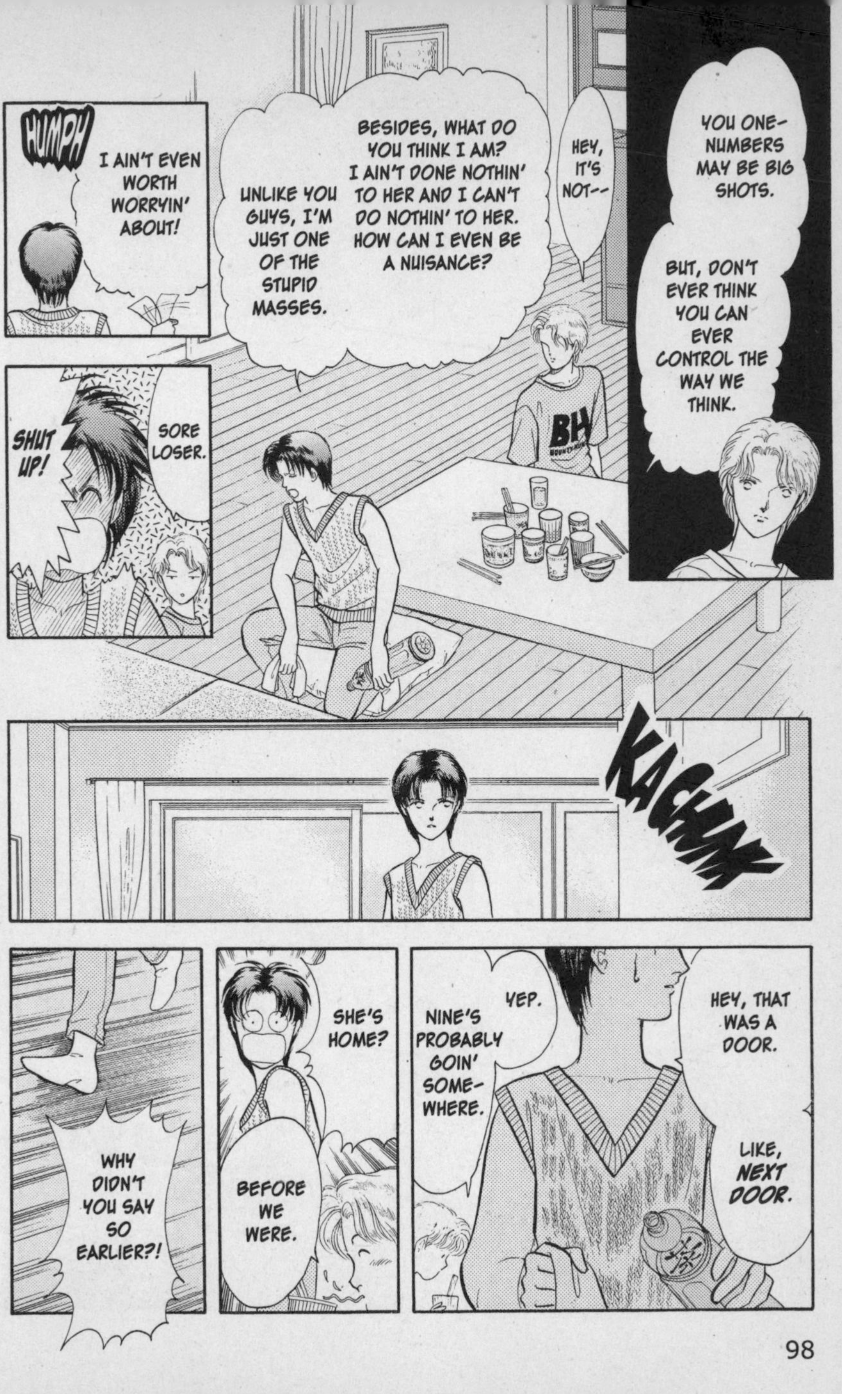
UNLIKE YOU GUYS, I'M JUST ONE OF THE STUPID MASSES.
BESIDES, WHAT DO YOU THINK I AM? I AIN'T DONE NOTHIN' TO HER AND I CAN'T DO NOTHIN' TO HER. HOW CAN I EVEN BE A NUISANCE?
HEY, IT'S NOT--
YOU ONE-NUMBERS MAY BE BIG SHOTS.
BUT, DON'T EVER THINK YOU CAN EVER CONTROL THE WAY WE THINK.
HUMPH
I AIN'T EVEN WORTH WORRYIN' ABOUT!
SORE LOSER.
SHUT UP!
KACHUNK
HEY, THAT WAS A DOOR.
LIKE, NEXT DOOR.
YEP.
NINE'S PROBABLY GOIN' SOMEWHERE.
SHE'S HOME?
BEFORE WE WERE.
WHY DIDN'T YOU SAY SO EARLIER?!

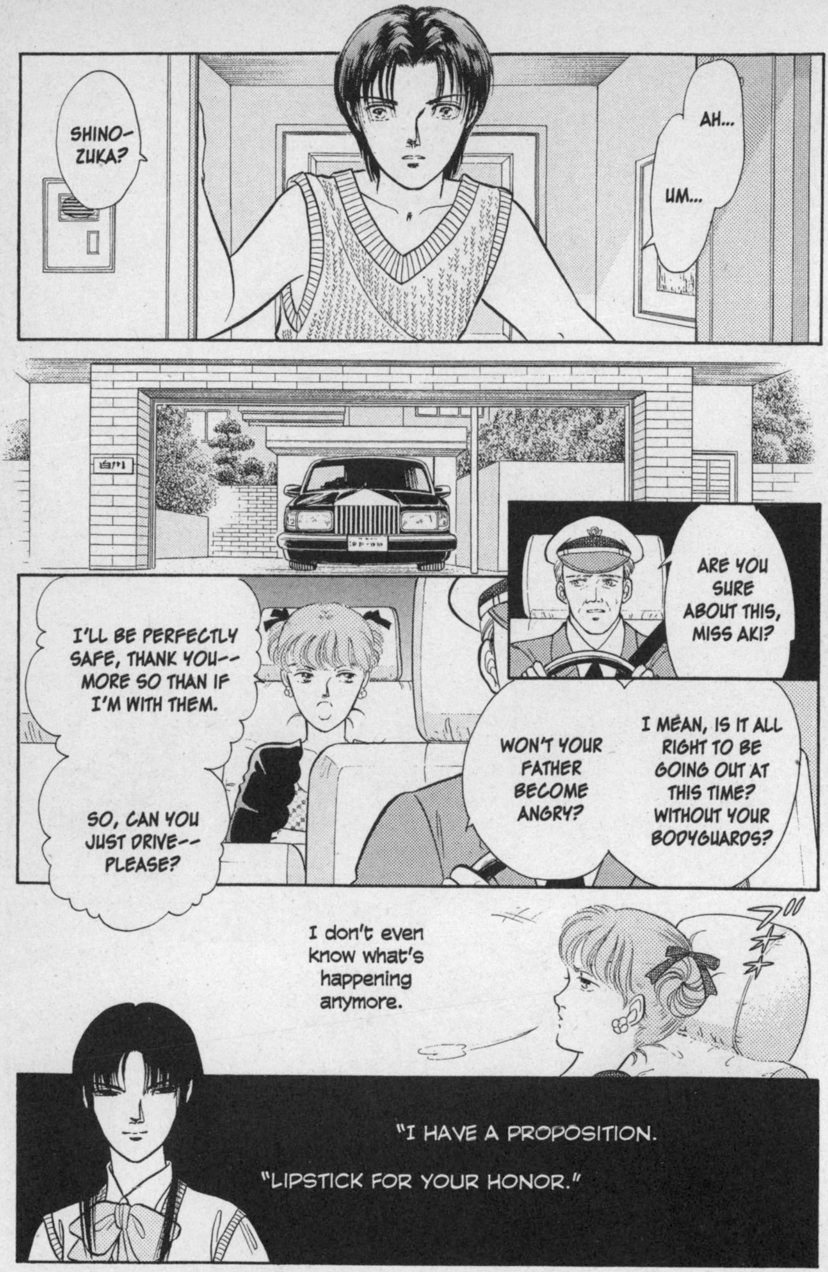
AH...
UM...
SHINO-ZUKA?
ARE YOU SURE ABOUT THIS, MISS AKI?
I MEAN, IS IT ALL RIGHT TO BE GOING OUT AT THIS TIME? WITHOUT YOUR BODYGUARDS?
WON'T YOUR FATHER BECOME ANGRY?
I'LL BE PERFECTLY SAFE, THANK YOU--MORE SO THAN IF I'M WITH THEM.
SO, CAN YOU JUST DRIVE--PLEASE?
I don't even know what's happening anymore.
"I HAVE A PROPOSITION.
"LIPSTICK FOR YOUR HONOR."

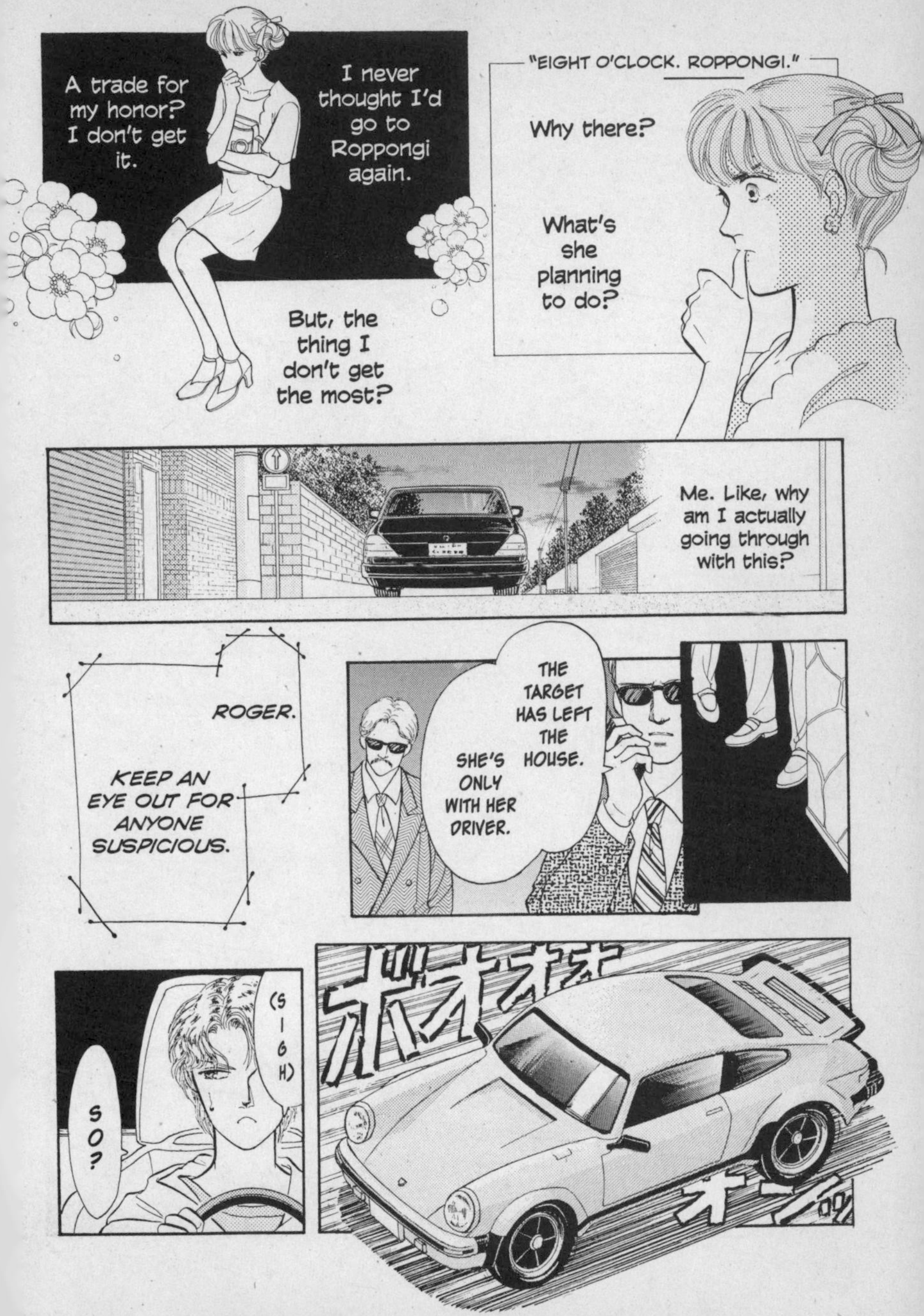
"EIGHT O'CLOCK. ROPPONGI."
Why there?
What's she planning to do?
I never thought I'd go to Roppongi again.
A trade for my honor? I don't get it.
But, the thing I don't get the most?
Me. Like, why am I actually going through with this?
THE TARGET HAS LEFT THE HOUSE.
SHE'S ONLY WITH HER DRIVER.
ROGER.
KEEP AN EYE OUT FOR ANYONE SUSPICIOUS.
ボオオオ
オン
(SIGH)
SO?

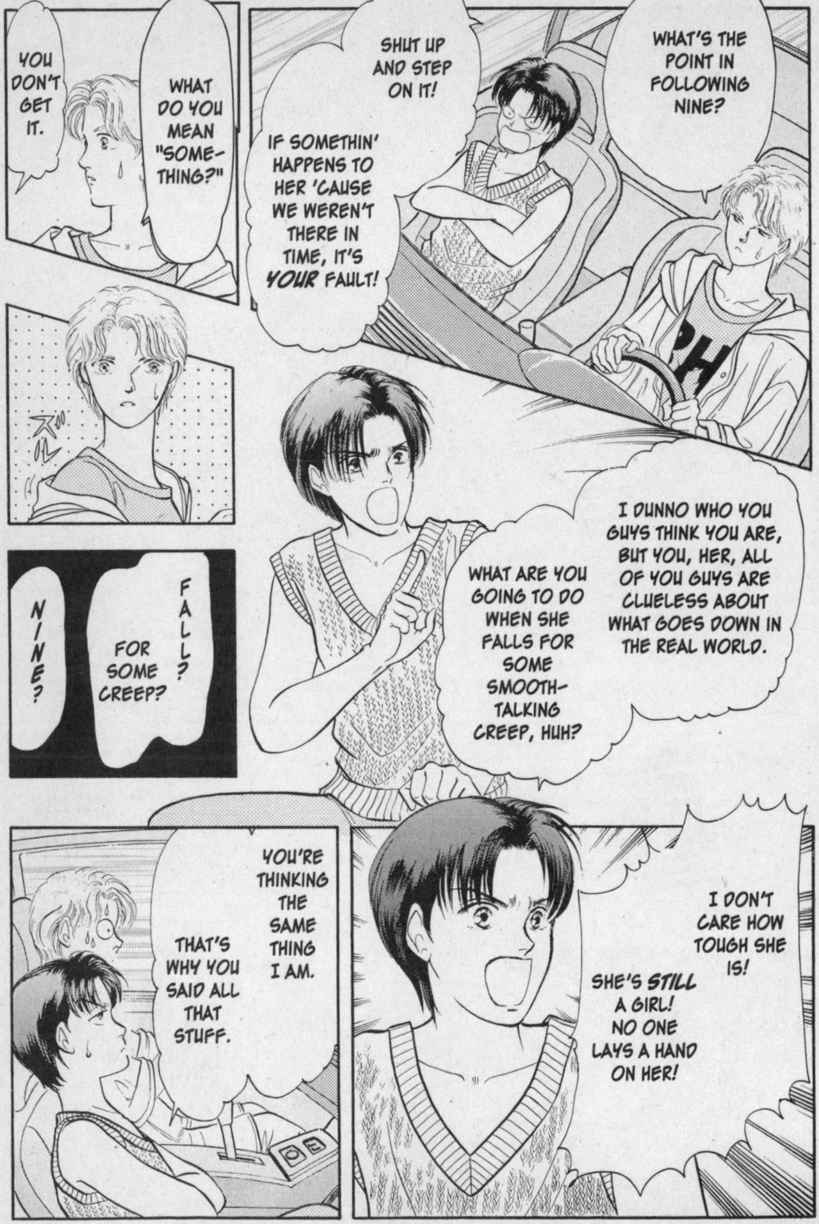
WHAT'S THE POINT IN FOLLOWING NINE?
SHUT UP AND STEP ON IT!
IF SOMETHIN' HAPPENS TO HER 'CAUSE WE WEREN'T THERE IN TIME, IT'S *YOUR* FAULT!
WHAT DO YOU MEAN "SOME-THING?"
YOU DON'T GET IT.
I DUNNO WHO YOU GUYS THINK YOU ARE, BUT YOU, HER, ALL OF YOU GUYS ARE CLUELESS ABOUT WHAT GOES DOWN IN THE REAL WORLD.
WHAT ARE YOU GOING TO DO WHEN SHE FALLS FOR SOME SMOOTH-TALKING CREEP, HUH?
FALL? FOR SOME CREEP?
NINE?
I DON'T CARE HOW TOUGH SHE IS!
SHE'S *STILL* A GIRL! NO ONE LAYS A HAND ON HER!
YOU'RE THINKING THE SAME THING I AM.
THAT'S WHY YOU SAID ALL THAT STUFF.

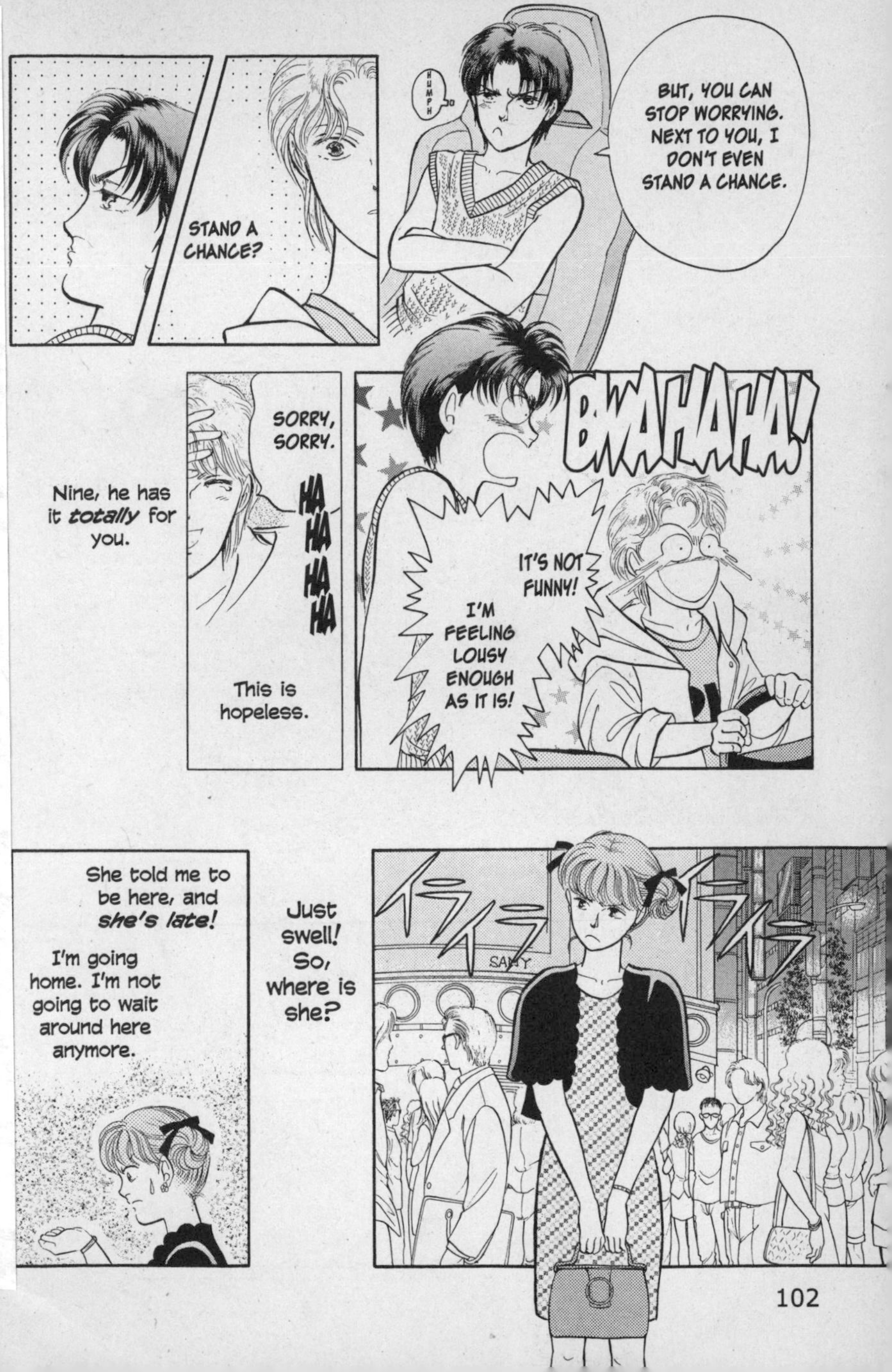
HUMPH
BUT, YOU CAN STOP WORRYING. NEXT TO YOU, I DON'T EVEN STAND A CHANCE.
STAND A CHANCE?
BWAHAHA!
IT'S NOT FUNNY!
I'M FEELING LOUSY ENOUGH AS IT IS!
SORRY, SORRY.
HA HA HA HA
Nine, he has it *totally* for you.
This is hopeless.
イライラ
イライラ
SANY
Just swell! So, where is she?
She told me to be here, and *she's late!*
I'm going home. I'm not going to wait around here anymore.

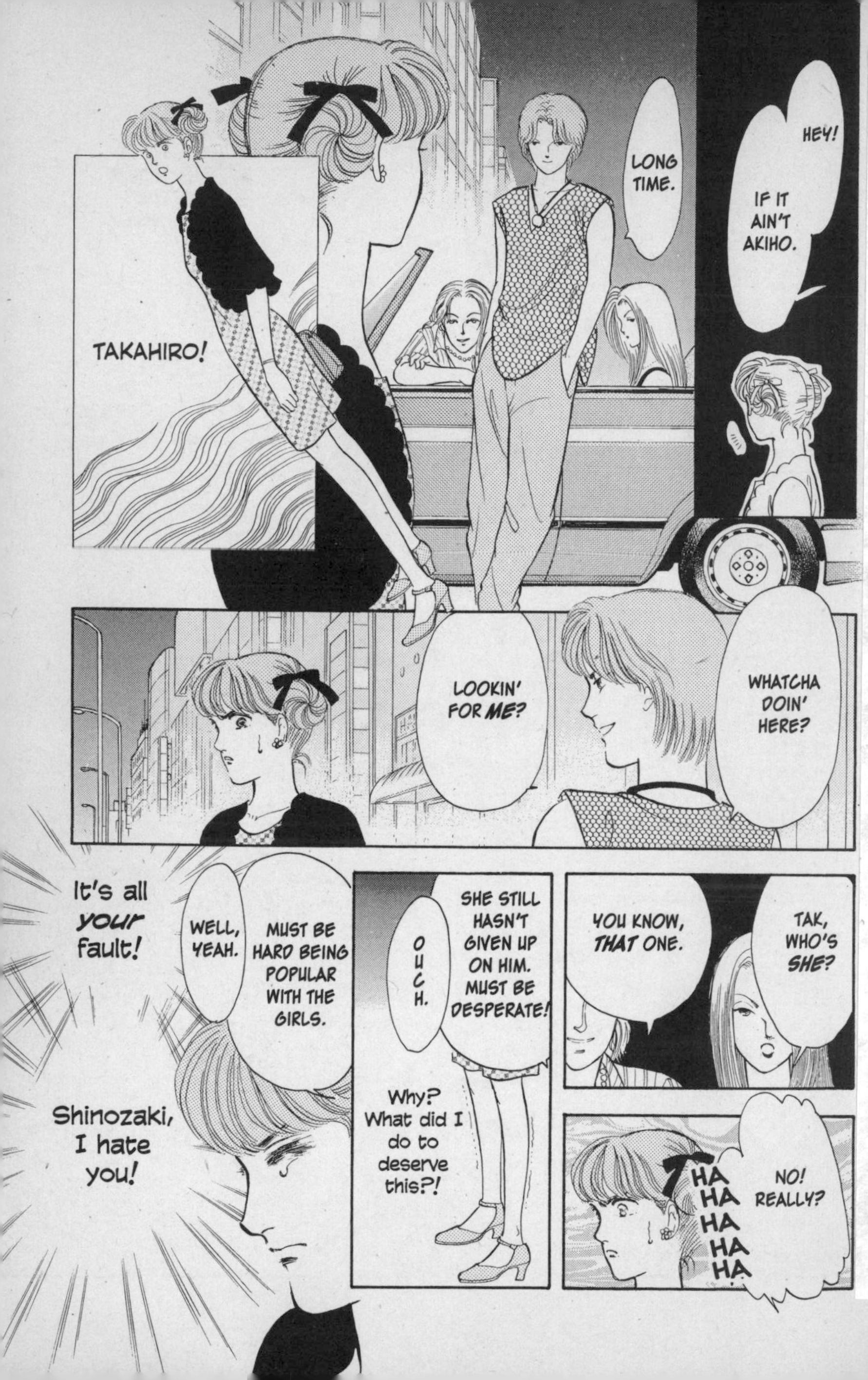
HEY!
IF IT AIN'T AKIHO.
LONG TIME.
TAKAHIRO!
WHATCHA DOIN' HERE?
LOOKIN' FOR *ME*?
TAK, WHO'S *SHE*?
YOU KNOW, *THAT* ONE.
NO! REALLY?
HA HA HA HA HA HA
SHE STILL HASN'T GIVEN UP ON HIM. MUST BE DESPERATE!
OUCH.
Why? What did I do to deserve this?!
MUST BE HARD BEING POPULAR WITH THE GIRLS.
WELL, YEAH.
It's all *your* fault!
Shinozaki, I hate you!

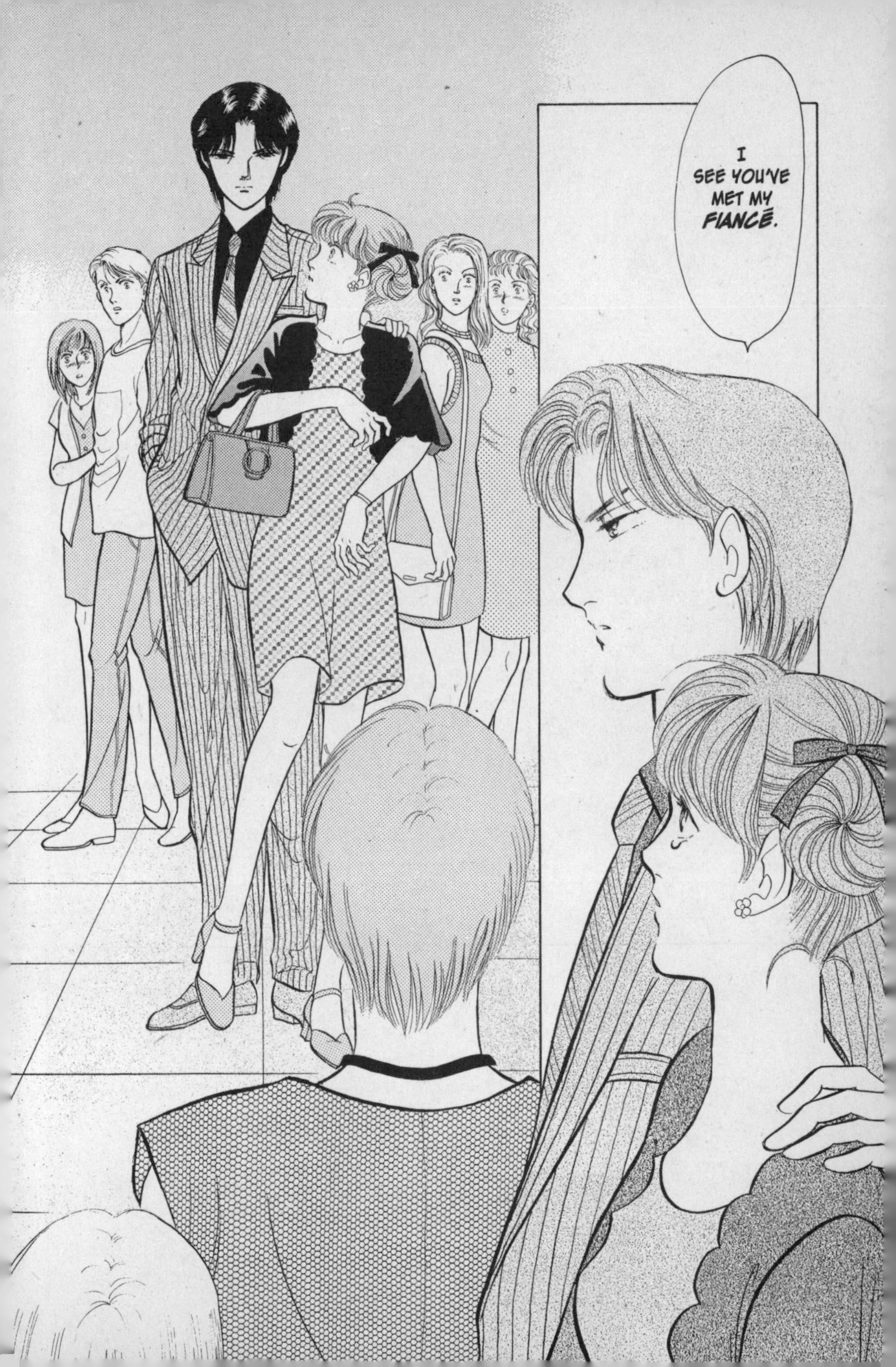
I SEE YOU'VE MET MY FIANCÉ.

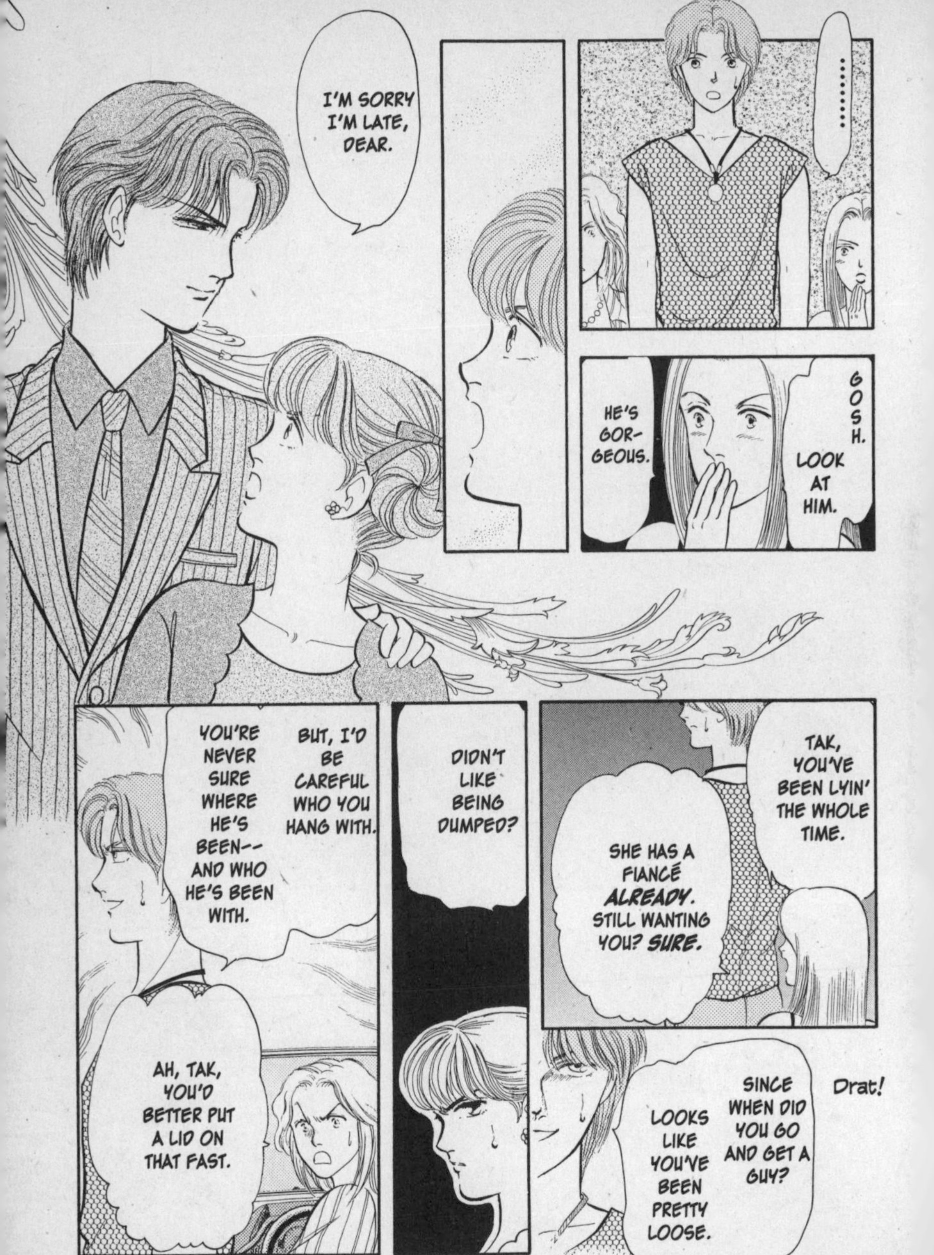
......
GOSH. LOOK AT HIM.
HE'S GOR-GEOUS.
I'M SORRY I'M LATE, DEAR.
TAK, YOU'VE BEEN LYIN' THE WHOLE TIME.
SHE HAS A FIANCÉ ***ALREADY***. STILL WANTING YOU? ***SURE.***
Drat!
SINCE WHEN DID YOU GO AND GET A GUY?
LOOKS LIKE YOU'VE BEEN PRETTY LOOSE.
DIDN'T LIKE BEING DUMPED?
BUT, I'D BE CAREFUL WHO YOU HANG WITH.
YOU'RE NEVER SURE WHERE HE'S BEEN-- AND WHO HE'S BEEN WITH.
AH, TAK, YOU'D BETTER PUT A LID ON THAT FAST.

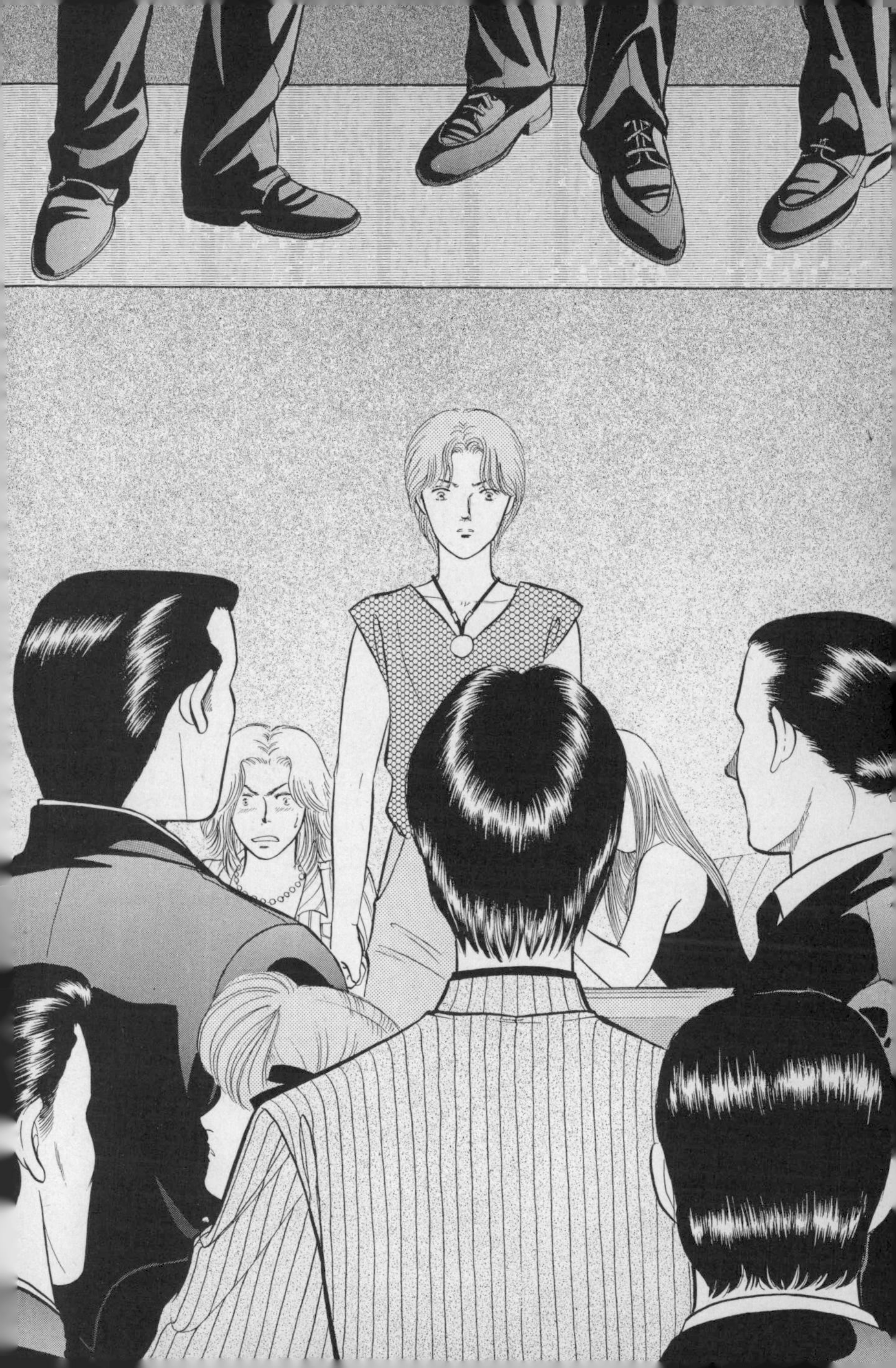

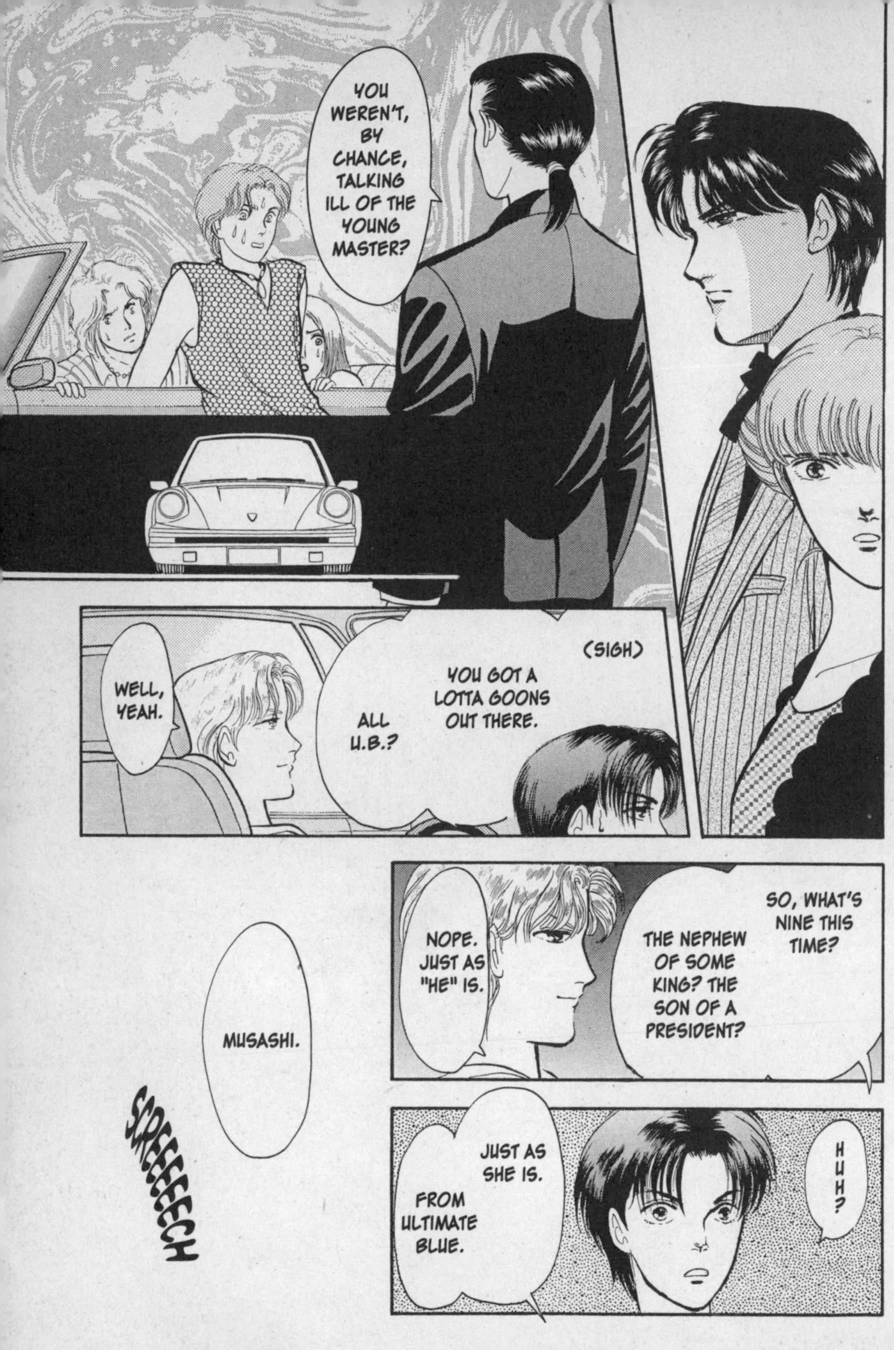
YOU WEREN'T, BY CHANCE, TALKING ILL OF THE YOUNG MASTER?
(SIGH)
YOU GOT A LOTTA GOONS OUT THERE.
ALL U.B.?
WELL, YEAH.
SO, WHAT'S NINE THIS TIME?
THE NEPHEW OF SOME KING? THE SON OF A PRESIDENT?
NOPE. JUST AS "HE" IS.
MUSASHI.
HUH?
JUST AS SHE IS.
FROM ULTIMATE BLUE.
SCREEEECH

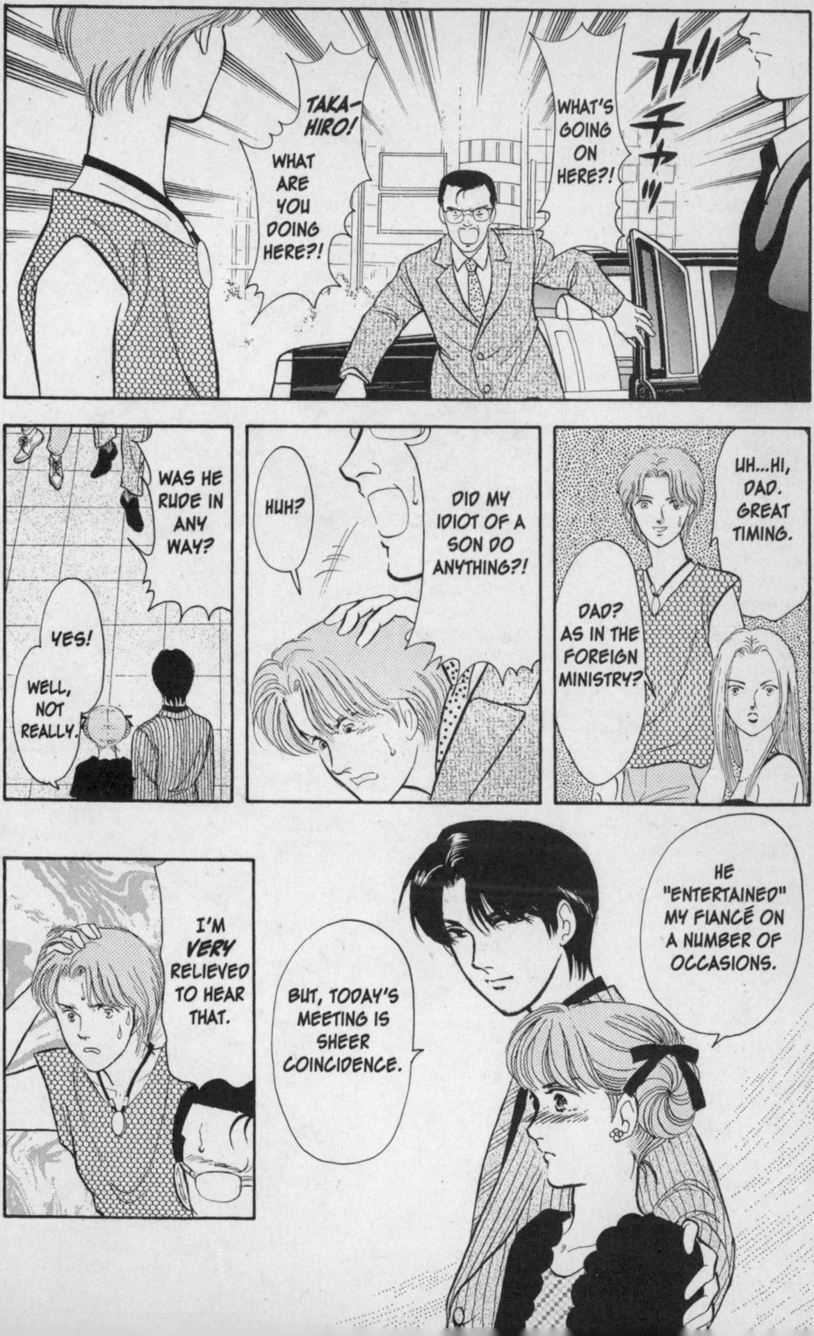
ガチャッ
WHAT'S GOING ON HERE?!
TAKA-HIRO!
WHAT ARE YOU DOING HERE?!
UH...HI, DAD. GREAT TIMING.
DAD? AS IN THE FOREIGN MINISTRY?
DID MY IDIOT OF A SON DO ANYTHING?!
HUH?
WAS HE RUDE IN ANY WAY?
YES!
WELL, NOT REALLY.
HE "ENTERTAINED" MY FIANCÉ ON A NUMBER OF OCCASIONS.
BUT, TODAY'S MEETING IS SHEER COINCIDENCE.
I'M *VERY* RELIEVED TO HEAR THAT.

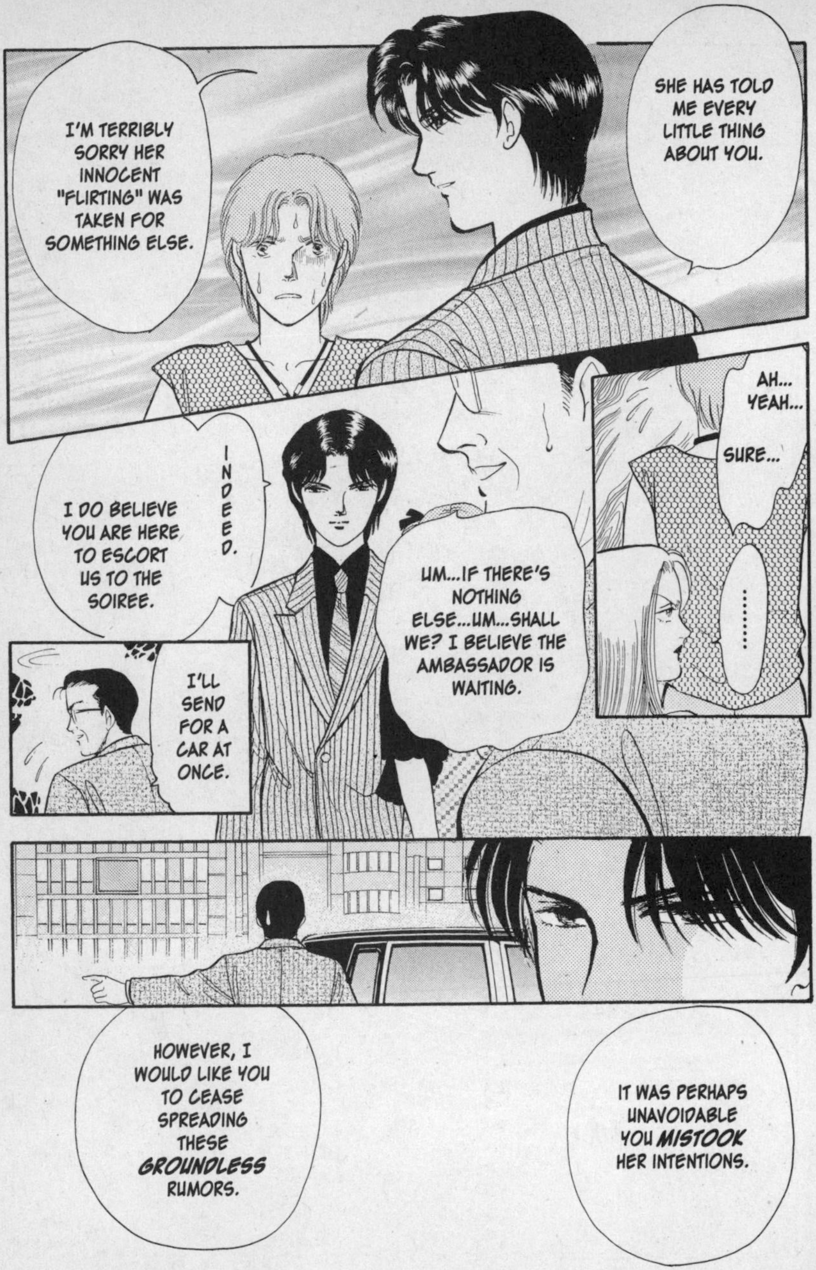

SHE HAS TOLD ME EVERY LITTLE THING ABOUT YOU.
I'M TERRIBLY SORRY HER INNOCENT "FLIRTING" WAS TAKEN FOR SOMETHING ELSE.
AH... YEAH...
SURE...
......
UM...IF THERE'S NOTHING ELSE...UM...SHALL WE? I BELIEVE THE AMBASSADOR IS WAITING.
INDEED.
I DO BELIEVE YOU ARE HERE TO ESCORT US TO THE SOIREE.
I'LL SEND FOR A CAR AT ONCE.
IT WAS PERHAPS UNAVOIDABLE YOU *MISTOOK* HER INTENTIONS.
HOWEVER, I WOULD LIKE YOU TO CEASE SPREADING THESE *GROUNDLESS* RUMORS.

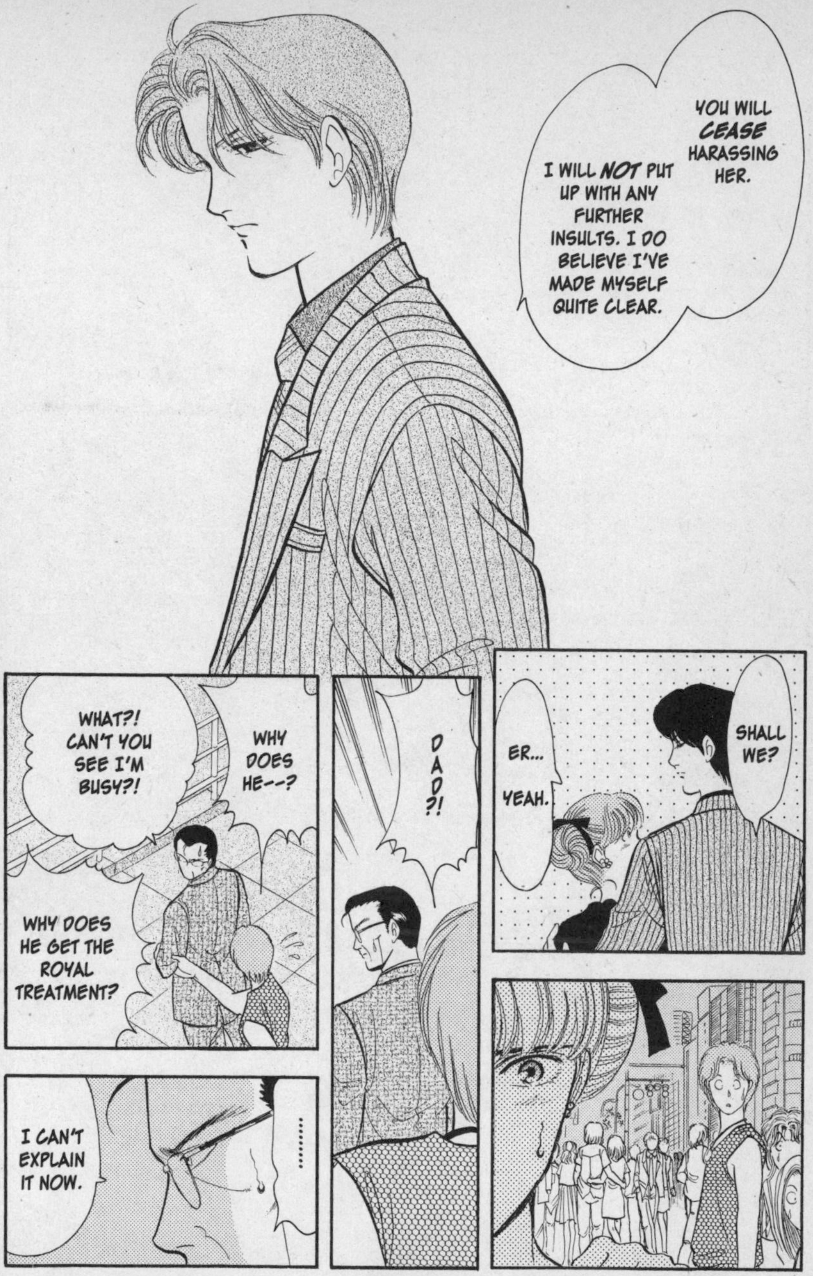
YOU WILL *CEASE* HARASSING HER.
I WILL ***NOT*** PUT UP WITH ANY FURTHER INSULTS. I DO BELIEVE I'VE MADE MYSELF QUITE CLEAR.
SHALL WE?
ER... YEAH.
DAD?!
WHAT?! CAN'T YOU SEE I'M BUSY?!
WHY DOES HE--?
WHY DOES HE GET THE ROYAL TREATMENT?
......
I CAN'T EXPLAIN IT NOW.

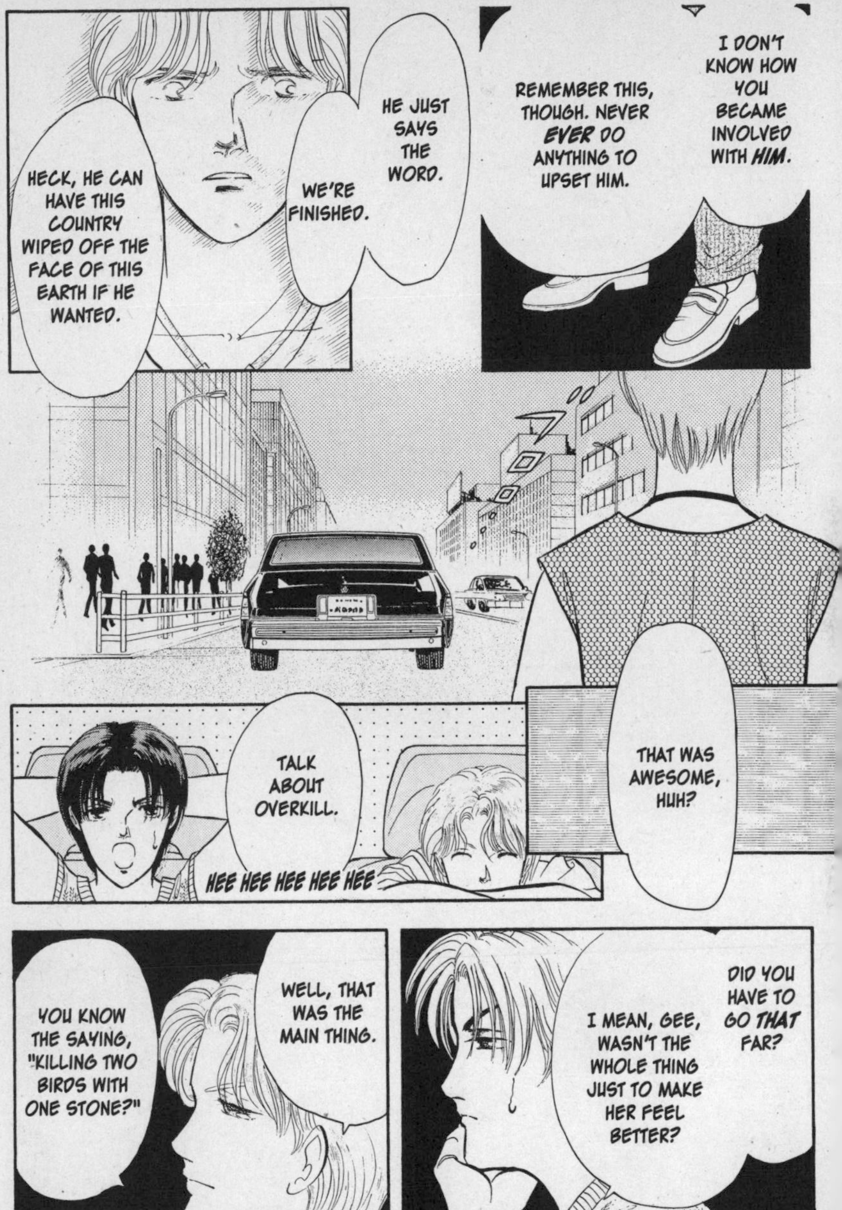
I DON'T KNOW HOW YOU BECAME INVOLVED WITH *HIM*.
REMEMBER THIS, THOUGH. NEVER *EVER* DO ANYTHING TO UPSET HIM.
HE JUST SAYS THE WORD.
WE'RE FINISHED.
HECK, HE CAN HAVE THIS COUNTRY WIPED OFF THE FACE OF THIS EARTH IF HE WANTED.
THAT WAS AWESOME, HUH?
TALK ABOUT OVERKILL.
HEE HEE HEE HEE HEE
DID YOU HAVE TO GO *THAT* FAR?
I MEAN, GEE, WASN'T THE WHOLE THING JUST TO MAKE HER FEEL BETTER?
WELL, THAT WAS THE MAIN THING.
YOU KNOW THE SAYING, "KILLING TWO BIRDS WITH ONE STONE?"

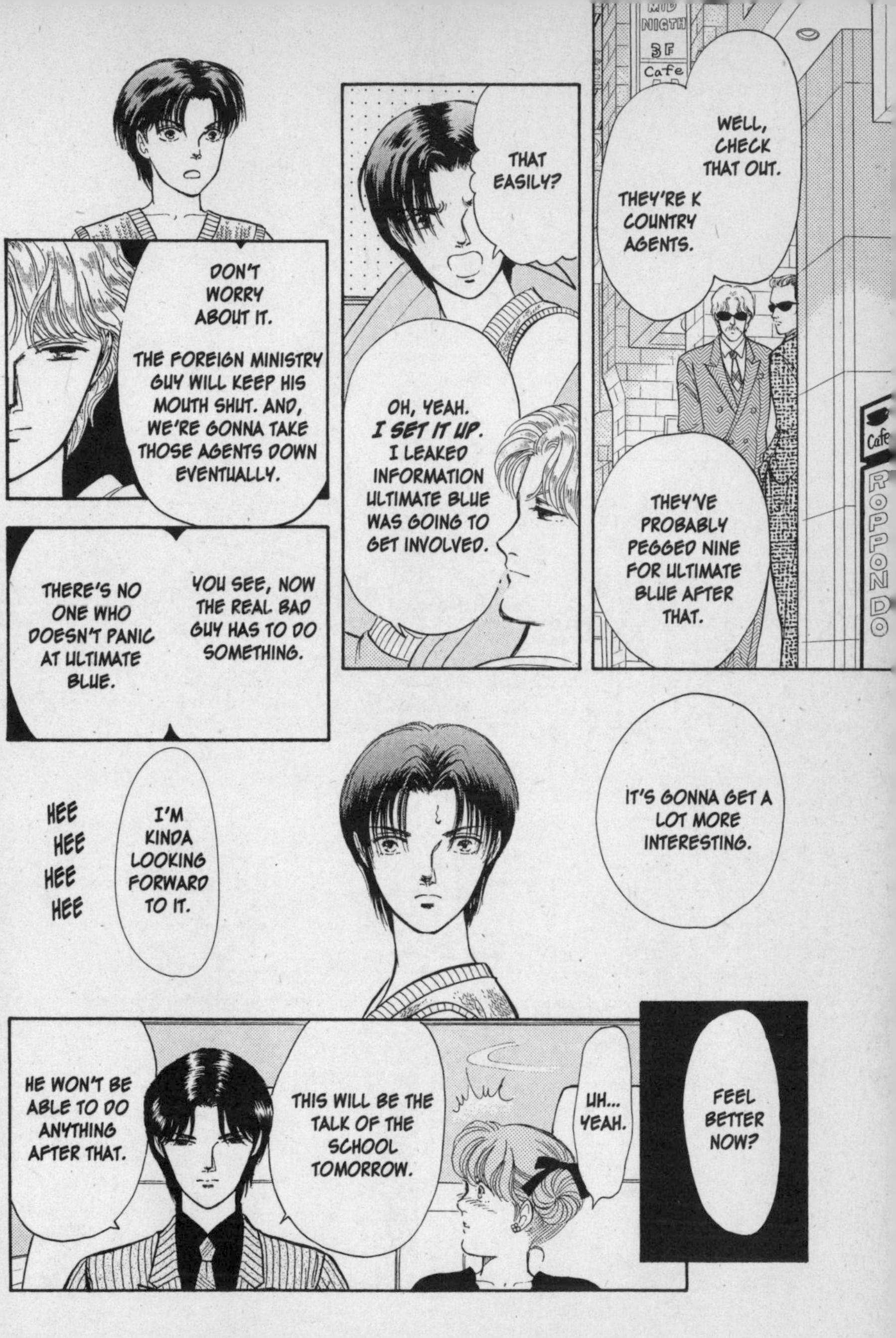
MID NIGTH
3F
Cafe
WELL, CHECK THAT OUT.
THEY'RE K COUNTRY AGENTS.
Cafe
ROPPONDO
THEY'VE PROBABLY PEGGED NINE FOR ULTIMATE BLUE AFTER THAT.
THAT EASILY?
OH, YEAH. *I SET IT UP.* I LEAKED INFORMATION ULTIMATE BLUE WAS GOING TO GET INVOLVED.
DON'T WORRY ABOUT IT.
THE FOREIGN MINISTRY GUY WILL KEEP HIS MOUTH SHUT. AND, WE'RE GONNA TAKE THOSE AGENTS DOWN EVENTUALLY.
YOU SEE, NOW THE REAL BAD GUY HAS TO DO SOMETHING.
THERE'S NO ONE WHO DOESN'T PANIC AT ULTIMATE BLUE.
IT'S GONNA GET A LOT MORE INTERESTING.
I'M KINDA LOOKING FORWARD TO IT.
HEE HEE HEE HEE
FEEL BETTER NOW?
UH... YEAH.
THIS WILL BE THE TALK OF THE SCHOOL TOMORROW.
HE WON'T BE ABLE TO DO ANYTHING AFTER THAT.

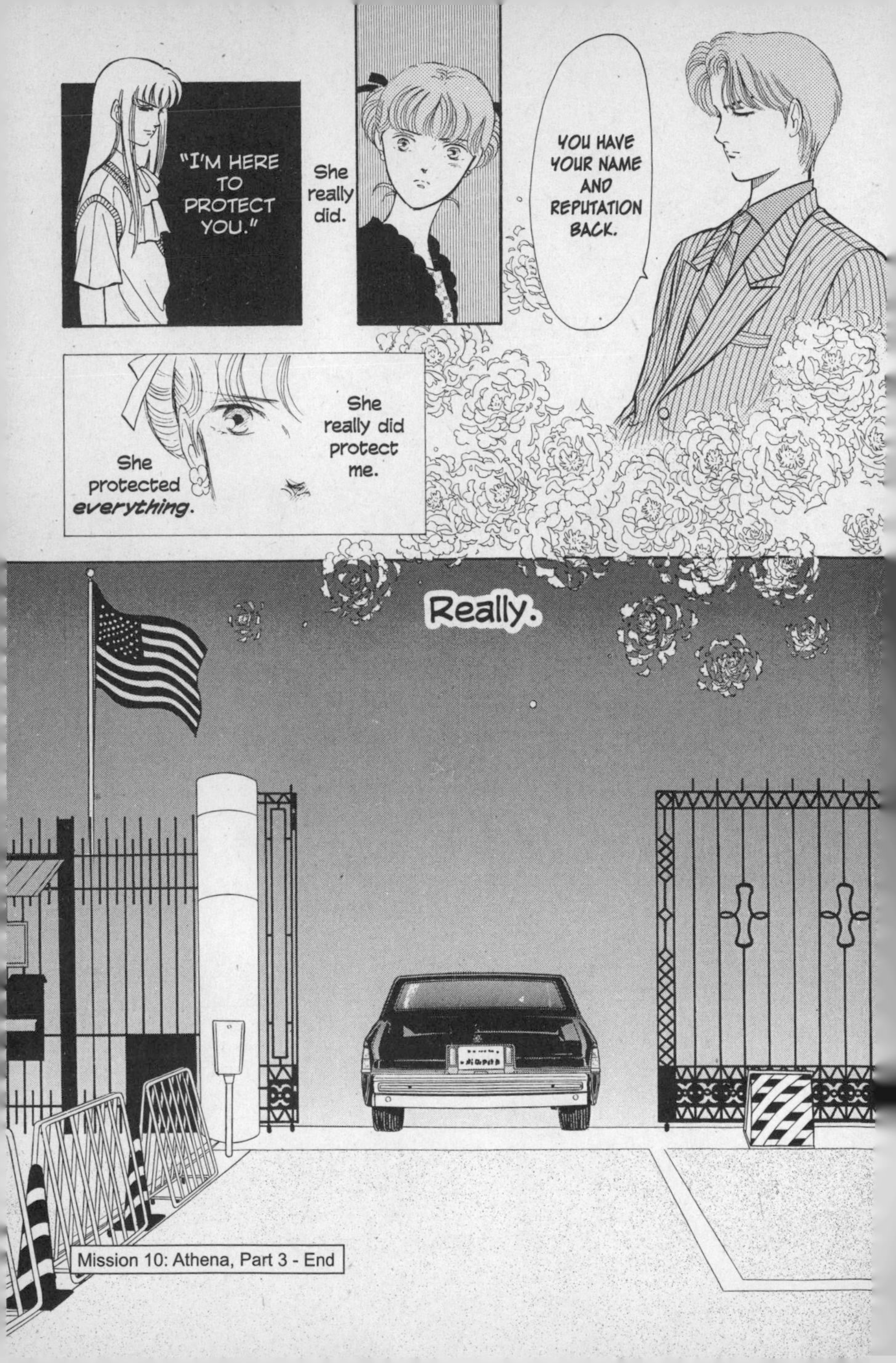

YOU HAVE YOUR NAME AND REPUTATION BACK.
She really did.
"I'M HERE TO PROTECT YOU."
She really did protect me.
She protected *everything*.
Really.
Mission 10: Athena, Part 3 - End

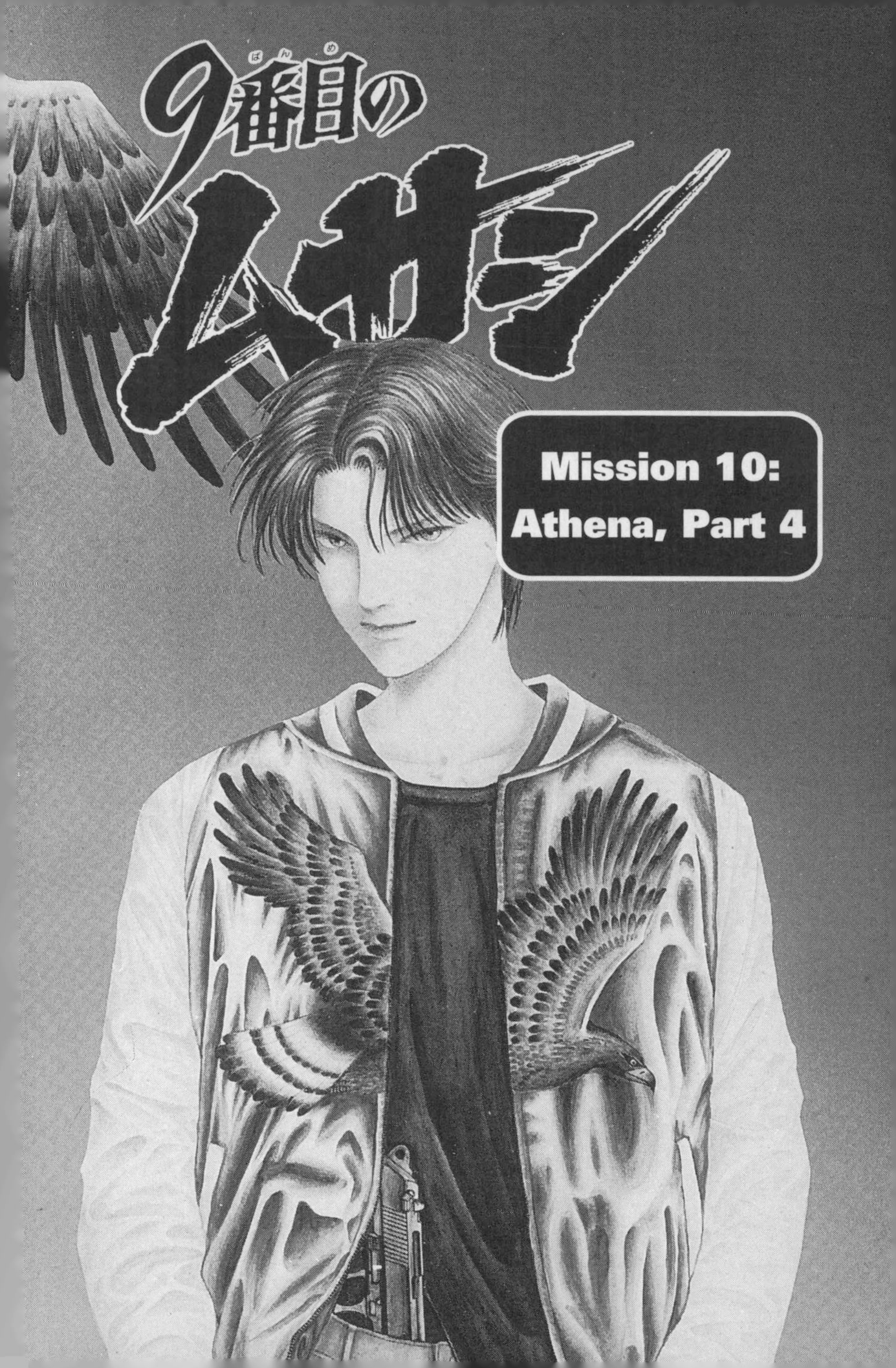
9番目のムサシ
Mission 10:
Athena, Part 4

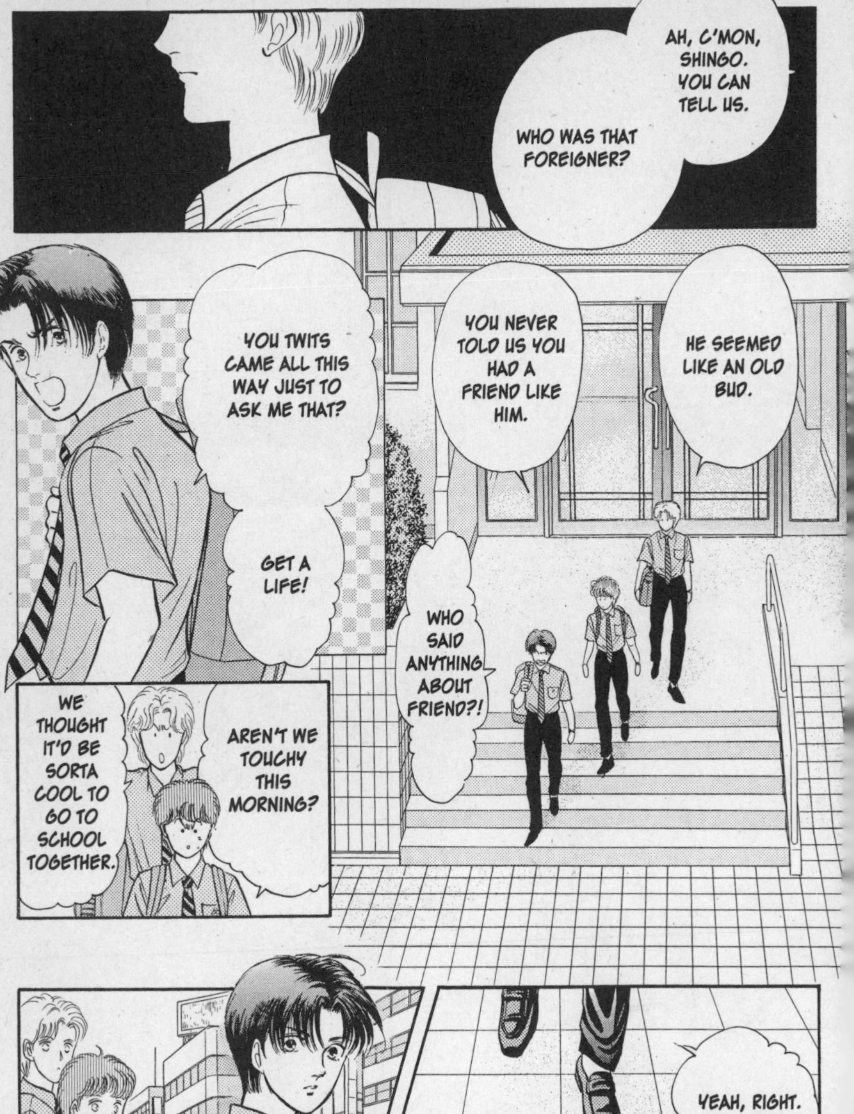
AH, C'MON, SHINGO. YOU CAN TELL US.
WHO WAS THAT FOREIGNER?
HE SEEMED LIKE AN OLD BUD.
YOU NEVER TOLD US YOU HAD A FRIEND LIKE HIM.
WHO SAID ANYTHING ABOUT FRIEND?!
YOU TWITS CAME ALL THIS WAY JUST TO ASK ME THAT?
GET A LIFE!
AREN'T WE TOUCHY THIS MORNING?
WE THOUGHT IT'D BE SORTA COOL TO GO TO SCHOOL TOGETHER.
YEAH, RIGHT. I'M NOT A STUPID LITTLE KID.

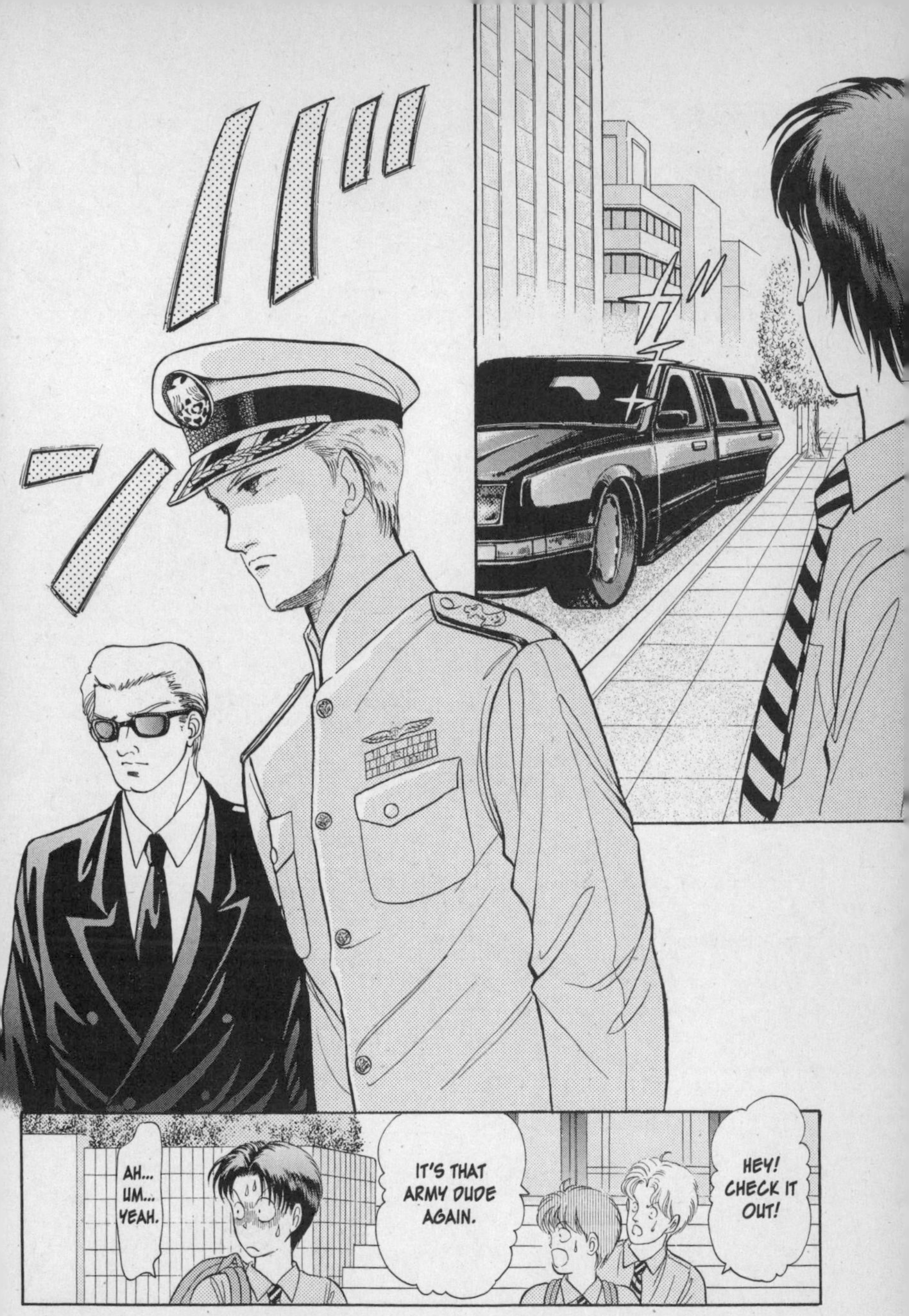
HEY! CHECK IT OUT!
IT'S THAT ARMY DUDE AGAIN.
AH... UM... YEAH.

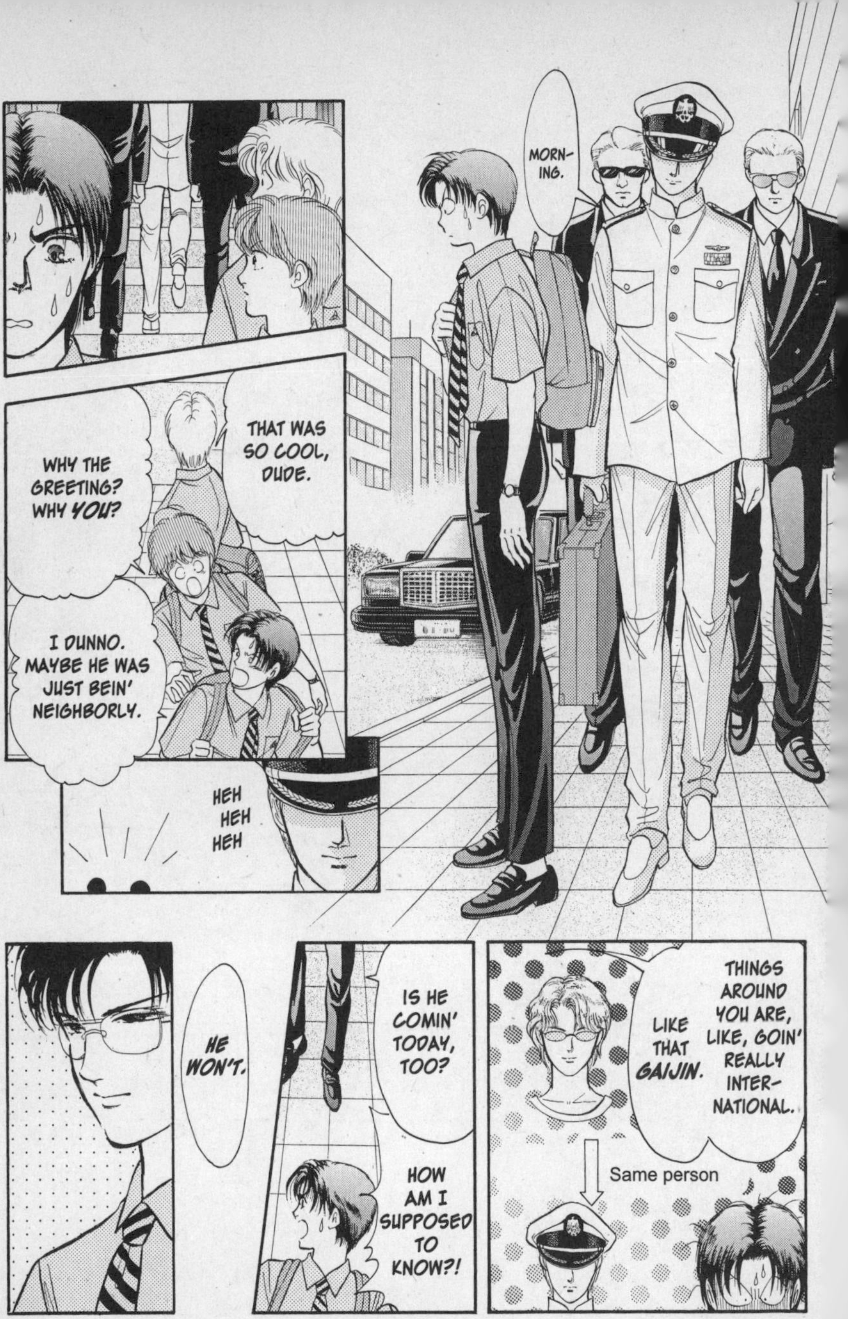
MORN-ING.
THAT WAS SO COOL, DUDE.
WHY THE GREETING? WHY *YOU?*
I DUNNO. MAYBE HE WAS JUST BEIN' NEIGHBORLY.
HEH HEH HEH
THINGS AROUND YOU ARE, LIKE, GOIN' REALLY INTER-NATIONAL.
LIKE THAT *GAIJIN*.
Same person
IS HE COMIN' TODAY, TOO?
HOW AM I SUPPOSED TO KNOW?!
HE WON'T.

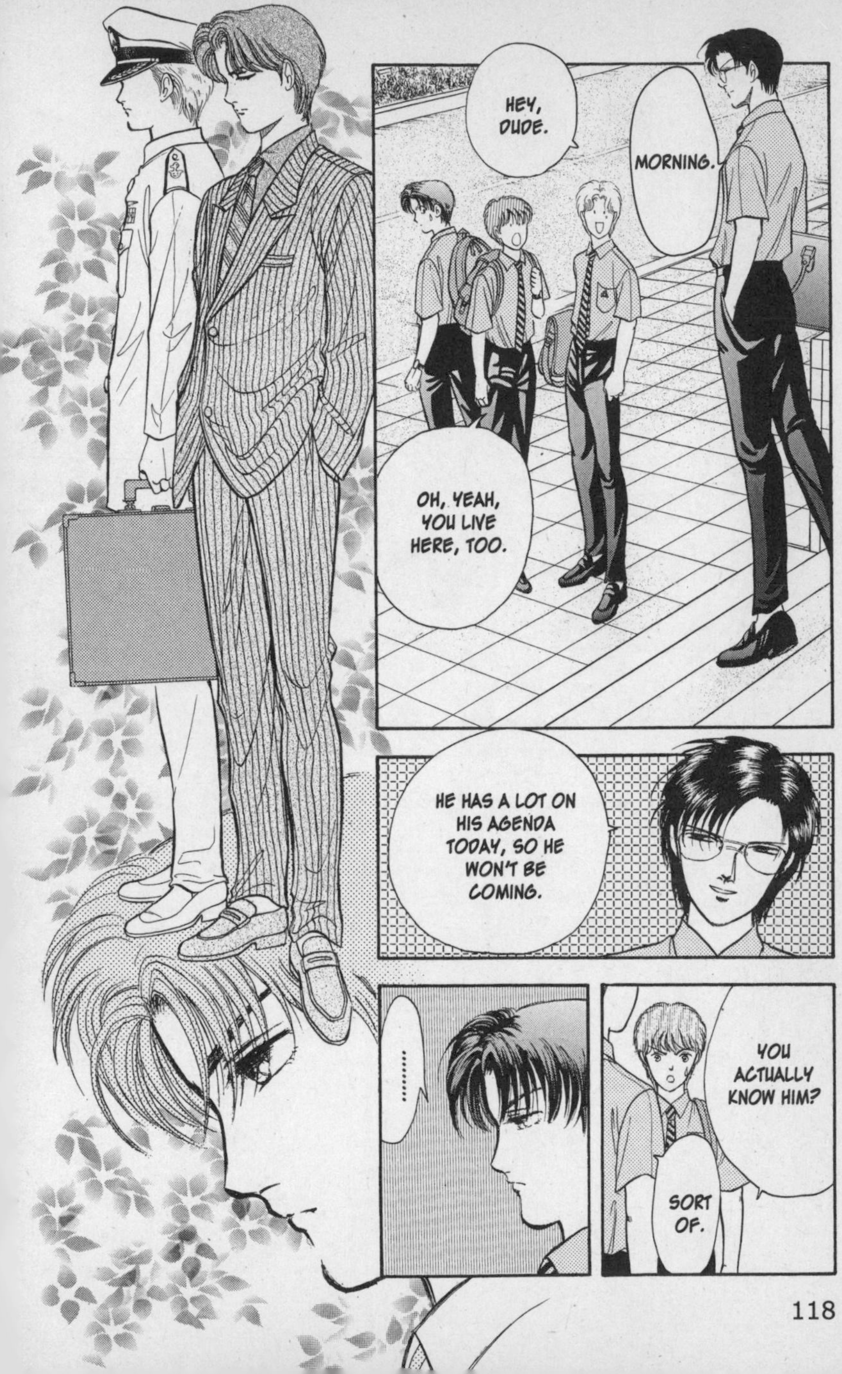
HEY, DUDE.
MORNING.
OH, YEAH, YOU LIVE HERE, TOO.
HE HAS A LOT ON HIS AGENDA TODAY, SO HE WON'T BE COMING.
YOU ACTUALLY KNOW HIM?
SORT OF.
......

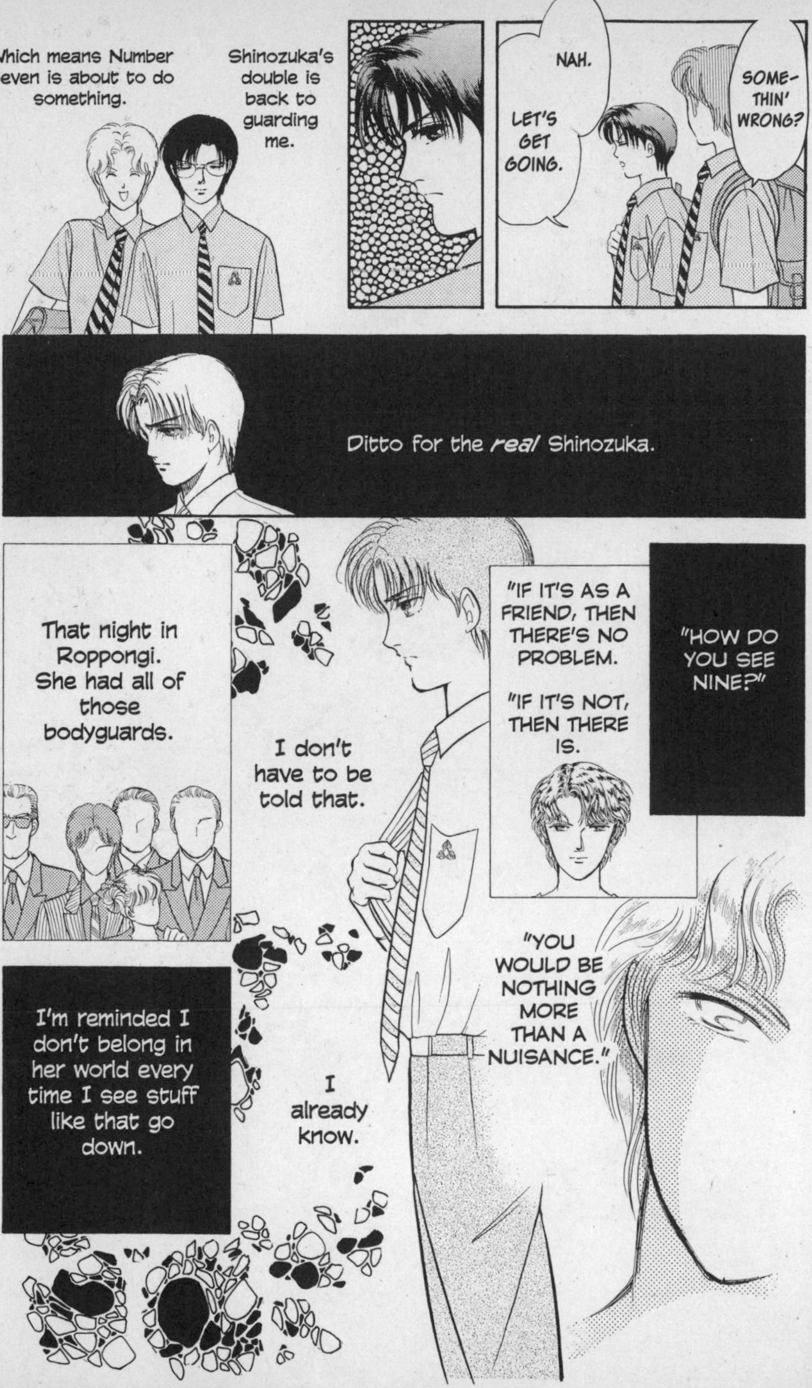
SOME-THIN' WRONG?
NAH.
LET'S GET GOING.
Shinozuka's double is back to guarding me.
Which means Number Seven is about to do something.
Ditto for the *real* Shinozuka.
"HOW DO YOU SEE NINE?"
"IF IT'S AS A FRIEND, THEN THERE'S NO PROBLEM.
"IF IT'S NOT, THEN THERE IS.
That night in Roppongi. She had all of those bodyguards.
I don't have to be told that.
"YOU WOULD BE NOTHING MORE THAN A NUISANCE."
I already know.
I'm reminded I don't belong in her world every time I see stuff like that go down.

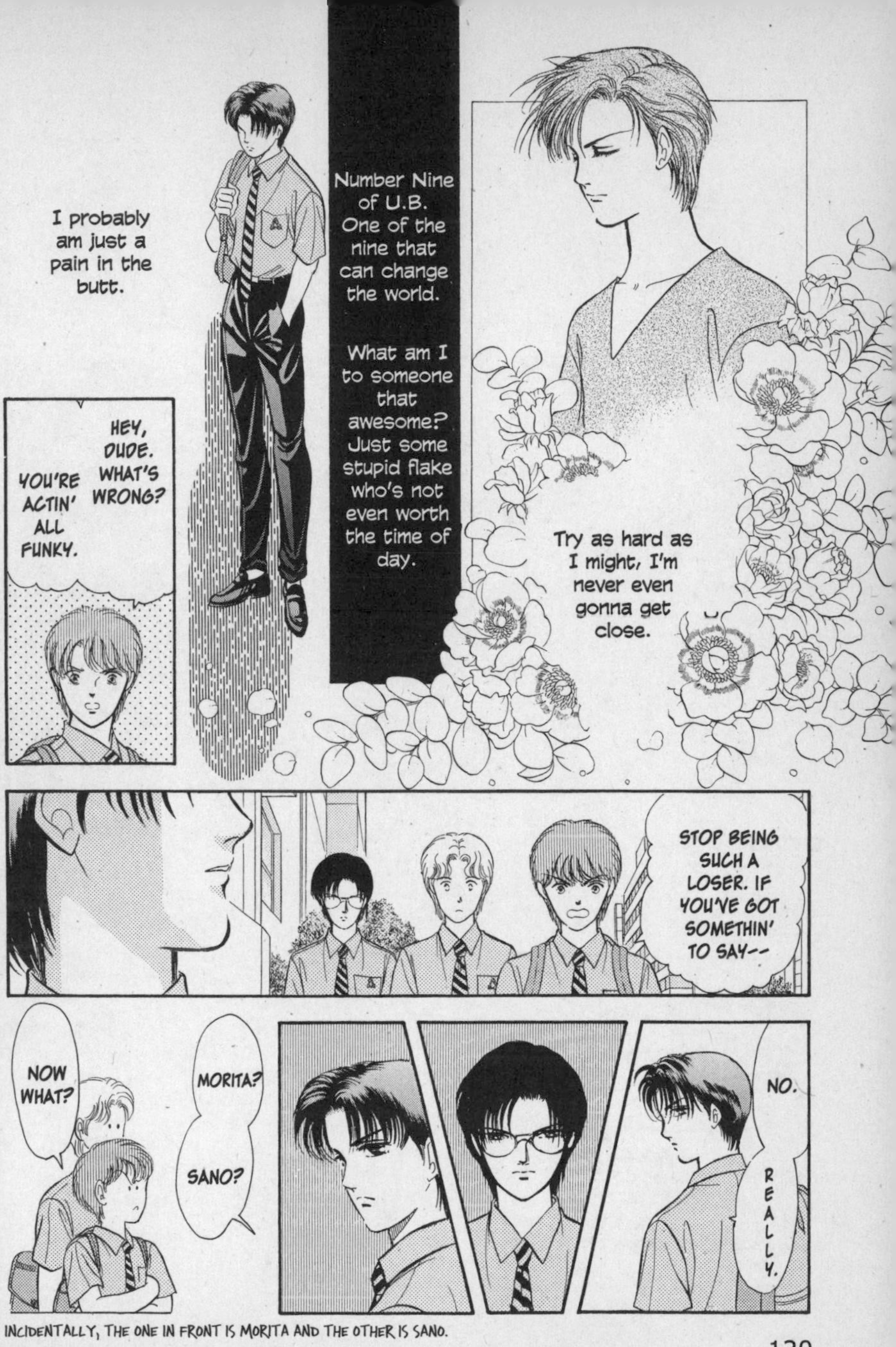
Number Nine of U.B. One of the nine that can change the world.
What am I to someone that awesome? Just some stupid flake who's not even worth the time of day.
Try as hard as I might, I'm never even gonna get close.
I probably am just a pain in the butt.
HEY, DUDE. WHAT'S WRONG?
YOU'RE ACTIN' ALL FUNKY.
STOP BEING SUCH A LOSER. IF YOU'VE GOT SOMETHIN' TO SAY--
NO.
REALLY.
MORITA?
SANO?
NOW WHAT?

INCIDENTALLY, THE ONE IN FRONT IS MORITA AND THE OTHER IS SANO.

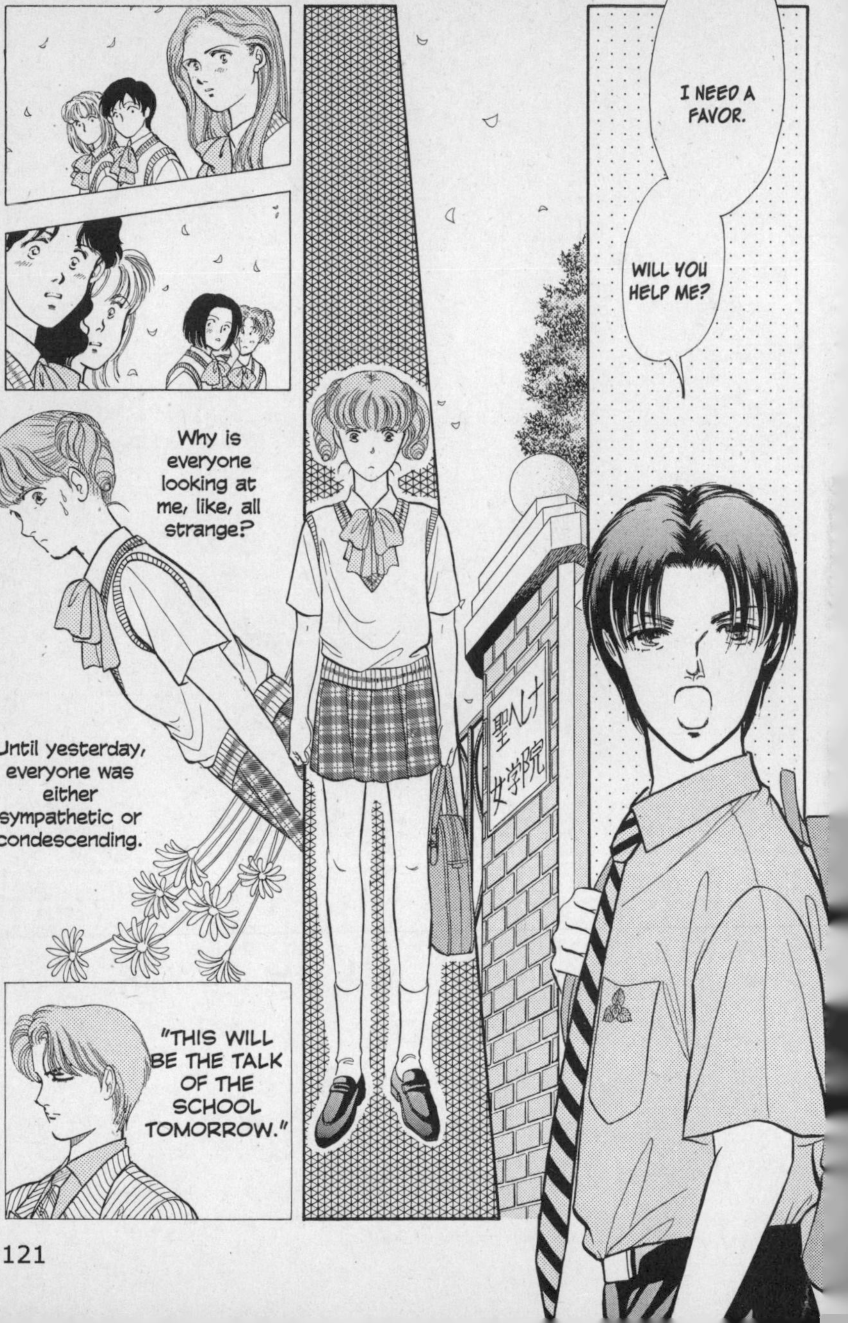

I NEED A FAVOR.
WILL YOU HELP ME?
聖ヘレナ女学院
Why is everyone looking at me, like, all strange?
Until yesterday, everyone was either sympathetic or condescending.
"THIS WILL BE THE TALK OF THE SCHOOL TOMORROW."

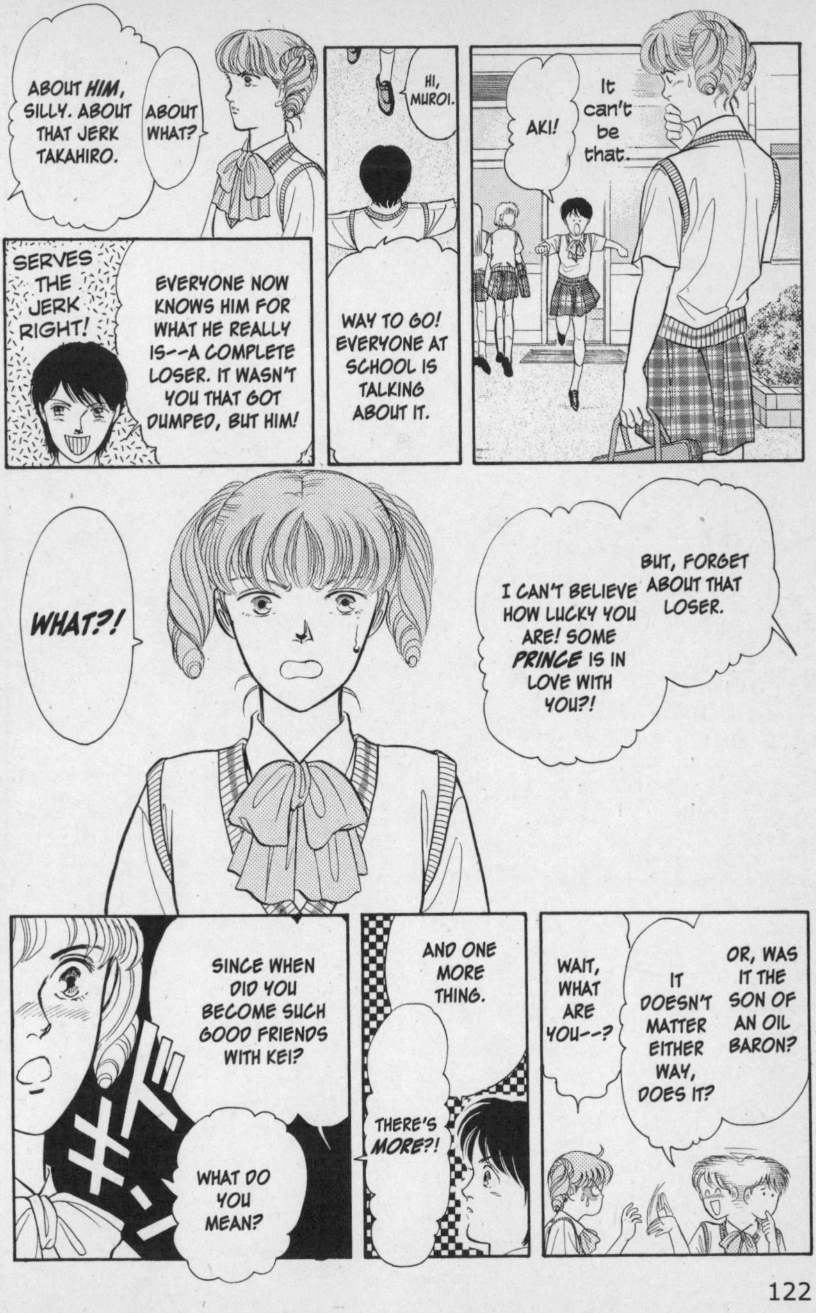
It can't be that.
AKI!
HI, MUROI.
WAY TO GO! EVERYONE AT SCHOOL IS TALKING ABOUT IT.
ABOUT WHAT?
ABOUT HIM, SILLY. ABOUT THAT JERK TAKAHIRO.
EVERYONE NOW KNOWS HIM FOR WHAT HE REALLY IS--A COMPLETE LOSER. IT WASN'T YOU THAT GOT DUMPED, BUT HIM!
SERVES THE JERK RIGHT!
BUT, FORGET ABOUT THAT LOSER.
I CAN'T BELIEVE HOW LUCKY YOU ARE! SOME PRINCE IS IN LOVE WITH YOU?!
WHAT?!
OR, WAS IT THE SON OF AN OIL BARON?
IT DOESN'T MATTER EITHER WAY, DOES IT?
WAIT, WHAT ARE YOU--?
AND ONE MORE THING.
THERE'S MORE?!
SINCE WHEN DID YOU BECOME SUCH GOOD FRIENDS WITH KEI?
WHAT DO YOU MEAN?

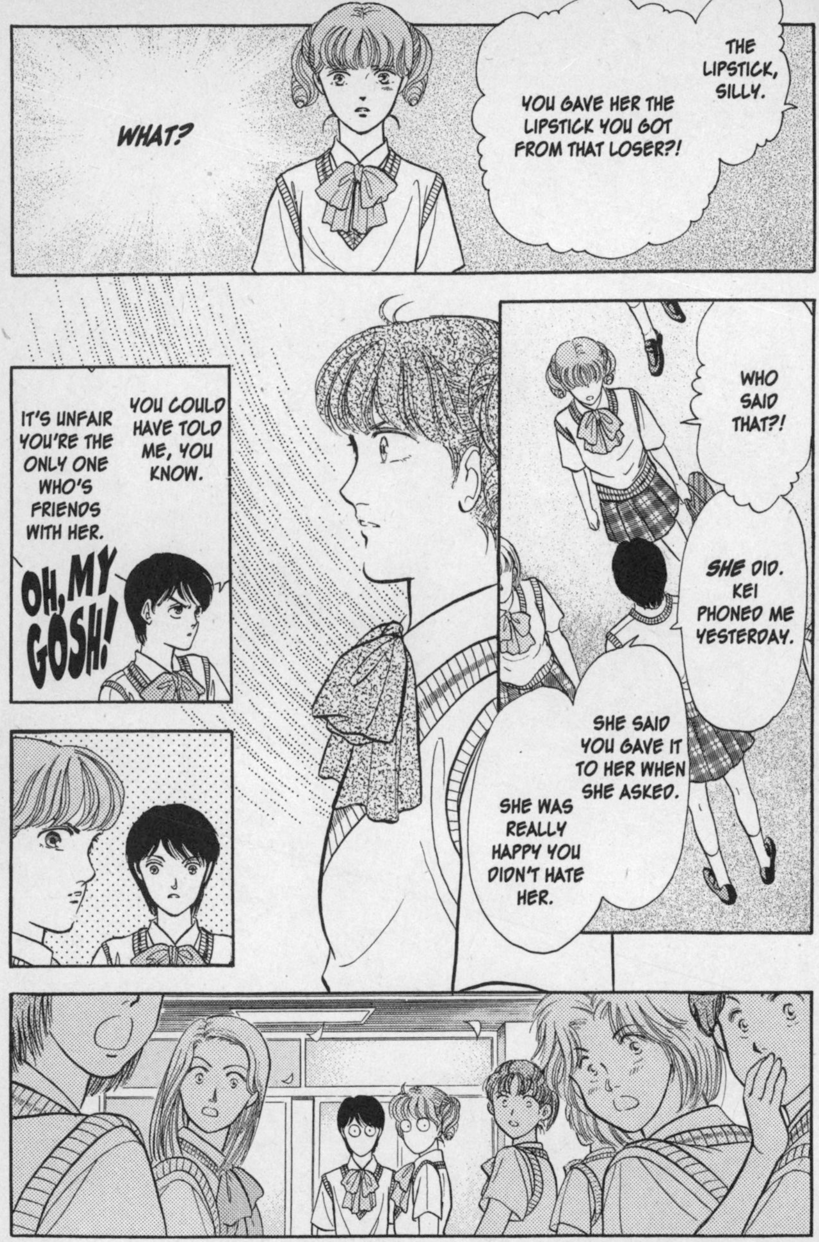
THE LIPSTICK, SILLY.
YOU GAVE HER THE LIPSTICK YOU GOT FROM THAT LOSER?!
WHAT?
WHO SAID THAT?!
SHE DID. KEI PHONED ME YESTERDAY.
SHE SAID YOU GAVE IT TO HER WHEN SHE ASKED.
SHE WAS REALLY HAPPY YOU DIDN'T HATE HER.
YOU COULD HAVE TOLD ME, YOU KNOW.
IT'S UNFAIR YOU'RE THE ONLY ONE WHO'S FRIENDS WITH HER.
OH, MY GOSH!

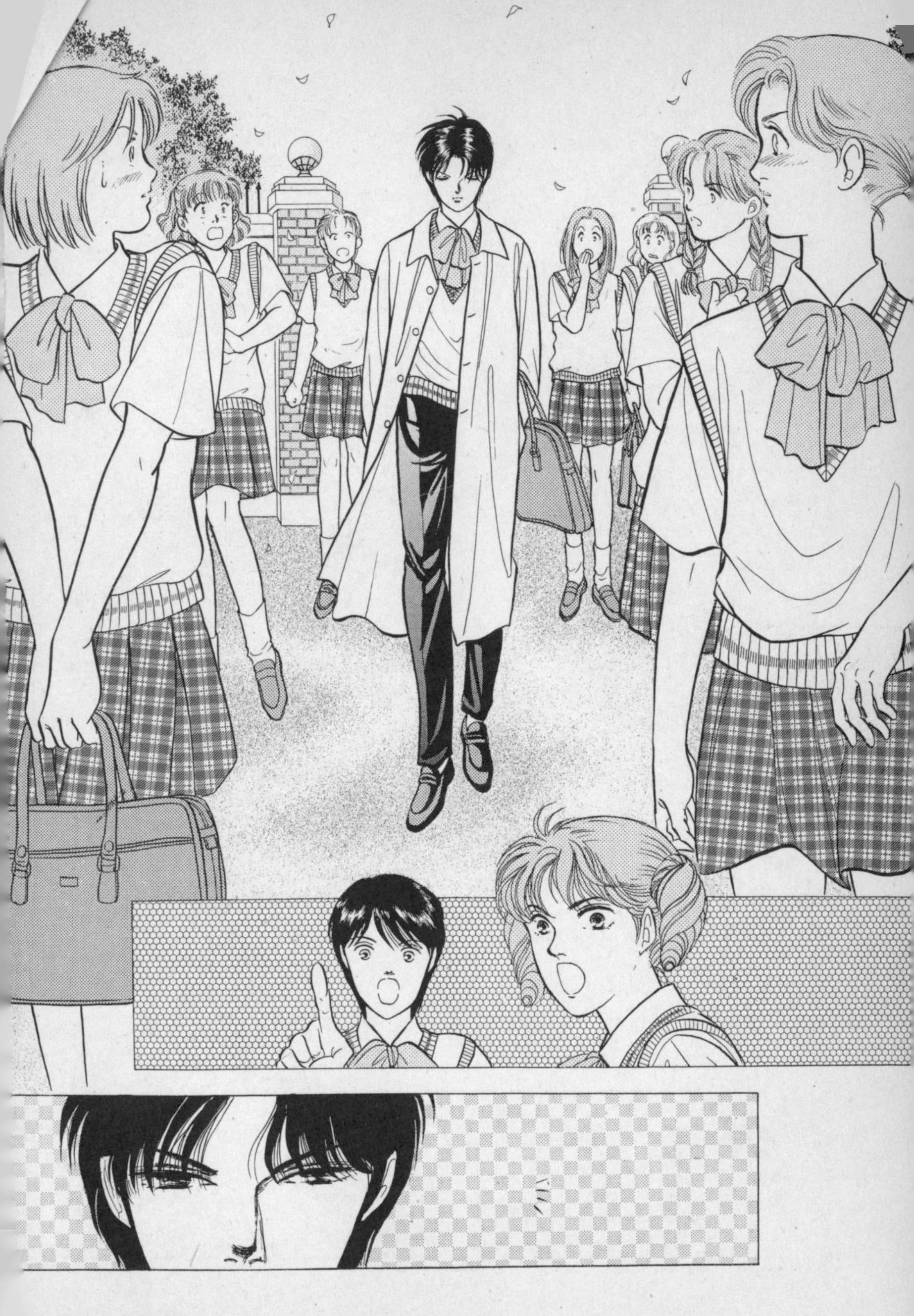

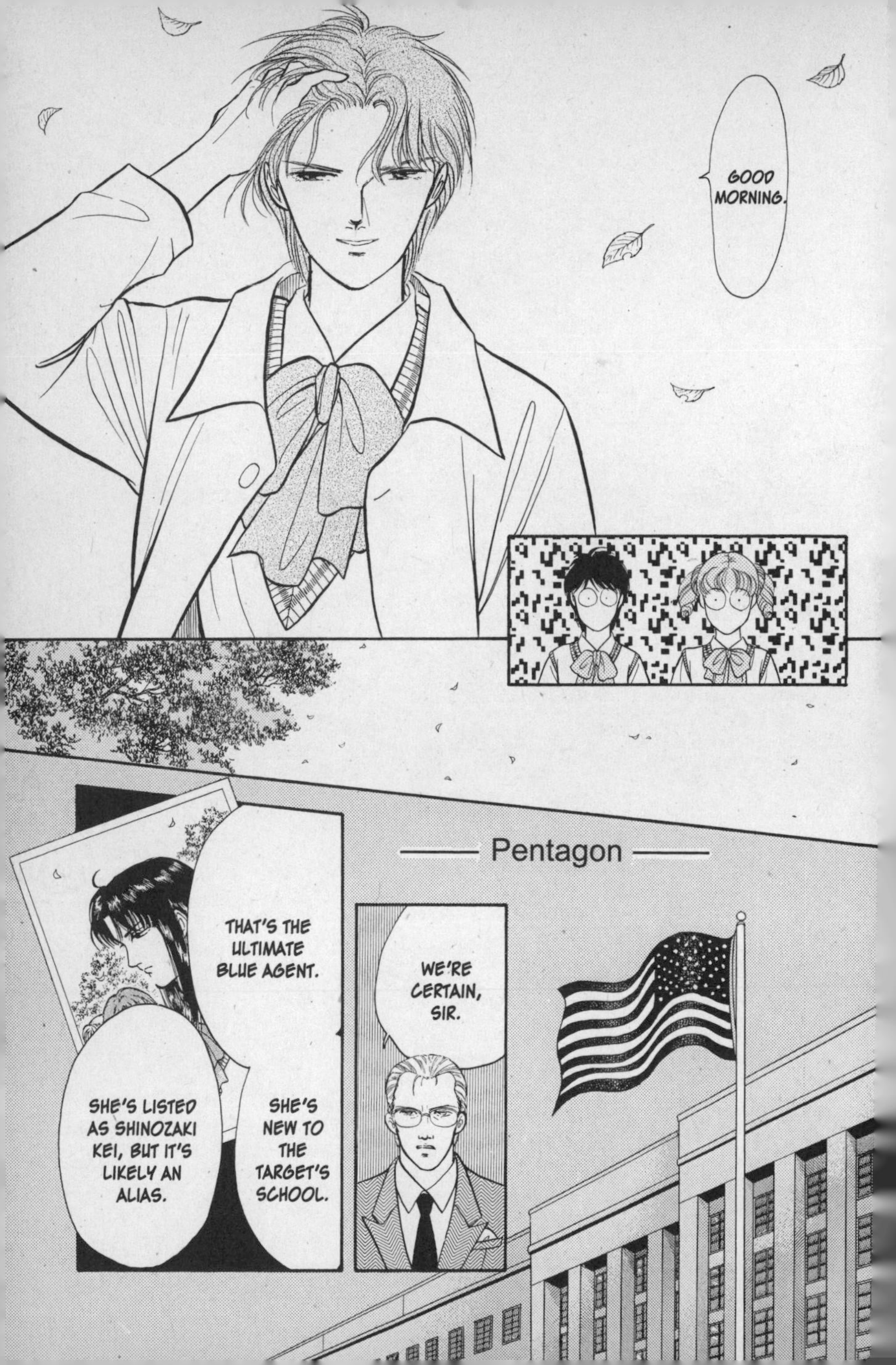
GOOD MORNING.
—— Pentagon ——
WE'RE CERTAIN, SIR.
THAT'S THE ULTIMATE BLUE AGENT.
SHE'S NEW TO THE TARGET'S SCHOOL.
SHE'S LISTED AS SHINOZAKI KEI, BUT IT'S LIKELY AN ALIAS.

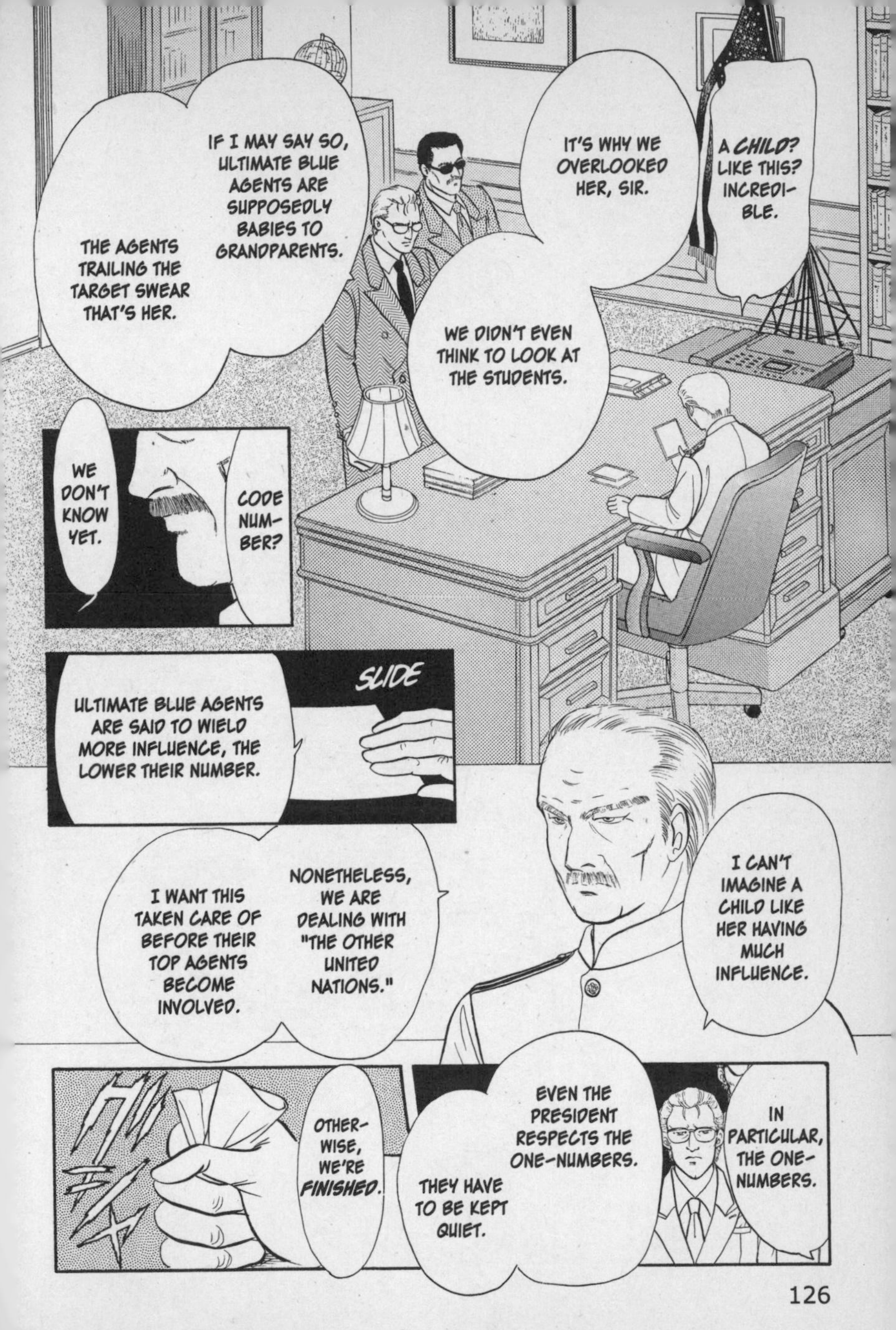
A CHILD? LIKE THIS? INCREDIBLE.
IT'S WHY WE OVERLOOKED HER, SIR.
WE DIDN'T EVEN THINK TO LOOK AT THE STUDENTS.
IF I MAY SAY SO, ULTIMATE BLUE AGENTS ARE SUPPOSEDLY BABIES TO GRANDPARENTS.
THE AGENTS TRAILING THE TARGET SWEAR THAT'S HER.
CODE NUMBER?
WE DON'T KNOW YET.
SLIDE
ULTIMATE BLUE AGENTS ARE SAID TO WIELD MORE INFLUENCE, THE LOWER THEIR NUMBER.
I CAN'T IMAGINE A CHILD LIKE HER HAVING MUCH INFLUENCE.
NONETHELESS, WE ARE DEALING WITH "THE OTHER UNITED NATIONS."
I WANT THIS TAKEN CARE OF BEFORE THEIR TOP AGENTS BECOME INVOLVED.
IN PARTICULAR, THE ONE-NUMBERS.
EVEN THE PRESIDENT RESPECTS THE ONE-NUMBERS.
THEY HAVE TO BE KEPT QUIET.
OTHER-WISE, WE'RE *FINISHED*.

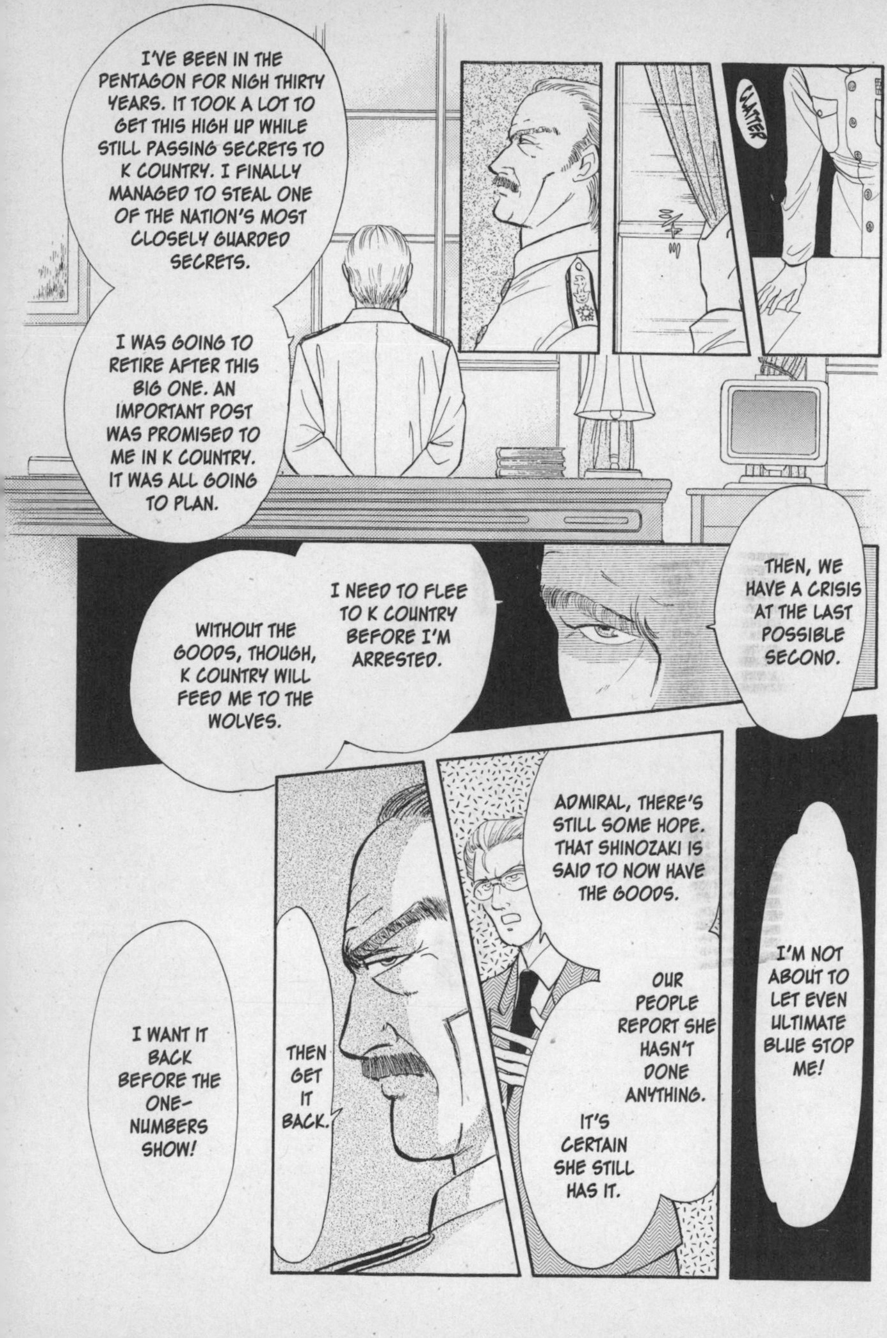
CLATTER
I'VE BEEN IN THE PENTAGON FOR NIGH THIRTY YEARS. IT TOOK A LOT TO GET THIS HIGH UP WHILE STILL PASSING SECRETS TO K COUNTRY. I FINALLY MANAGED TO STEAL ONE OF THE NATION'S MOST CLOSELY GUARDED SECRETS.
I WAS GOING TO RETIRE AFTER THIS BIG ONE. AN IMPORTANT POST WAS PROMISED TO ME IN K COUNTRY. IT WAS ALL GOING TO PLAN.
THEN, WE HAVE A CRISIS AT THE LAST POSSIBLE SECOND.
I NEED TO FLEE TO K COUNTRY BEFORE I'M ARRESTED.
WITHOUT THE GOODS, THOUGH, K COUNTRY WILL FEED ME TO THE WOLVES.
I'M NOT ABOUT TO LET EVEN ULTIMATE BLUE STOP ME!
ADMIRAL, THERE'S STILL SOME HOPE. THAT SHINOZAKI IS SAID TO NOW HAVE THE GOODS.
OUR PEOPLE REPORT SHE HASN'T DONE ANYTHING.
IT'S CERTAIN SHE STILL HAS IT.
THEN GET IT BACK.
I WANT IT BACK BEFORE THE ONE-NUMBERS SHOW!

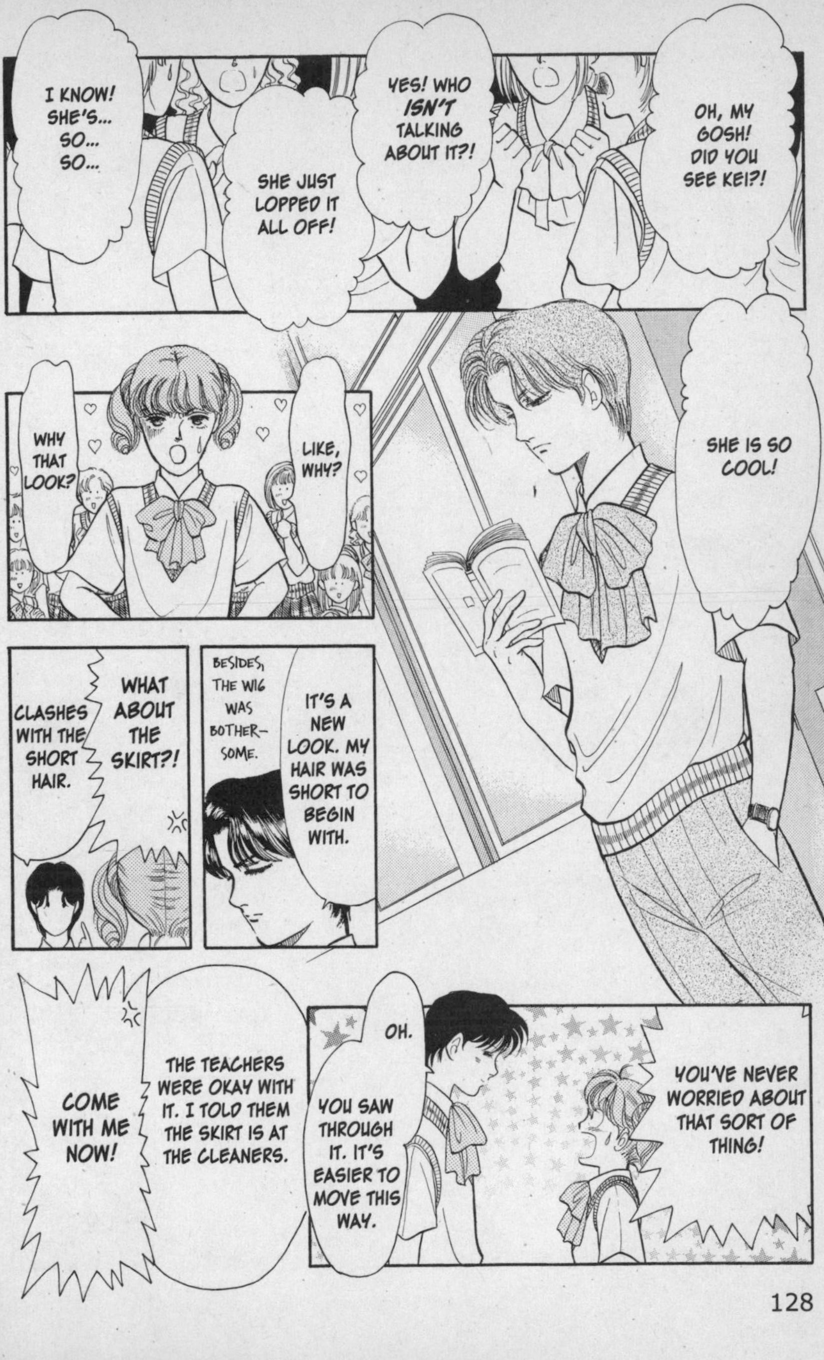
OH, MY GOSH! DID YOU SEE KEI?!
YES! WHO ISN'T TALKING ABOUT IT?!
SHE JUST LOPPED IT ALL OFF!
I KNOW! SHE'S... SO... SO...
SHE IS SO COOL!
LIKE, WHY?
WHY THAT LOOK?
IT'S A NEW LOOK. MY HAIR WAS SHORT TO BEGIN WITH.
BESIDES, THE WIG WAS BOTHER-SOME.
WHAT ABOUT THE SKIRT?!
CLASHES WITH THE SHORT HAIR.
YOU'VE NEVER WORRIED ABOUT THAT SORT OF THING!
OH.
YOU SAW THROUGH IT. IT'S EASIER TO MOVE THIS WAY.
THE TEACHERS WERE OKAY WITH IT. I TOLD THEM THE SKIRT IS AT THE CLEANERS.
COME WITH ME NOW!

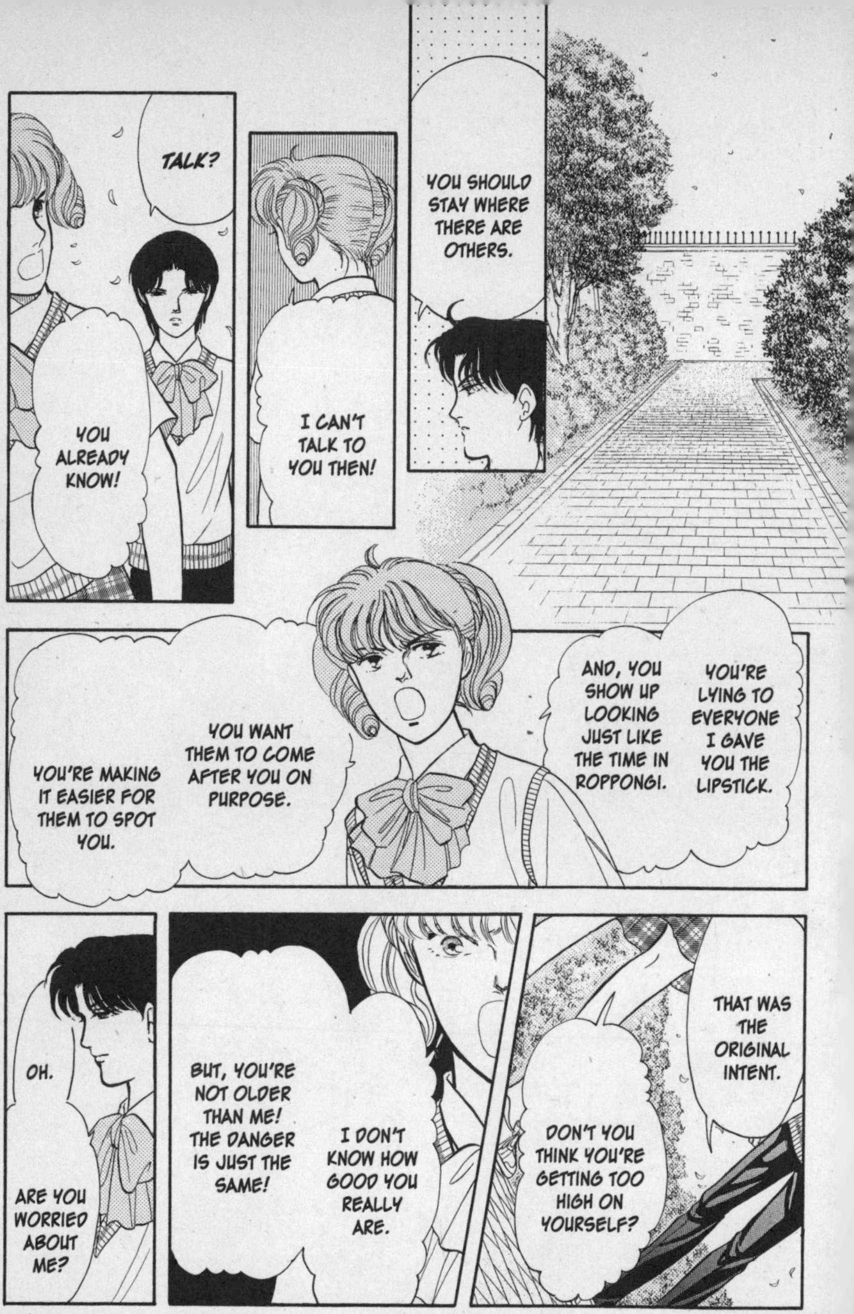
YOU SHOULD STAY WHERE THERE ARE OTHERS.
I CAN'T TALK TO YOU THEN!
TALK?
YOU ALREADY KNOW!
YOU'RE LYING TO EVERYONE I GAVE YOU THE LIPSTICK.
AND, YOU SHOW UP LOOKING JUST LIKE THE TIME IN ROPPONGI.
YOU WANT THEM TO COME AFTER YOU ON PURPOSE.
YOU'RE MAKING IT EASIER FOR THEM TO SPOT YOU.
THAT WAS THE ORIGINAL INTENT.
DON'T YOU THINK YOU'RE GETTING TOO HIGH ON YOURSELF?
I DON'T KNOW HOW GOOD YOU REALLY ARE.
BUT, YOU'RE NOT OLDER THAN ME! THE DANGER IS JUST THE SAME!
OH.
ARE YOU WORRIED ABOUT ME?

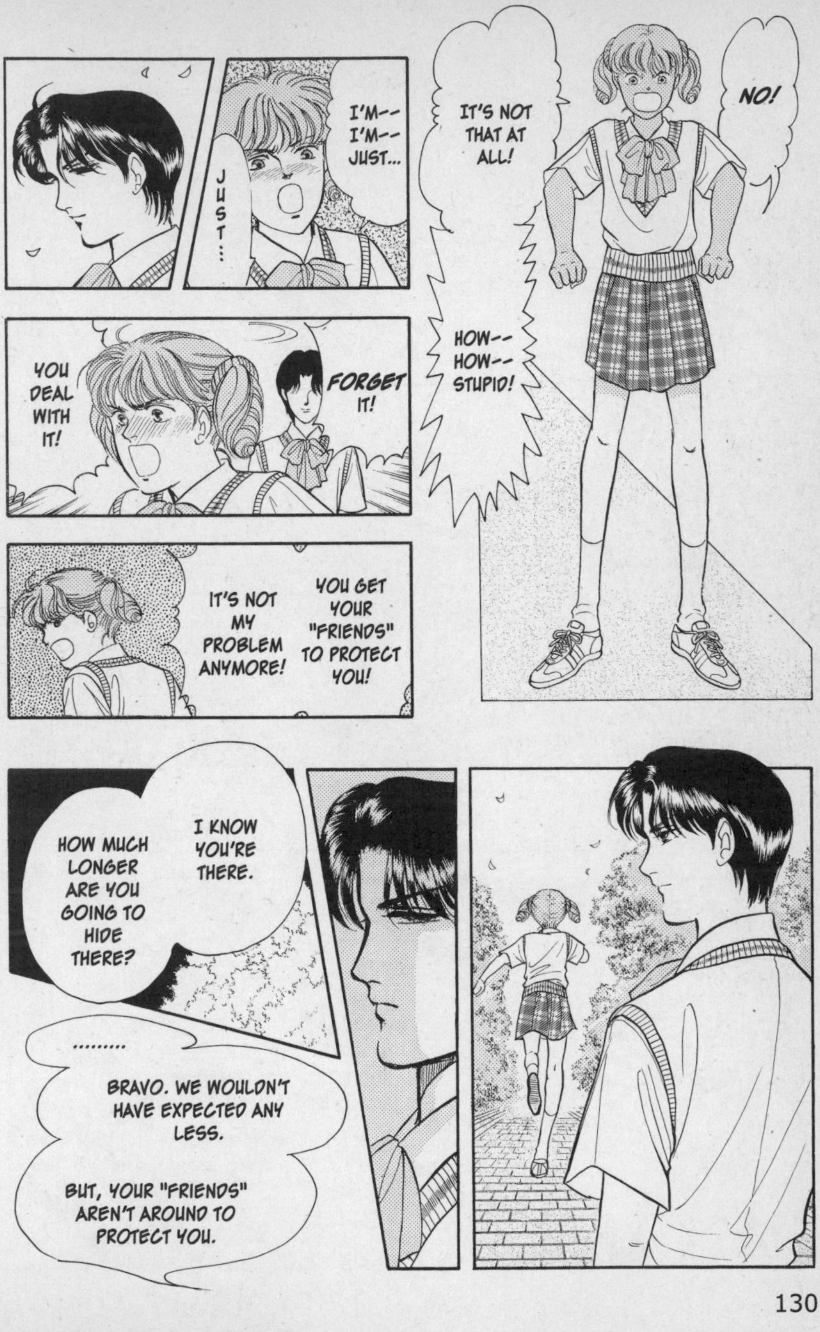
NO!
IT'S NOT THAT AT ALL!
HOW-- HOW-- STUPID!
I'M-- I'M-- JUST...
JUST...
FORGET IT!
YOU DEAL WITH IT!
YOU GET YOUR "FRIENDS" TO PROTECT YOU!
IT'S NOT MY PROBLEM ANYMORE!
I KNOW YOU'RE THERE.
HOW MUCH LONGER ARE YOU GOING TO HIDE THERE?
....
BRAVO. WE WOULDN'T HAVE EXPECTED ANY LESS.
BUT, YOUR "FRIENDS" AREN'T AROUND TO PROTECT YOU.

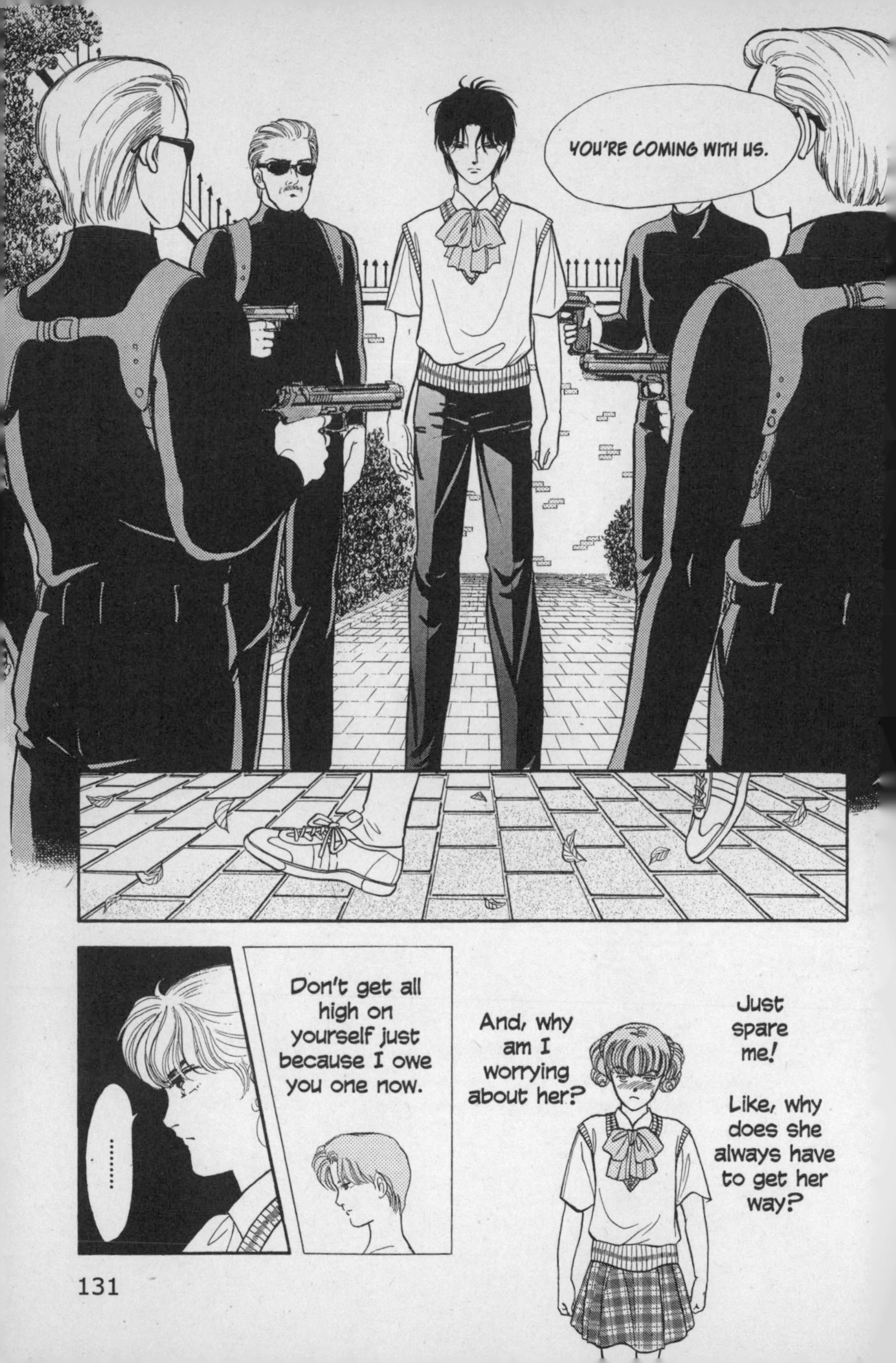
YOU'RE COMING WITH US.
Just spare me!
And, why am I worrying about her?
Like, why does she always have to get her way?
Don't get all high on yourself just because I owe you one now.
……

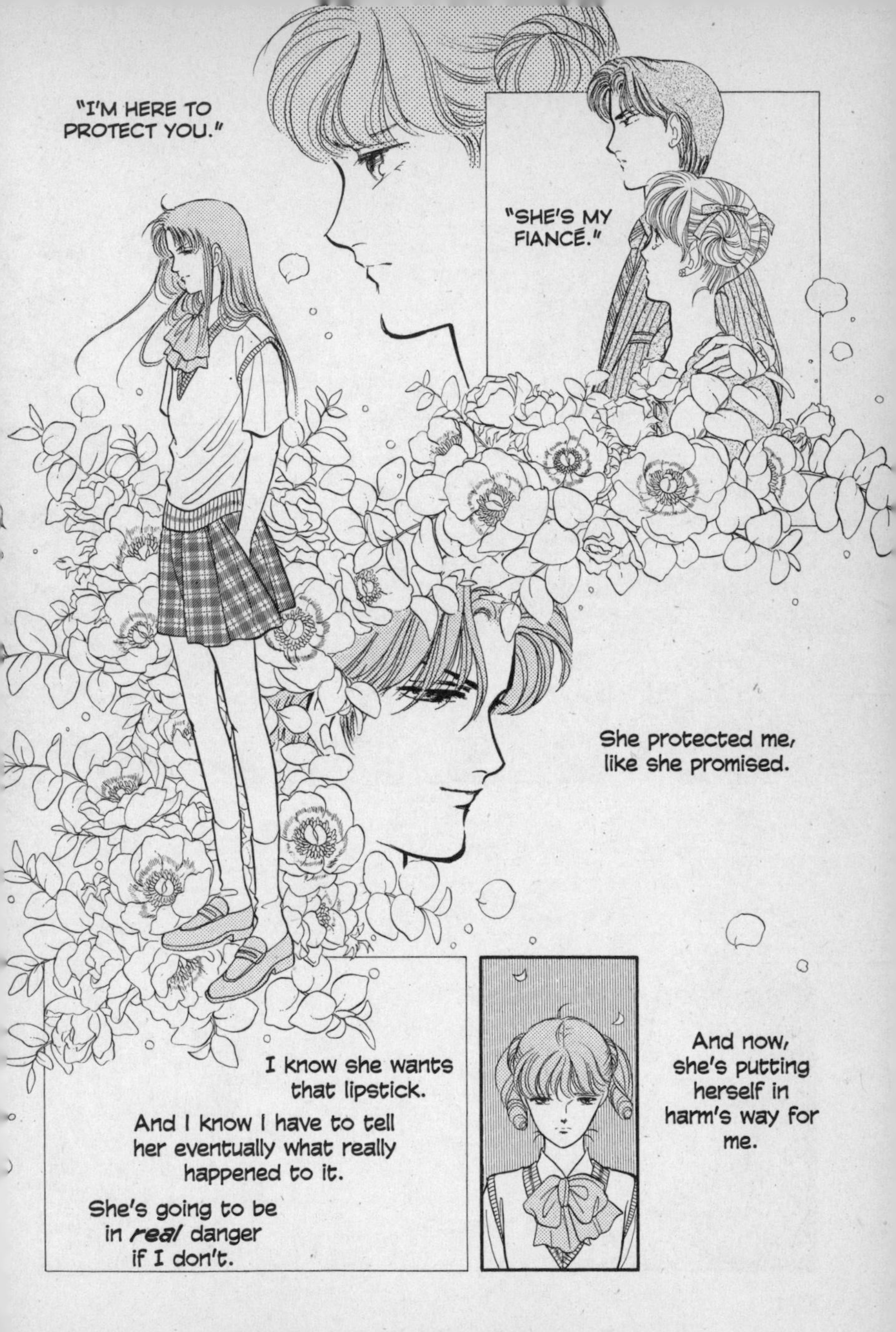
"SHE'S MY FIANCÉ."
"I'M HERE TO PROTECT YOU."
She protected me, like she promised.
And now, she's putting herself in harm's way for me.
I know she wants that lipstick.
And I know I have to tell her eventually what really happened to it.
She's going to be in *real* danger if I don't.

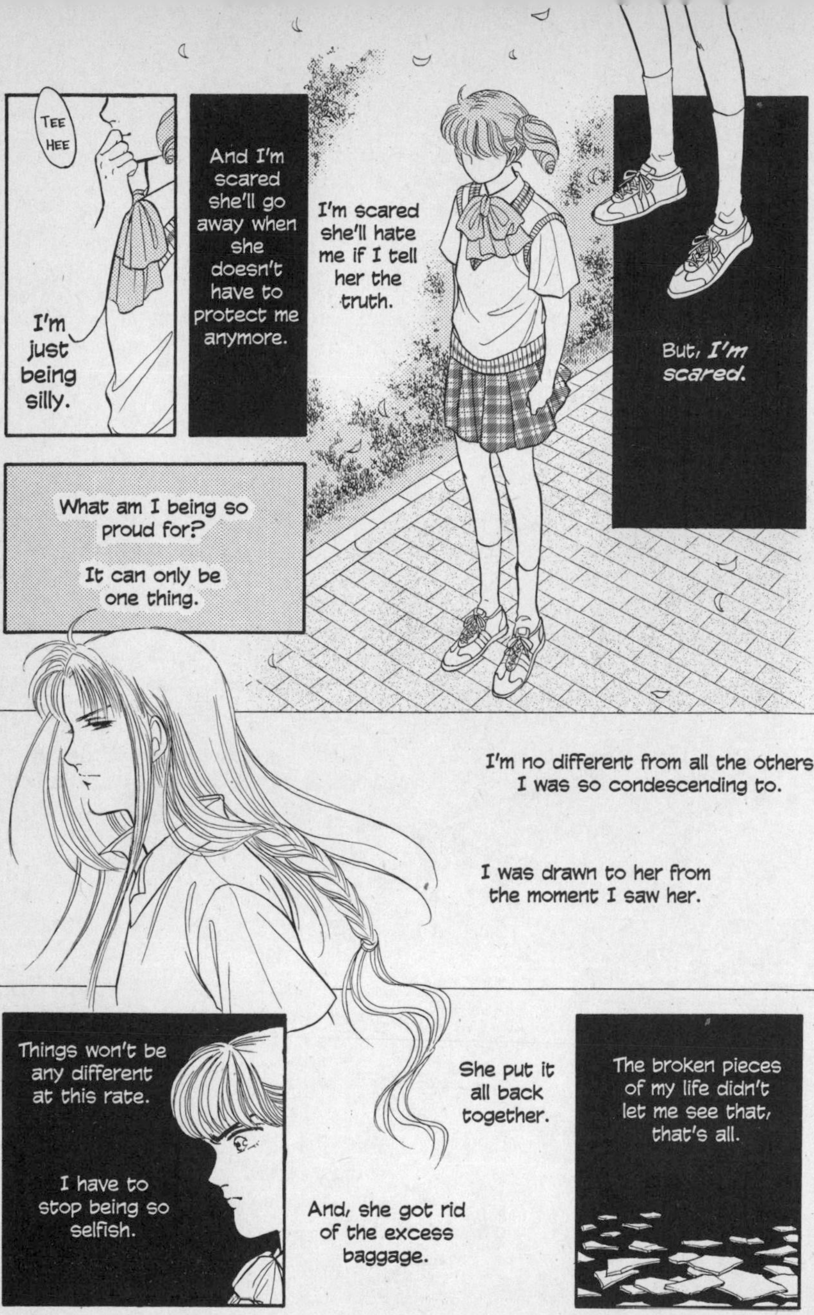
But, *I'm scared.*
I'm scared she'll hate me if I tell her the truth.
And I'm scared she'll go away when she doesn't have to protect me anymore.
TEE HEE
I'm just being silly.
What am I being so proud for?
It can only be one thing.
I'm no different from all the others I was so condescending to.
I was drawn to her from the moment I saw her.
The broken pieces of my life didn't let me see that, that's all.
She put it all back together.
And, she got rid of the excess baggage.
Things won't be any different at this rate.
I have to stop being so selfish.

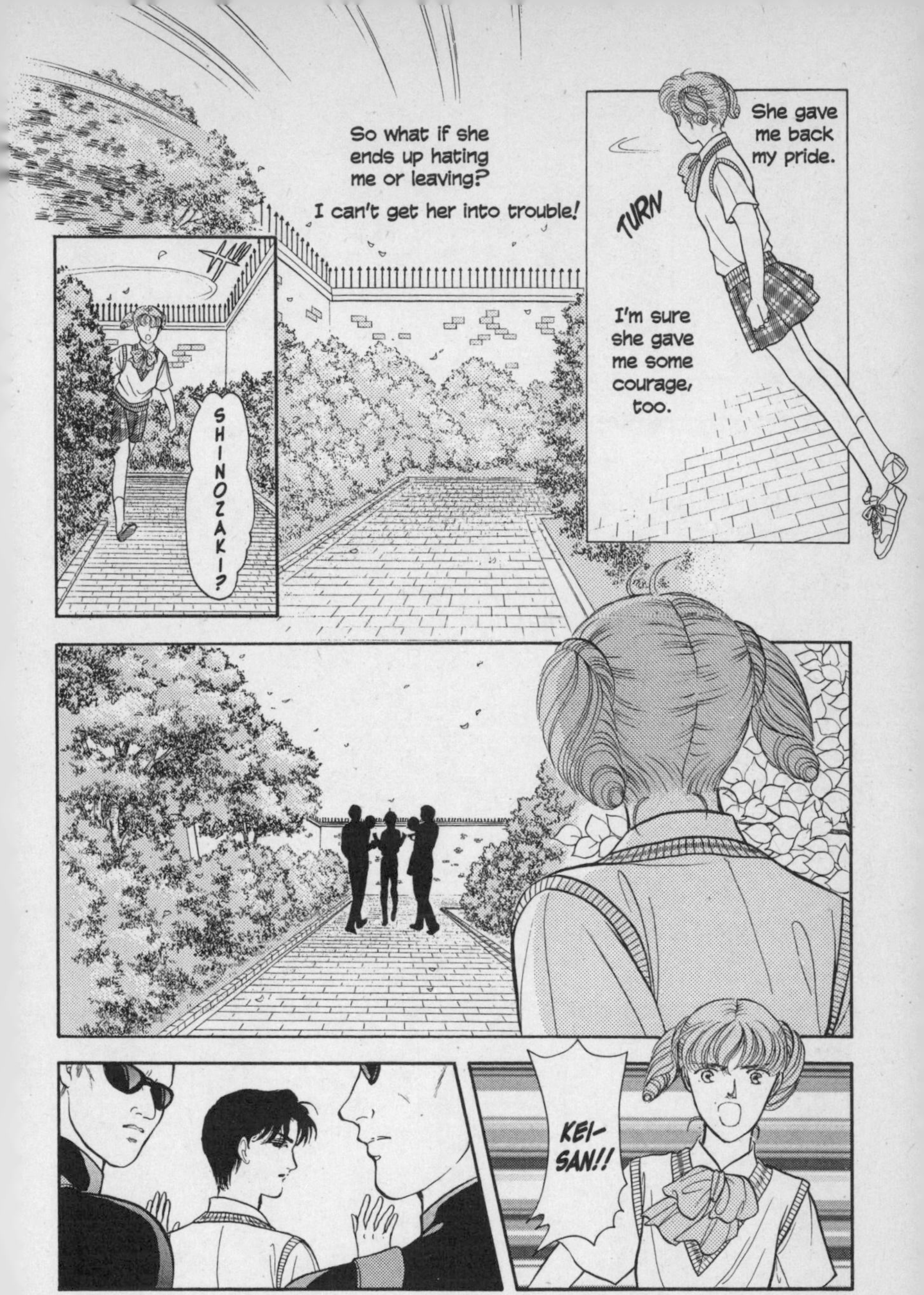
She gave me back my pride.
TURN
I'm sure she gave me some courage, too.
So what if she ends up hating me or leaving?
I can't get her into trouble!
SHINOZAKI?
KEI-SAN!!

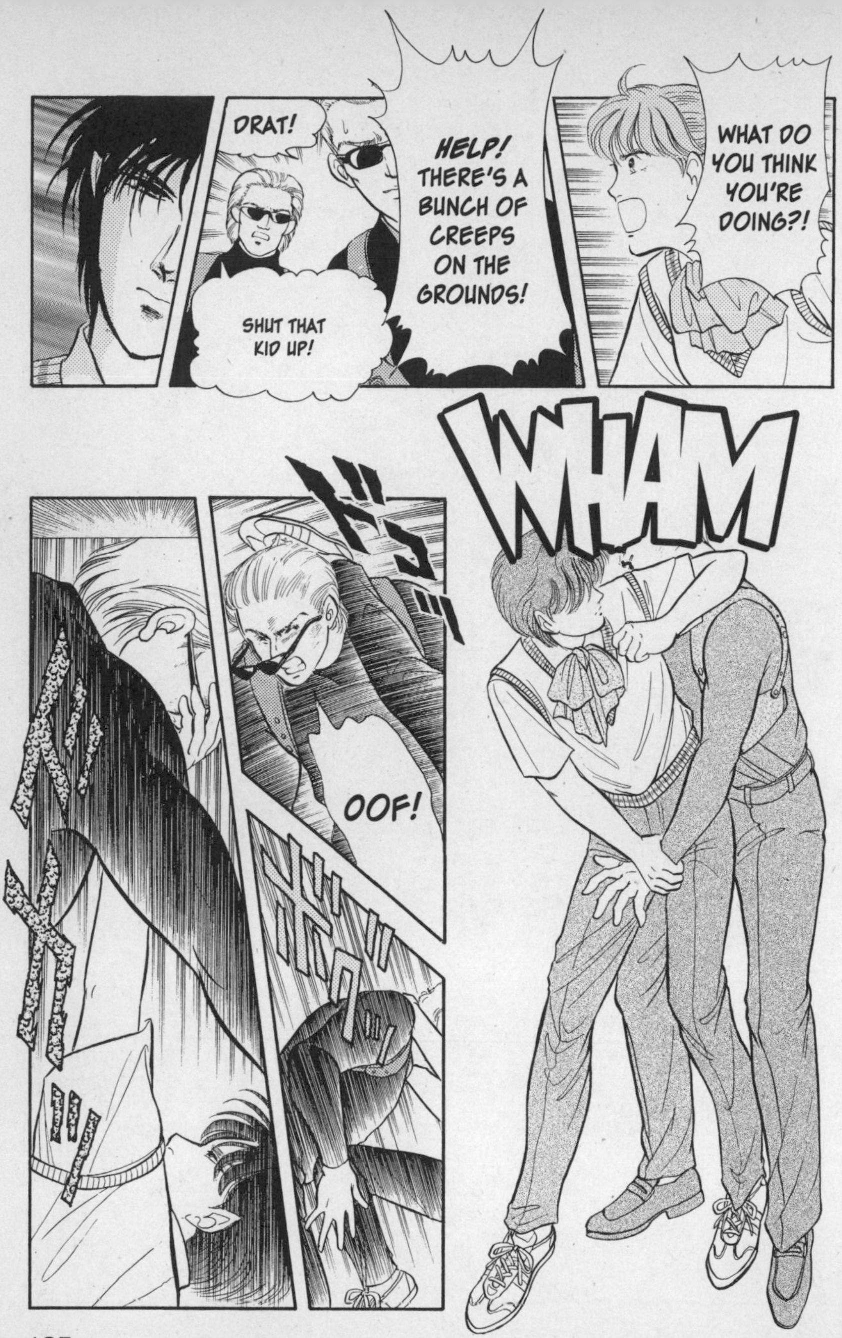
WHAT DO YOU THINK YOU'RE DOING?!
HELP! THERE'S A BUNCH OF CREEPS ON THE GROUNDS!
DRAT!
SHUT THAT KID UP!
WHAM
OOF!

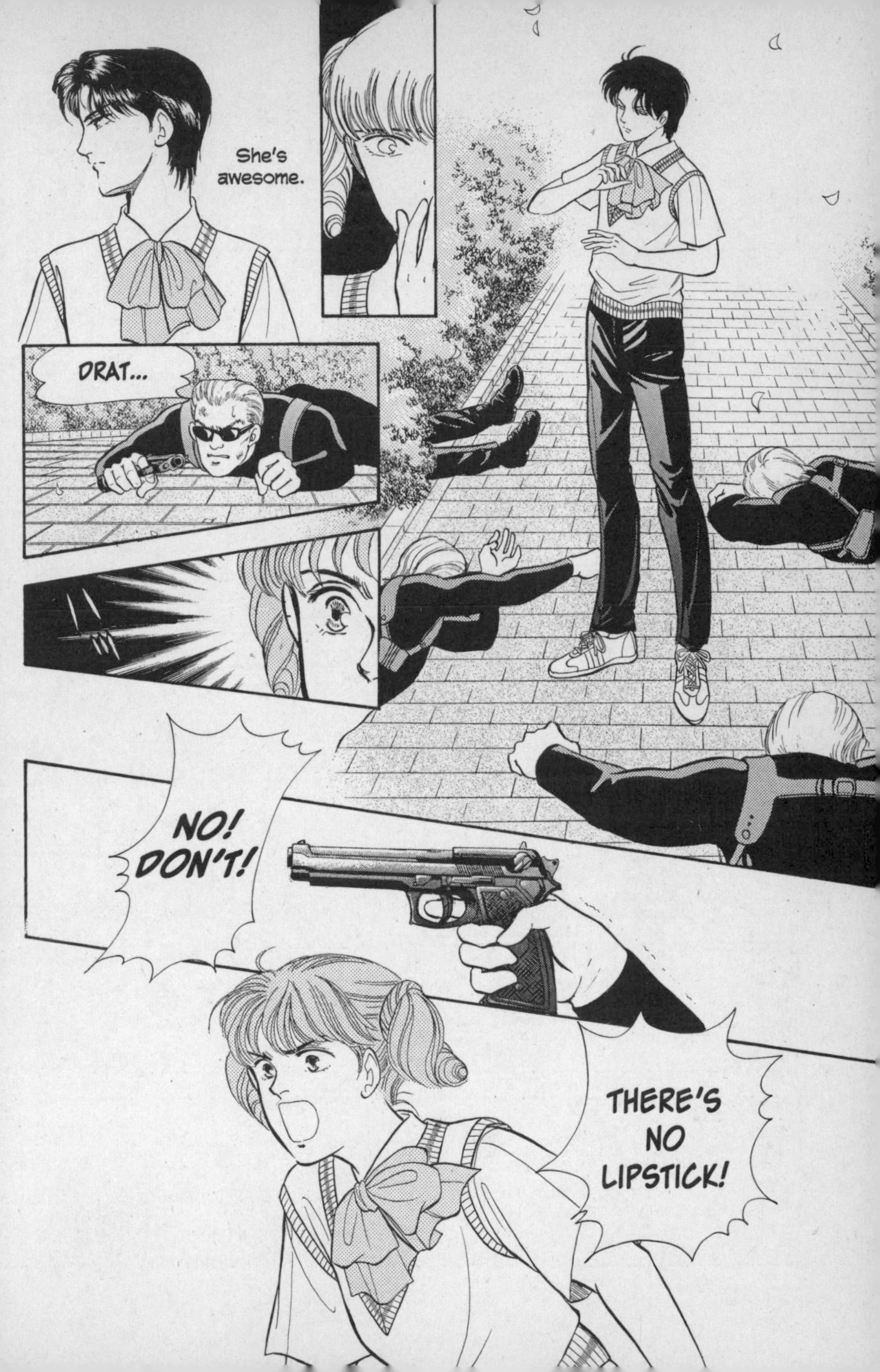
She's awesome.
DRAT...
NO! DON'T!
THERE'S NO LIPSTICK!

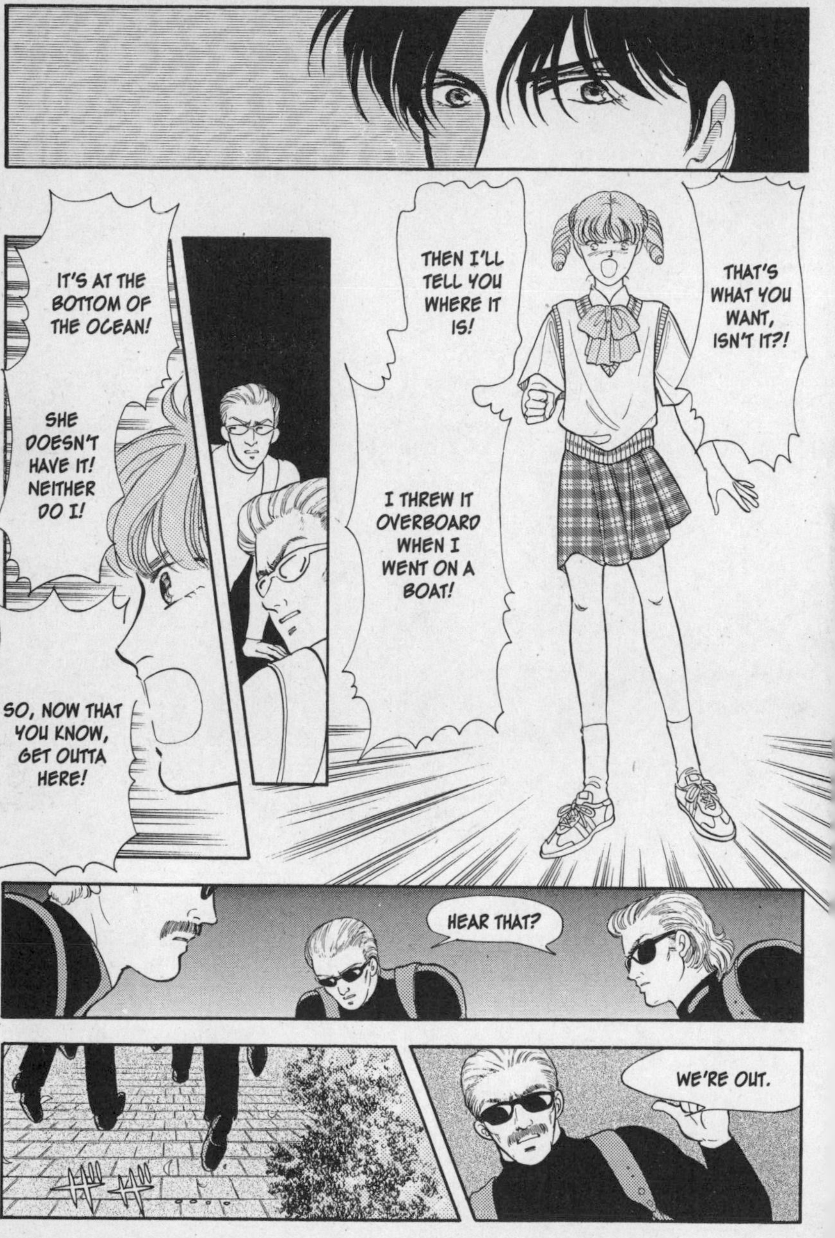
THAT'S WHAT YOU WANT, ISN'T IT?!
THEN I'LL TELL YOU WHERE IT IS!
I THREW IT OVERBOARD WHEN I WENT ON A BOAT!
IT'S AT THE BOTTOM OF THE OCEAN!
SHE DOESN'T HAVE IT! NEITHER DO I!
SO, NOW THAT YOU KNOW, GET OUTTA HERE!
HEAR THAT?
WE'RE OUT.

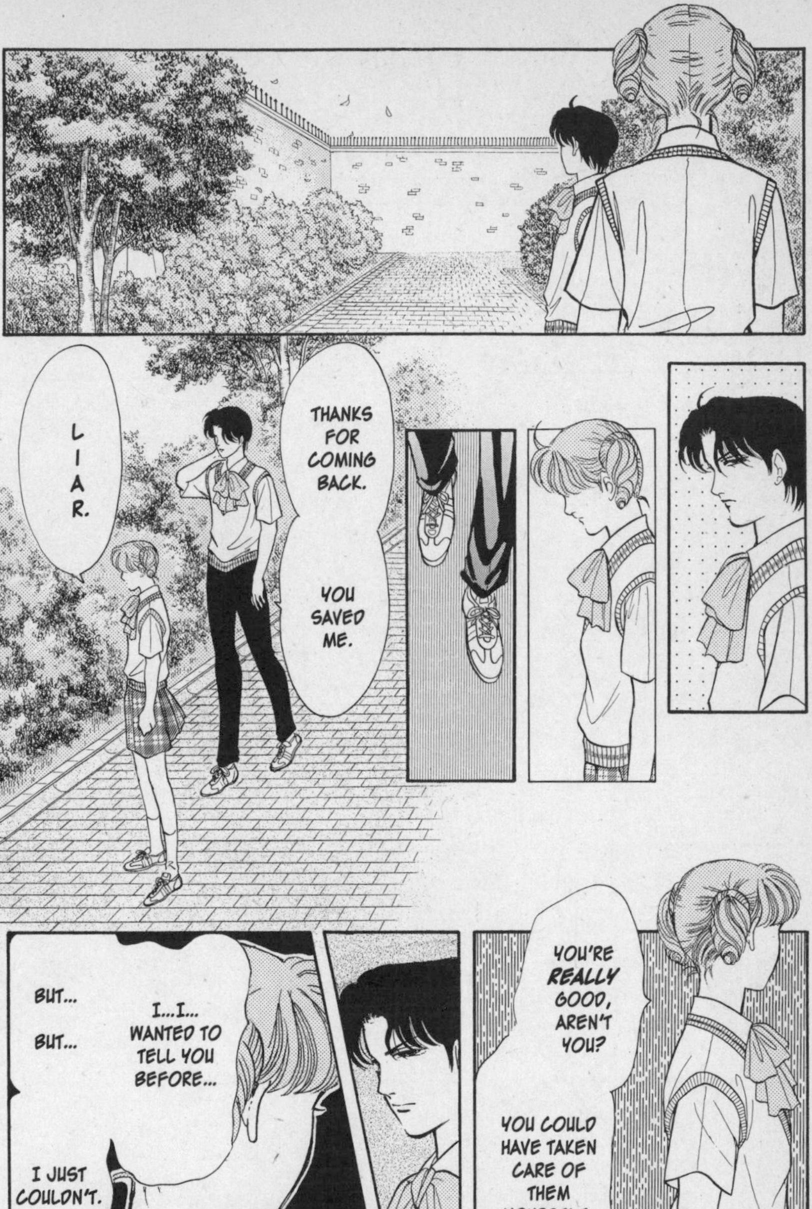
THANKS FOR COMING BACK.
YOU SAVED ME.
LIAR.
YOU'RE *REALLY* GOOD, AREN'T YOU?
YOU COULD HAVE TAKEN CARE OF THEM YOURSELF.
I...I... WANTED TO TELL YOU BEFORE...
BUT...
BUT...
I JUST COULDN'T.

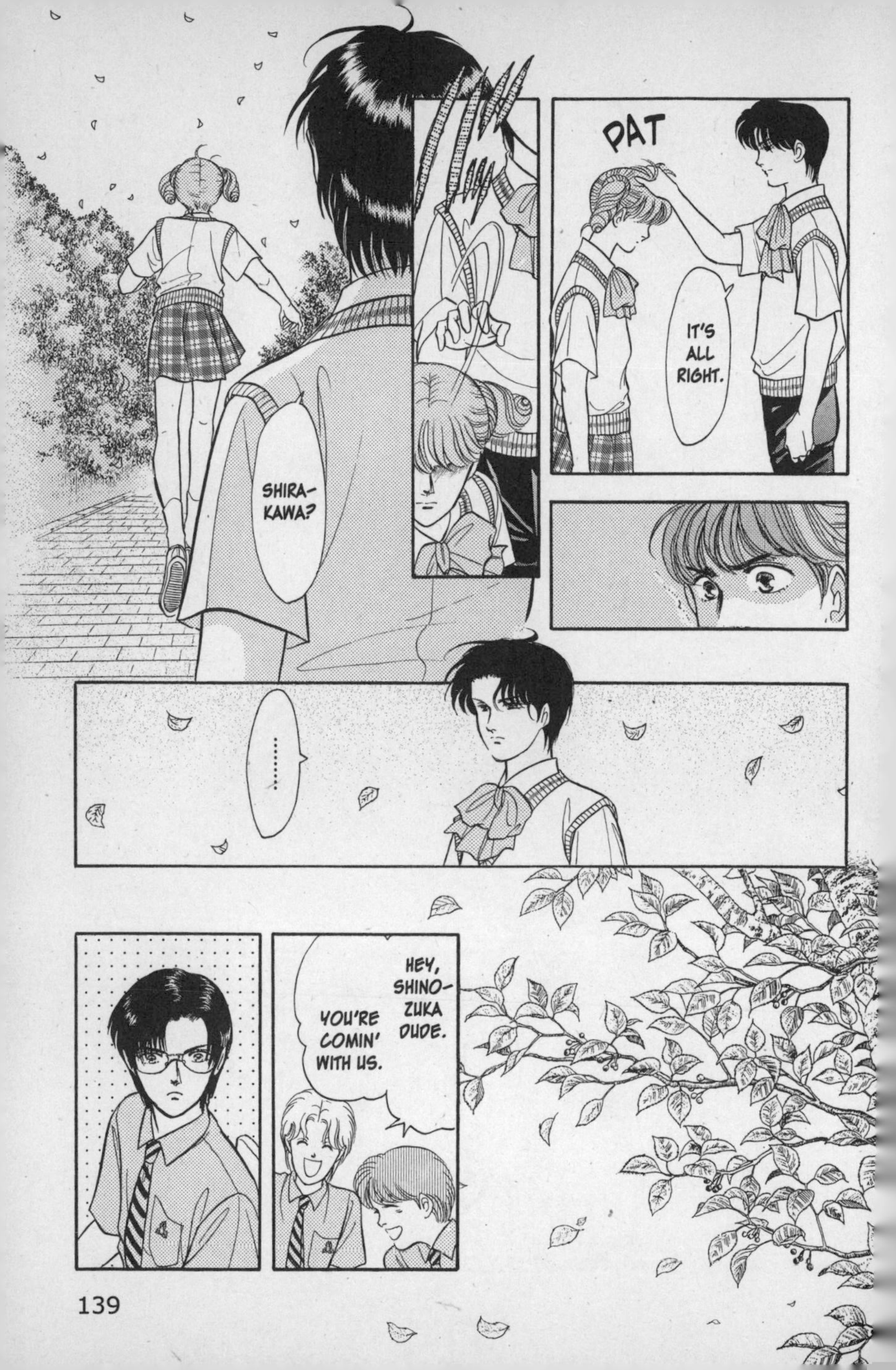
PAT
IT'S ALL RIGHT.
SHIRA-KAWA?
......
HEY, SHINO-ZUKA DUDE.
YOU'RE COMIN' WITH US.

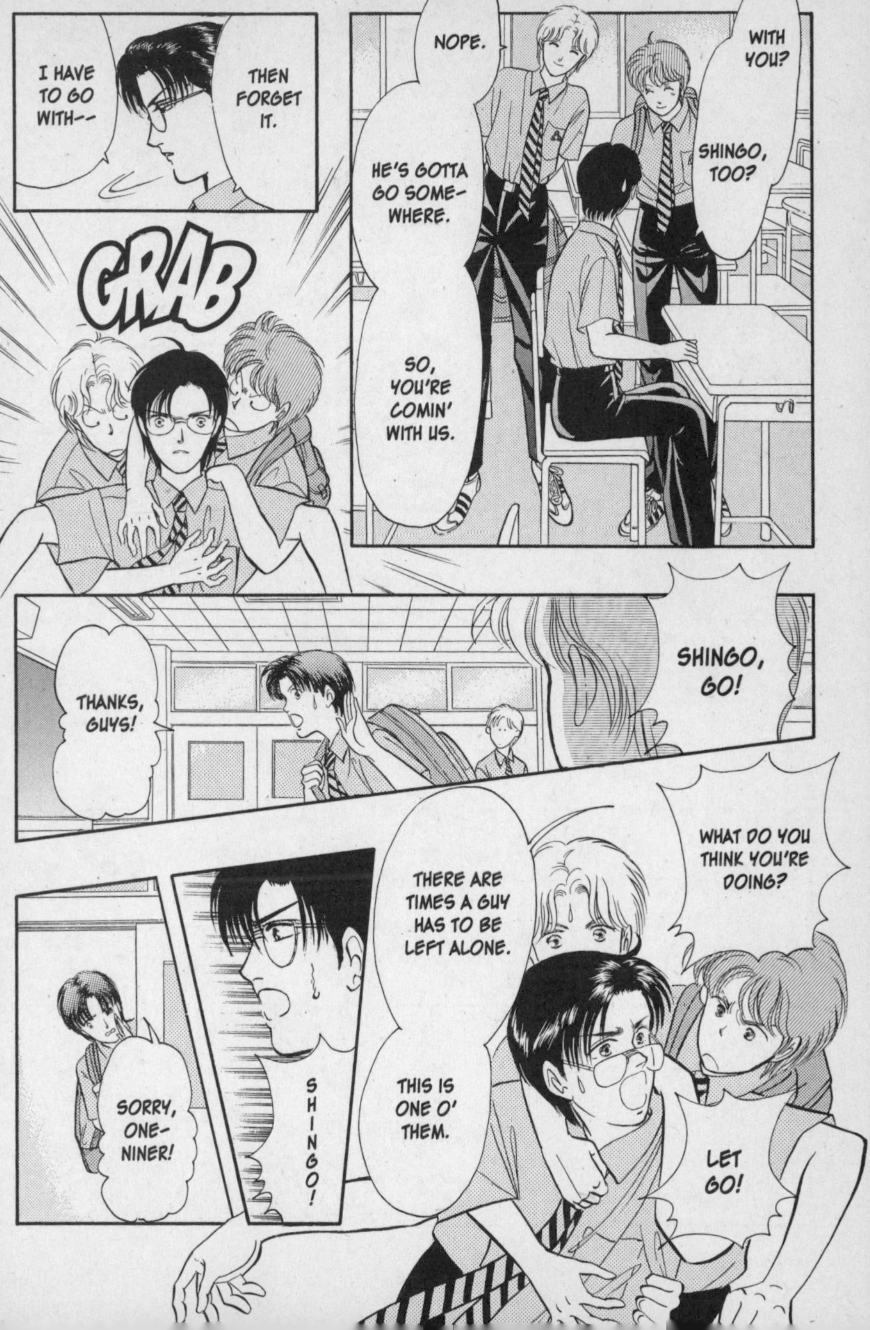
WITH YOU?
SHINGO, TOO?
NOPE.
HE'S GOTTA GO SOME-WHERE.
SO, YOU'RE COMIN' WITH US.
THEN FORGET IT.
I HAVE TO GO WITH--
GRAB
SHINGO, GO!
THANKS, GUYS!
WHAT DO YOU THINK YOU'RE DOING?
THERE ARE TIMES A GUY HAS TO BE LEFT ALONE.
THIS IS ONE O' THEM.
LET GO!
SHINGO!
SORRY, ONE-NINER!

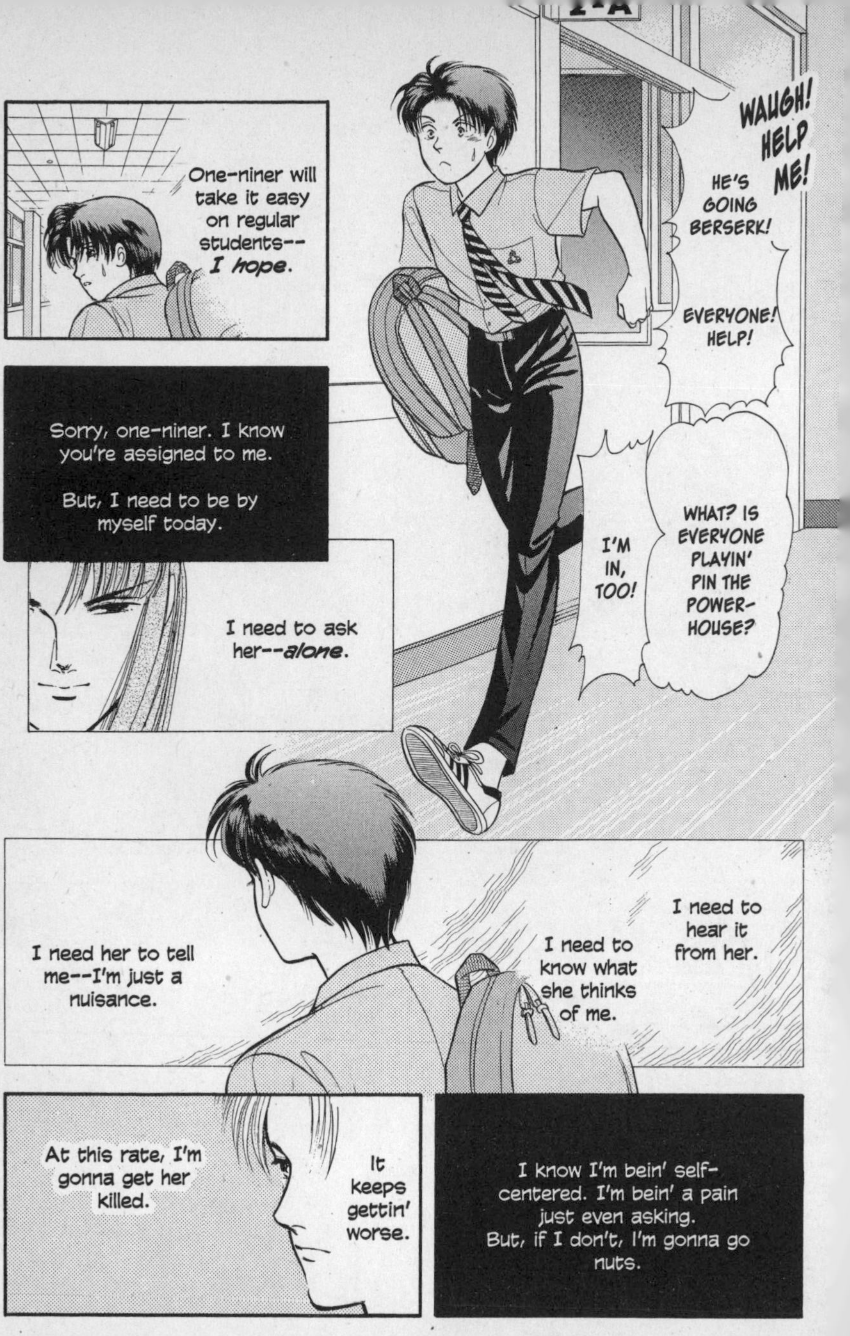
WAUGH! HELP ME!
HE'S GOING BERSERK!
EVERYONE! HELP!
WHAT? IS EVERYONE PLAYIN' PIN THE POWER-HOUSE?
I'M IN, TOO!
One-niner will take it easy on regular students-- *I hope*.
Sorry, one-niner. I know you're assigned to me.
But, I need to be by myself today.
I need to ask her--*alone*.
I need to hear it from her.
I need to know what she thinks of me.
I need her to tell me--I'm just a nuisance.
I know I'm bein' self-centered. I'm bein' a pain just even asking.
But, if I don't, I'm gonna go nuts.
It keeps gettin' worse.
At this rate, I'm gonna get her killed.

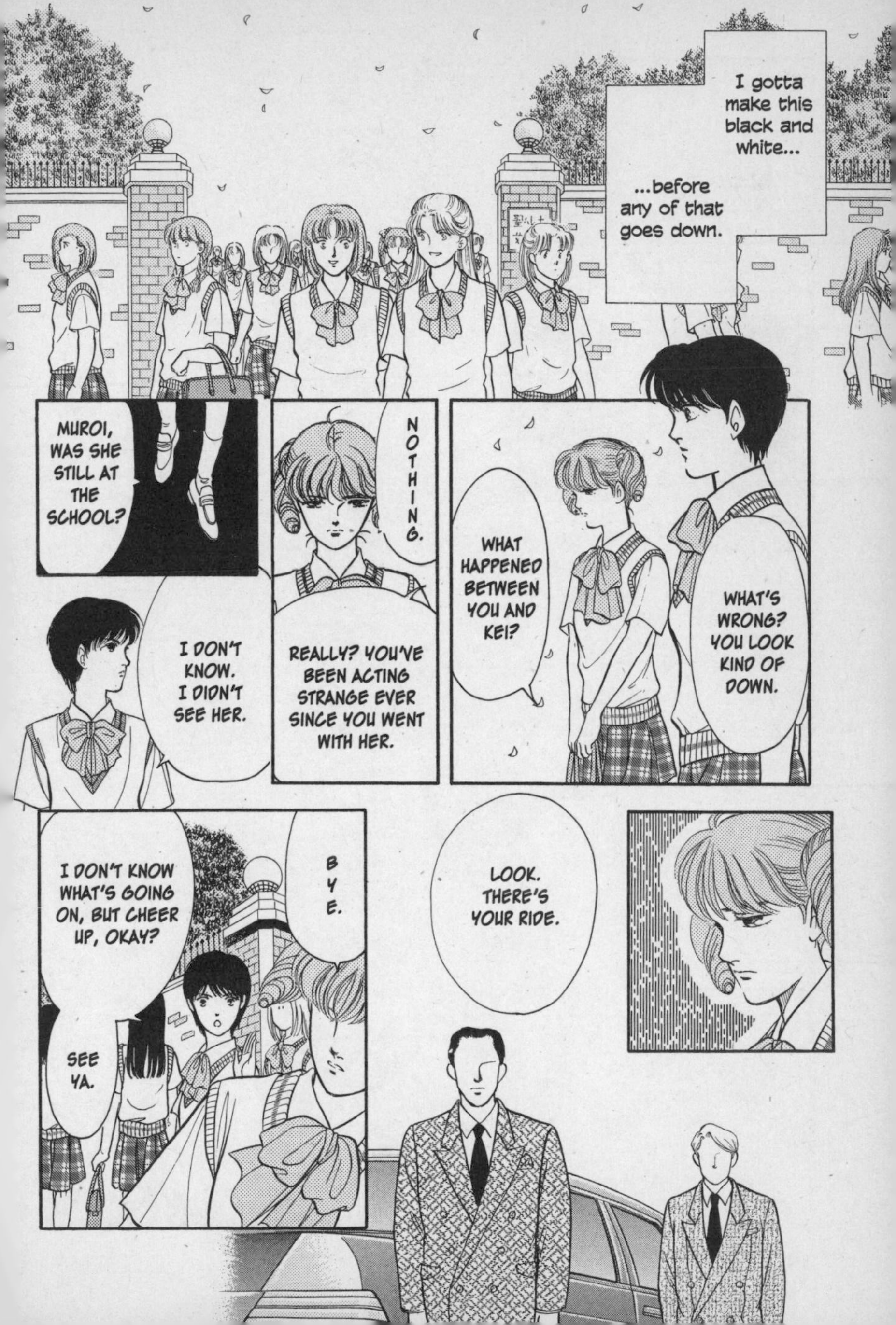
I gotta make this black and white...
...before any of that goes down.
WHAT'S WRONG? YOU LOOK KIND OF DOWN.
WHAT HAPPENED BETWEEN YOU AND KEI?
NOTHING.
REALLY? YOU'VE BEEN ACTING STRANGE EVER SINCE YOU WENT WITH HER.
MUROI, WAS SHE STILL AT THE SCHOOL?
I DON'T KNOW. I DIDN'T SEE HER.
LOOK. THERE'S YOUR RIDE.
BYE.
I DON'T KNOW WHAT'S GOING ON, BUT CHEER UP, OKAY?
SEE YA.

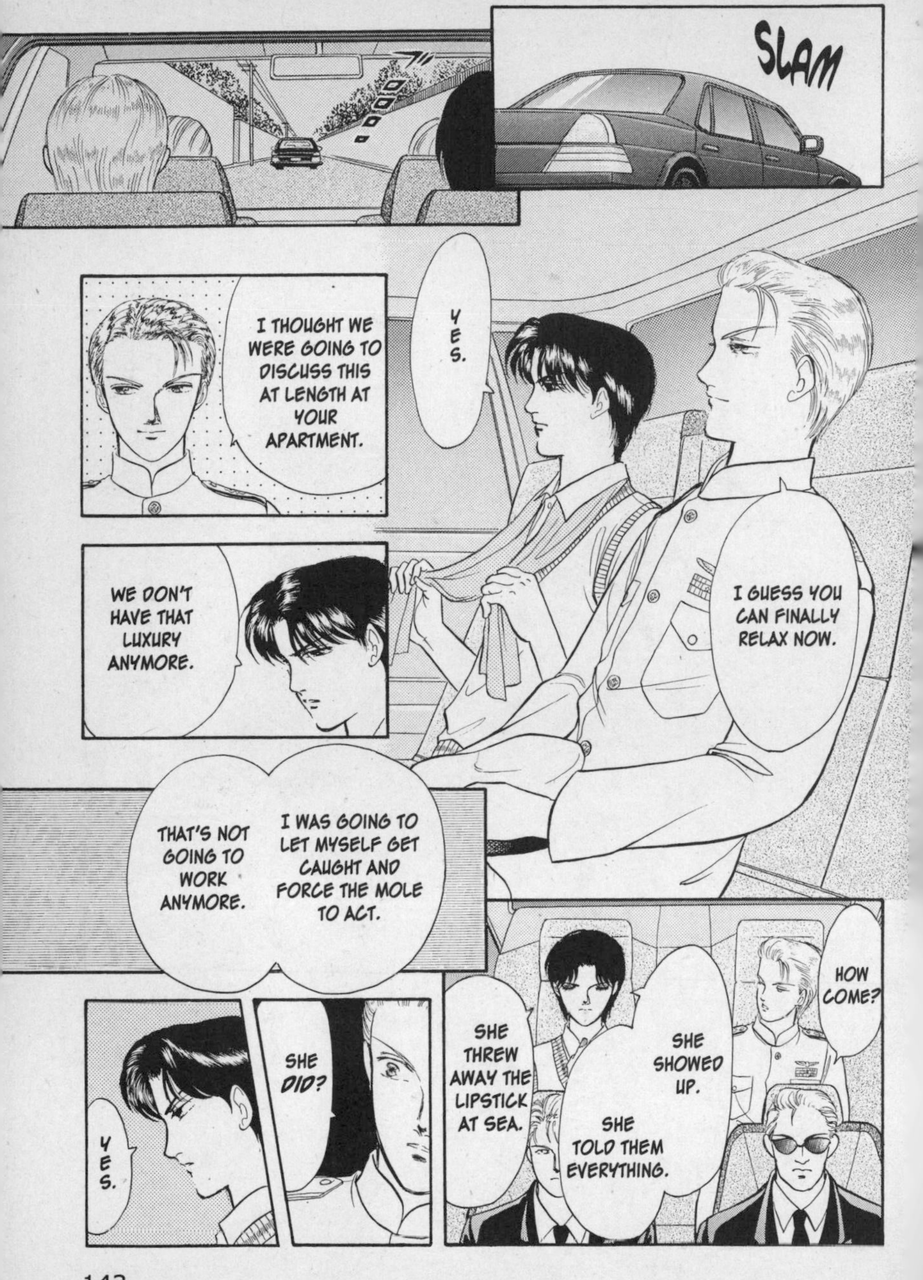
SLAM
I GUESS YOU CAN FINALLY RELAX NOW.
YES.
I THOUGHT WE WERE GOING TO DISCUSS THIS AT LENGTH AT YOUR APARTMENT.
WE DON'T HAVE THAT LUXURY ANYMORE.
I WAS GOING TO LET MYSELF GET CAUGHT AND FORCE THE MOLE TO ACT.
THAT'S NOT GOING TO WORK ANYMORE.
HOW COME?
SHE SHOWED UP.
SHE TOLD THEM EVERYTHING.
SHE THREW AWAY THE LIPSTICK AT SEA.
SHE DID?
YES.

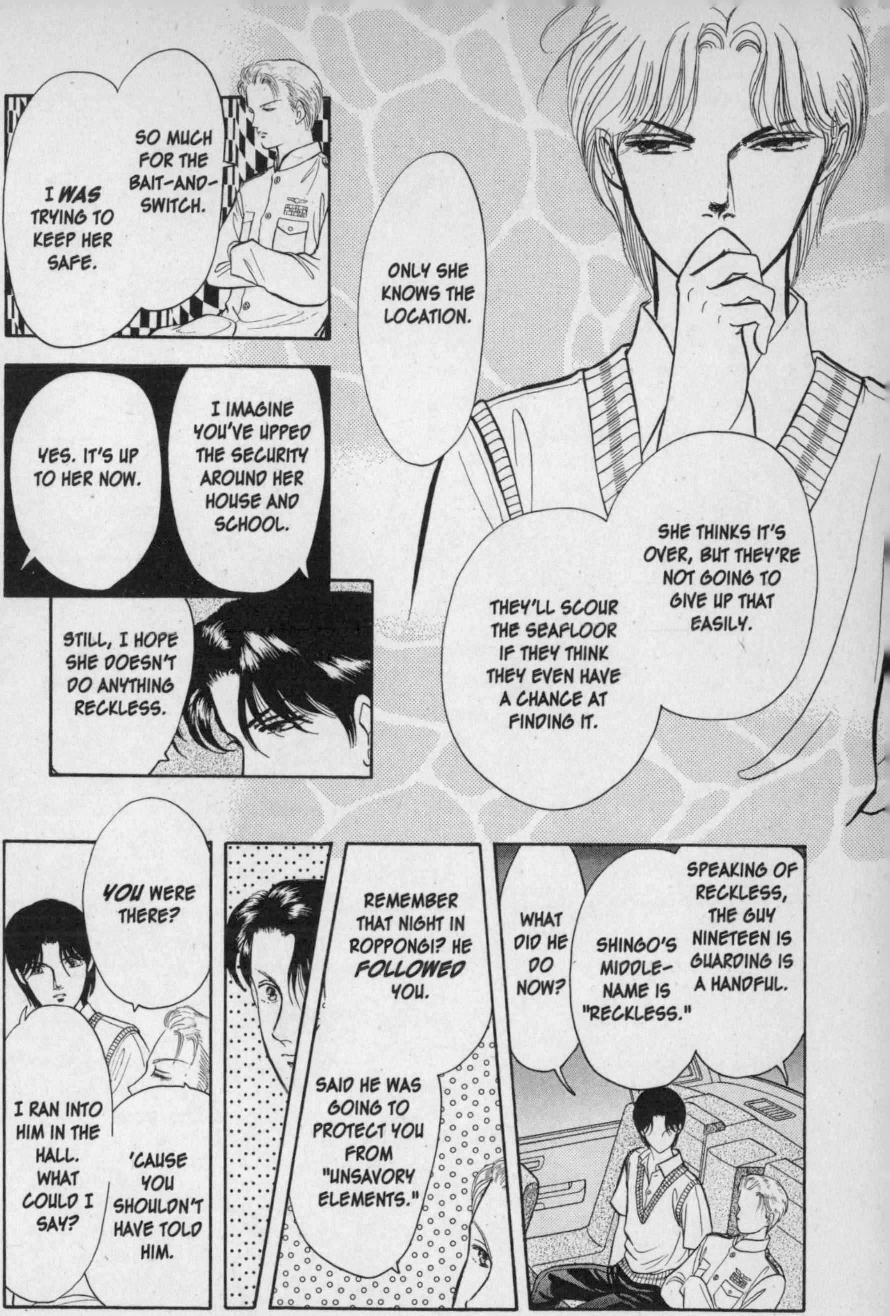
ONLY SHE KNOWS THE LOCATION.
SHE THINKS IT'S OVER, BUT THEY'RE NOT GOING TO GIVE UP THAT EASILY.
THEY'LL SCOUR THE SEAFLOOR IF THEY THINK THEY EVEN HAVE A CHANCE AT FINDING IT.
SO MUCH FOR THE BAIT-AND-SWITCH.
I *WAS* TRYING TO KEEP HER SAFE.
I IMAGINE YOU'VE UPPED THE SECURITY AROUND HER HOUSE AND SCHOOL.
YES. IT'S UP TO HER NOW.
STILL, I HOPE SHE DOESN'T DO ANYTHING RECKLESS.
SPEAKING OF RECKLESS, THE GUY NINETEEN IS GUARDING IS A HANDFUL.
SHINGO'S MIDDLE-NAME IS "RECKLESS."
WHAT DID HE DO NOW?
REMEMBER THAT NIGHT IN ROPPONGI? HE *FOLLOWED* YOU.
SAID HE WAS GOING TO PROTECT YOU FROM "UNSAVORY ELEMENTS."
YOU WERE THERE?
'CAUSE YOU SHOULDN'T HAVE TOLD HIM.
I RAN INTO HIM IN THE HALL. WHAT COULD I SAY?

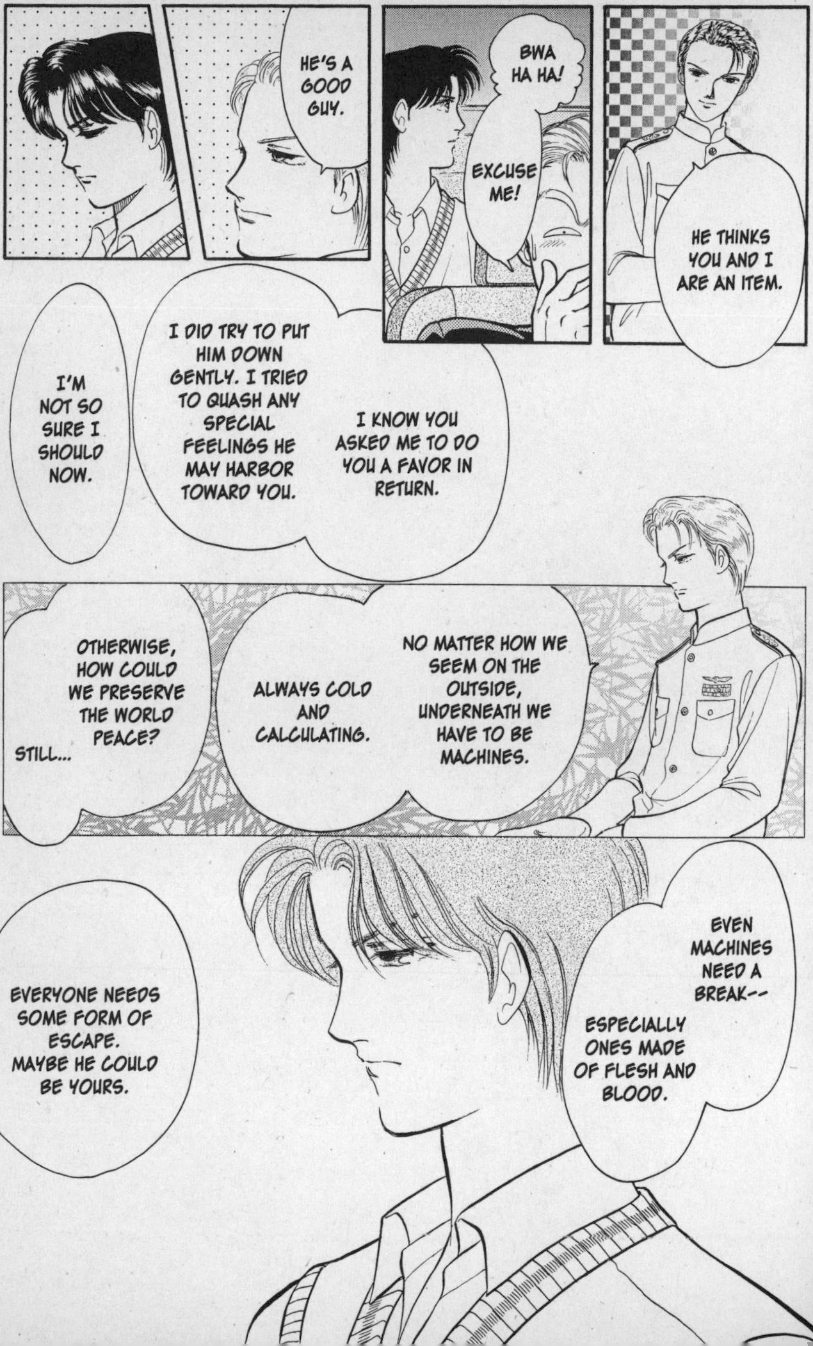

HE THINKS YOU AND I ARE AN ITEM.
BWA HA HA!
EXCUSE ME!
HE'S A GOOD GUY.
I KNOW YOU ASKED ME TO DO YOU A FAVOR IN RETURN.
I DID TRY TO PUT HIM DOWN GENTLY. I TRIED TO QUASH ANY SPECIAL FEELINGS HE MAY HARBOR TOWARD YOU.
I'M NOT SO SURE I SHOULD NOW.
NO MATTER HOW WE SEEM ON THE OUTSIDE, UNDERNEATH WE HAVE TO BE MACHINES.
ALWAYS COLD AND CALCULATING.
OTHERWISE, HOW COULD WE PRESERVE THE WORLD PEACE?
STILL...
EVEN MACHINES NEED A BREAK--
ESPECIALLY ONES MADE OF FLESH AND BLOOD.
EVERYONE NEEDS SOME FORM OF ESCAPE. MAYBE HE COULD BE YOURS.

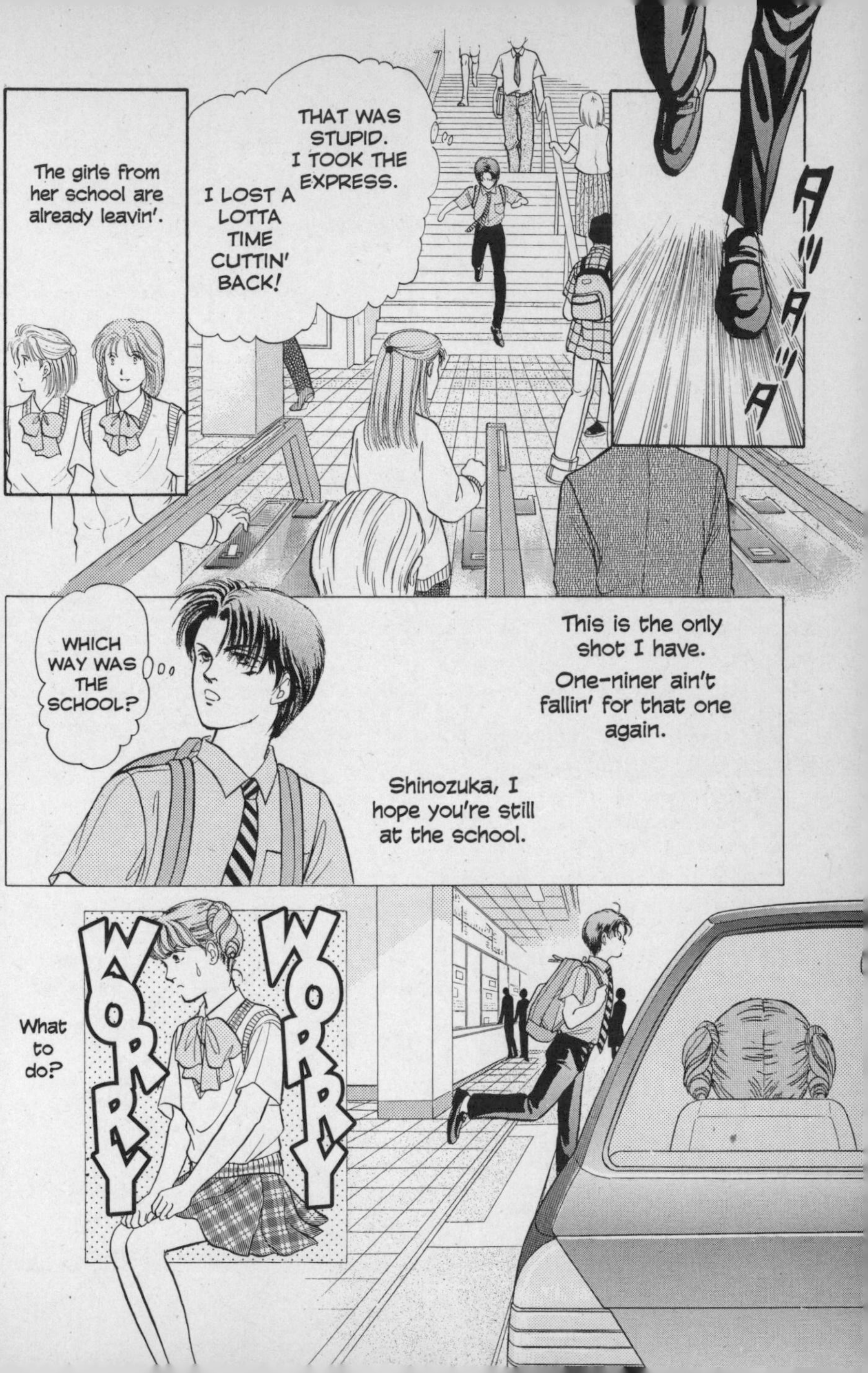
THAT WAS STUPID. I TOOK THE EXPRESS.
I LOST A LOTTA TIME CUTTIN' BACK!
The girls from her school are already leavin'.
This is the only shot I have.
One-niner ain't fallin' for that one again.
Shinozuka, I hope you're still at the school.
WHICH WAY WAS THE SCHOOL?
WORRY
WORRY
What to do?

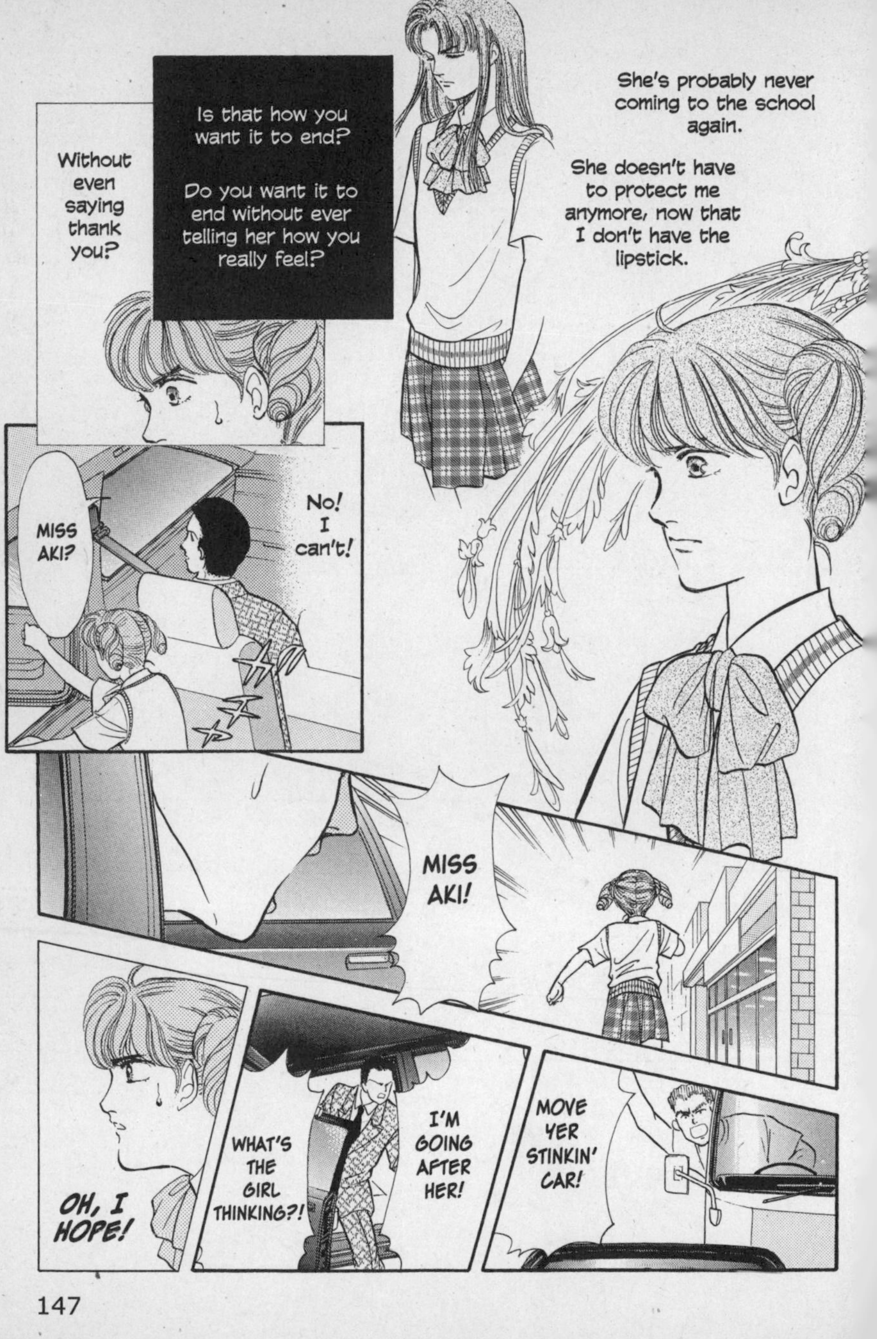
She's probably never coming to the school again.
She doesn't have to protect me anymore, now that I don't have the lipstick.
Is that how you want it to end?
Do you want it to end without ever telling her how you really feel?
Without even saying thank you?
No! I can't!
MISS AKI?
MISS AKI!
MOVE YER STINKIN' CAR!
I'M GOING AFTER HER!
WHAT'S THE GIRL THINKING?!
OH, I HOPE!

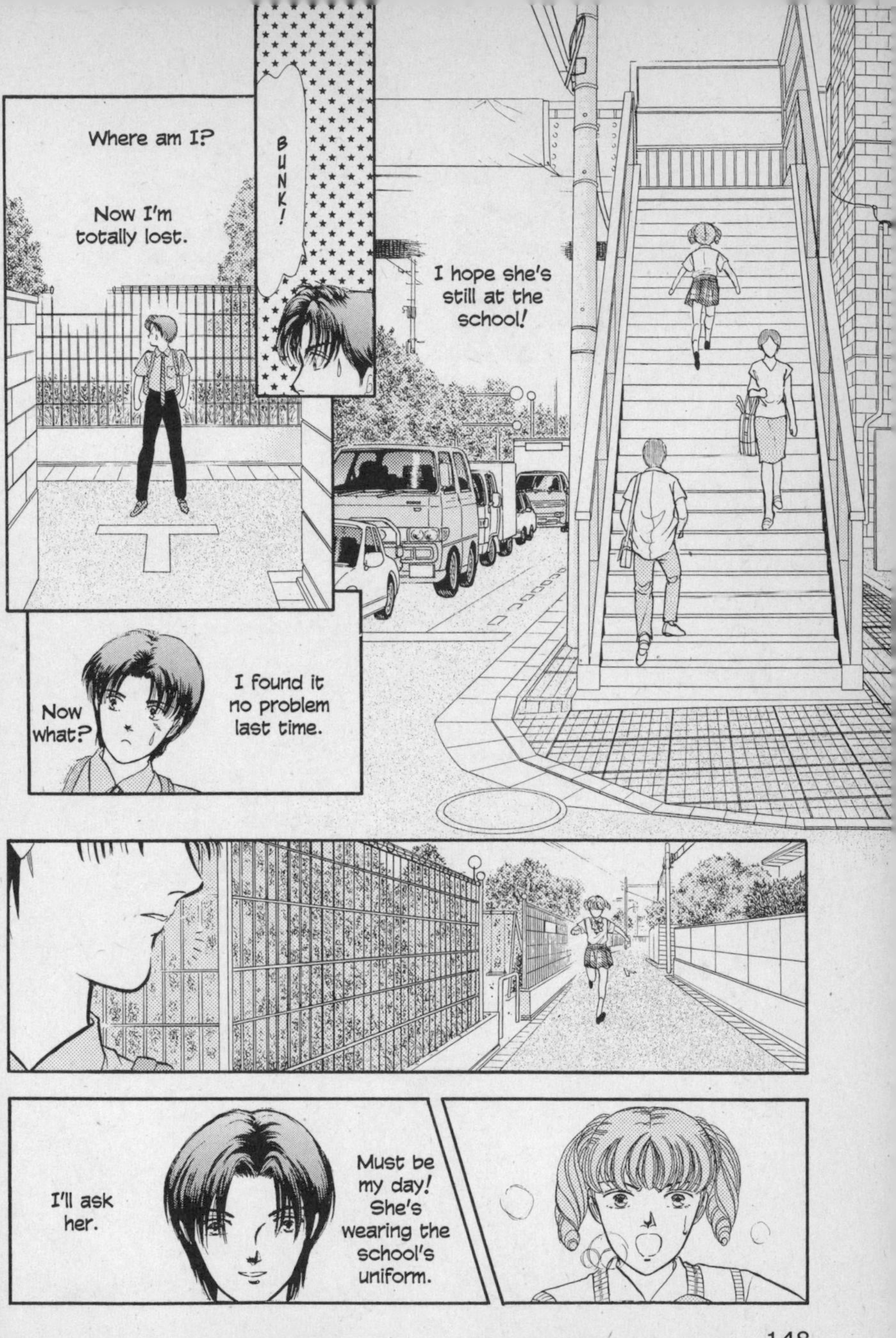
I hope she's still at the school!
BUNK!
Where am I?
Now I'm totally lost.
I found it no problem last time.
Now what?
Must be my day! She's wearing the school's uniform.
I'll ask her.

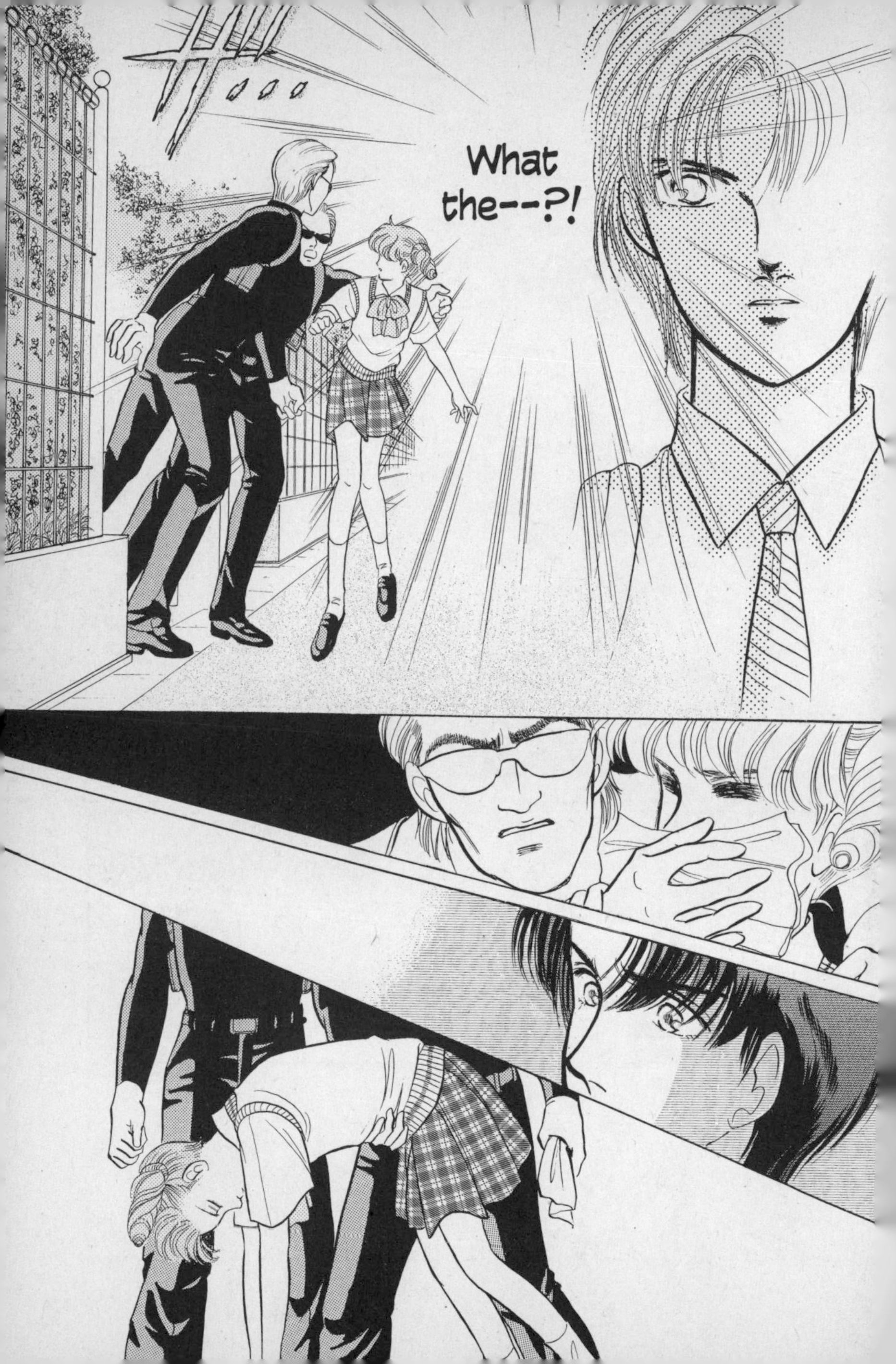
What the--?!

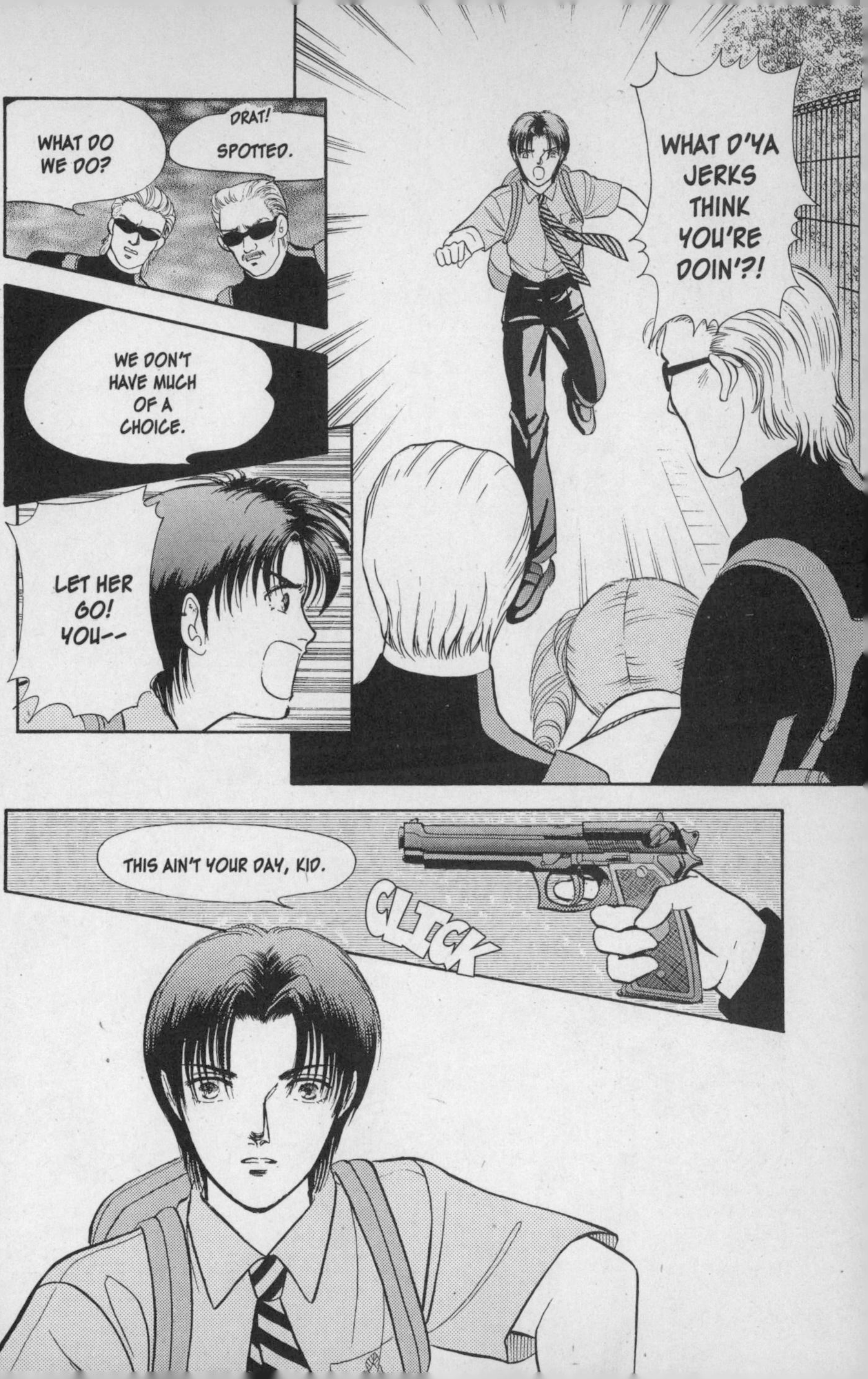
WHAT D'YA JERKS THINK YOU'RE DOIN'?!
DRAT! SPOTTED.
WHAT DO WE DO?
WE DON'T HAVE MUCH OF A CHOICE.
LET HER GO! YOU--
THIS AIN'T YOUR DAY, KID.
CLICK

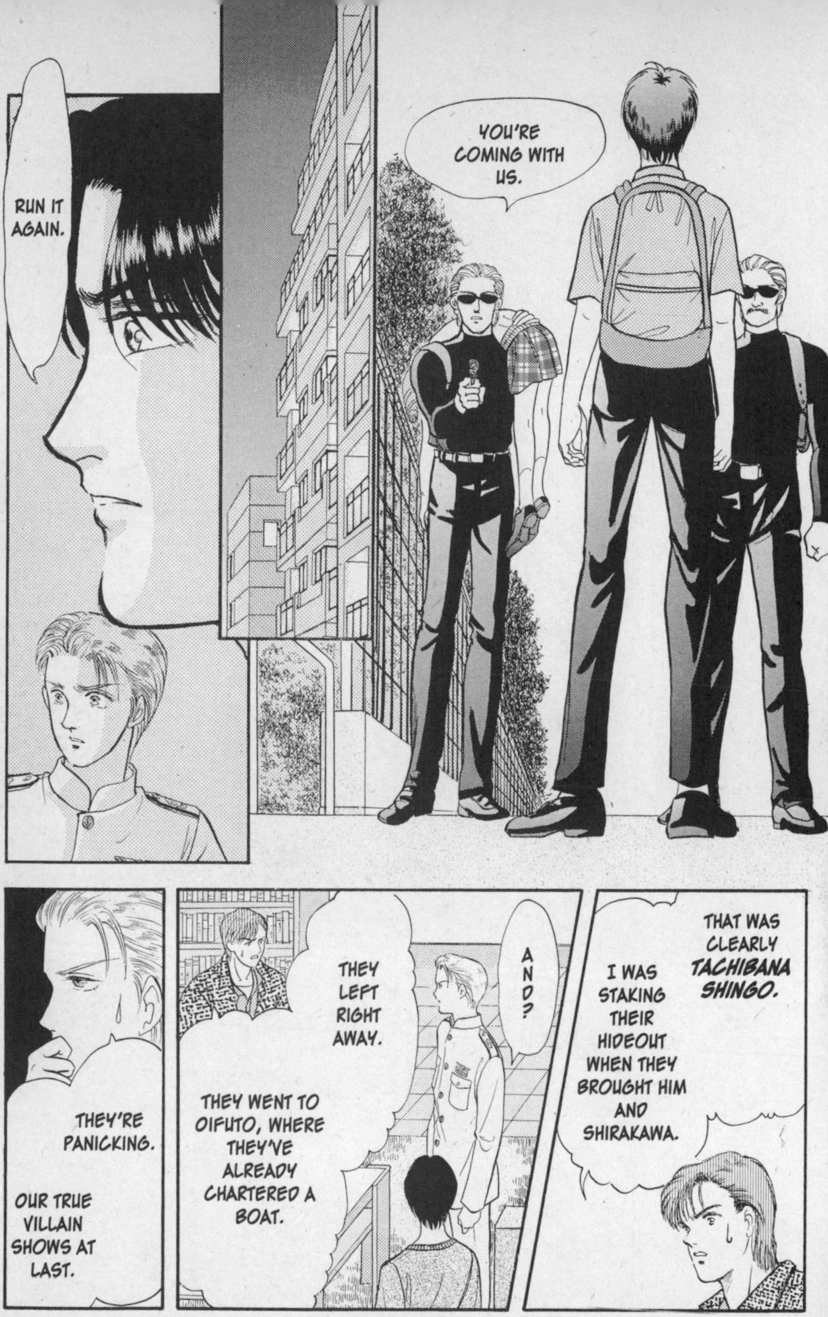
YOU'RE COMING WITH US.
RUN IT AGAIN.
THAT WAS CLEARLY *TACHIBANA SHINGO.*
I WAS STAKING THEIR HIDEOUT WHEN THEY BROUGHT HIM AND SHIRAKAWA.
AND?
THEY LEFT RIGHT AWAY.
THEY WENT TO OIFUTO, WHERE THEY'VE ALREADY CHARTERED A BOAT.
THEY'RE PANICKING.
OUR TRUE VILLAIN SHOWS AT LAST.

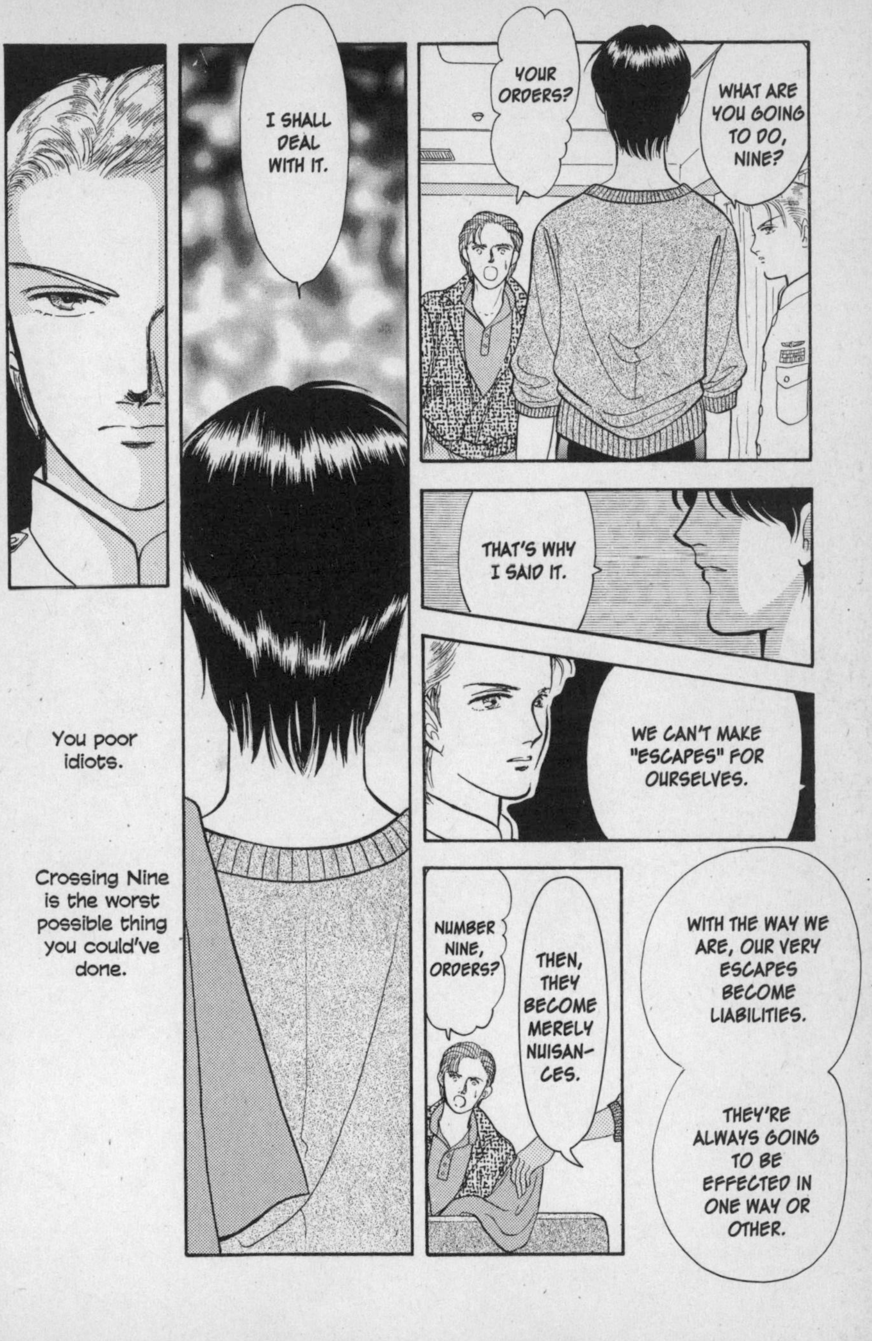
WHAT ARE YOU GOING TO DO, NINE?
YOUR ORDERS?
THAT'S WHY I SAID IT.
WE CAN'T MAKE "ESCAPES" FOR OURSELVES.
WITH THE WAY WE ARE, OUR VERY ESCAPES BECOME LIABILITIES.
THEY'RE ALWAYS GOING TO BE EFFECTED IN ONE WAY OR OTHER.
THEN, THEY BECOME MERELY NUISAN-CES.
NUMBER NINE, ORDERS?
I SHALL DEAL WITH IT.
You poor idiots.
Crossing Nine is the worst possible thing you could've done.

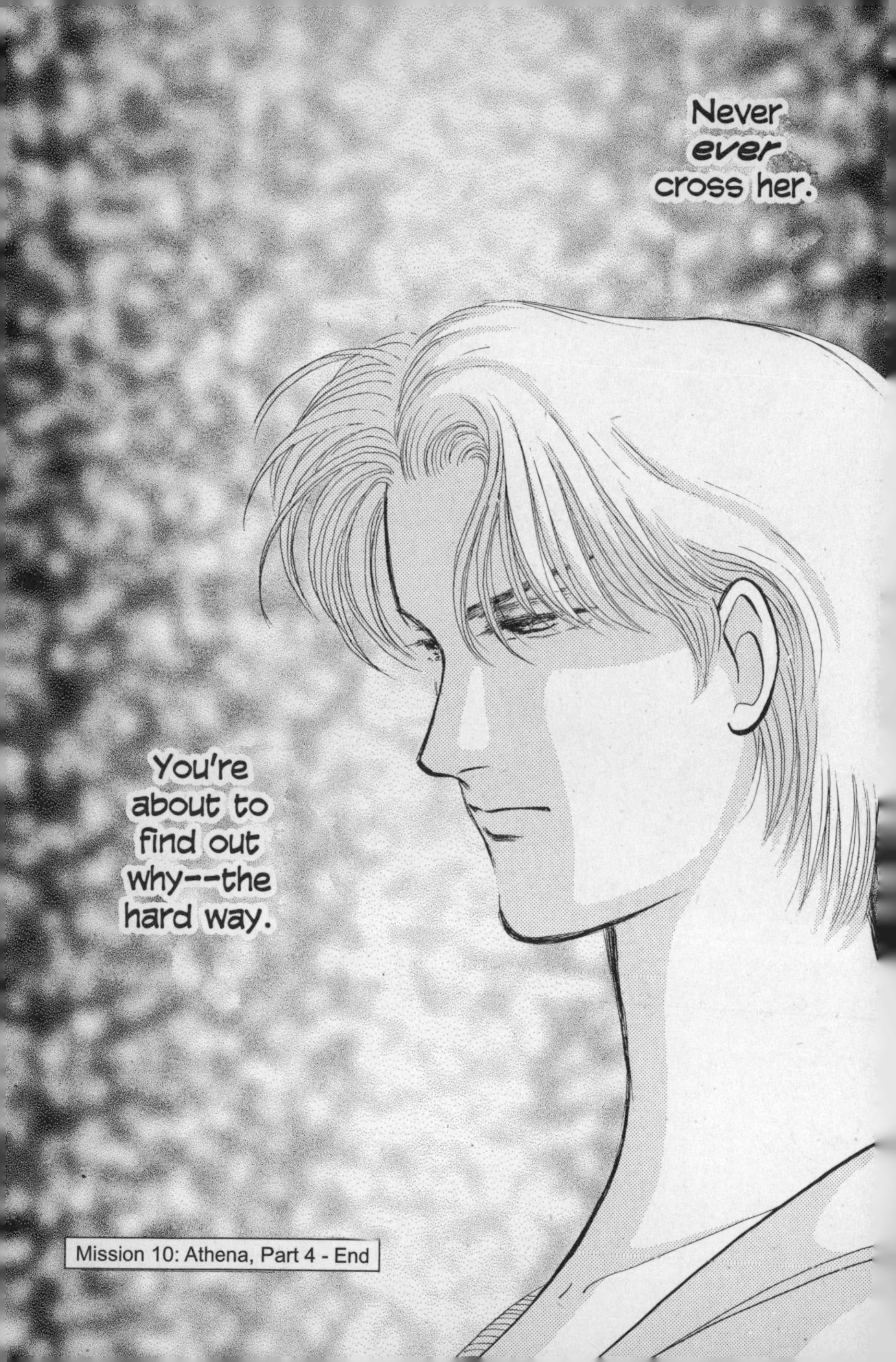
Never *ever* cross her.
You're about to find out why--the hard way.
Mission 10: Athena, Part 4 - End

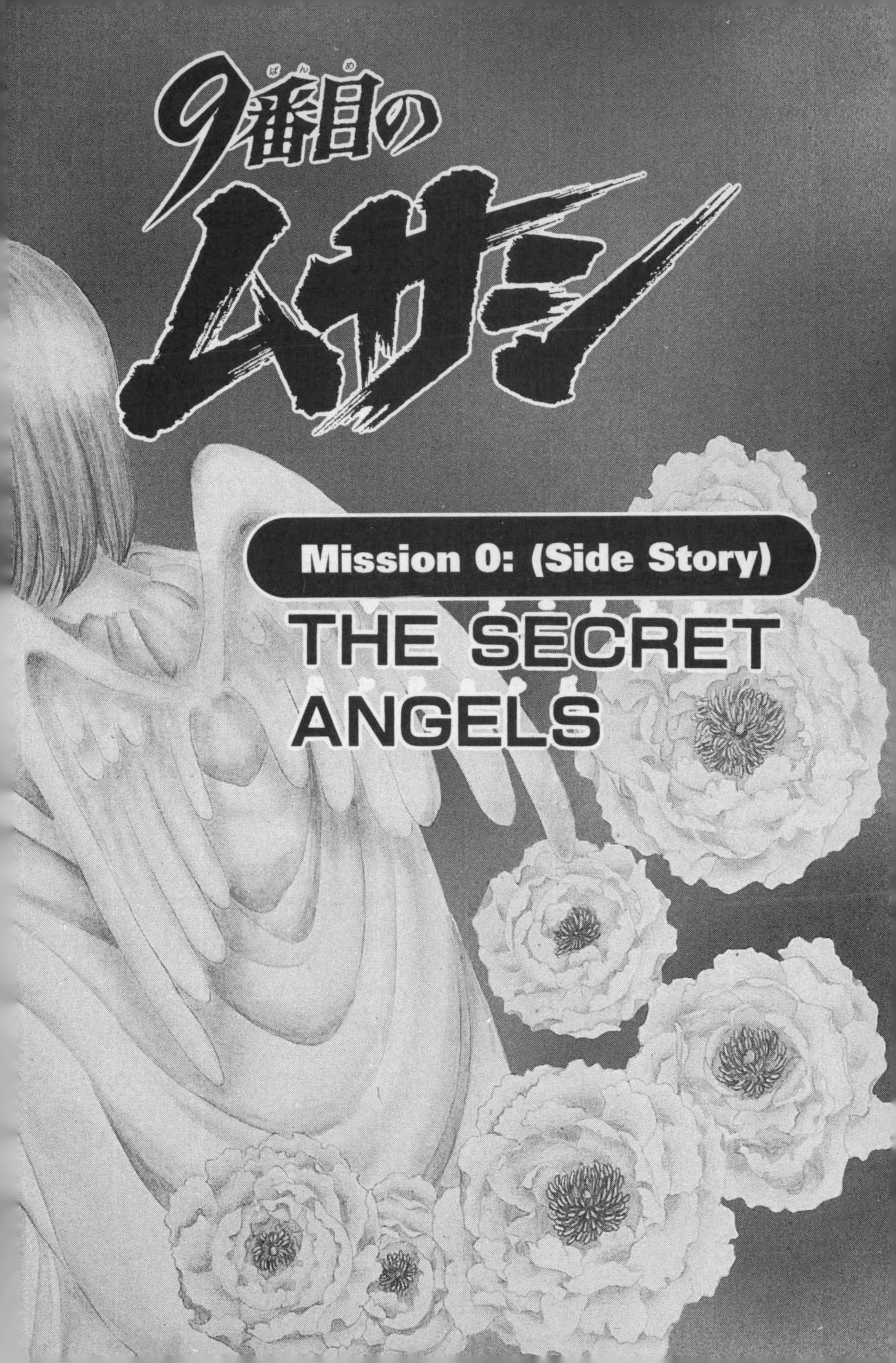
9番目のムサシ
Mission 0: (Side Story)
THE SECRET ANGELS

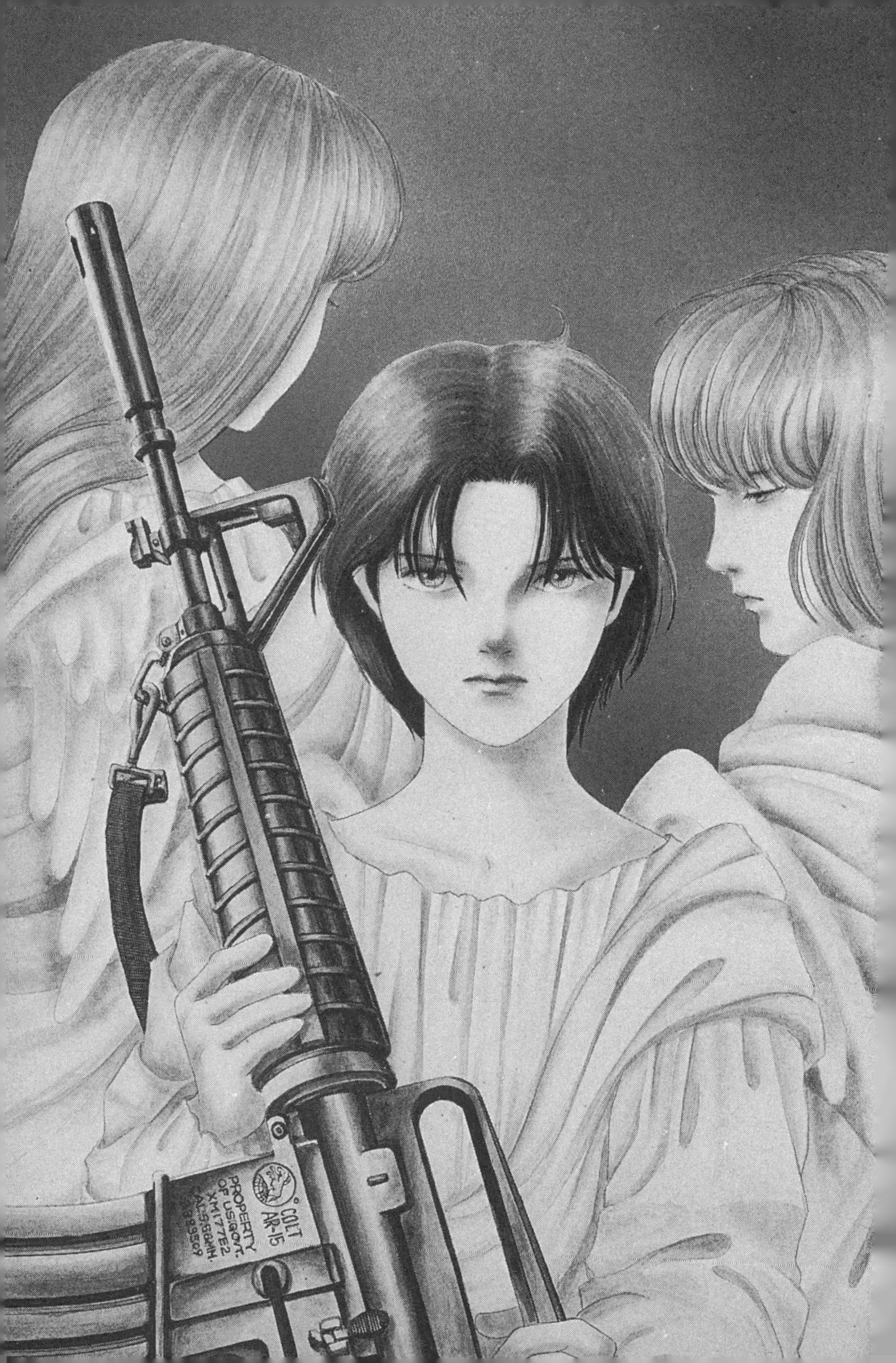
COLT
AR-15
PROPERTY
OF U.S.GOVT.
XM177E2

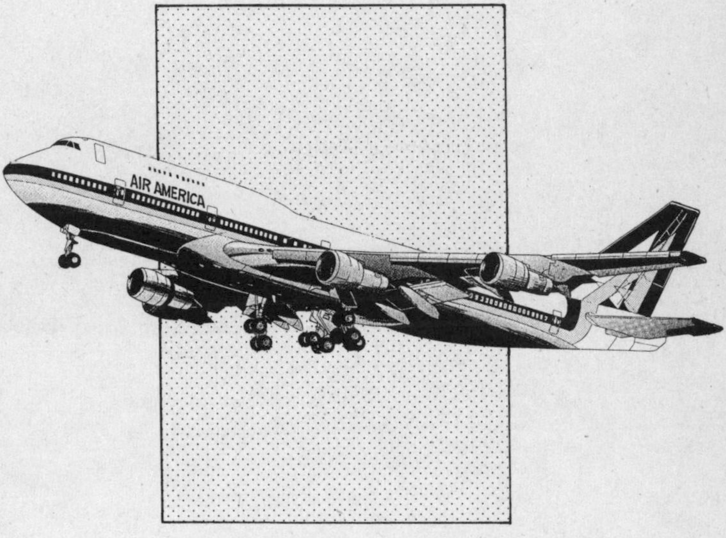
AIR AMERICA

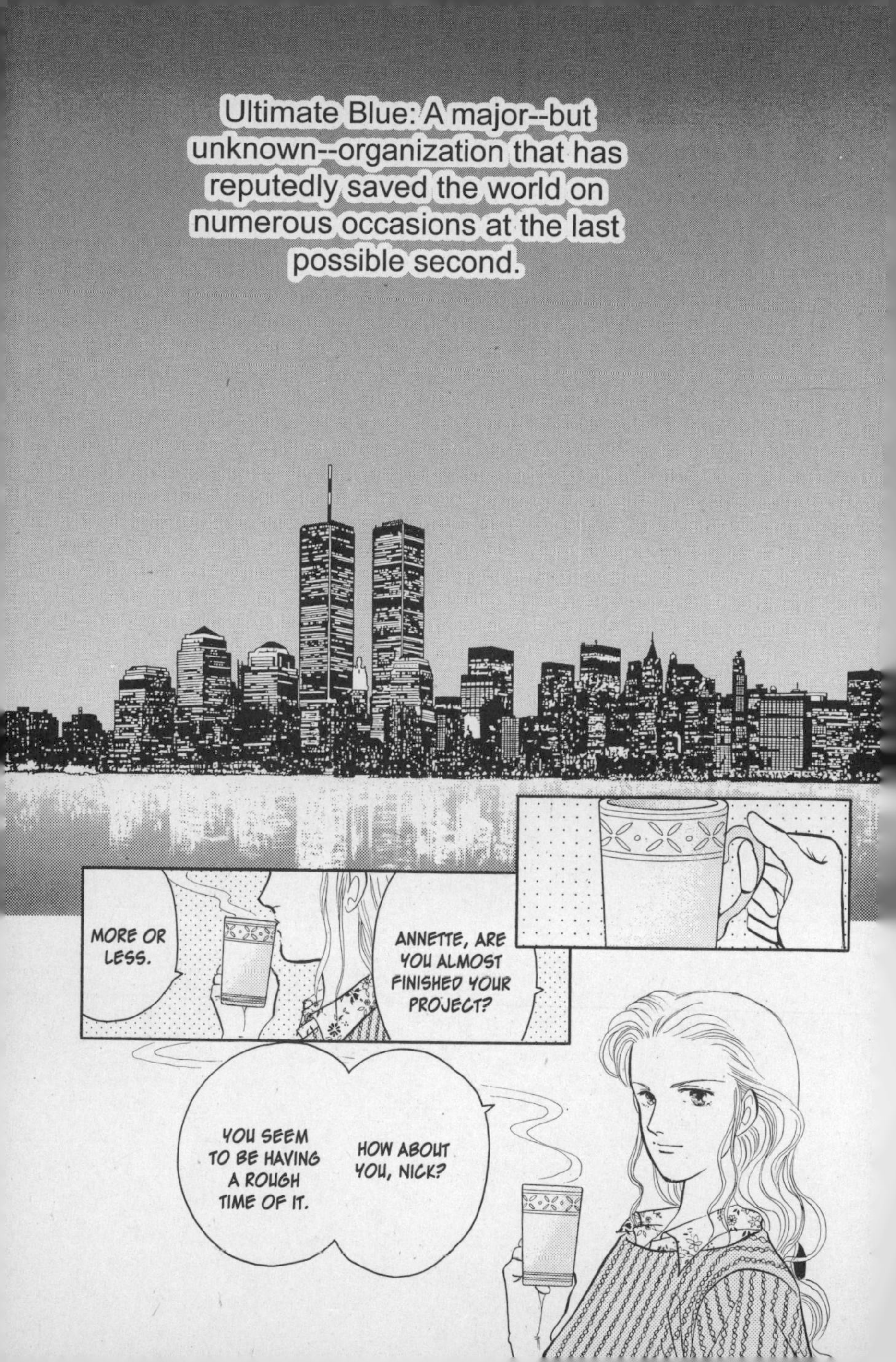
Ultimate Blue: A major--but unknown--organization that has reputedly saved the world on numerous occasions at the last possible second.
ANNETTE, ARE YOU ALMOST FINISHED YOUR PROJECT?
MORE OR LESS.
HOW ABOUT YOU, NICK?
YOU SEEM TO BE HAVING A ROUGH TIME OF IT.

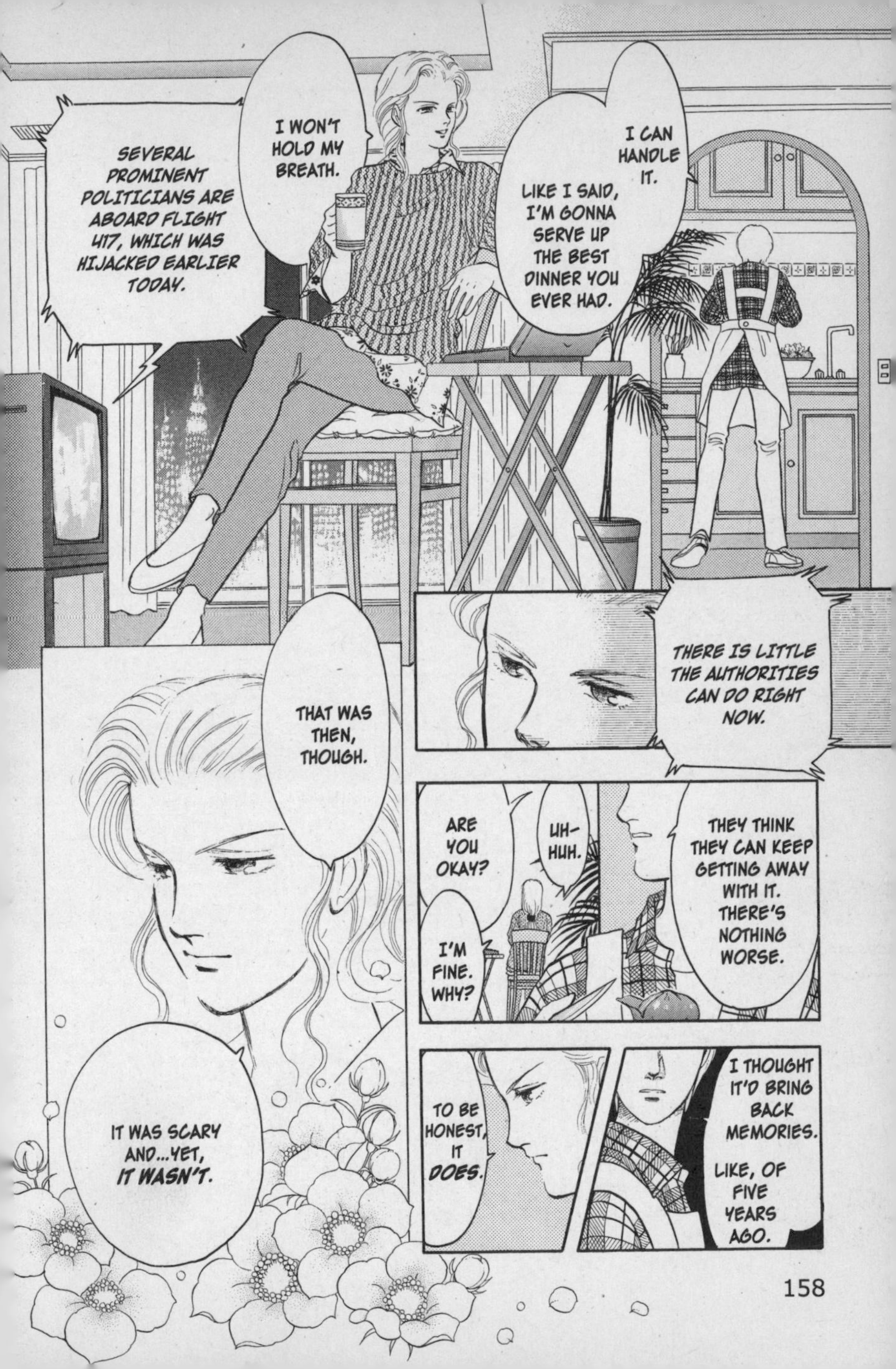
I CAN HANDLE IT.
LIKE I SAID, I'M GONNA SERVE UP THE BEST DINNER YOU EVER HAD.
I WON'T HOLD MY BREATH.
SEVERAL PROMINENT POLITICIANS ARE ABOARD FLIGHT 417, WHICH WAS HIJACKED EARLIER TODAY.
THERE IS LITTLE THE AUTHORITIES CAN DO RIGHT NOW.
THEY THINK THEY CAN KEEP GETTING AWAY WITH IT. THERE'S NOTHING WORSE.
UH-HUH.
ARE YOU OKAY?
I'M FINE. WHY?
I THOUGHT IT'D BRING BACK MEMORIES.
LIKE, OF FIVE YEARS AGO.
TO BE HONEST, IT *DOES*.
THAT WAS THEN, THOUGH.
IT WAS SCARY AND...YET, *IT WASN'T*.

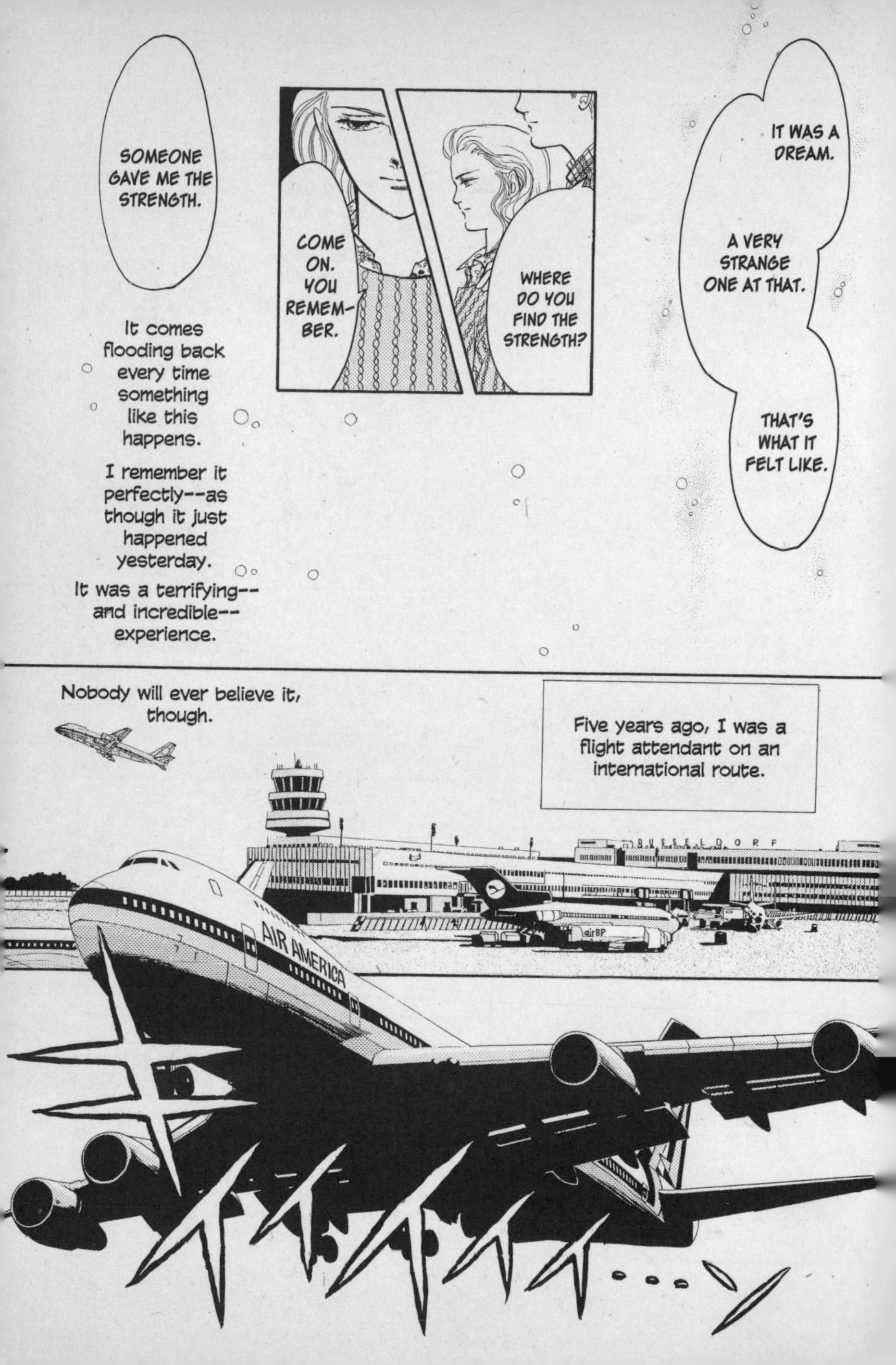
IT WAS A DREAM.
A VERY STRANGE ONE AT THAT.
THAT'S WHAT IT FELT LIKE.
WHERE DO YOU FIND THE STRENGTH?
COME ON. YOU REMEMBER.
SOMEONE GAVE ME THE STRENGTH.
It comes flooding back every time something like this happens.
I remember it perfectly--as though it just happened yesterday.
It was a terrifying--and incredible--experience.
Nobody will ever believe it, though.
Five years ago, I was a flight attendant on an international route.
DUSSELDORF
AIR AMERICA
airBP

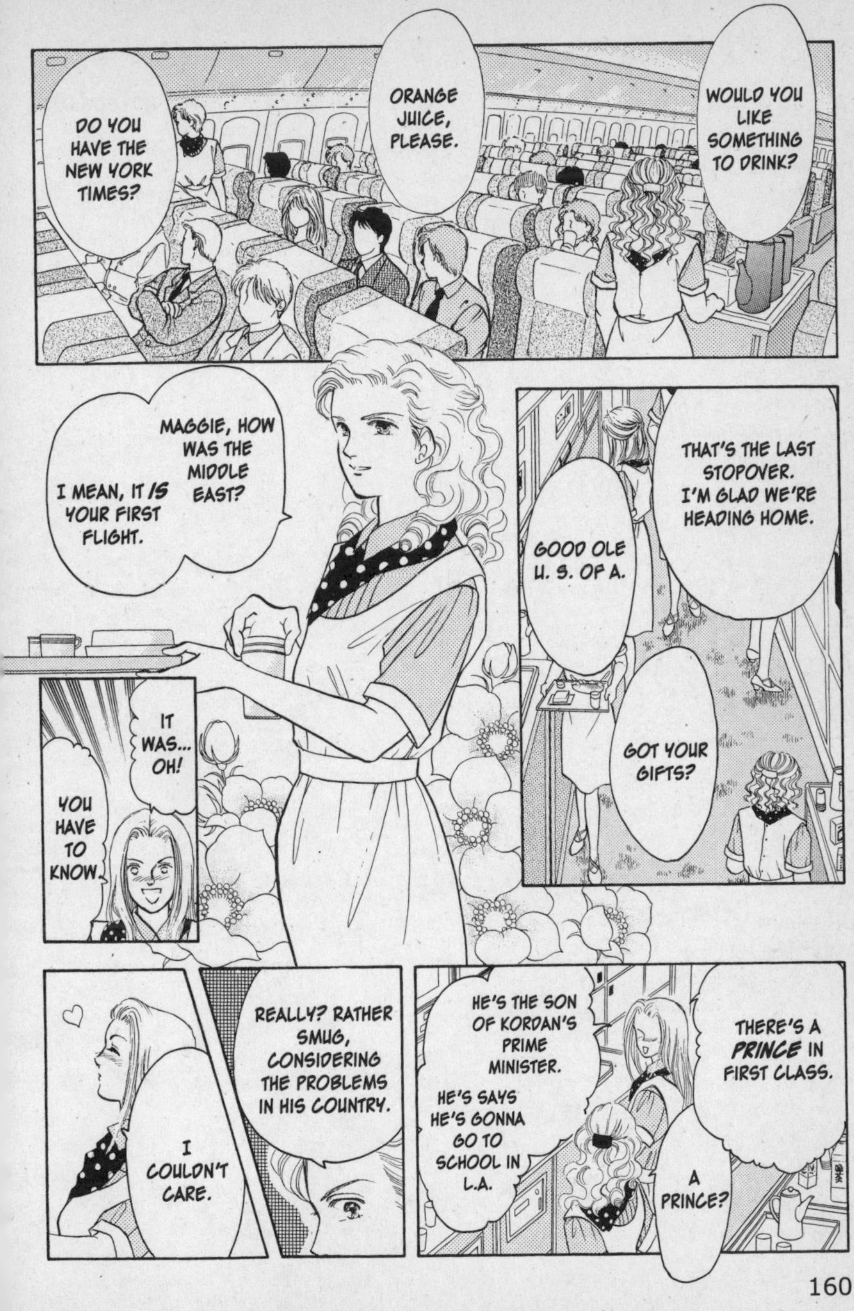
WOULD YOU LIKE SOMETHING TO DRINK?
ORANGE JUICE, PLEASE.
DO YOU HAVE THE NEW YORK TIMES?
THAT'S THE LAST STOPOVER. I'M GLAD WE'RE HEADING HOME.
GOOD OLE U. S. OF A.
GOT YOUR GIFTS?
MAGGIE, HOW WAS THE MIDDLE EAST?
I MEAN, IT *IS* YOUR FIRST FLIGHT.
IT WAS... OH!
YOU HAVE TO KNOW.
THERE'S A *PRINCE* IN FIRST CLASS.
A PRINCE?
HE'S THE SON OF KORDAN'S PRIME MINISTER.
HE'S SAYS HE'S GONNA GO TO SCHOOL IN L.A.
REALLY? RATHER SMUG, CONSIDERING THE PROBLEMS IN HIS COUNTRY.
I COULDN'T CARE.

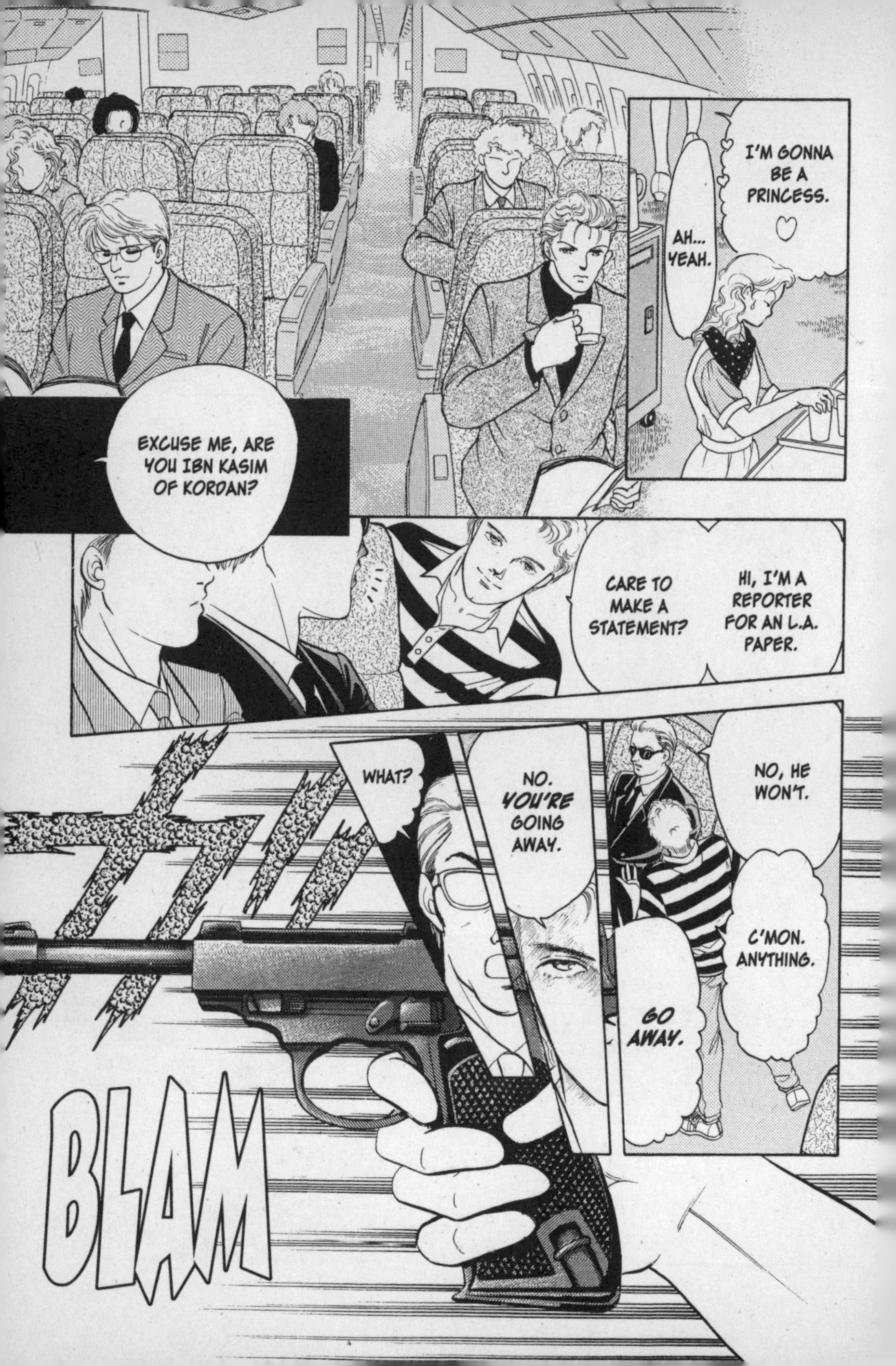
I'M GONNA BE A PRINCESS.
AH... YEAH.
EXCUSE ME, ARE YOU IBN KASIM OF KORDAN?
HI, I'M A REPORTER FOR AN L.A. PAPER.
CARE TO MAKE A STATEMENT?
NO, HE WON'T.
C'MON. ANYTHING.
GO AWAY.
NO. *YOU'RE* GOING AWAY.
WHAT?
BLAM

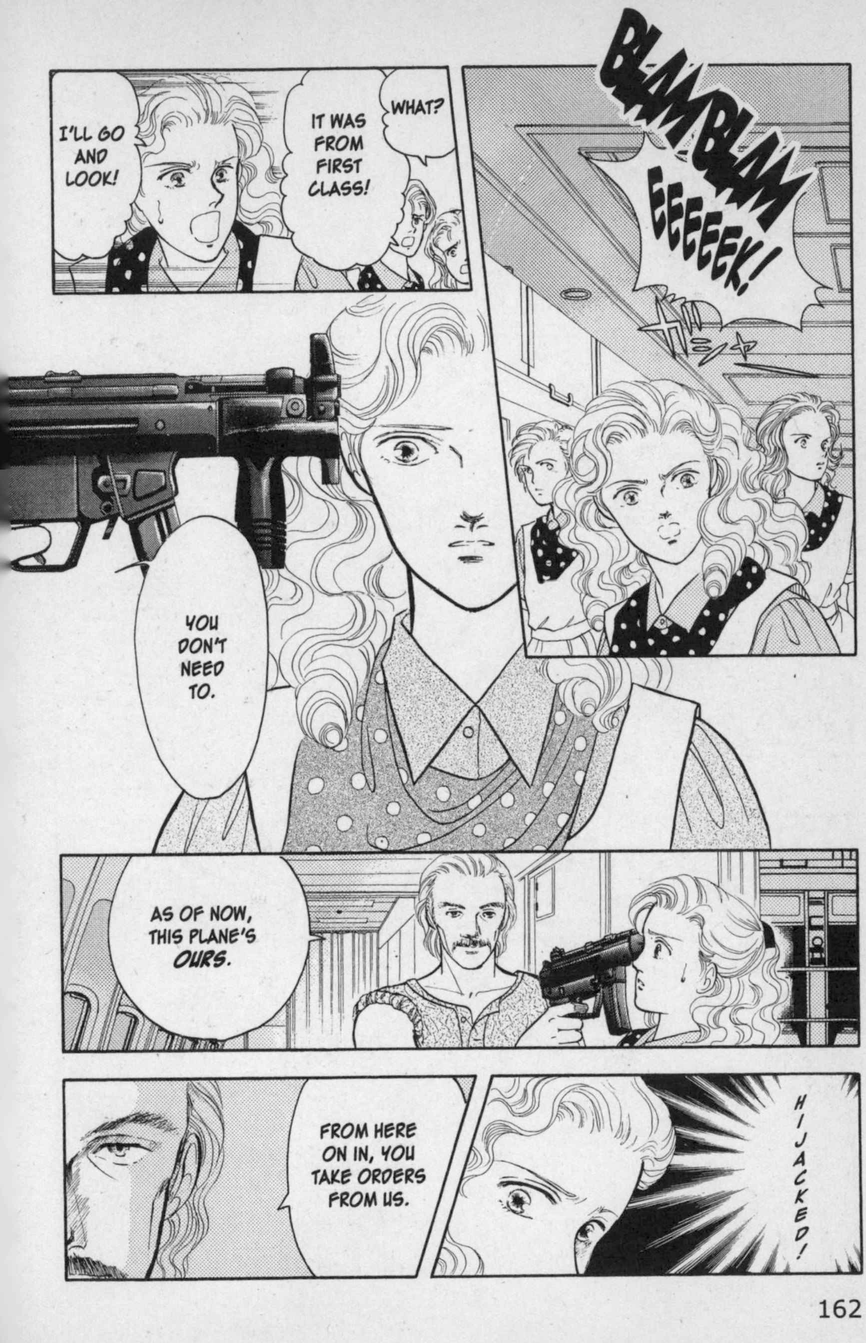

BLAM BLAM
EEEEEK!
WHAT?
IT WAS FROM FIRST CLASS!
I'LL GO AND LOOK!
YOU DON'T NEED TO.
AS OF NOW, THIS PLANE'S *OURS*.
HIJACKED!
FROM HERE ON IN, YOU TAKE ORDERS FROM US.

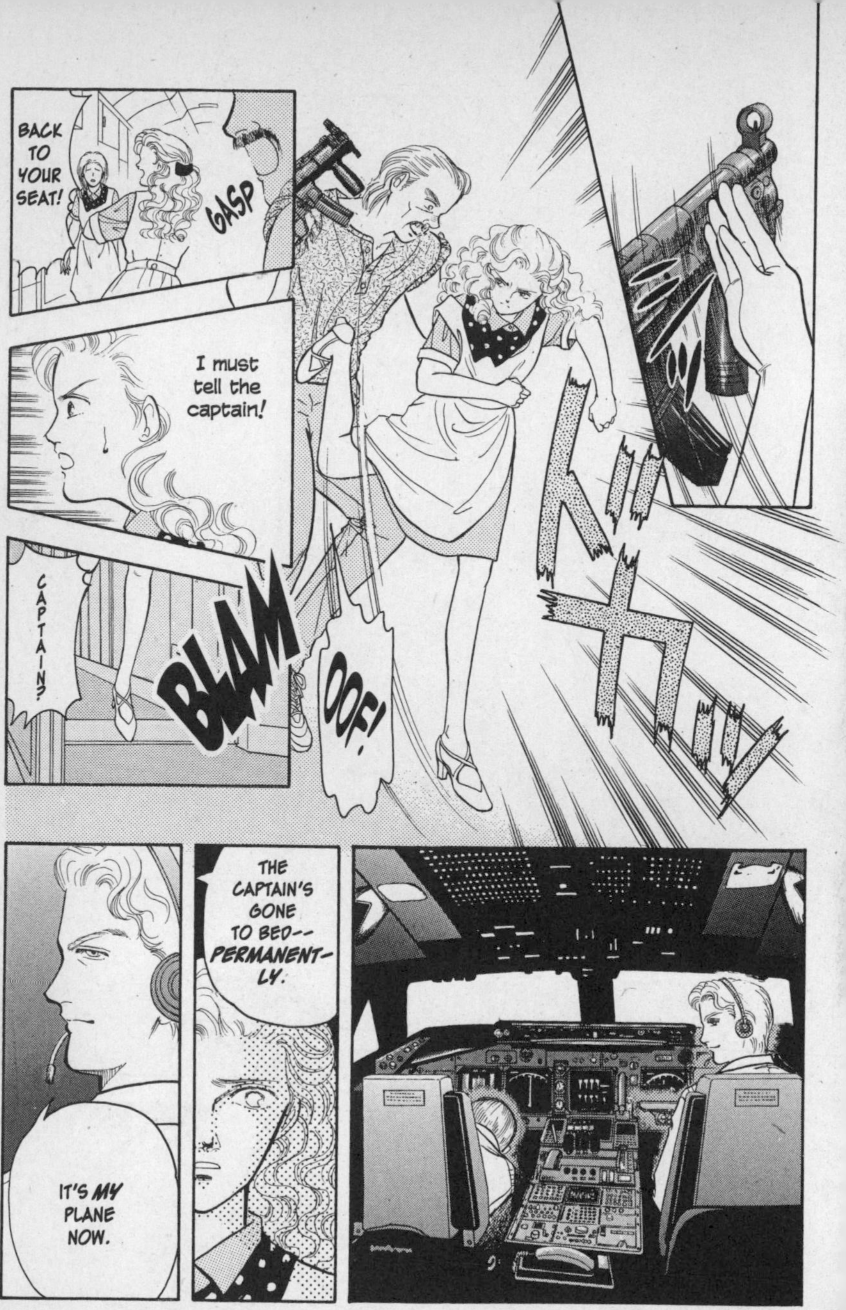
BLAM
OOF!
BACK TO YOUR SEAT!
GASP
I must tell the captain!
CAPTAIN?
THE CAPTAIN'S GONE TO BED--*PERMANENTLY*.
IT'S *MY* PLANE NOW.

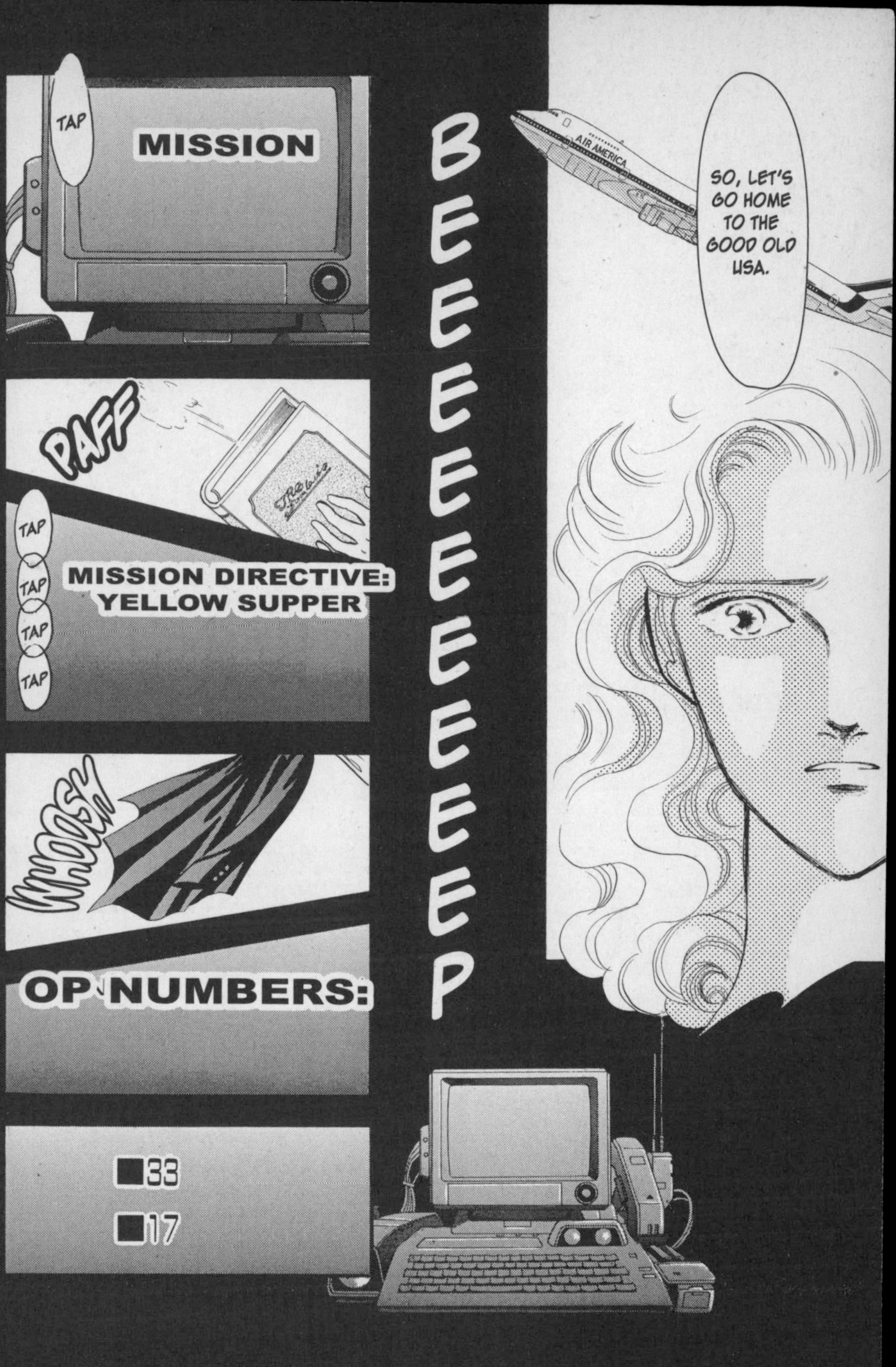
AIR AMERICA
SO, LET'S GO HOME TO THE GOOD OLD USA.
BEEEEEEEEEEP
TAP
MISSION
PAFF
TAP
TAP
TAP
TAP
MISSION DIRECTIVE: YELLOW SUPPER
WHOOSH
OP NUMBERS:
■33
■17

9

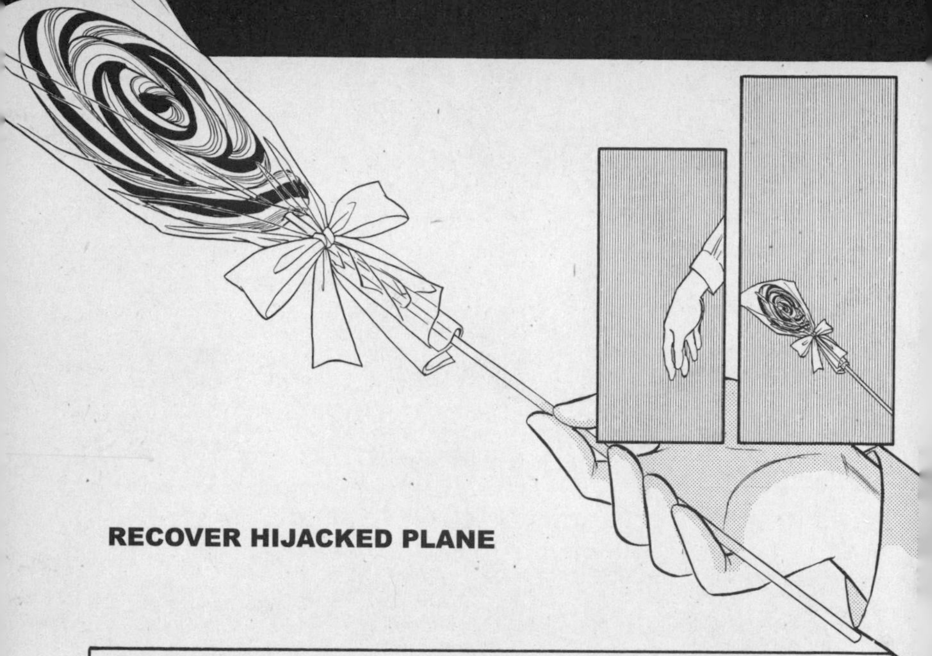

RECOVER HIJACKED PLANE

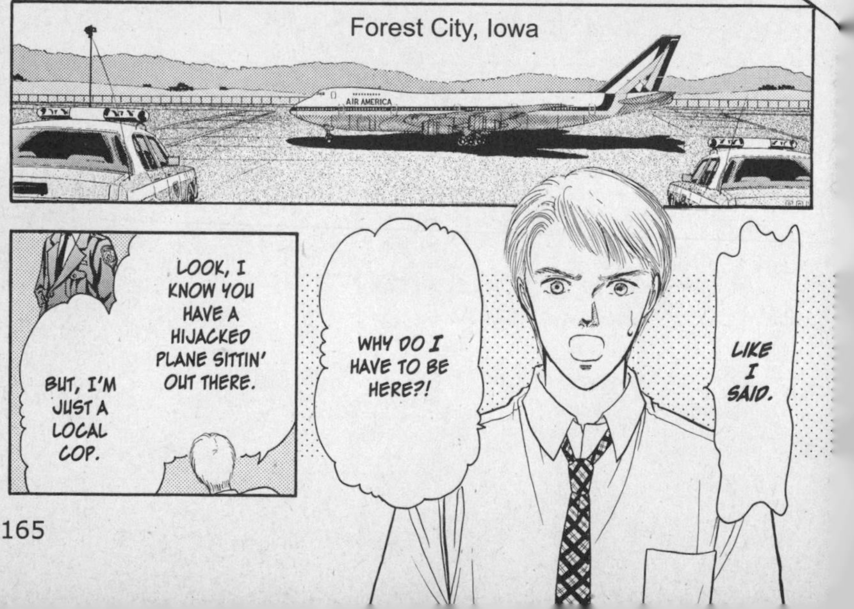
Forest City, Iowa
AIR AMERICA
LIKE I SAID.
WHY DO I HAVE TO BE HERE?!
LOOK, I KNOW YOU HAVE A HIJACKED PLANE SITTIN' OUT THERE.
BUT, I'M JUST A LOCAL COP.

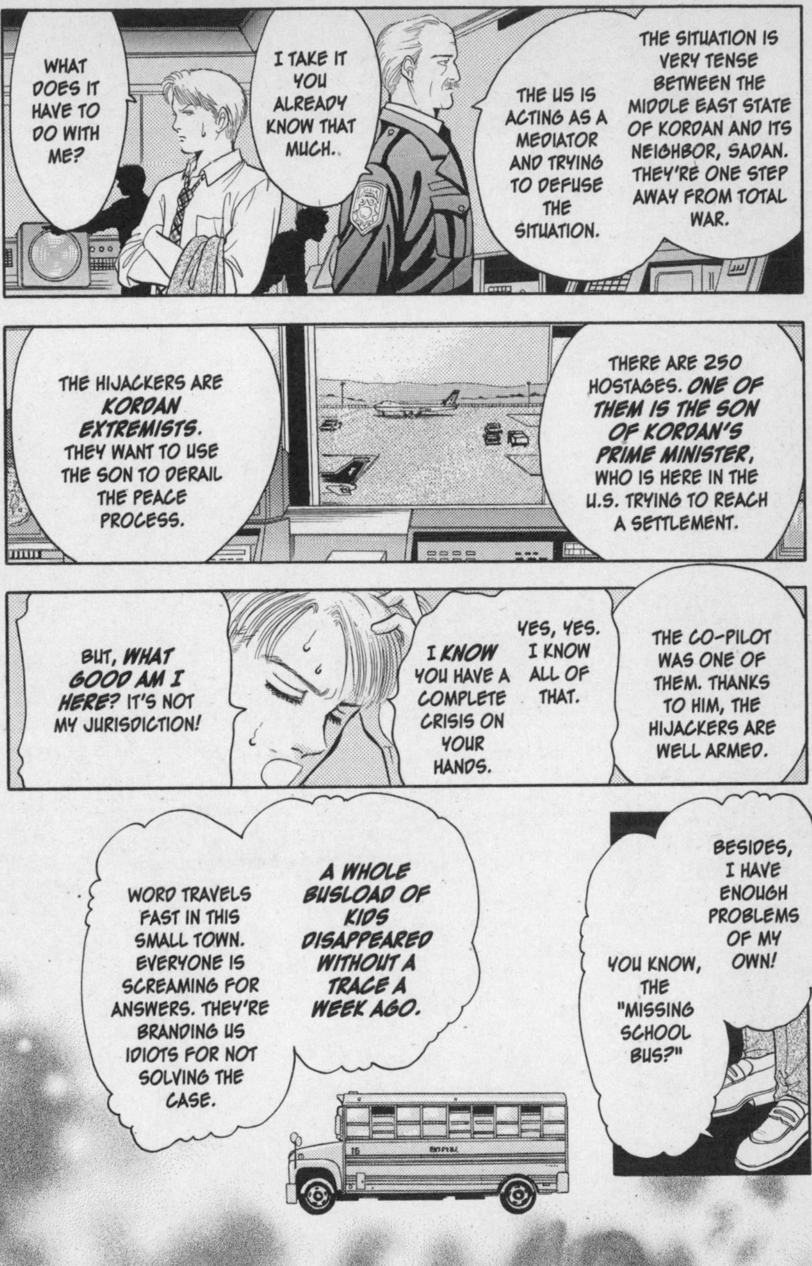
THE SITUATION IS VERY TENSE BETWEEN THE MIDDLE EAST STATE OF KORDAN AND ITS NEIGHBOR, SADAN. THEY'RE ONE STEP AWAY FROM TOTAL WAR.
THE US IS ACTING AS A MEDIATOR AND TRYING TO DEFUSE THE SITUATION.
I TAKE IT YOU ALREADY KNOW THAT MUCH.
WHAT DOES IT HAVE TO DO WITH ME?
THERE ARE 250 HOSTAGES. *ONE OF THEM IS THE SON OF KORDAN'S PRIME MINISTER*, WHO IS HERE IN THE U.S. TRYING TO REACH A SETTLEMENT.
THE HIJACKERS ARE *KORDAN EXTREMISTS*. THEY WANT TO USE THE SON TO DERAIL THE PEACE PROCESS.
THE CO-PILOT WAS ONE OF THEM. THANKS TO HIM, THE HIJACKERS ARE WELL ARMED.
YES, YES. I KNOW ALL OF THAT.
I *KNOW* YOU HAVE A COMPLETE CRISIS ON YOUR HANDS.
BUT, *WHAT GOOD AM I HERE?* IT'S NOT MY JURISDICTION!
BESIDES, I HAVE ENOUGH PROBLEMS OF MY OWN!
YOU KNOW, THE "MISSING SCHOOL BUS?"
A WHOLE BUSLOAD OF KIDS DISAPPEARED WITHOUT A TRACE A WEEK AGO.
WORD TRAVELS FAST IN THIS SMALL TOWN. EVERYONE IS SCREAMING FOR ANSWERS. THEY'RE BRANDING US IDIOTS FOR NOT SOLVING THE CASE.

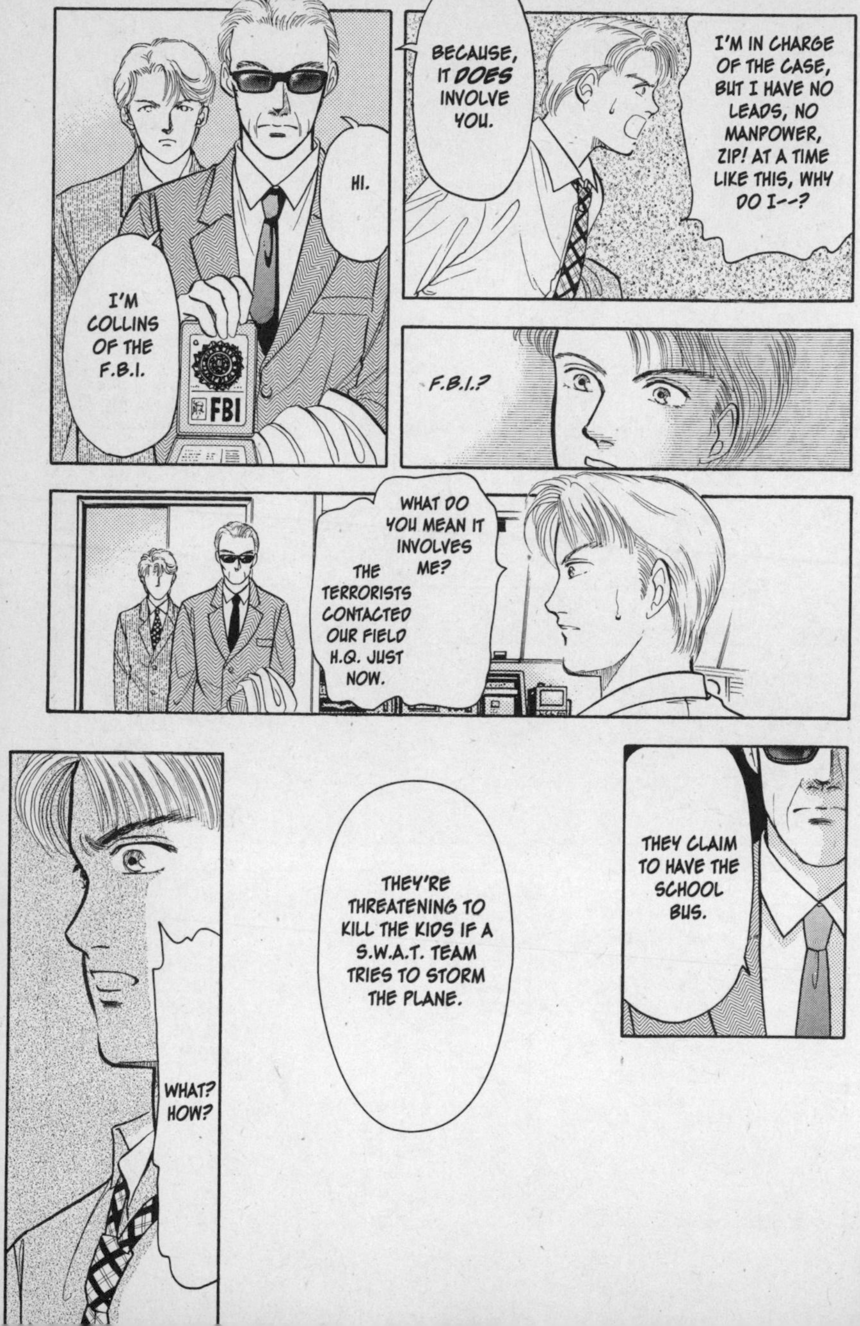
I'M IN CHARGE OF THE CASE, BUT I HAVE NO LEADS, NO MANPOWER, ZIP! AT A TIME LIKE THIS, WHY DO I--?
BECAUSE, IT *DOES* INVOLVE YOU.
F.B.I.?
HI.
I'M COLLINS OF THE F.B.I.
FBI
WHAT DO YOU MEAN IT INVOLVES ME?
THE TERRORISTS CONTACTED OUR FIELD H.Q. JUST NOW.
THEY CLAIM TO HAVE THE SCHOOL BUS.
THEY'RE THREATENING TO KILL THE KIDS IF A S.W.A.T. TEAM TRIES TO STORM THE PLANE.
WHAT? HOW?

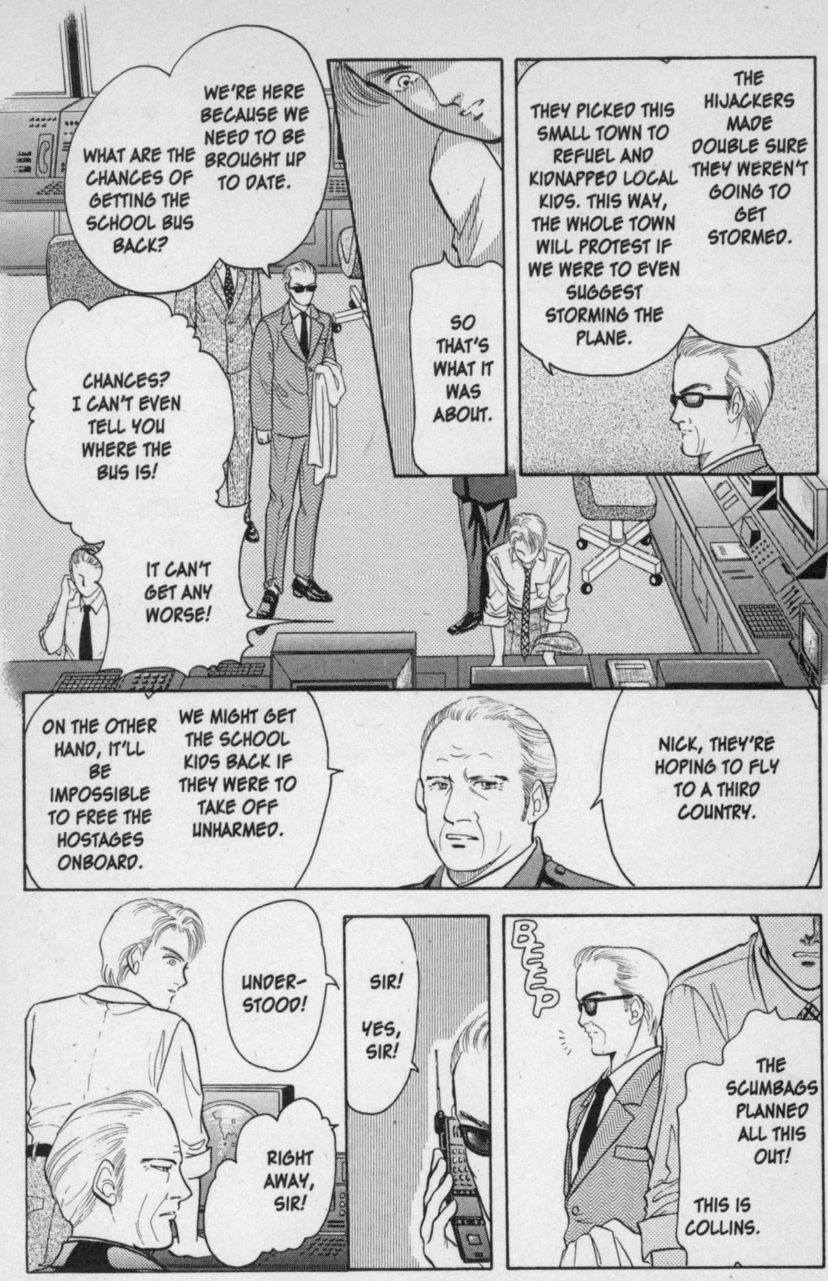
THE HIJACKERS MADE DOUBLE SURE THEY WEREN'T GOING TO GET STORMED.
THEY PICKED THIS SMALL TOWN TO REFUEL AND KIDNAPPED LOCAL KIDS. THIS WAY, THE WHOLE TOWN WILL PROTEST IF WE WERE TO EVEN SUGGEST STORMING THE PLANE.
SO THAT'S WHAT IT WAS ABOUT.
WE'RE HERE BECAUSE WE NEED TO BE BROUGHT UP TO DATE.
WHAT ARE THE CHANCES OF GETTING THE SCHOOL BUS BACK?
CHANCES? I CAN'T EVEN TELL YOU WHERE THE BUS IS!
IT CAN'T GET ANY WORSE!
NICK, THEY'RE HOPING TO FLY TO A THIRD COUNTRY.
WE MIGHT GET THE SCHOOL KIDS BACK IF THEY WERE TO TAKE OFF UNHARMED.
ON THE OTHER HAND, IT'LL BE IMPOSSIBLE TO FREE THE HOSTAGES ONBOARD.
BEEP
THE SCUMBAGS PLANNED ALL THIS OUT!
THIS IS COLLINS.
SIR!
YES, SIR!
UNDER-STOOD!
RIGHT AWAY, SIR!

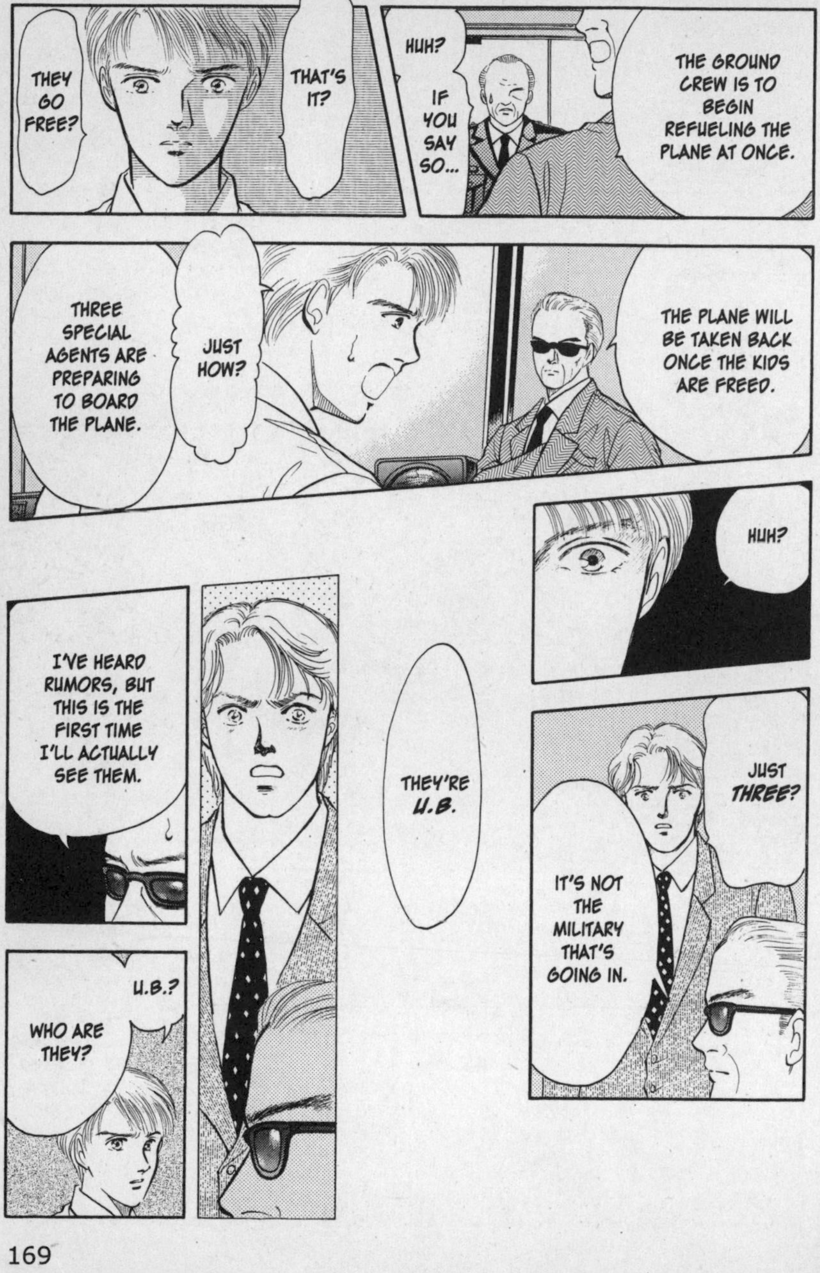

THE GROUND CREW IS TO BEGIN REFUELING THE PLANE AT ONCE.
HUH?
IF YOU SAY SO...
THAT'S IT?
THEY GO FREE?
THE PLANE WILL BE TAKEN BACK ONCE THE KIDS ARE FREED.
JUST HOW?
THREE SPECIAL AGENTS ARE PREPARING TO BOARD THE PLANE.
HUH?
JUST *THREE?*
IT'S NOT THE MILITARY THAT'S GOING IN.
THEY'RE *U.B.*
I'VE HEARD RUMORS, BUT THIS IS THE FIRST TIME I'LL ACTUALLY SEE THEM.
U.B.?
WHO ARE THEY?

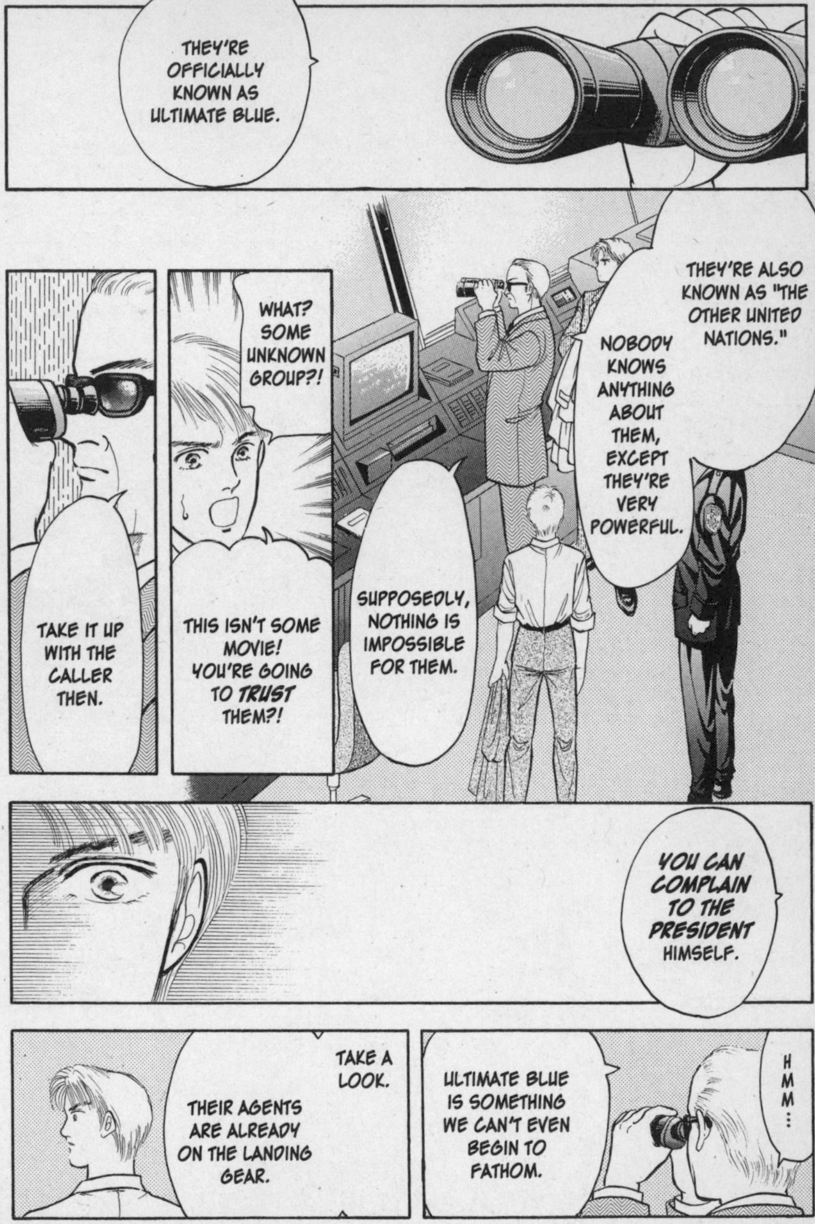
THEY'RE OFFICIALLY KNOWN AS ULTIMATE BLUE.
THEY'RE ALSO KNOWN AS "THE OTHER UNITED NATIONS."
NOBODY KNOWS ANYTHING ABOUT THEM, EXCEPT THEY'RE VERY POWERFUL.
SUPPOSEDLY, NOTHING IS IMPOSSIBLE FOR THEM.
WHAT? SOME UNKNOWN GROUP?!
THIS ISN'T SOME MOVIE! YOU'RE GOING TO *TRUST* THEM?!
TAKE IT UP WITH THE CALLER THEN.
YOU CAN COMPLAIN TO THE PRESIDENT HIMSELF.
HMM...
ULTIMATE BLUE IS SOMETHING WE CAN'T EVEN BEGIN TO FATHOM.
TAKE A LOOK.
THEIR AGENTS ARE ALREADY ON THE LANDING GEAR.

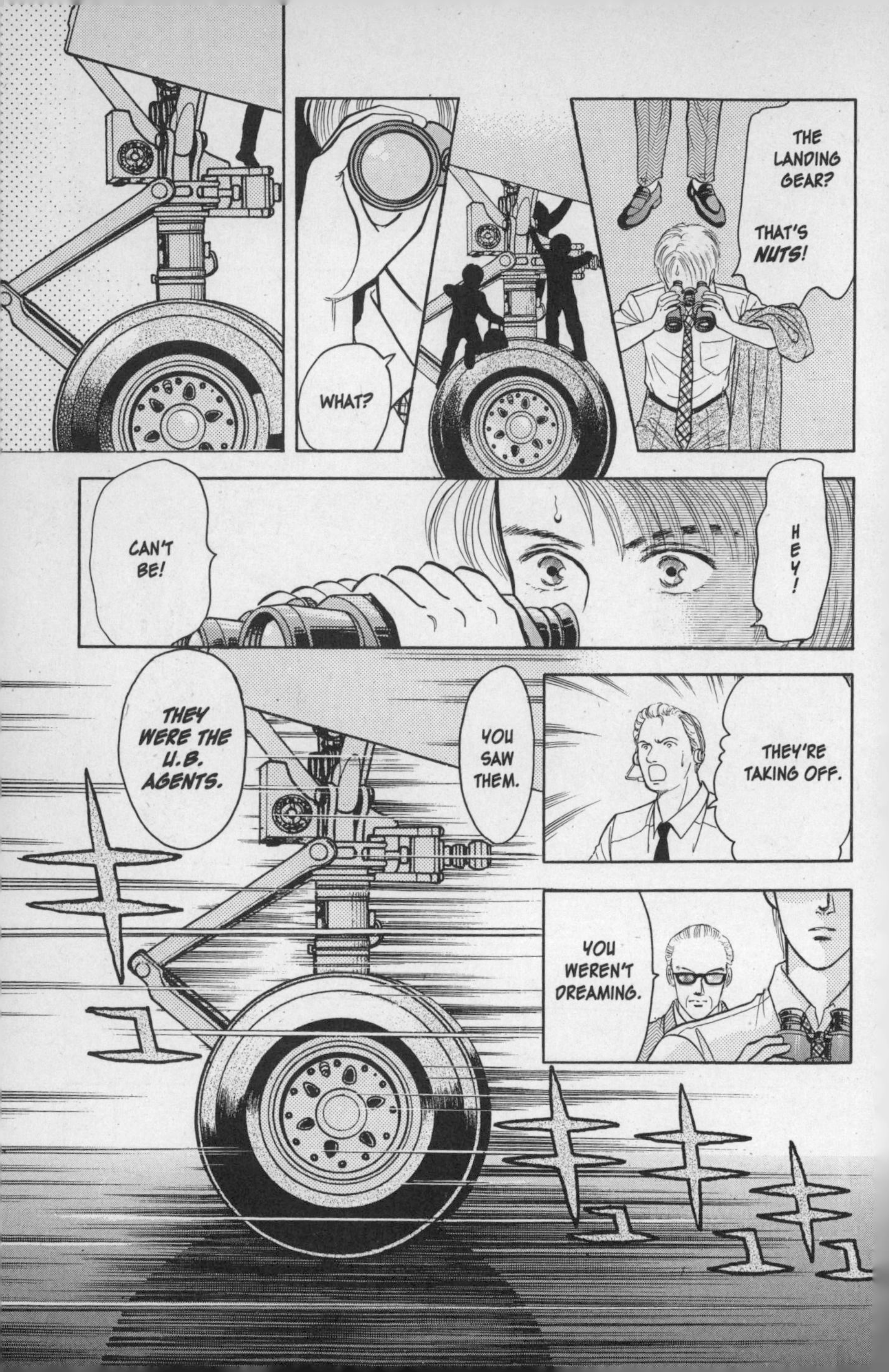
THE LANDING GEAR?
THAT'S NUTS!
WHAT?
HEY!
CAN'T BE!
THEY'RE TAKING OFF.
YOU WEREN'T DREAMING.
YOU SAW THEM.
THEY WERE THE U.B. AGENTS.

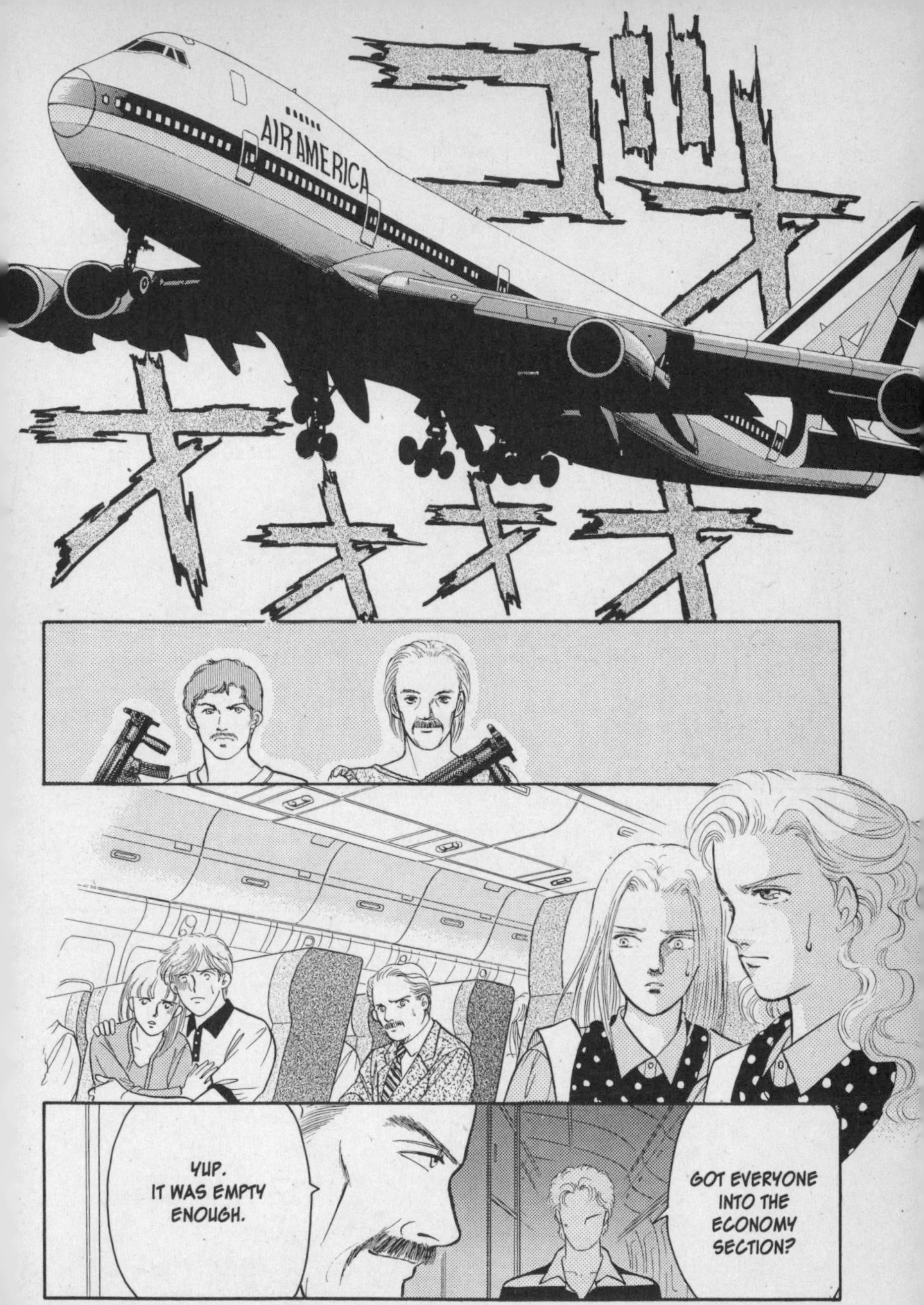
AIR AMERICA
GOT EVERYONE INTO THE ECONOMY SECTION?
YUP. IT WAS EMPTY ENOUGH.

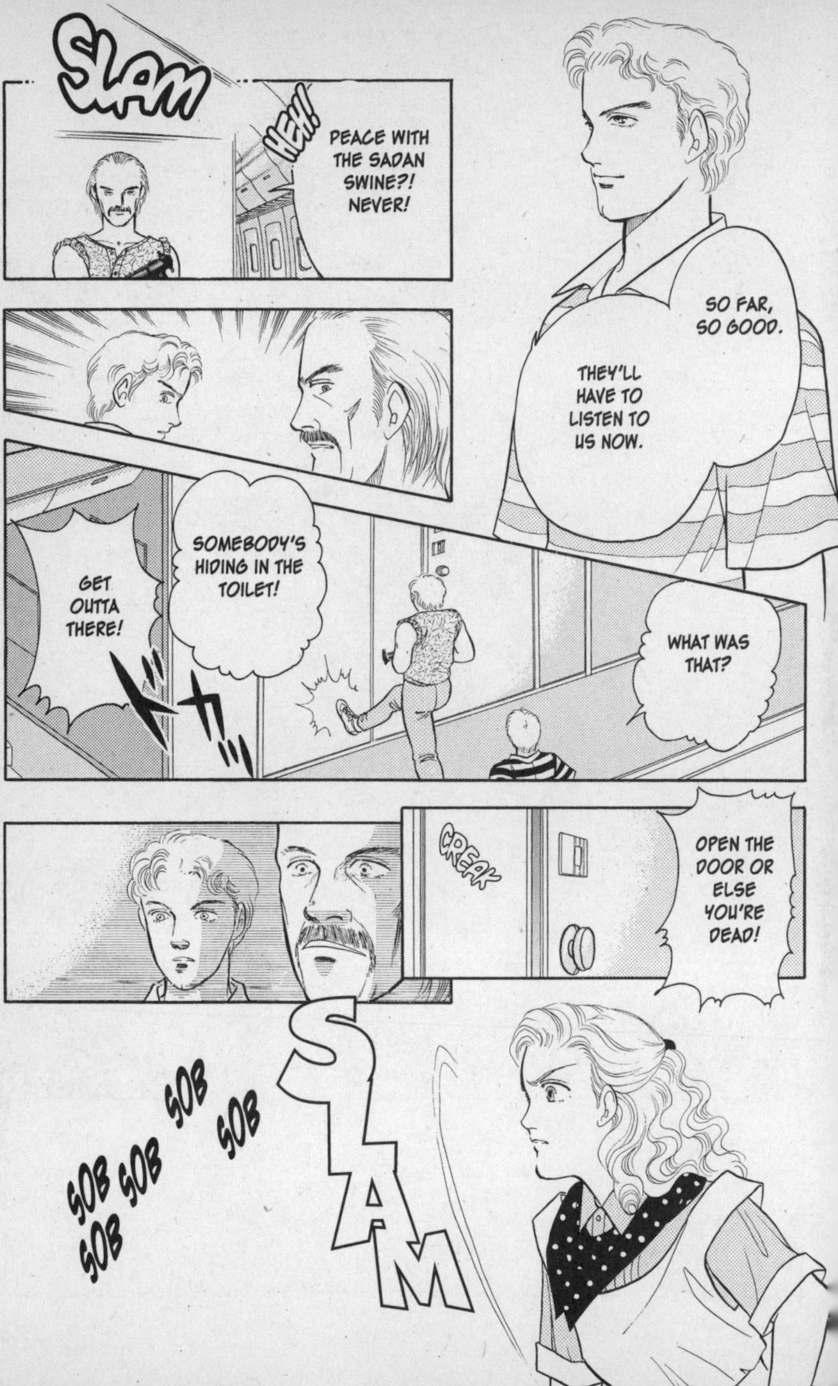
SO FAR, SO GOOD.
THEY'LL HAVE TO LISTEN TO US NOW.
SLAM
HEH!
PEACE WITH THE SADAN SWINE?! NEVER!
WHAT WAS THAT?
SOMEBODY'S HIDING IN THE TOILET!
GET OUTTA THERE!
OPEN THE DOOR OR ELSE YOU'RE DEAD!
CREAK
SLAM
SOB SOB
SOB SOB
SOB SOB

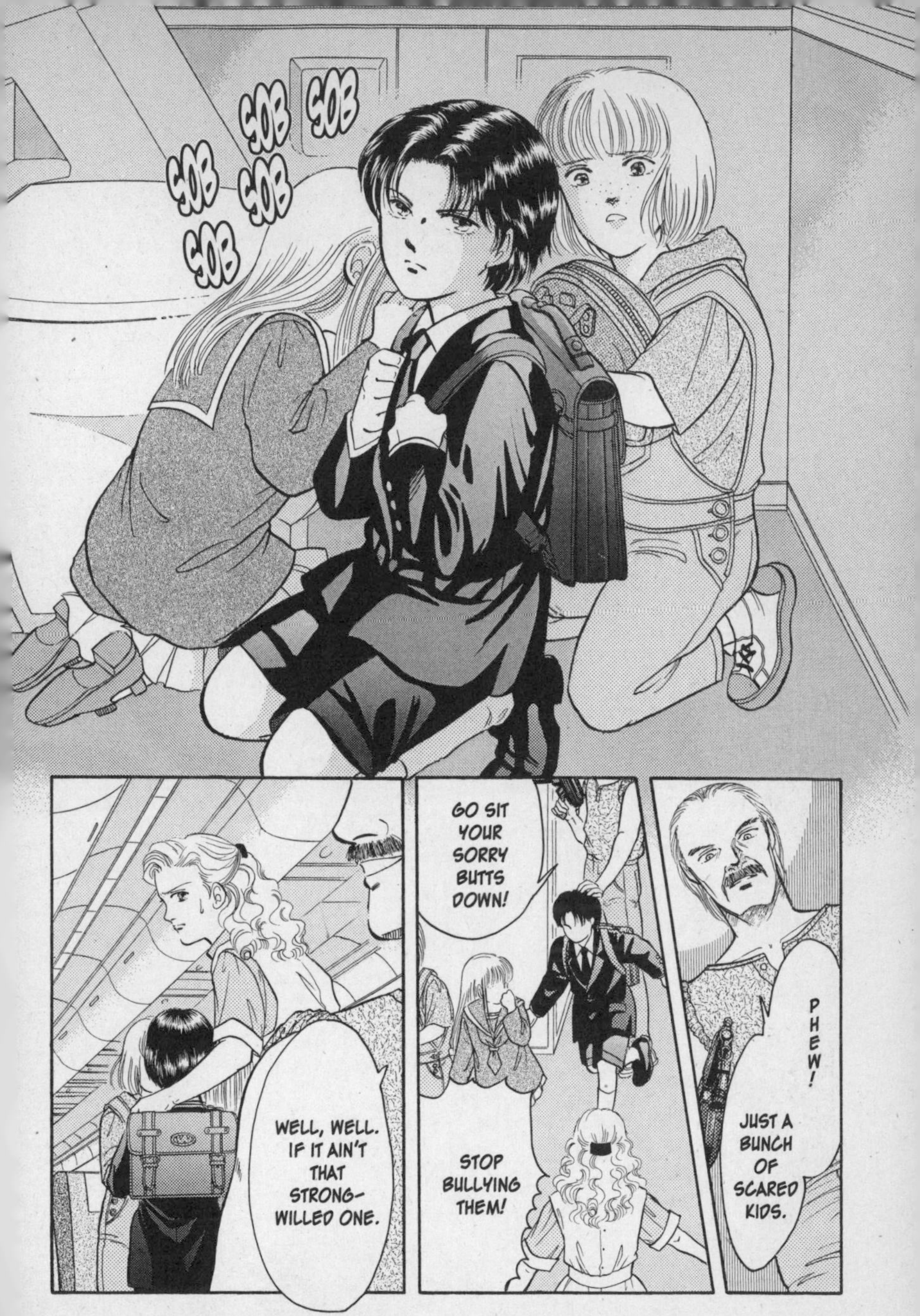
SOB SOB
SOB SOB
SOB SOB
PHEW!
JUST A BUNCH OF SCARED KIDS.
GO SIT YOUR SORRY BUTTS DOWN!
STOP BULLYING THEM!
WELL, WELL. IF IT AIN'T THAT STRONG-WILLED ONE.

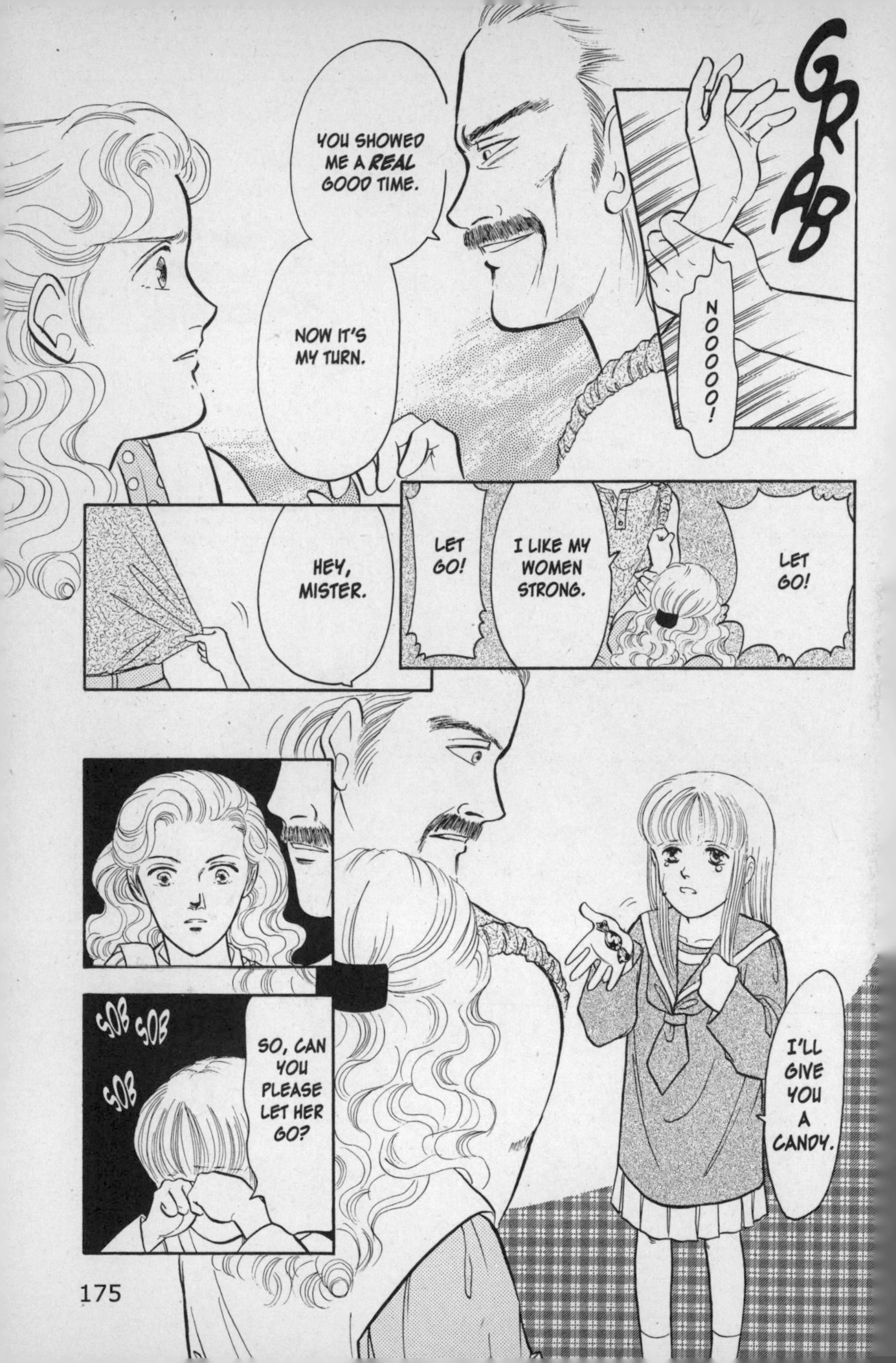
GRAB
NOOOOOO!
YOU SHOWED ME A REAL GOOD TIME.
NOW IT'S MY TURN.
LET GO!
I LIKE MY WOMEN STRONG.
LET GO!
HEY, MISTER.
I'LL GIVE YOU A CANDY.
SOB SOB SOB
SO, CAN YOU PLEASE LET HER GO?

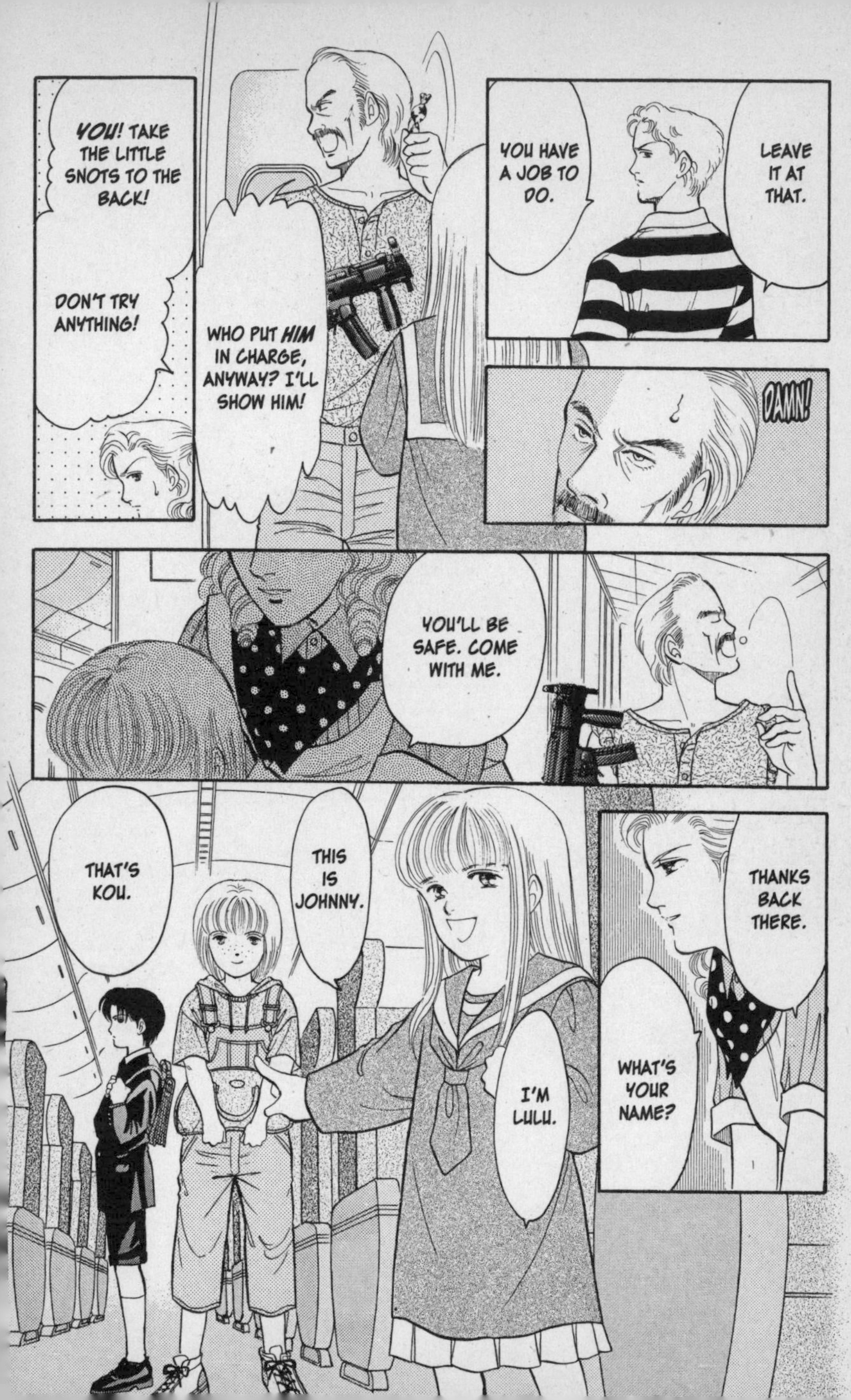
LEAVE IT AT THAT.
YOU HAVE A JOB TO DO.
DAMN!
WHO PUT HIM IN CHARGE, ANYWAY? I'LL SHOW HIM!
YOU! TAKE THE LITTLE SNOTS TO THE BACK!
DON'T TRY ANYTHING!
YOU'LL BE SAFE. COME WITH ME.
THANKS BACK THERE.
WHAT'S YOUR NAME?
I'M LULU.
THIS IS JOHNNY.
THAT'S KOU.

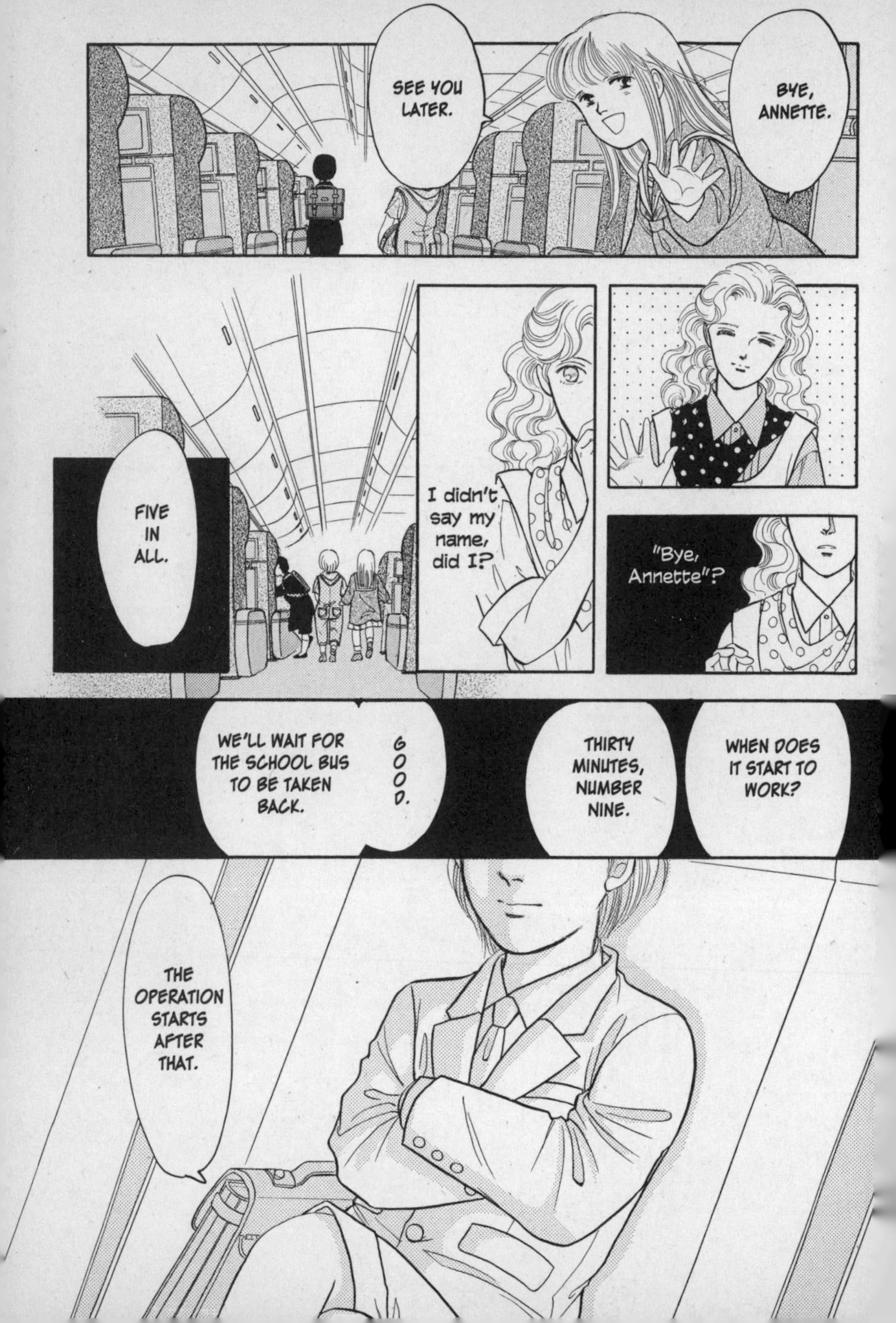

BYE, ANNETTE.
SEE YOU LATER.
"Bye, Annette"?
I didn't say my name, did I?
FIVE IN ALL.
WHEN DOES IT START TO WORK?
THIRTY MINUTES, NUMBER NINE.
GOOD.
WE'LL WAIT FOR THE SCHOOL BUS TO BE TAKEN BACK.
THE OPERATION STARTS AFTER THAT.

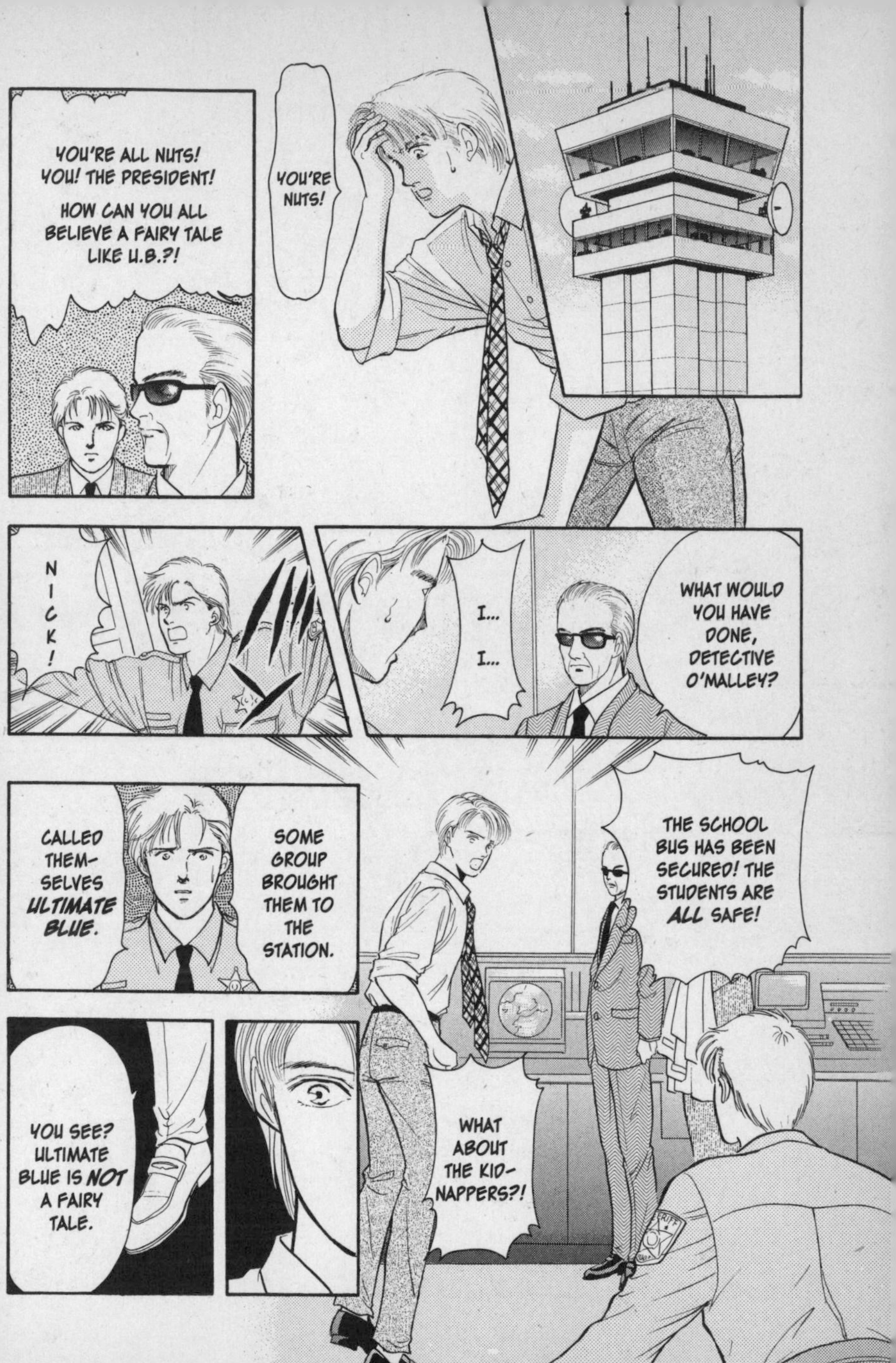
YOU'RE NUTS!
YOU'RE ALL NUTS! YOU! THE PRESIDENT!
HOW CAN YOU ALL BELIEVE A FAIRY TALE LIKE U.B.?!
WHAT WOULD YOU HAVE DONE, DETECTIVE O'MALLEY?
I... I...
NICK!
THE SCHOOL BUS HAS BEEN SECURED! THE STUDENTS ARE ALL SAFE!
WHAT ABOUT THE KID-NAPPERS?!
SOME GROUP BROUGHT THEM TO THE STATION.
CALLED THEM-SELVES ULTIMATE BLUE.
YOU SEE? ULTIMATE BLUE IS NOT A FAIRY TALE.

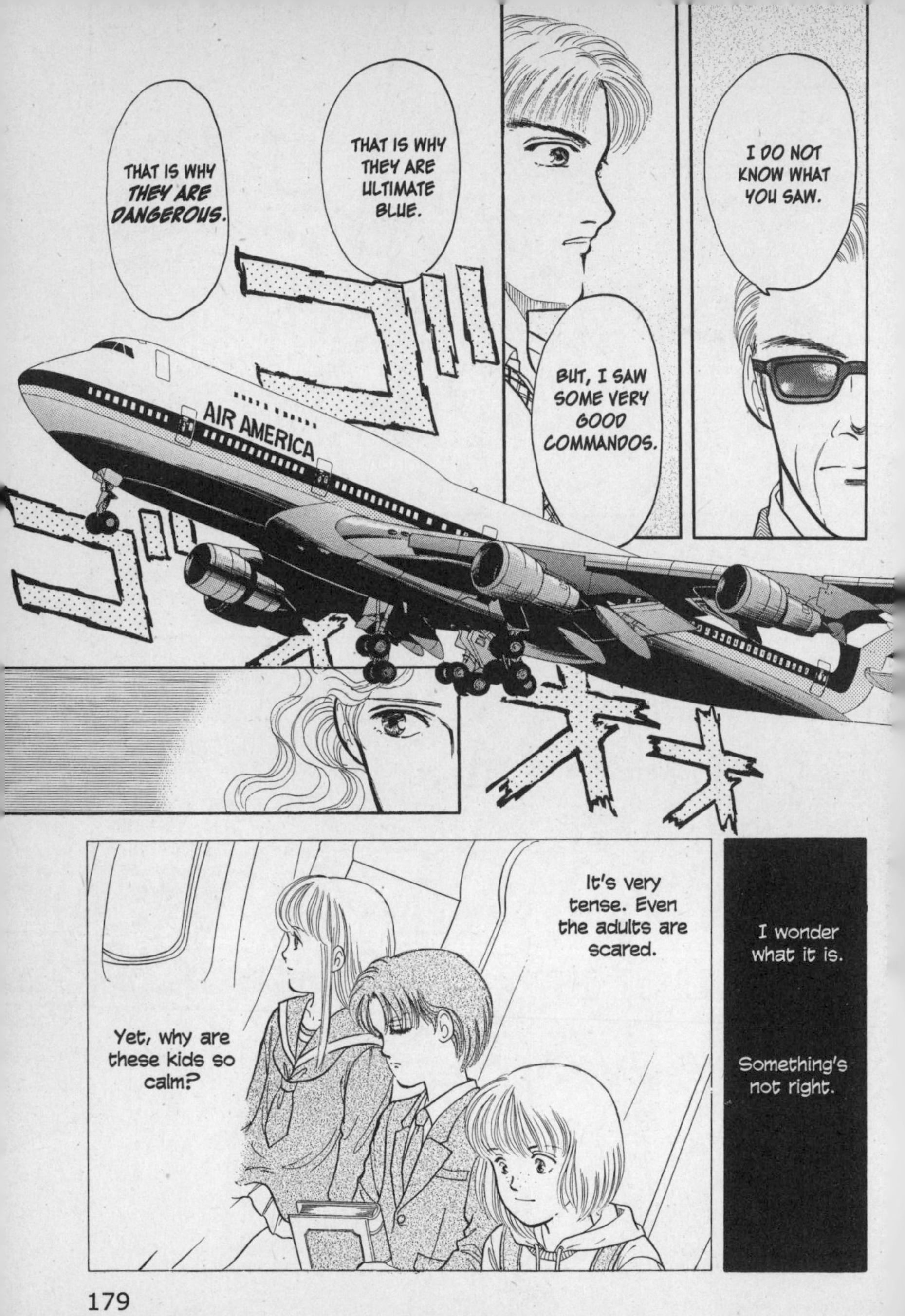

I DO NOT KNOW WHAT YOU SAW.
BUT, I SAW SOME VERY GOOD COMMANDOS.
THAT IS WHY THEY ARE ULTIMATE BLUE.
THAT IS WHY *THEY ARE DANGEROUS.*
AIR AMERICA
I wonder what it is.
Something's not right.
It's very tense. Even the adults are scared.
Yet, why are these kids so calm?

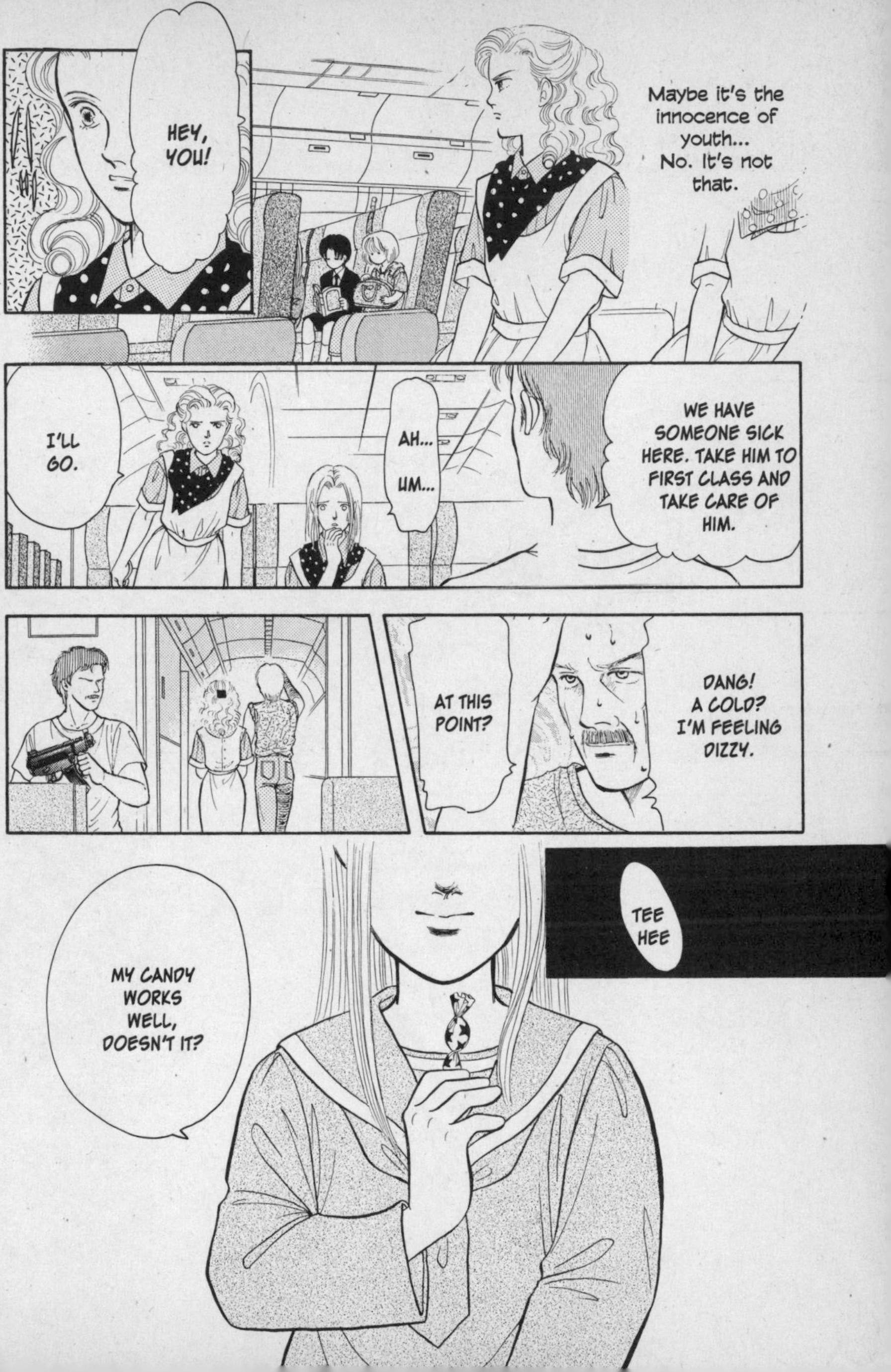
Maybe it's the innocence of youth... No. It's not that.
HEY, YOU!
WE HAVE SOMEONE SICK HERE. TAKE HIM TO FIRST CLASS AND TAKE CARE OF HIM.
AH... UM...
I'LL GO.
DANG! A COLD? I'M FEELING DIZZY.
AT THIS POINT?
TEE HEE
MY CANDY WORKS WELL, DOESN'T IT?

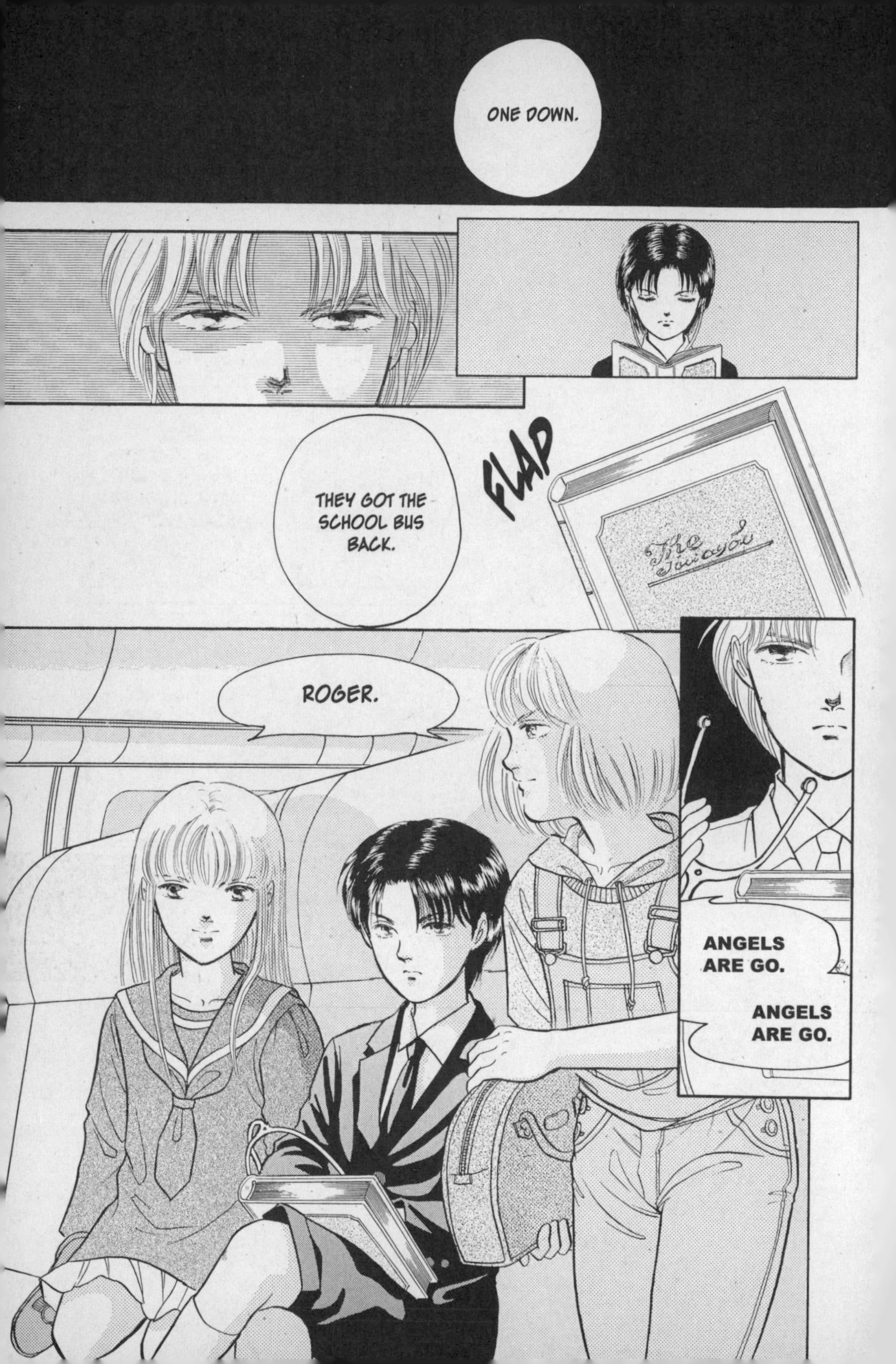
ONE DOWN.
FLAP
THEY GOT THE SCHOOL BUS BACK.
ANGELS ARE GO.
ANGELS ARE GO.
ROGER.

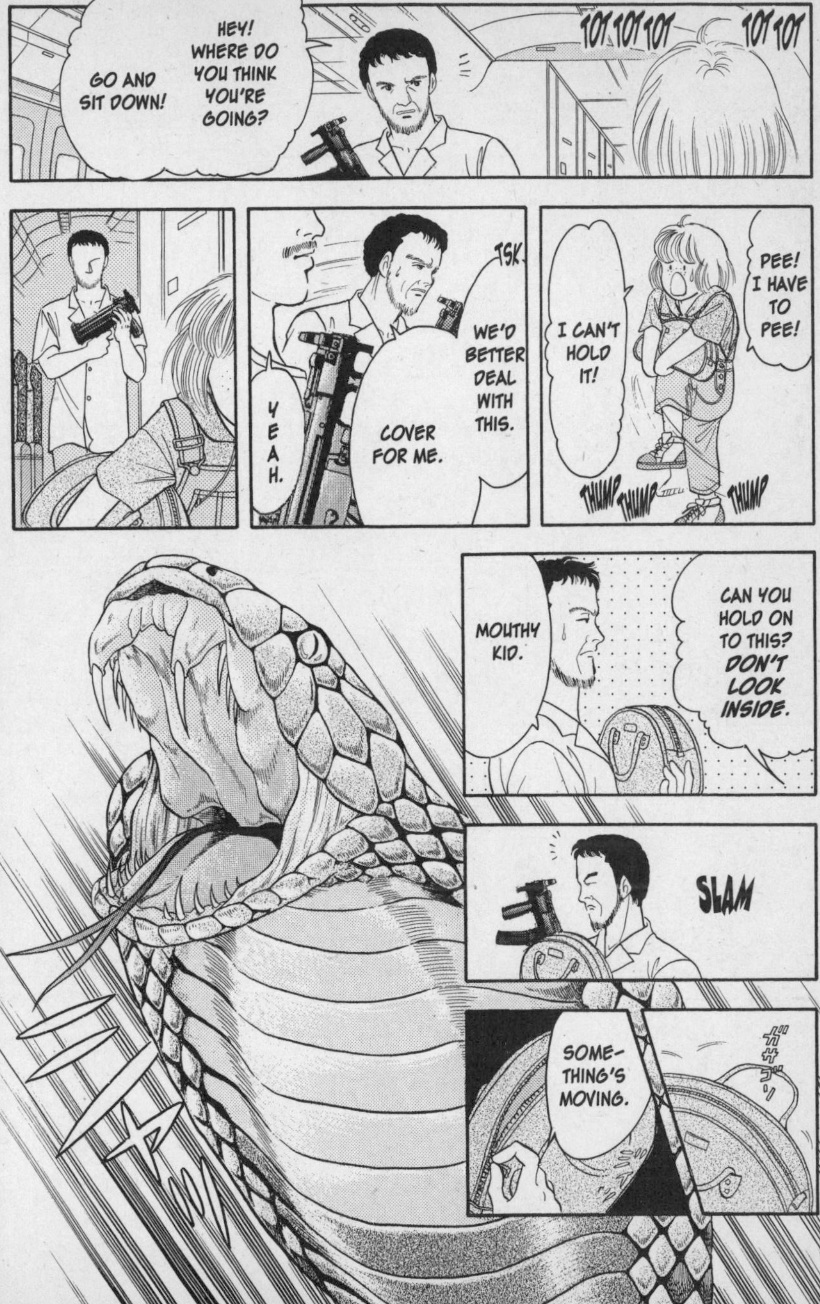
TOT TOT
TOT TOT TOT
HEY! WHERE DO YOU THINK YOU'RE GOING?
GO AND SIT DOWN!
PEE! I HAVE TO PEE!
I CAN'T HOLD IT!
THUMP THUMP THUMP
TSK
WE'D BETTER DEAL WITH THIS.
COVER FOR ME.
YEAH.
CAN YOU HOLD ON TO THIS? DON'T LOOK INSIDE.
MOUTHY KID.
SLAM
SOME-THING'S MOVING.

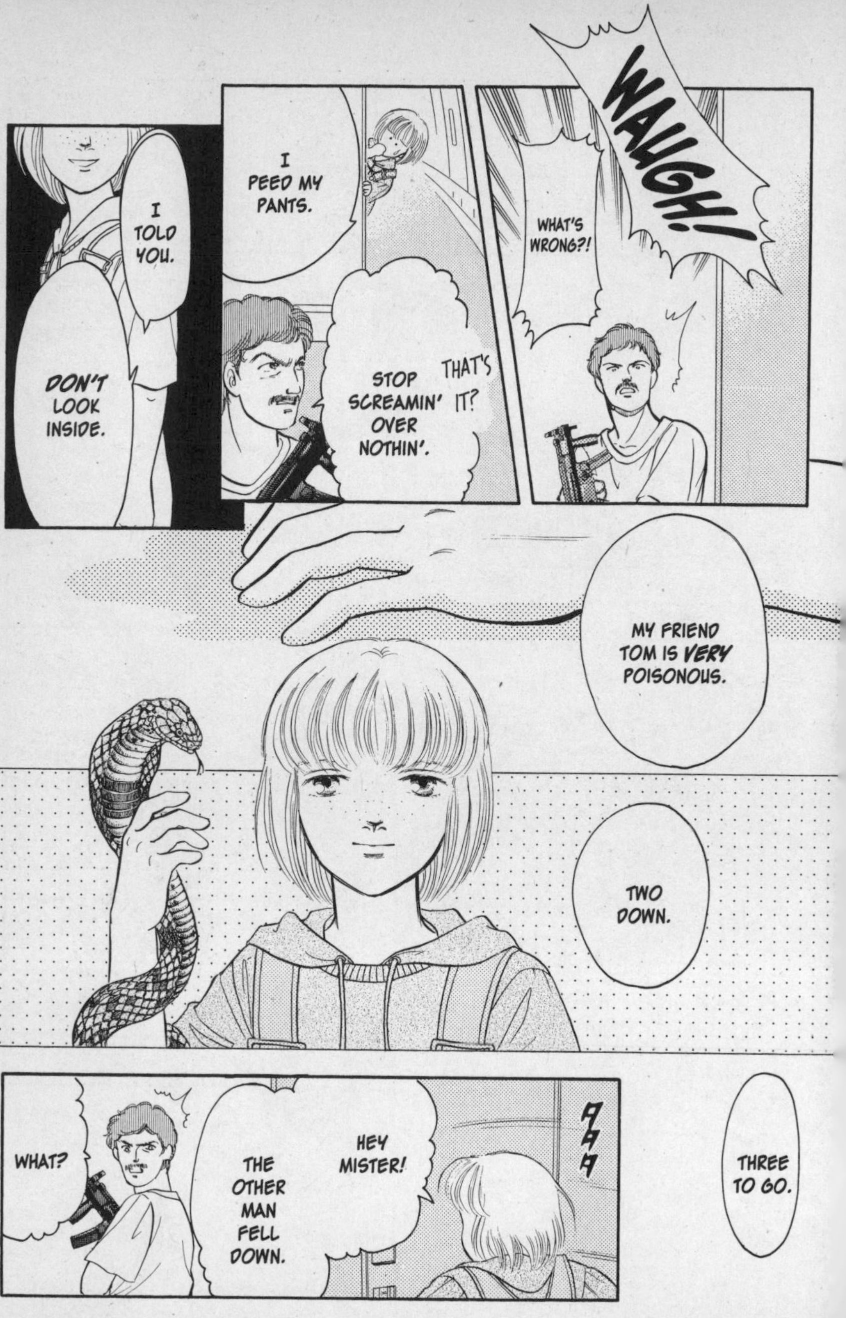
WAUGH!
WHAT'S WRONG?!
I PEED MY PANTS.
THAT'S IT?
STOP SCREAMIN' OVER NOTHIN'.
I TOLD YOU.
DON'T LOOK INSIDE.
MY FRIEND TOM IS VERY POISONOUS.
TWO DOWN.
THREE TO GO.
タタタ
HEY MISTER!
THE OTHER MAN FELL DOWN.
WHAT?

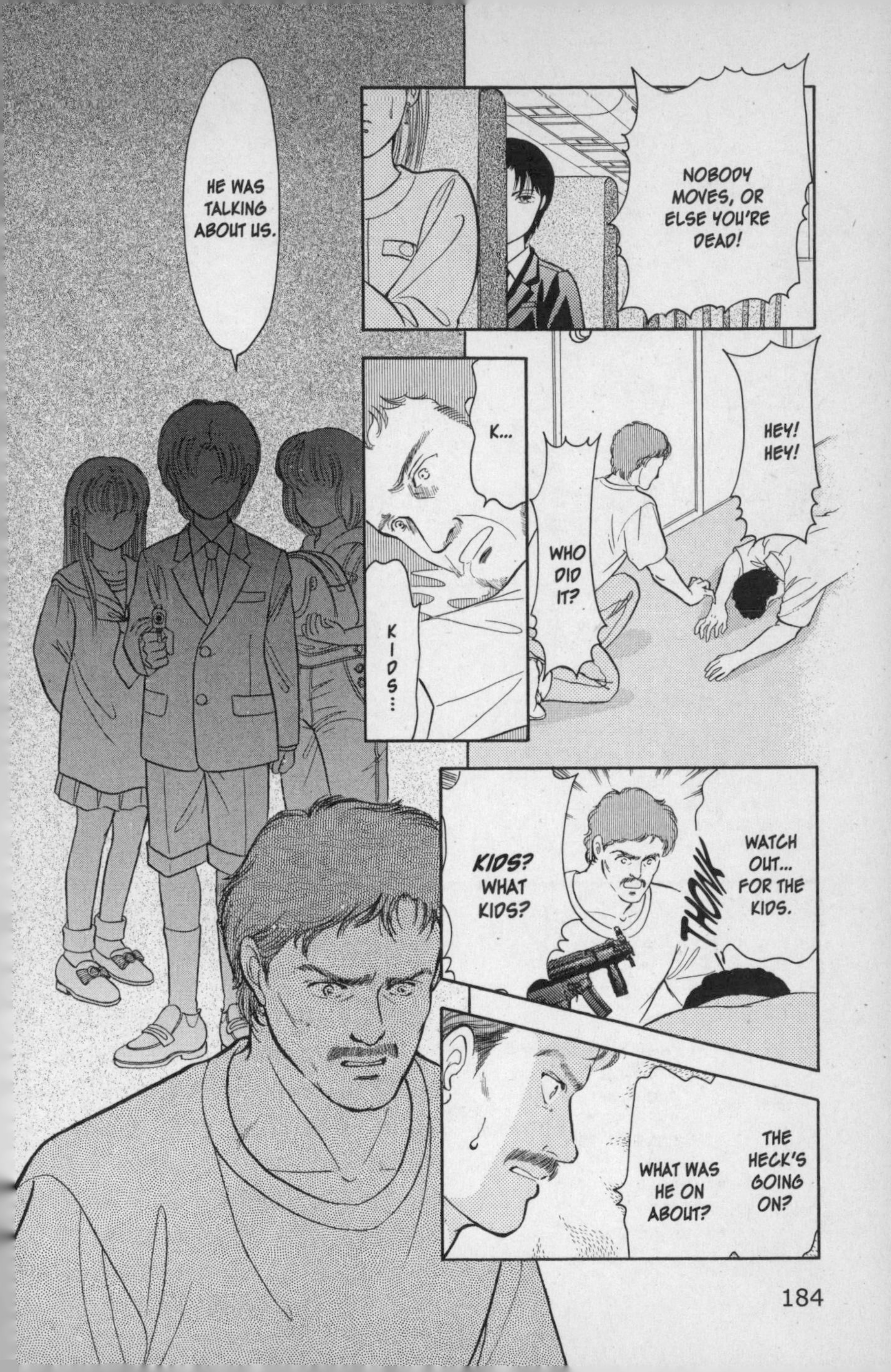
NOBODY MOVES, OR ELSE YOU'RE DEAD!
HEY! HEY!
WHO DID IT?
K...
KIDS...
WATCH OUT... FOR THE KIDS.
THONK
KIDS? WHAT KIDS?
THE HECK'S GOING ON?
WHAT WAS HE ON ABOUT?
HE WAS TALKING ABOUT US.

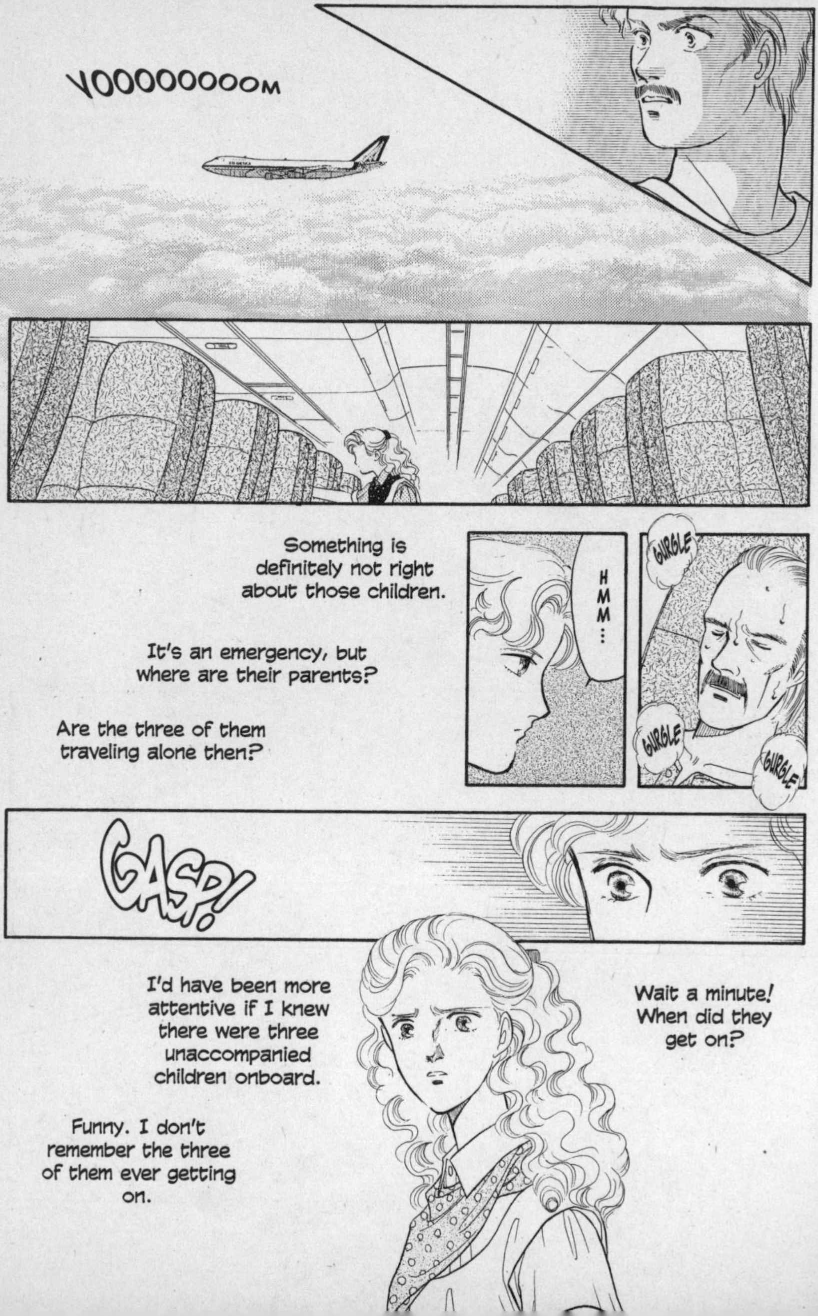
VOOOOOOOOM
GURGLE
GURGLE
GURGLE
HMM...
Something is definitely not right about those children.
It's an emergency, but where are their parents?
Are the three of them traveling alone then?
GASP!
Wait a minute! When did they get on?
I'd have been more attentive if I knew there were three unaccompanied children onboard.
Funny. I don't remember the three of them ever getting on.

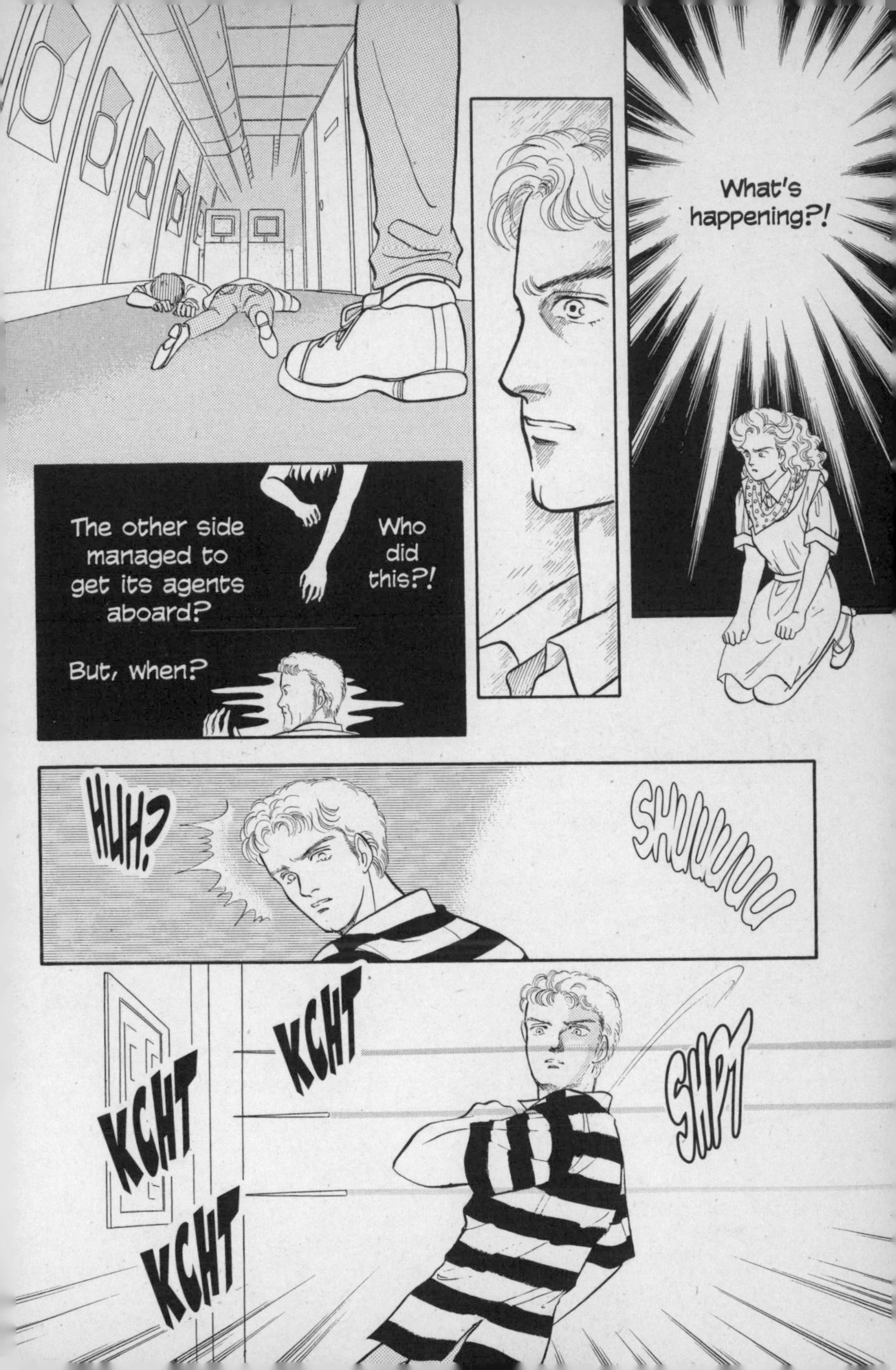

What's happening?!
Who did this?!
The other side managed to get its agents aboard?
But, when?
SHUUUUU
HUH?
SHPT
KCHT
KCHT
KCHT

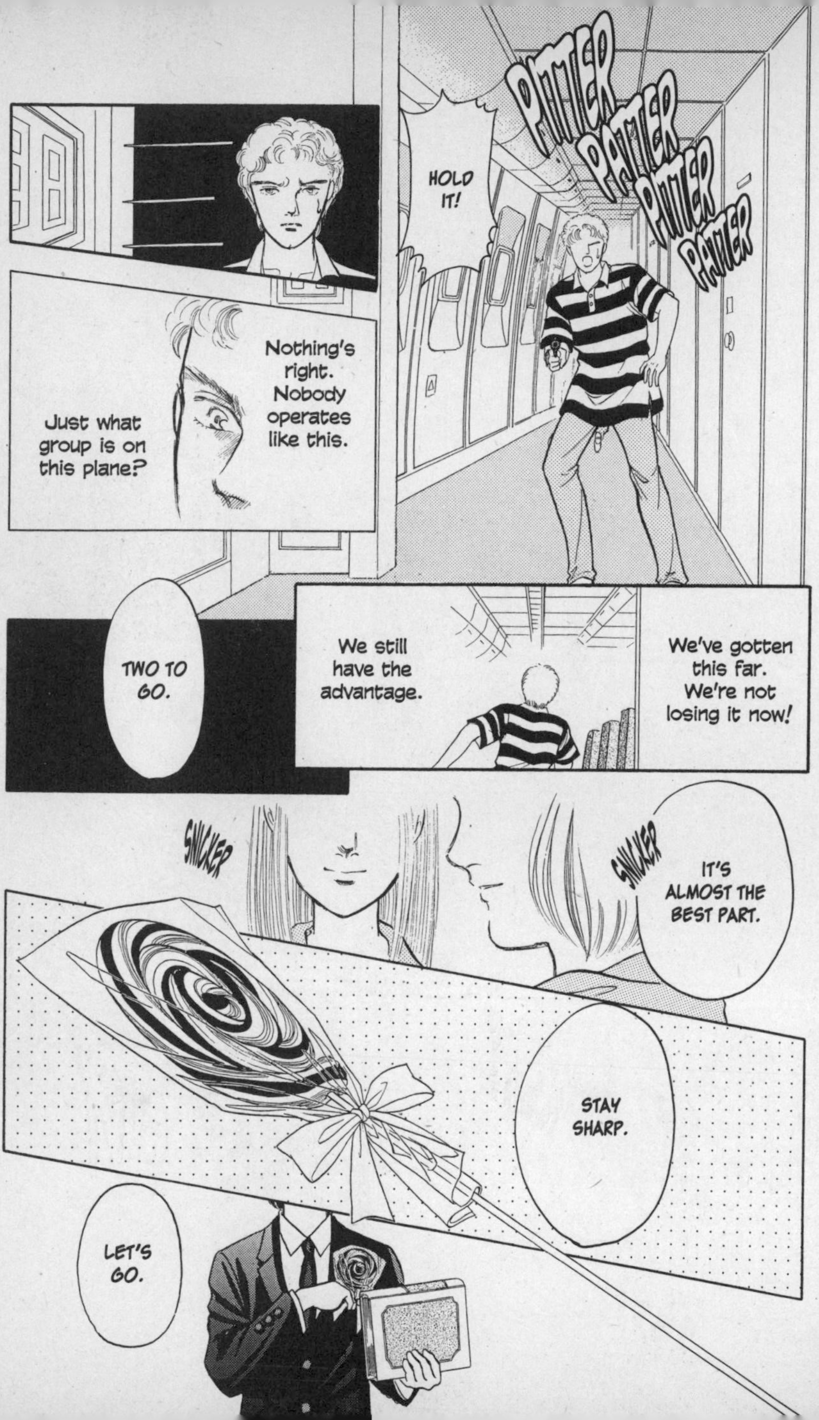
PITTER PATTER PITTER PATTER
HOLD IT!
Nothing's right. Nobody operates like this.
Just what group is on this plane?
We've gotten this far. We're not losing it now!
We still have the advantage.
TWO TO GO.
IT'S ALMOST THE BEST PART.
SNICKER
SNICKER
STAY SHARP.
LET'S GO.

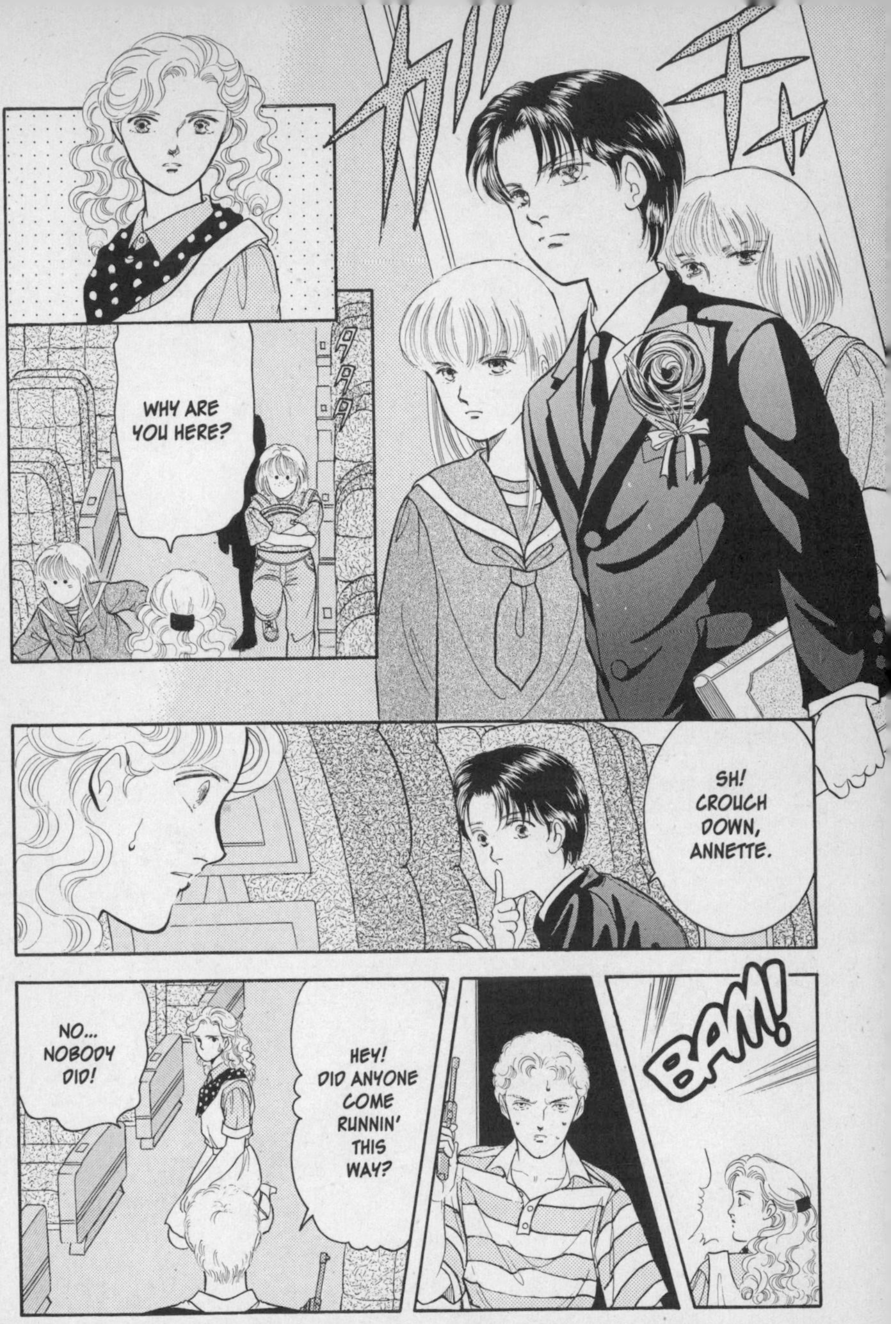
WHY ARE YOU HERE?
SH! CROUCH DOWN, ANNETTE.
BAM!
HEY! DID ANYONE COME RUNNIN' THIS WAY?
NO... NOBODY DID!

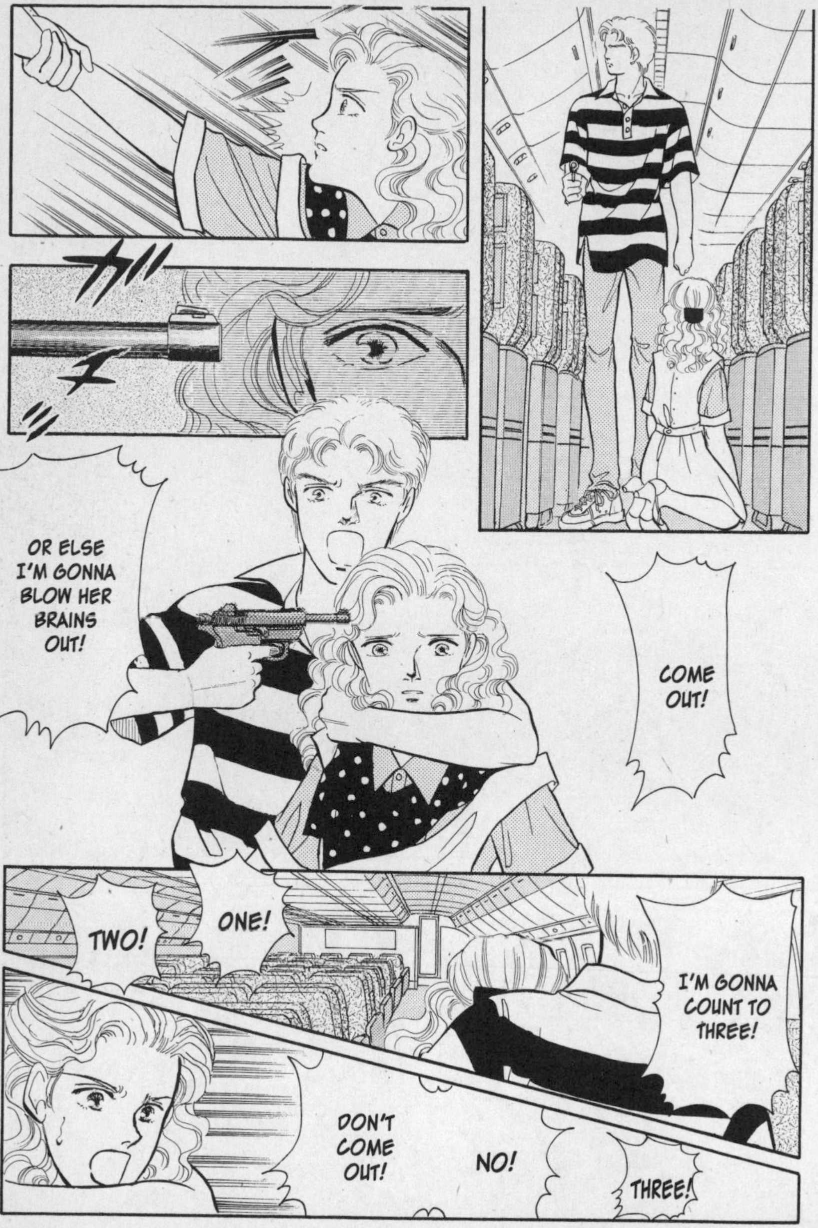
COME OUT!
OR ELSE I'M GONNA BLOW HER BRAINS OUT!
I'M GONNA COUNT TO THREE!
ONE!
TWO!
THREE!
NO!
DON'T COME OUT!

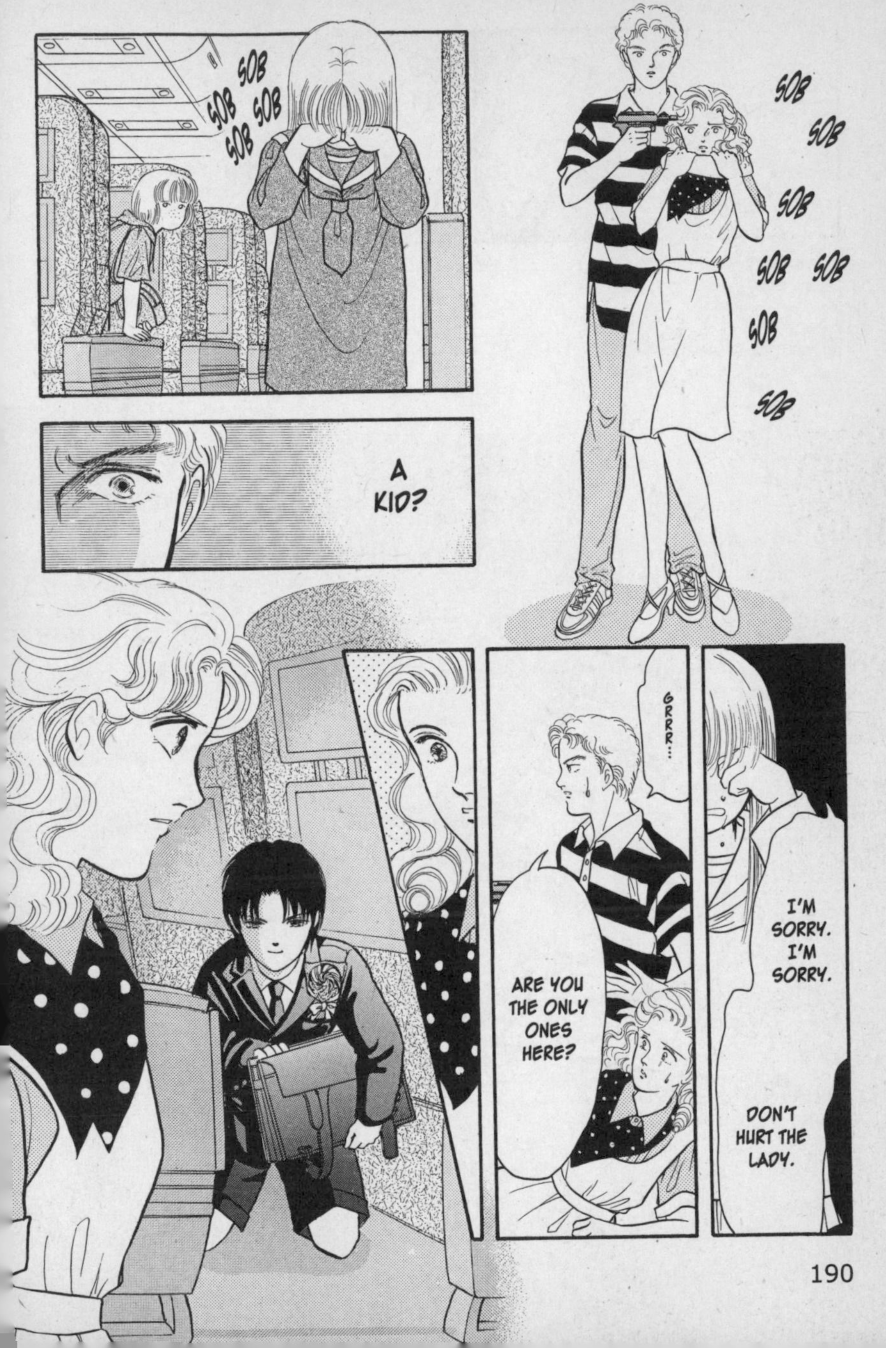
SOB
SOB
SOB
SOB SOB
SOB
SOB
SOB SOB SOB SOB SOB
A KID?
I'M SORRY. I'M SORRY.
DON'T HURT THE LADY.
GRRR...
ARE YOU THE ONLY ONES HERE?

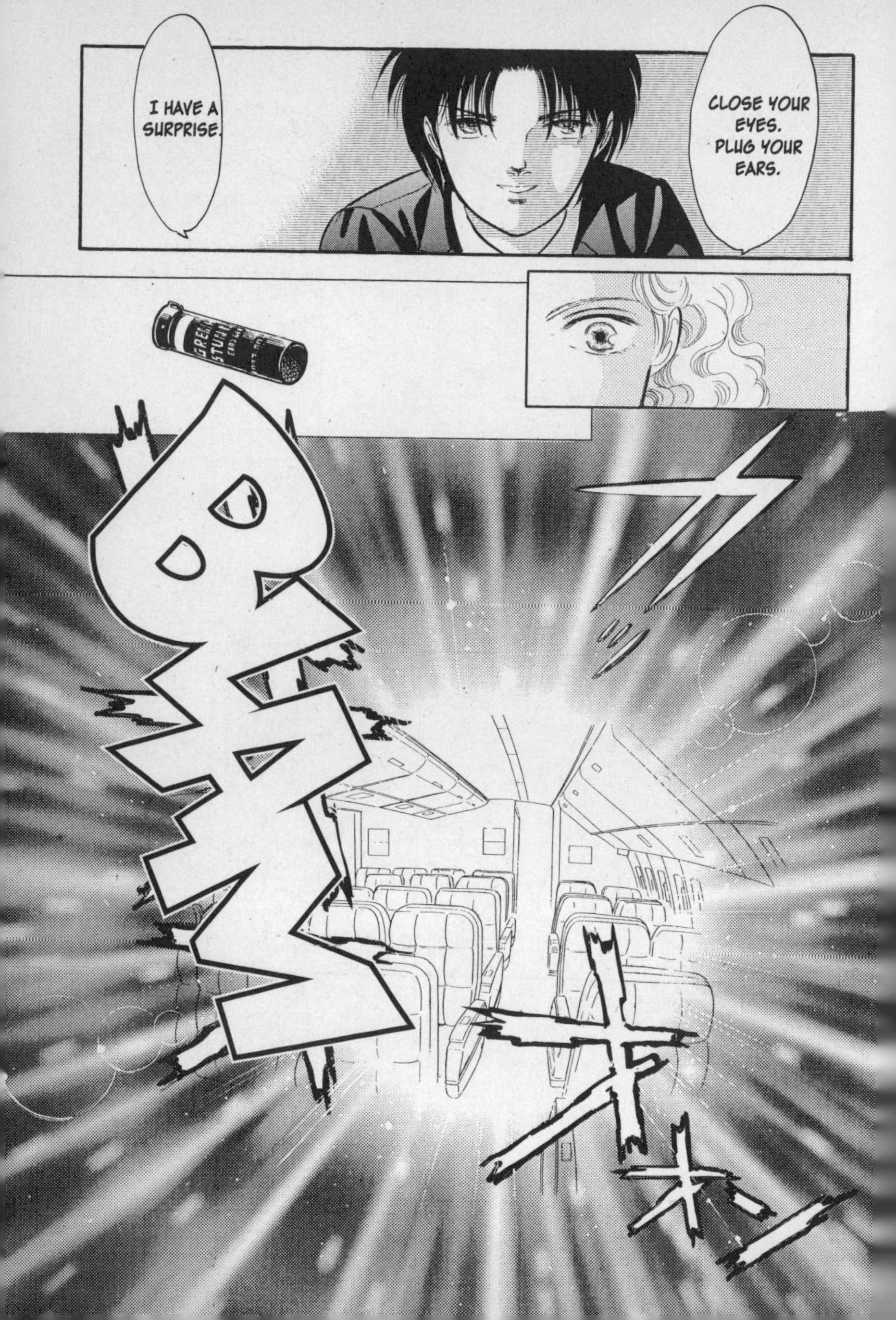
CLOSE YOUR EYES. PLUG YOUR EARS.
I HAVE A SURPRISE.
BAM

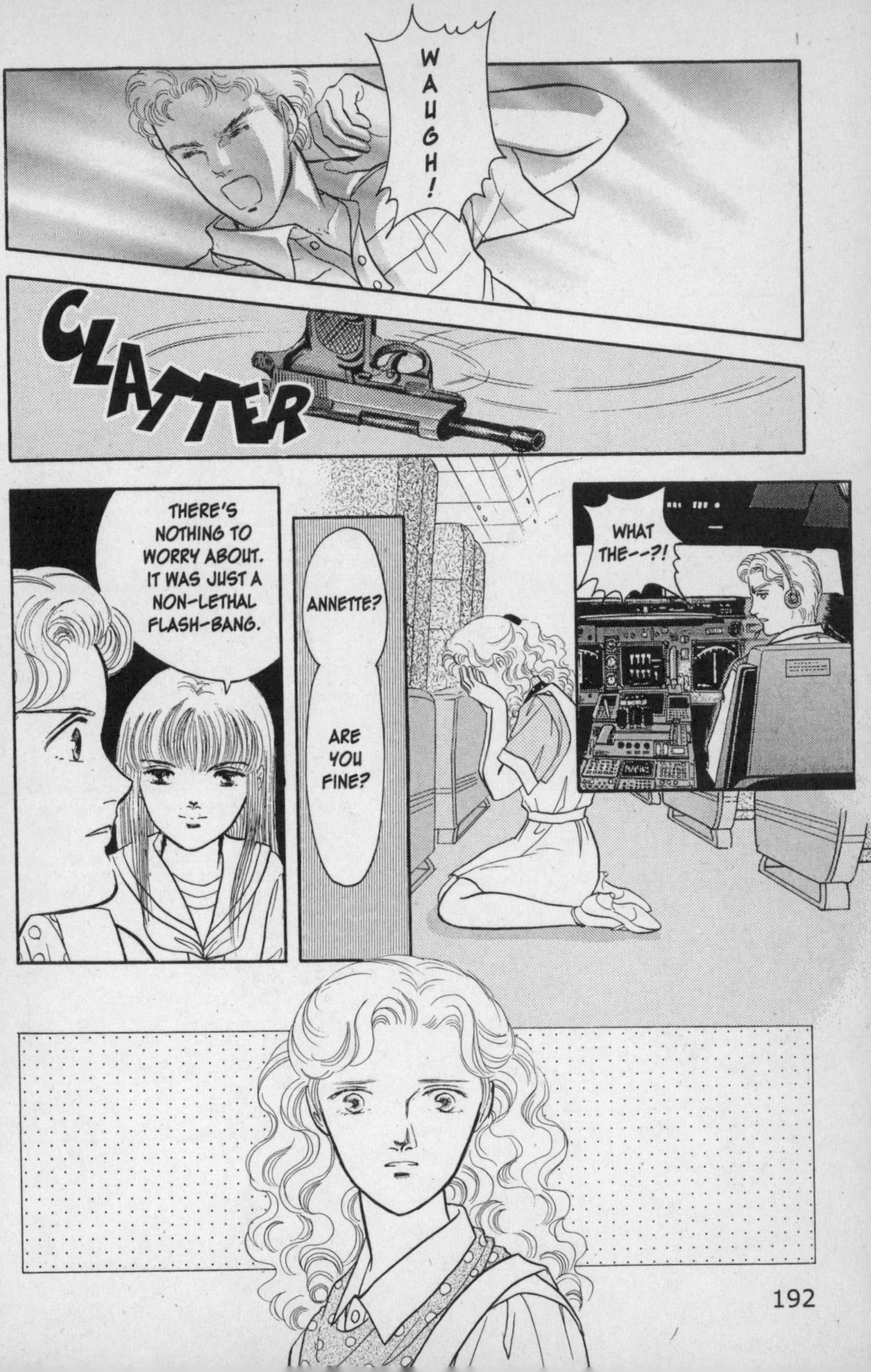
WAUGH!
CLATTER
WHAT THE--?!
ANNETTE?
ARE YOU FINE?
THERE'S NOTHING TO WORRY ABOUT. IT WAS JUST A NON-LETHAL FLASH-BANG.

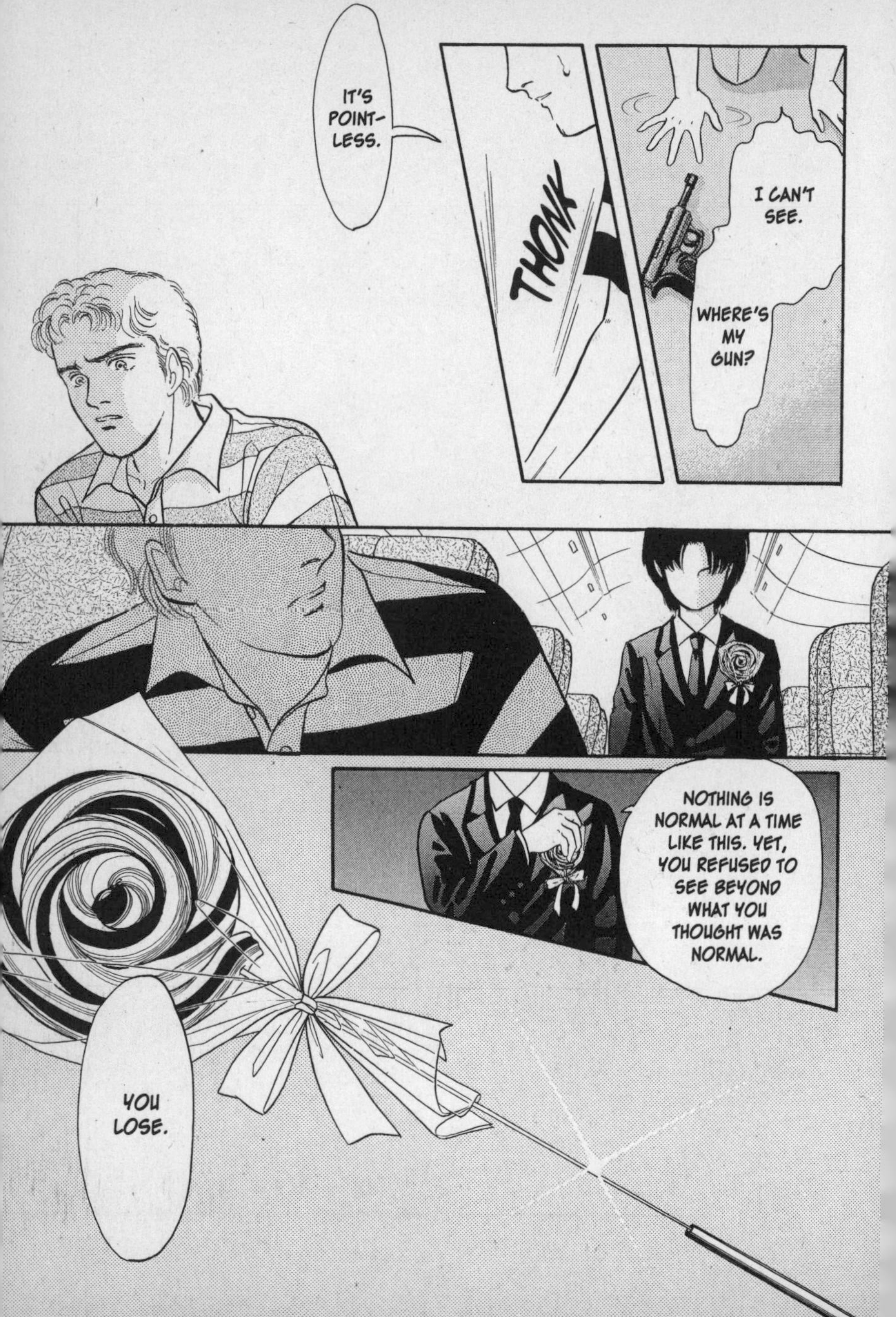
I CAN'T SEE.
WHERE'S MY GUN?
THONK
IT'S POINT-LESS.
NOTHING IS NORMAL AT A TIME LIKE THIS. YET, YOU REFUSED TO SEE BEYOND WHAT YOU THOUGHT WAS NORMAL.
YOU LOSE.

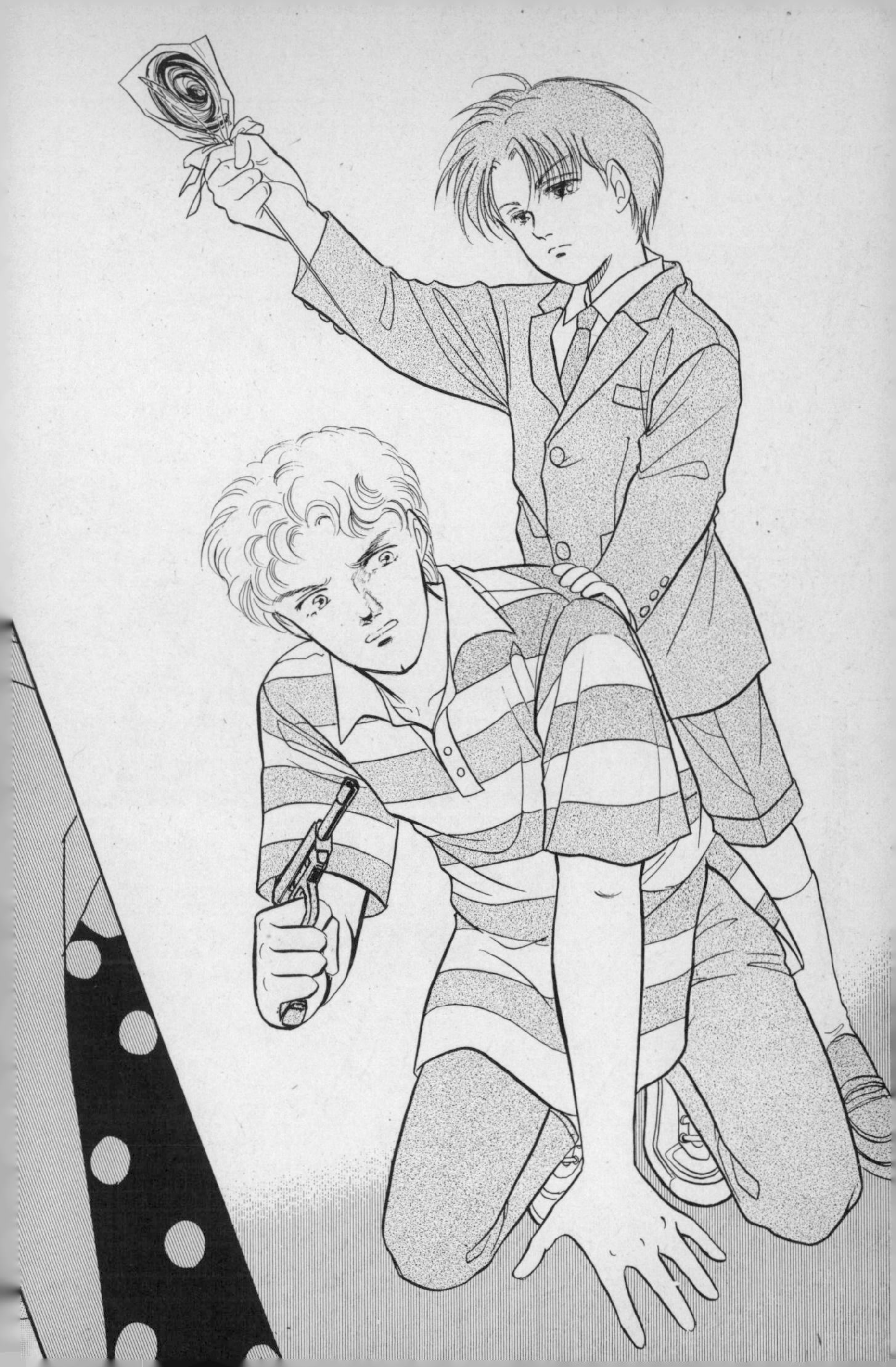

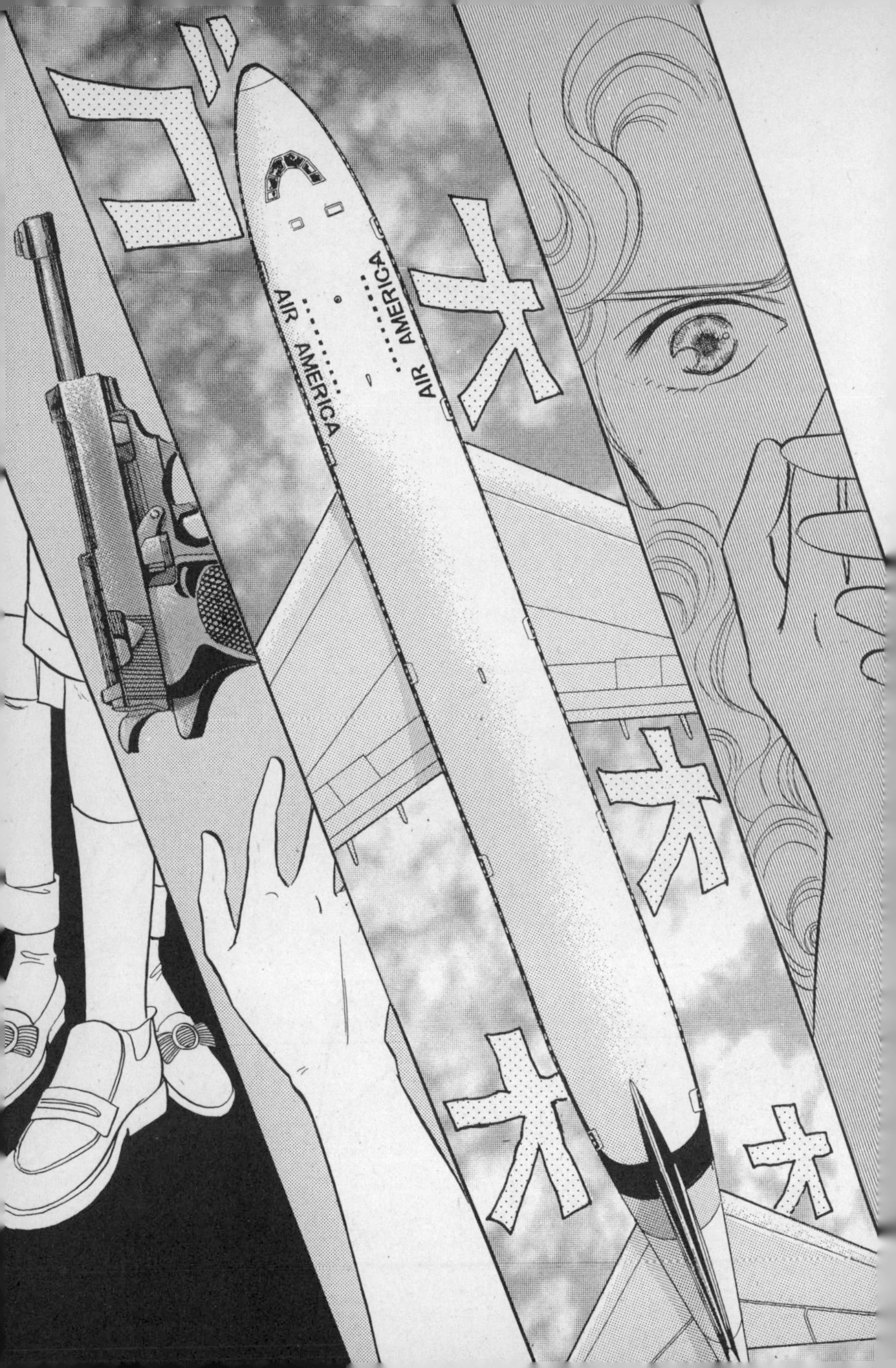
ゴオオオオ
AIR AMERICA
AIR AMERICA

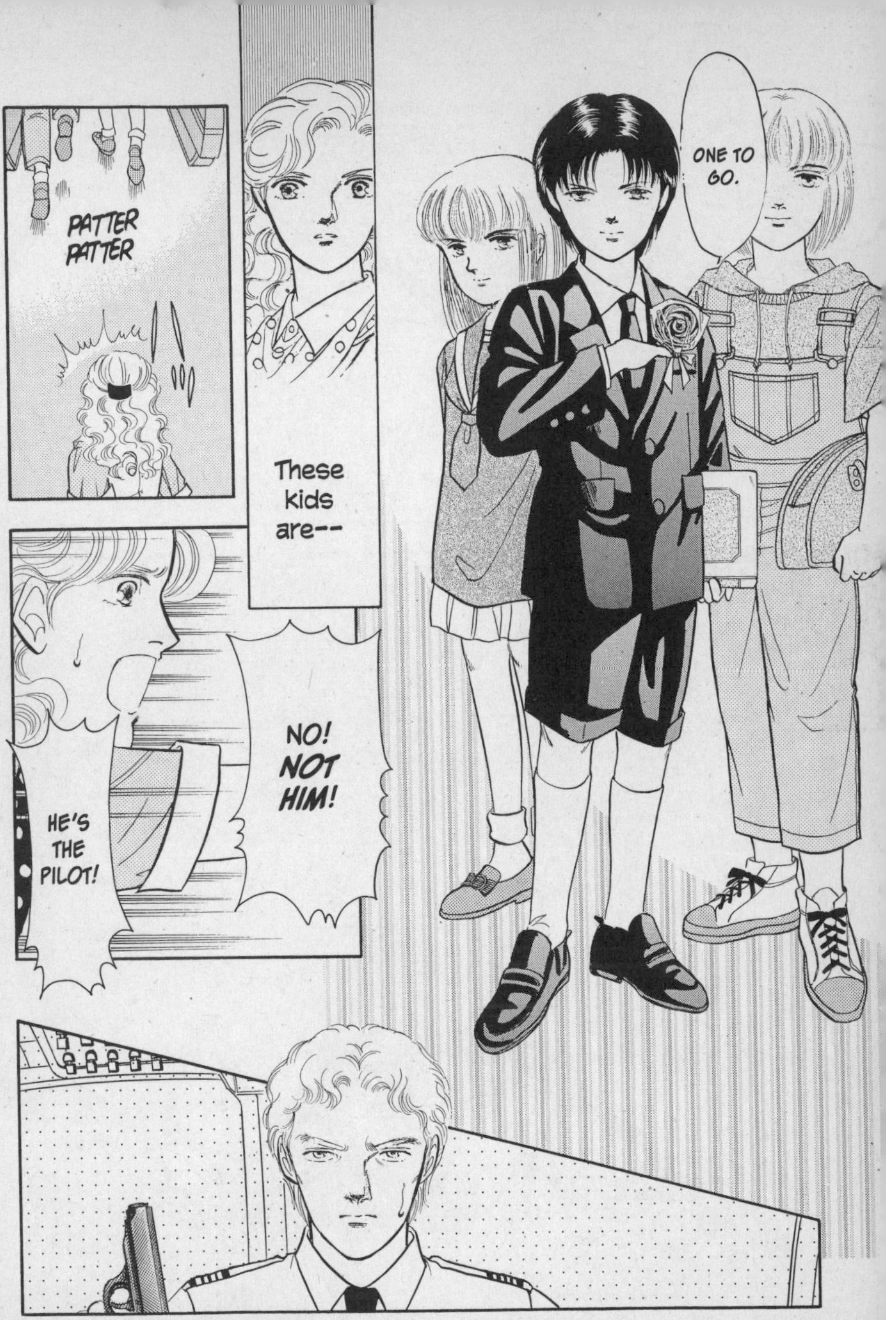
ONE TO GO.
These kids are--
PATTER PATTER
NO! NOT HIM!
HE'S THE PILOT!

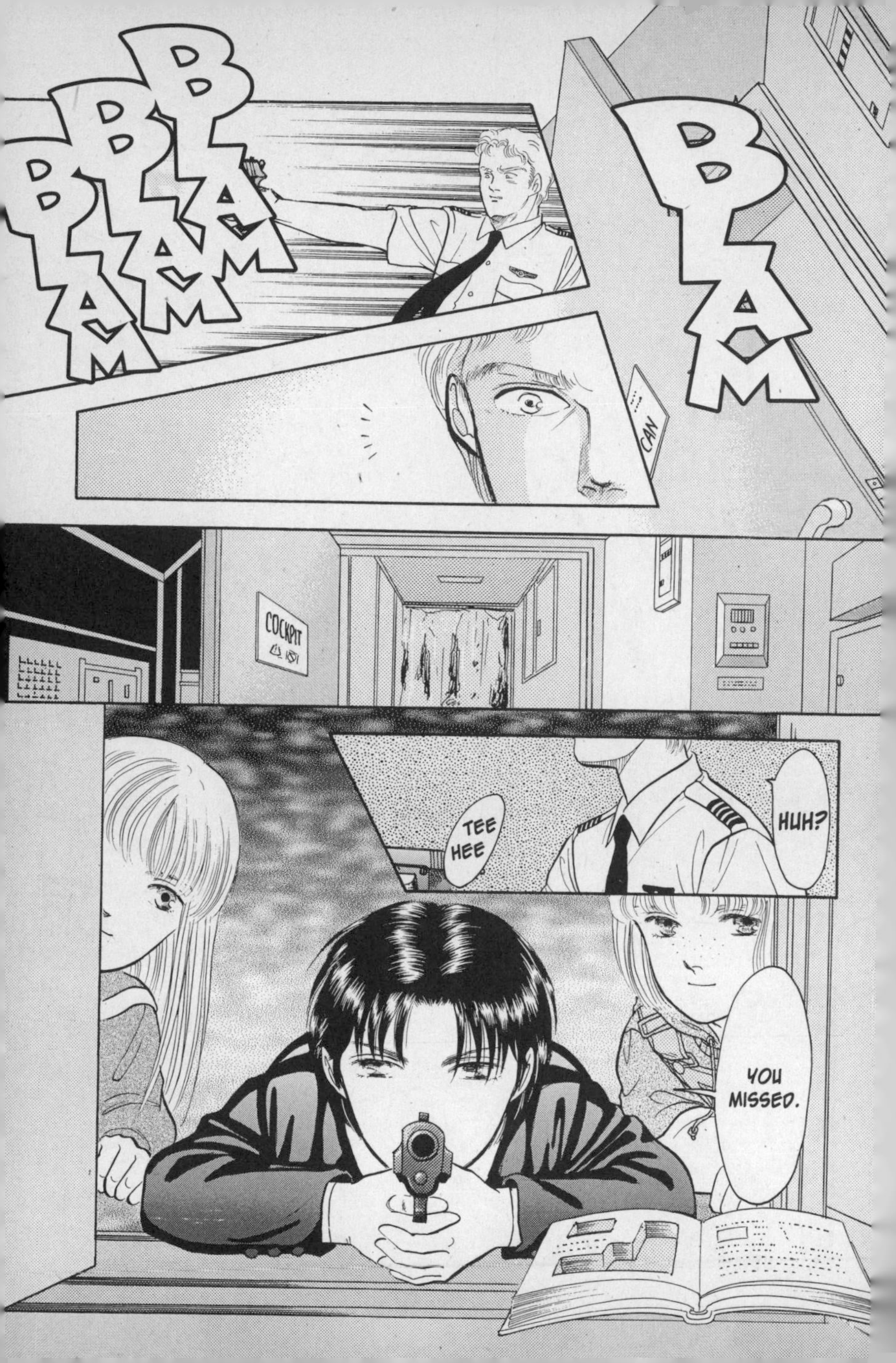
BLAM
BLAM
BLAM
BLAM
CAN
COCKPIT
HUH?
TEE HEE
YOU MISSED.

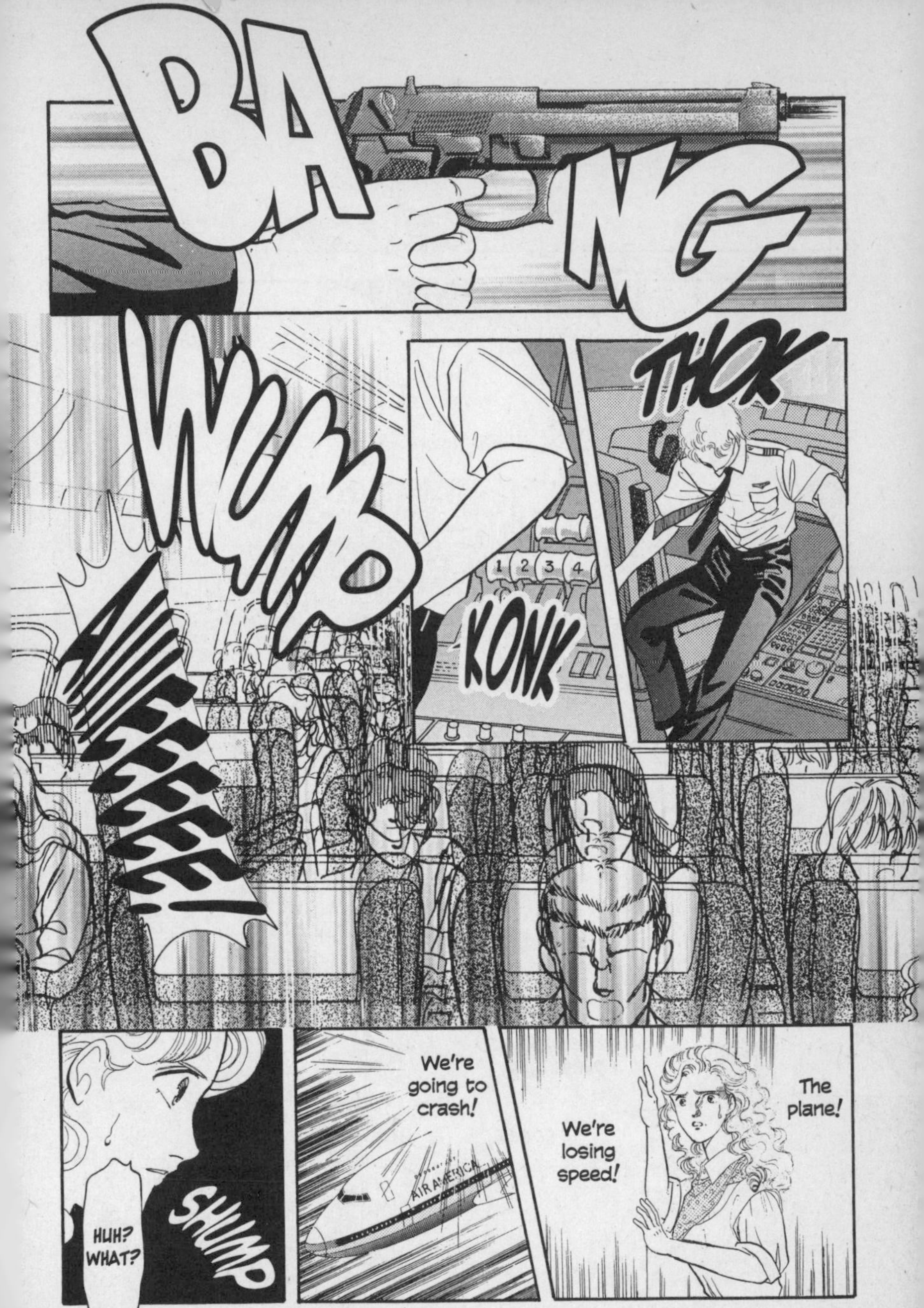
BANG
THOK
KONK
WHUMP
AIIIIEEEEE!
The plane!
We're losing speed!
We're going to crash!
AIR AMERICA
SHUMP
HUH? WHAT?

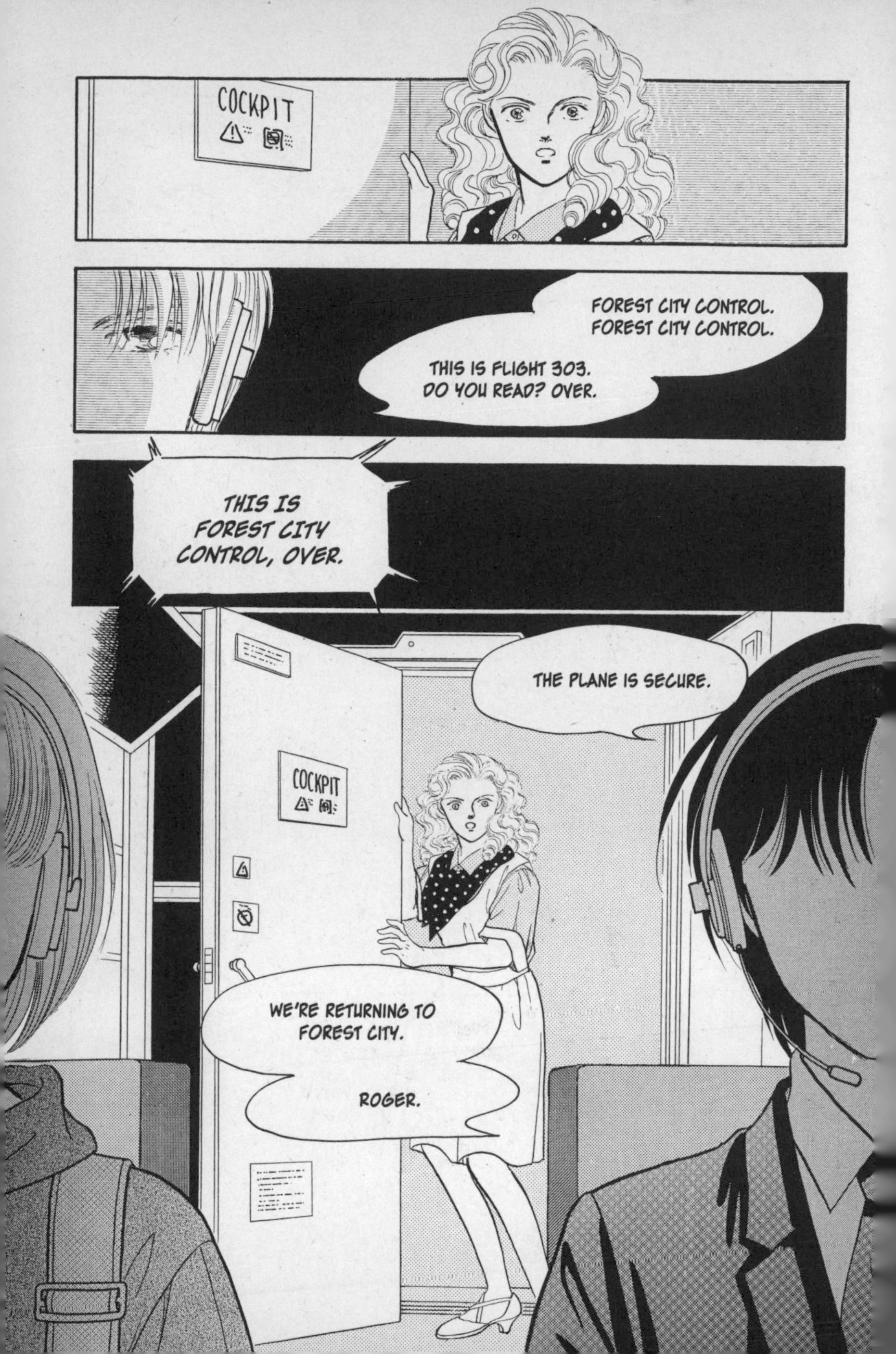
COCKPIT
FOREST CITY CONTROL. FOREST CITY CONTROL.
THIS IS FLIGHT 303. DO YOU READ? OVER.
THIS IS FOREST CITY CONTROL, OVER.
THE PLANE IS SECURE.
COCKPIT
WE'RE RETURNING TO FOREST CITY.
ROGER.

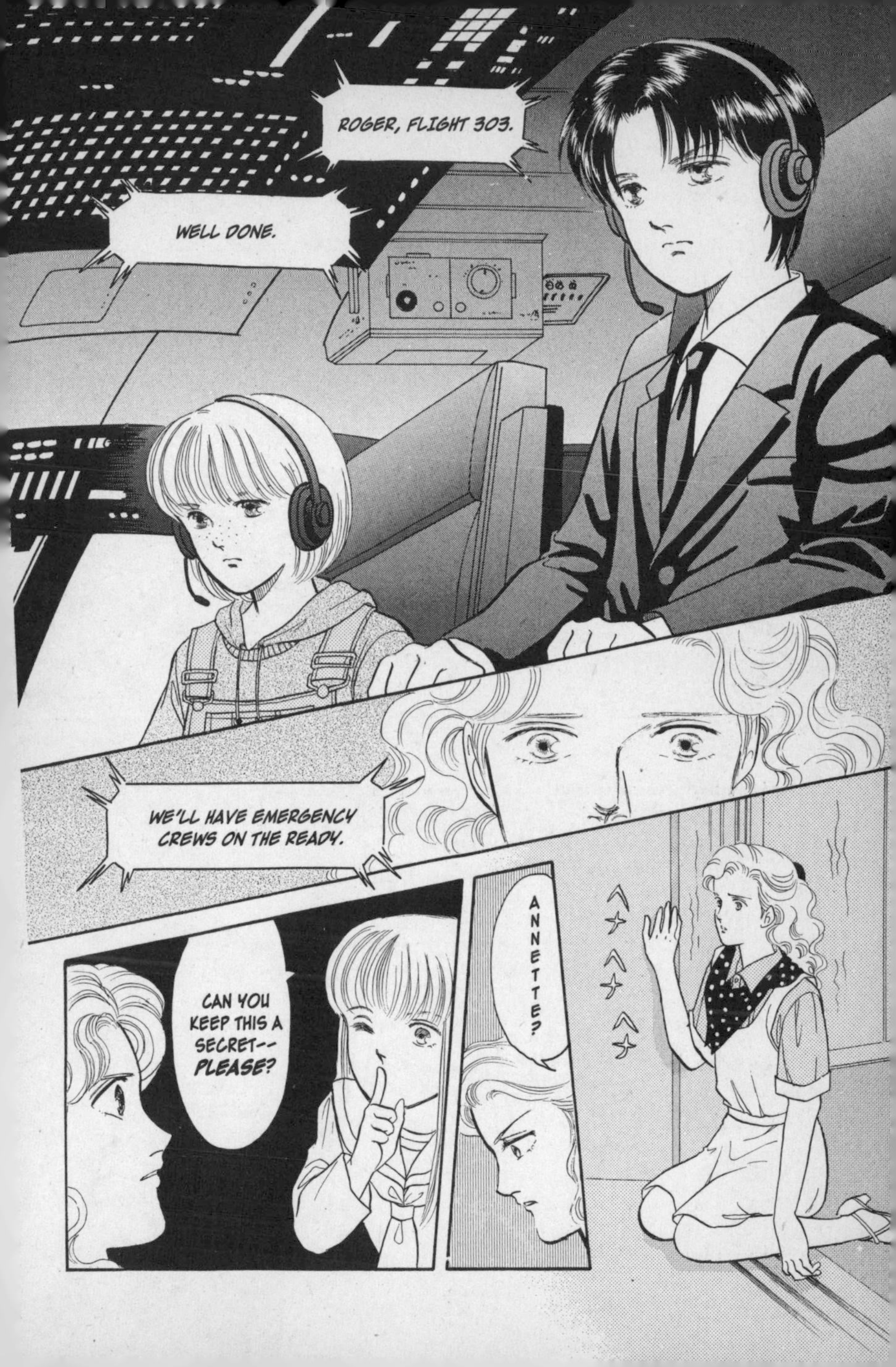
ROGER, FLIGHT 303.
WELL DONE.
WE'LL HAVE EMERGENCY CREWS ON THE READY.
ANNETTE?
CAN YOU KEEP THIS A SECRET-- PLEASE?

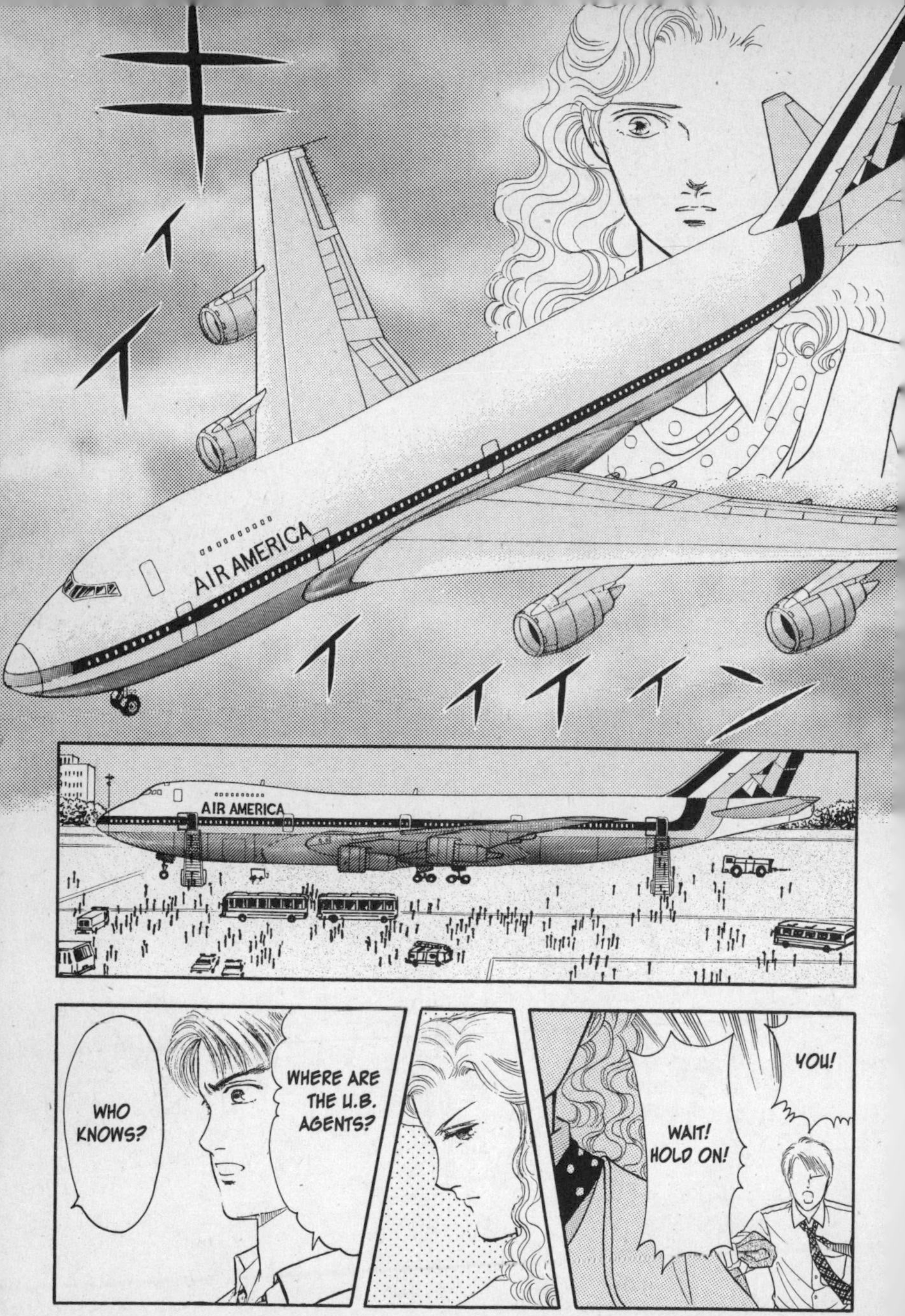
キイイイイイイン
AIR AMERICA
AIR AMERICA
YOU!
WAIT! HOLD ON!
WHERE ARE THE U.B. AGENTS?
WHO KNOWS?

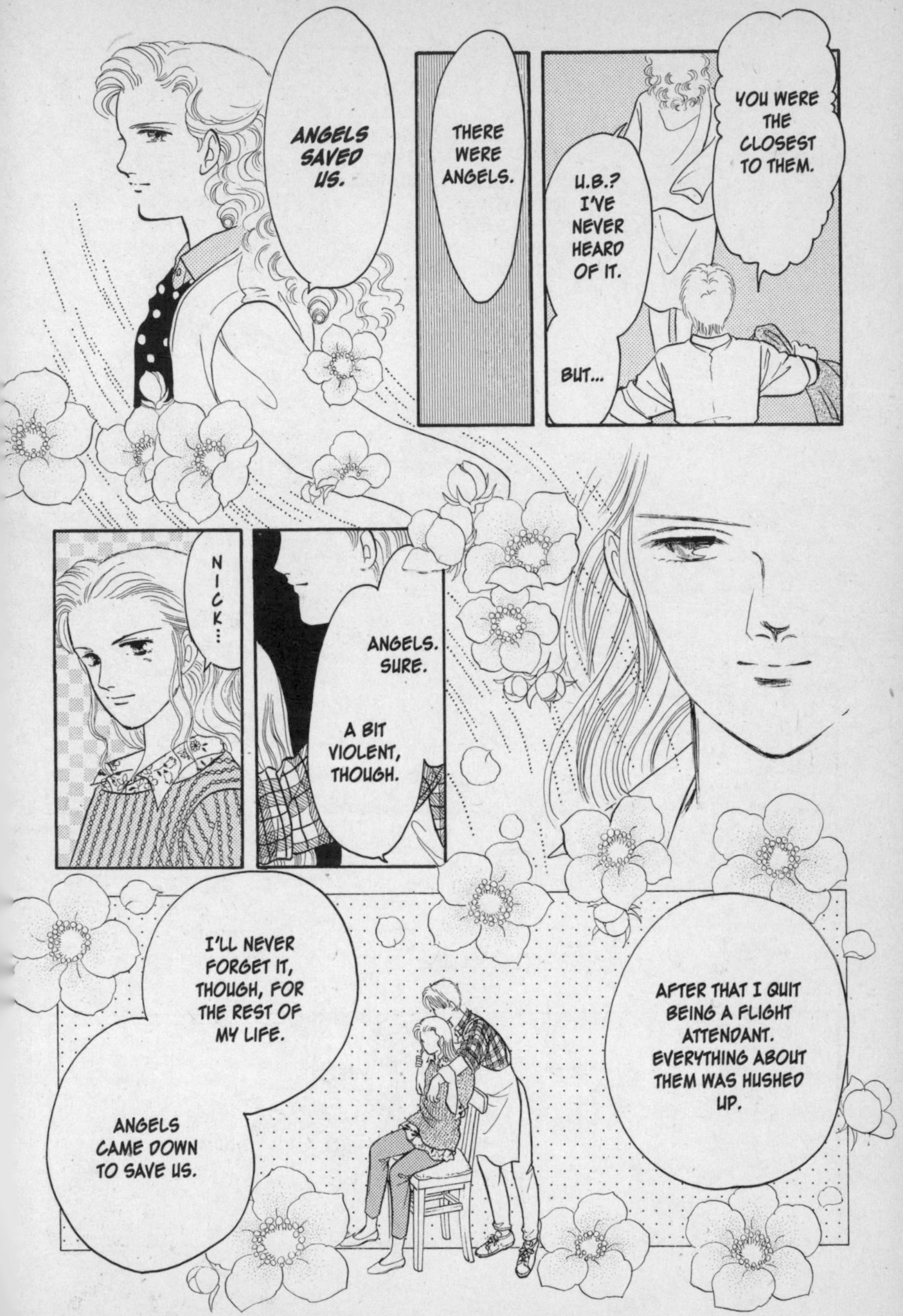
YOU WERE THE CLOSEST TO THEM.
U.B.? I'VE NEVER HEARD OF IT.
BUT...
THERE WERE ANGELS.
ANGELS SAVED US.
ANGELS. SURE.
A BIT VIOLENT, THOUGH.
NICK...
AFTER THAT I QUIT BEING A FLIGHT ATTENDANT. EVERYTHING ABOUT THEM WAS HUSHED UP.
I'LL NEVER FORGET IT, THOUGH, FOR THE REST OF MY LIFE.
ANGELS CAME DOWN TO SAVE US.

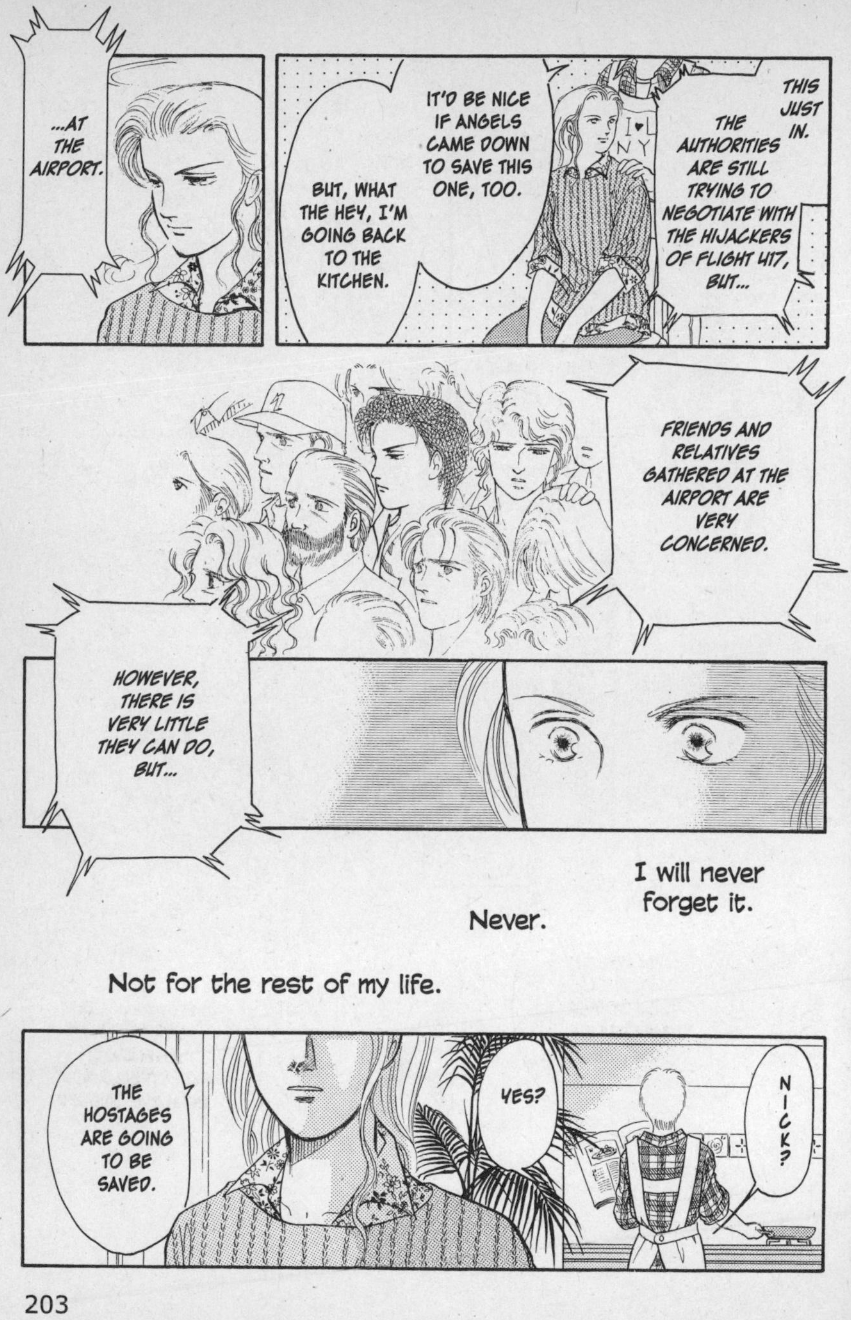
THIS JUST IN.
THE AUTHORITIES ARE STILL TRYING TO NEGOTIATE WITH THE HIJACKERS OF FLIGHT 417, BUT...
IT'D BE NICE IF ANGELS CAME DOWN TO SAVE THIS ONE, TOO.
BUT, WHAT THE HEY, I'M GOING BACK TO THE KITCHEN.
...AT THE AIRPORT.
FRIENDS AND RELATIVES GATHERED AT THE AIRPORT ARE VERY CONCERNED.
HOWEVER, THERE IS VERY LITTLE THEY CAN DO, BUT...
I will never forget it.
Never.
Not for the rest of my life.
NICK?
YES?
THE HOSTAGES ARE GOING TO BE SAVED.

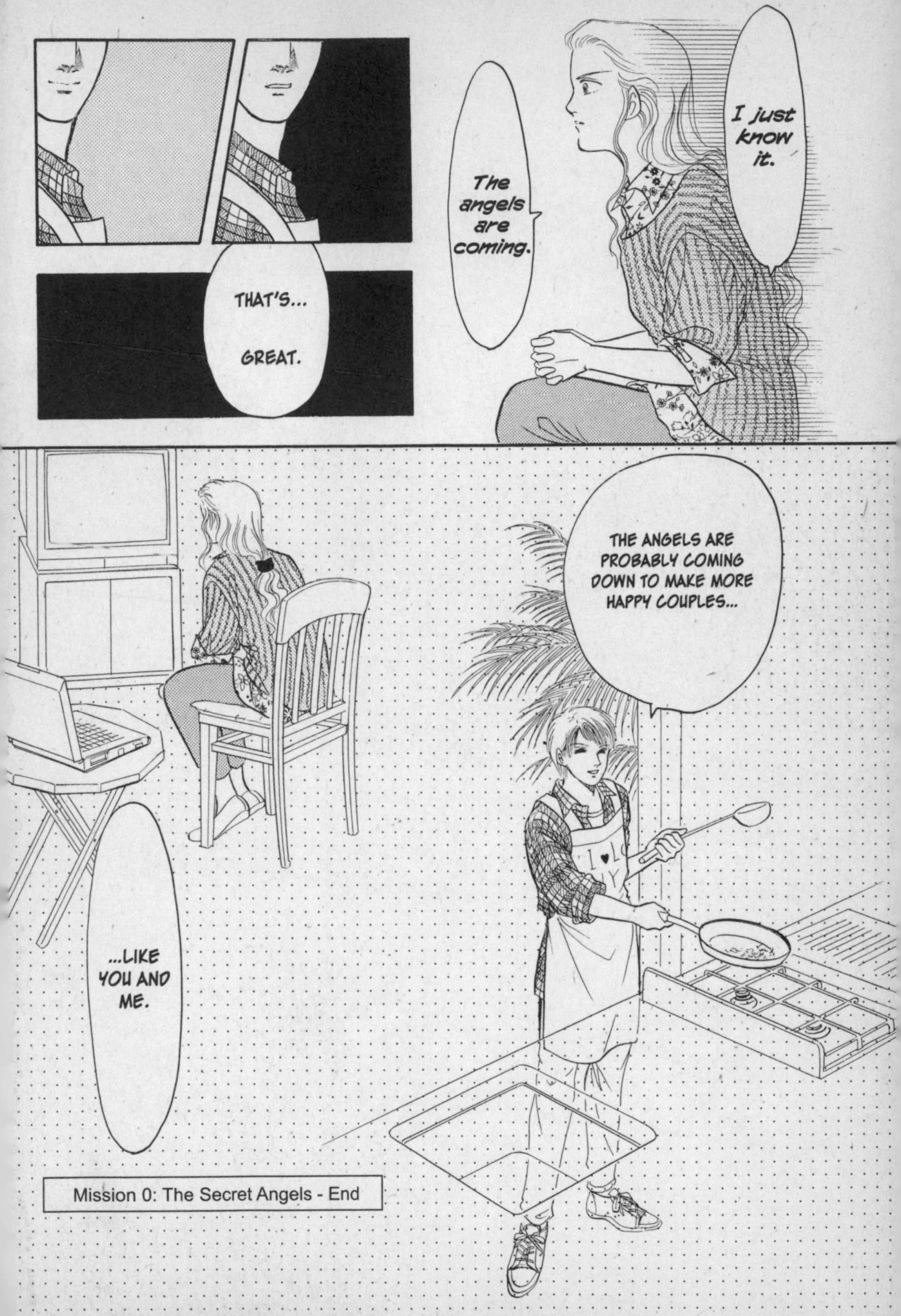
I just know it.
The angels are coming.
THAT'S... GREAT.
THE ANGELS ARE PROBABLY COMING DOWN TO MAKE MORE HAPPY COUPLES...
...LIKE YOU AND ME.
Mission 0: The Secret Angels - End

cmx

Jim Lee
  Editorial Director
John Nee
  VP—Business Development
Hank Kanalz
  VP—General Manager, WildStorm
Jonathan Tarbox
  Group Editor
Paul Levitz
  President & Publisher
Georg Brewer
  VP—Design & Retail Product Development
Richard Bruning
  Senior VP—Creative Director
Patrick Caldon
  Senior VP—Finance & Operations
Chris Caramalis
  VP—Finance
Terri Cunningham
  VP—Managing Editor
Stephanie Fierman
  Senior VP—Sales & Marketing
Alison Gill
  VP—Manufacturing
Rich Johnson
  VP—Book Trade Sales
Lillian Laserson
  Senior VP & General Counsel
Paula Lowitt,
  Senior VP– Business & Legal Affairs
David McKillips
  VP—Advertising & Custom Publishing
Gregory Noveck
  Senior VP—Creative Affairs
Cheryl Rubin
  Senior VP—Brand Management
Bob Wayne
  VP—Sales

 DC Comics, a Warner Bros.
Entertainment Company.

Translation and Adaptation by
Tony Ogasawara

William F. Schuch — Lettering
John J. Hill — CMX Logo & Publication Design
Larry Berry — Additional Design

ISBN: 1-4012-0543-7

FLIP IT!!

All the pages in this book were created—and are printed here—in Japanese RIGHT-to-LEFT format. No artwork has been reversed, so you can read the stories the way the creators meant for them to be read.

JAPANESE NAMES

Authentic Japanese name order is family name first, given name second. In the CMX books and on the covers, we will list the names of all characters as well as the manga creators in Japanese order, unless otherwise instructed by the author.

RIGHT TO LEFT?!

Traditional Japanese manga starts at the upper right-hand corner, and moves right-to-left as it goes down the page. Follow this guide for an easy understanding.

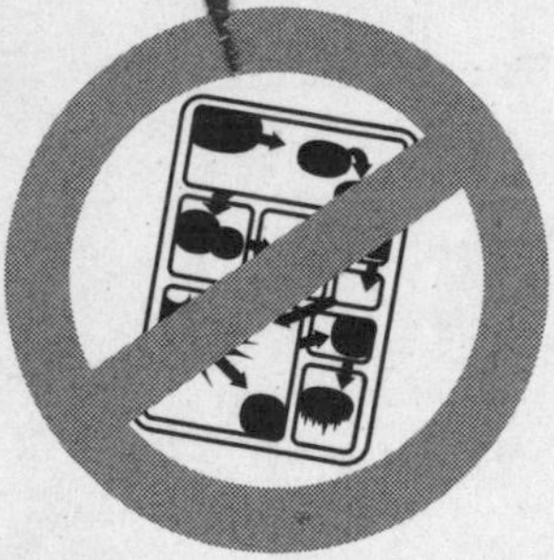

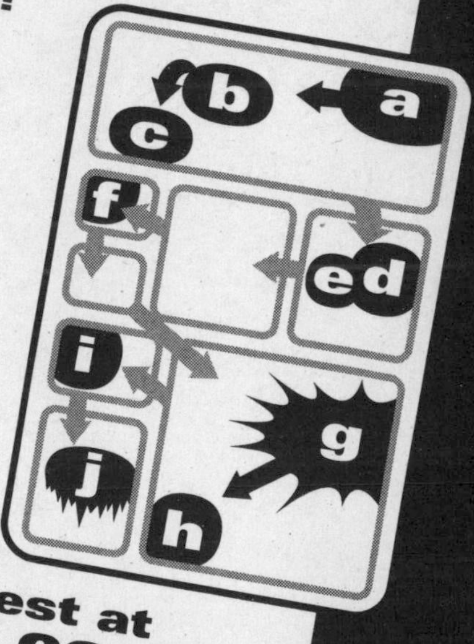
a
b
c
d
e
f
g
h
i
j

Catch the latest at cmxmanga.com!